Journal of My Life

Journal de Mavie

Ecris par moy an Lan 1764 menetra
le tout
Sans Obstentation Et Sans Reflexition

Ecrire Laverité Selou moy Se la doit etre
ne parlé ni darme et deblasou
oublier ce que toit Ses ancetre
et desert Vain Titre neu decæe Son nom

Je Suis née le 13 juillet 1738 natif de cette grande
Cité mon pere etoit dela clase dese que lon
apelle ordinairemeul artisaut il profesoit Letat
deVitrie cest donc deluy que jetabliray La Souche
Demafamille et ne parlerez nulemeut de mes
ancetre mou pere Semaria et Setablit en meme
Temps et epousa une fille Vertueuse quy luy
donna quatre enfaut trois fille et un garsou dout cest
demoy que jevais ecrire toute Les petite fredaine
mon pere devint veuf que javoit deux aus Lou
mavoit mis en nourice magraud mere quy
ma toujour beaucoup aimee et meme idolátrée

Journal of My Life

by Jacques-Louis Ménétra

with an introduction and
commentary by
Daniel Roche

translated by
Arthur Goldhammer

foreword by
Robert Darnton

COLUMBIA UNIVERSITY PRESS
NEW YORK
1986

Library of Congress Cataloging-in-Publication Data

Ménétra, Jacques-Louis, b. 1738.
Journal of my life.

Translation of: Journal de ma vie.
Includes bibliographical references.
1. Ménétra, Jacques-Louis, b. 1738.   2. Glass-workers
—France—History—18th century.   3. Glass-workers—
France—Biography.   4. France—Social conditions—18th
century.   I. Roche,   Daniel.   II. Title.   III. Series.
HD8039.G52F7313   1986   666'.1'0924   [B]   85-28068
ISBN 0-231-06128-5
ISBN 0-231-06129-3 (pbk.)

Columbia University Press
New York   Oxford

Journal de ma vie

Text copyright © 1982, Editions Montalba;
English edition: copyright © 1986, Columbia University Press.
Foreword reprinted with permission from
The New York Review of Books. Copyright © 1984, Robert Darnton.

Printed in the United States of America

Book design by Ken Venezio

Contents

Foreword

Jacques-Louis Ménétra's *Journal de ma vie* reads like a historian's dream
come true. It fits perfectly into the current picture of Old Regime demog-
raphy (Ménétra married at twenty-seven and had four children of whom
two died in infancy). It also conforms to the standard view of the sans-
culotte (Ménétra worked with his hands but earned enough to support a
family as an independent artisan). And best of all, it is told in Ménétra's
own words. It conveys his own understanding of what it meant to grow
up in Paris, where he was born in 1738; to tramp around provincial shops
on a journeyman's *tour de France*; to settle down as a Parisian master with
a shop and family of his own; and to live through the great events of the
Revolution as a militant in his local Section.

It seems astounding that such a document should turn up after being
buried for nearly two centuries. But three other working-class autobiogra-
phies from the Old Regime have surfaced in the last few years,[1] and others
may still be lying undiscovered in archives and attics. The autobiographical urge extended far deeper in French society than we ever suspected.

So did literacy and exposure to all sorts of literature. Ménétra mentions
as a matter of course that he learned the three Rs and singing in parish
schools. Paris had about five hundred free elementary schools—one for
every 1,200 inhabitants—in the eighteenth century. In a previous book,
based on notarial archives, Roche found that 98 percent of the domestic
servants who left wills were literate; and of them, two-thirds owned
writing desks complete with inkstands, pens, and papers kept on file.

Ménétra and his companions on the *tour de France* were always writing
letters—to keep in touch with their families, to woo their girl friends, and
to find out about jobs in shops farther down the road. When Ménétra
tramped, he sometimes carried a book in the sack slung over his back.
When he settled down in a town, he improvised songs and staged skits

with the other workers. Back in Paris, he spent many evenings in the boulevard theaters and sometimes went drinking with vaudeville stars like Gaspard Taconnet, an author of *poissard* farces, and Pierre Gourlin, a popular harlequin. Literature and the written word were part of his daily life, so it does not seem incredible that he should have put his life into writing.

But how did a man of the people understand autobiography in the eighteenth century? Ménétra did not follow any obvious model. In fact, he broke with literary convention by refusing to divide his story into chapters and paragraphs and even to use punctuation. Instead of address-ing an explicit audience, he dedicated his text to himself ("a mon esprit") and filled it with allusions and expressions that make no sense today. Thus the *Journal de ma vie* makes difficult reading. Roche helps us over the hardest parts with some well-placed footnotes, but the story comes from an almost inaccessible world. That is what makes it so fascinating—as strange and mysterious in its way as Rousseau's *Confessions*.

The comparison with Rosseau is difficult to avoid, although Jean-Jacques rose to the top of Parisian society while Ménétra remained in obscurity, a layer or two from the bottom. The two men crossed paths. According to Ménétra they took a few walks around Paris together in 1770 and once stopped by the Café de la Régence to play checkers (Rousseau won). Both of them came from humble homes (Rousseau's father was a watchmaker). Both lost their mothers as infants. Both had troubled rela-tions with their fathers and spent much of their youth on the road. Both confessed.

But where Rousseau wallowed in guilt, Ménétra boasted. Like Jean-Jacques, he had left a string of illegitimate children behind him, but he was proud of it. He, too, had a weakness for a "maman," but his ran a whore house. He was also surrounded by conspirators, but he beat them off with a broom handle. Ménétra swaggered through life with such zest that his Journal reads like Rousseau turned upside down and rewritten in the language of the working man: the confessions of a *titi parisien*.

It also can be read as a tall tale. At the outset, Ménétra announces, "I am going to write about all my pranks." The theme of joking—*fredaines, niches, espiègleries*—runs throughout the narrative and provides Ménétra with a way of organizing it. He presents his life as a series of pranks, which all demonstrate the same happy conclusion: no matter what he does, he comes out on top. He outwits the *mamans* and wins free bed and breakfast in the best brothels of Paris. He seduces the wives of friends and thus restores domestic tranquility to some frustrated households. He bamboozles the intendant of Bordeaux and thereby saves his companions from being drafted into the army.

Ménétra triumphs over everything. Small in stature but a "Hercule en amour," he seduces all the girls, wins all the fights, rescues all the drowning children, puts out all the fires, dupes all the yokels, confounds all the priests, and even buys a surprising share of successful lottery tickets, using the proceeds to regale his friends in the finest taverns and houses of pleasure in Paris. Ménétra is so successful, in fact, that he seems too good to be true.

Much of the Journal is patently false. As Roche points out, Ménétra could not have exchanged greetings with the folk-hero-bandit Louis Mandrin in 1762, because Mandrin had been executed in 1755. It seems equally unlikely that Ménétra led 500 members of his workers' association, the *compagnonnage du Devoir*, against 750 of the rival *Gavots* in a pitched battle near Angers, leaving seven dead and fifty-seven wounded. Journeymen on the *tour de France* certainly brawled among themselves, but not on such a scale and probably not without leaving some trace of their disturbances in the archives.

That Ménétra made up some of the incidents in his narrative is clear from his account of a murder in one of the inns on his route. Shortly before his arrival, he recounts, the innkeeper's son returned after twenty year's absence in the army. Instead of revealing his identity, the son took a room and gave his parents a purse full of gold for safekeeping over the night. They could not resist the opportunity for sudden wealth. So they killed him in his bed, only to discover from word that arrived the next day that they had murdered their own son. The tale came from a common *canard* or broadside that had been hawked throughout the country in various editions since 1618, but Ménétra incorporated it in the story of his life as if it had happened under his nose.

How much make-believe did he weave into his Journal? One cannot say, but its unreliability as fact seems less important than its artistry as fantasy. If Ménétra was a sort of eighteenth-century Walter Mitty, he gives us a chance to see what eighteenth-century dreams were made of.

He took a great deal of his material from the popular literature of his time, which featured the sort of thing that he passed off as everyday occurrences on his travels: hideous crimes, encounters with ghosts, black magic, dramatic rescues, practical jokes (the funniest at the expenses of priests), and orgies (the juiciest in nunneries). Ménétra's favorite genre was the sexual yarn. It gave him a chance to assert his own prowess, because he always cast himself as the seducer; yet it often seems to come straight out of Boccaccio or from the oral equivalents of the *Decamerone* that circulated among the story tellers of the Old Regime.

The journeymen swapped stories on the road and in the inns patronized by their *compagnonnage*. They often slept two to a bed with several beds to a room and exchanged burlesque "confessions" before dozing off. Sometimes, like Ulysses, they spun yarns before well-born hosts. For example, after repairing windows in one château, Ménétra spent an evening at the seigneur's table: "He took pleasure in getting us to recount all our pranks and everything we had done on our *tour de France*. I told a few stories for them. The seigneur and his wife laughed until the tears ran down their cheeks."

The Journal seems to be an extension of these bull sessions, translated awkwardly into writing in 1764, when Ménétra returned from his last tour of the provinces and drafted the bulk of the manuscript. In sections written later, he provided information about his life after 1765, when he set up his own shop in Paris. But he devoted most of the text to the period that he considered his happiest, the seven years that he spent on the road with occasional forays back on the boulevards at home.

Ménétra narrates his tour de France as a series of seductions, strung out in geographical order: the plump widow in Vendôme, the saddler's wife in Tours, the delicious servant girl in Angers, and the nuns in Agen who at first made him wear a bell as a warning signal while he repaired their windows and then, once he had got beneath their skirts, took to knitting his stockings. The travelogue is marked off with bedroom farces. Thus the story of the old prude in Lyon, who though deaf was "still fresh": Ménétra blows out the candle and "took her by assault" just before a knock announces her husband. As he enters, Ménétra hides behind the door, "happy invention." The wife sends the husband to fetch a new candle. Then Ménétra scrambles into his breeches and dashes to safety, dodging the old man on his way down the stairs.

Part boulevard *parade*, part Boccaccio, part dirty joke, the stories suggest that Ménétra was above all a story teller, a working-class Casanova or Leporello. But he drew on his experiences, and it was something more than one long romp through boudoirs and haystacks. The text often works against itself, so that behind the braggadocio our hero looks small, weak, and lonely—the very opposite of the eighteenth-century he-man whom he puts up front.

If we put together the biographical information interspersed between the jokes, we see that Ménétra, like most Parisian babies, spent his first years with a wet nurse outside the city. His mother died before he reached the age of two. When his father and grandmother came to visit him one day, they found him begging outside a church. The wet nurse had taught him to imitate a deaf-mute in order to pick up some extra pennies. He returned with his grandmother and lived with her until the age of eleven. Then he moved in with his father, who had acquired a new wife, and learned the glazier's craft. Little Jacques-Louis also learned to dodge blows and to sleep under the bridges of the Seine when his father became too violent.

The brutality increased as the boy turned into an adolescent and the father, widowed for the second time, took to drink. In one brawl, the old man broke the son's jaw. In another he dislocated a leg, and the son drew a knife in a third. It was time to leave home. After drifting from shop to shop in Paris for a few years, Ménétra left on his *tour de France,* aged eighteen. After his return, he married a girl with enough of a dowry to help him establish his own shop. And soon he was quarreling with his own children, a boy and a girl, just as his father had quarreled with him.

Ménétra narrates the whole cycle in a matter-of-fact way, without self-pity or guilt, but in doing so he undercuts the notion of life as a laugh. In the end, it transpires that he has been disowned by his father, betrayed by his comrades, deserted by his wife, and abandoned by his son, who ran off to another shop as soon as he learned the trade. What has become of all the women? we wonder; and we notice that Ménétra almost never mentions them by name, not even his wife. They make an impressive string of conquests—fifty-two seductions before his wedding and a dozen afterward, not counting liaisons with prostitutes—but they are interchangeable, like the faceless nuns and farmers' daughters of the standard jokes. In looking back over them, Ménétra thinks of the glazier's widow he had left in Nîmes, who had offered him her heart as well as her bed. Had be been wrong to run away from the opportunity to link his life with hers? Had he missed something all along—namely, love? "I knew love only as pleasure and not as perfect friendship." Perhaps ultimately the joke was on him.

This second aspect of the Journal, the anxiety beneath the swagger, makes us feel that we have come in contact with a believable human being, someone like ourselves. But we do not close the book with a reassuring refrain, *homo sum,* ringing in our ears, because a third element in Ménétra's narrative makes it strangely disturbing. It constantly brings us up

short against things we cannot fathom—everything from expressions beyond the range of our dictionaries (what is so insulting about saying
"bougie à l'huile" to a monk?) to behavior outside the scope of our experience (why does Ménétra take such delight in poking a cat in a cage and in
stealing chickens from a Jew?)

We cannot even get most of Ménétra's jokes. What is so funny, we
wonder, about the scene in Bayonne that seemed hilarious to him: half-
naked prostitutes shut in an iron cage and dumped into a river? Where is
the charm in the "charming farce" that he encountered in Lyon: a nobleman rounds up all the hunchbacks of the city and forces them to share a
meal while being served and serenaded by equally deformed townsmen?
Why does Ménétra find it impossible to contain his laughter when his boss
stumbles while carrying a load of glass panes above his head: "As he
wasn't wearing a wig, his head went right through the panes, and he was
collared; the bits of glass tore into his neck; the slightest movement caused
him excruiciating pain. . . . I couldn't prevent myself from bursting into
laughter and telling him he should have worn a hat"?

Laughter does not echo unambiguously across the ages. When it reaches
us from the distant past, it makes us sense the gap between our ancestors
and ourselves rather than our common humanity. Ménétra's jokes are usually cruel, and they often suggest that he expressed the brotherhood of
man through the spoliation of women. In a typical "prank," he and his pal
Gombeaut raped a girl whom they had found making love with her boyfriend in the woods outside Paris. Each of them took a turn while the
other held the boyfriend at bay, using a sword that he had left in the grass.
This feat consummated a pact that the two friends had made over a bottle
of wine a few days earlier. "We are great friends, but we must become
brothers," they declared. So they sold their silver shoe buckles and spent
the proceeds on a night together with a whore.

Now, the male animal may not have abandoned bestiality, but I doubt
that he behaves like that today, or at least that he would boast about it.
The peculiar character of Ménétra's boasting calls for an explanation. We
might, for example, glimpse an element of class conflict behind it. Ménétra
and his fellow workers made a specialty of cuckolding their bosses: that
was the funniest joke of all. When he arrived in Auch, Ménétra transmitted some venereal disease to the wife of his "bourgeois," as the workers
called their master. She passed it on to her husband, who, thinking, it had
come from another source, took his problem to Ménétra. Our hero was
skilled in folk medicine as in the arts of love. So he cured the grateful

couple and left town with the blessing of the bourgeois, who never suspected that he owed his disease to his doctor.

We also might explain the pranks as variations on the theme of social
and economic advancement. In the glazier's trade, as in many other skilled
crafts, masterships were restricted in number and transmissable through
widows. As the masters grew old and died, their widows took up with
journeymen, who in turn took over the shops. Ménétra bragged that he
could have fornicated his way to the top of many businesses on his *tour de
France*. When one of his mates broke up with a master's wife, Ménétra
took him to a tavern and consoled him with a proposition: "I'll buy her
from you for a bottle of wine and a salad."After sharing the food and later
the woman, they considered themselves "brothers."

That episode suggests another explanation: male bonding. The fellow
travelers often expressed their fellowship by sharing women. They even
felt united by venereal disease, which made them accomplices in a common dirty joke. After seducing a cook, Ménétra discovered that he had
come down with a case of the clap that was also afflicting two of his
drinking partners. Having traced it to the same source, they proclaimed
laughingly that they, too, had become "brothers," and they toasted their
fraternity in the tavern before undergoing a mercury treatment together.

But whatever sociological gloss you apply to the text—class rivalry,
social mobility, or peer group solidarity—it remains irreducibly strange.
Ménétra lived in a world so saturated with violence and death that we can
barely imagine it. We may have had some hard knocks in the subways of
New York or the throughways of Los Angeles, but how many of us encounter corpses on our daily rounds? Ménétra ran into them all the time, being
fished out of the Seine, exposed on gibbets, and carted through the streets
after fights or funerals. When he woke up one morning in an inn frequented by his *compagnonnage,* he found that his bedmate was dead. In
another inn, when his mate got up to urinate he tripped over a corpse that
had been stashed under the bed before their arrival.

Ménétra begins his life story by remarking casually that two of his three
siblings died at their wet nurses—a common experience according to the
historical demographers. He goes on to recount all sorts of violent incidents. A friend blows off his nose while playing with firecrackers. Two
others blind themselves. A cousin kills a scullery maid in the kitchen
while toying with a pistol. A fellow worker, sotted with drink, falls asleep
by the Pont Neuf and kills himself by tumbling into the Seine. Another
drinking partner dies after downing a bottle of poison that he mistook for

brandy. A woman in an apartment upstairs quarrels with her husband and jumps out the window, impaling herself on the wrought-iron sign of the shop below. The body count of the Journal looks nearly as impressive as the toll of seductions.

Ménétra probably inflated it in the course of the story telling, but his rhetoric is significant in itself. It shows that he assumed familiarity with death on the part of his readers and that he drew on the macabre element in the popular culture of his time. For example, he relates the crimes of La Giroux, a notorious murderess, in a manner like that of the broadsides sold at her execution. He describes buying a broadside himself and then adds a characteristic touch: during her last moments he worried that she would inculpate him by revealing that he had had her maidenhead. Ménétra reports the crimes and punishment of the Duhamel gang in similar fashion, dwelling on the most sensational details. "The monster Duhamel" killed his mistress, grilled her heart, and ate it. "During his interrogation, he boldly said to the lieutenant-criminal of police, 'Monsieur, if you had tasted it but once, you could never get enough.'"

Many other elements of popular culture also shape the narrative. Like most Parisians, Ménétra was fascinated with the public hangman, Henri Samson, who supposedly possessed extraordinary healing powers owing to his familiarity with death. When Ménétra fell into a kind of paralysis, "Monsieur Henri" put him back on his feet by administering a potion brewed from the body of a freshly executed criminal.

Whenever Ménétra consumes food in the Journal, he is doing something significant—curing a disease, seducing a woman, cementing a friendship, or finding a job. The tavern was more important than the church in the culture of his craft. It provided a fraternal atmosphere for the ceremonies of the *compagnonnage*. Ménétra ate and drank his way through many rites of passage and even invented one of his own, a burlesque version of baptism and the Eucharist. It was such a hit, he claimed, that the leaders of the *compagnonnage* took it seriously and reprimanded him for flooding their association with schismatic "journeymen of the crust."

He also acted in earnest as a master or ceremonies. His production of the glazier's feast of Saint Luke in Lyons seemed in retrospect to have been the high point of his life. He had all the glazier's shops hung in flowers and all the journeymen decked out in grey suits with white gloves and stockings, their hair curled and done up in white ribbons. They paraded through the streets carrying bouquets and the insignia of their craft to the sound of violins and oboes. Then, for nearly a week, they ate, drank, and danced.

The cost came to three hundred days' worth of labor, but they did not worry about it because they did not calculate time and money as modern workers do. Instead, they believed in excess—overeating, heavy drinking, extravagant spending, profligate wenching, hard brawling, big talking, and belly laughing.

All these attitudes fit together in a plebeian culture that was essentially Rabelaisian. While the upper classes snickered over Voltaire or wept over Rousseau, the working men, and perhaps many of the women, lived in a rowdy world that Rabelais had captured in writing two centuries earlier. Mikhail Bakhtin has shown that popular Rabelaisianism had a revolutionary edge to it. Could it have been the source of the ideology that Ménétra brought into the Revolution?

We cannot answer that question definitively, because Ménétra wrote only a short and garbled account of his experience as a sans-culotte. He saw the Terror at street level, where party lines disappeared in neighborhood feuds and politics degenerated into *règlements de compte*. Robespierre and the others do not appear in his narrative, but the people swarm through it—the common people, masters and journeymen alike—storming the Bastille, marching on the Tuileries Palace, leaving to face the invading armies at the border. This popular revolution did not derive from the Enlightenment, but it realized some of the principles that Ménétra had assimilated under the Old Regime. We can hear the future sans-culotte in the orator who toasted his fellow glaziers at the feast of Saint Luke in Lyons: "My friends, today we are all comrades together, and we all act in unison."

Similar ideas can be found in the *Social Contract*. But to understand the way they resonated in the revolutionary Sections of Paris, we need to go beyond Rousseau to Rabelais. Liberty and equality appear in *Gargantua* and *Pantagruel* as a festive throwing off of constraints and sharing of the good things in life—the values that the sans-culottes expressed as *liberté sans gêne* and *égalité dans les jouissances*.[2] Seen through Rabelais, Ménétra can help us grasp the third component of the sans-culotte trinity, the one that seems most alien today: fraternity. Ménétra did not learn brotherhood from books but from drinking and wenching his way around *tour de France*. His kind of fraternity could be violent and cruel, but in the supreme test of 1793–1794 it bound the common people together in a common effort not merely to fill the belly and rescue the republic but to save a way of life.

Because that way of life was transmitted on the road and in the tavern by men who did not write books, historians have had trouble tracking it down. They usually reconstruct the past from what they find in libraries. As professor succeeds professor, a pattern spreads from book to book. The process is probably healthy and in any case is inevitable. But sometimes in the course of it the life goes out of history. Daniel Roche has made a new life accessible, one so strange and yet authentic that it challenges our understanding of what it meant to be a man two centuries ago.

Robert Darnton

A Note on the Text

The holograph of Jacques-Louis Ménétra's journal consists of 331 folio sheets containing an unpunctuated, phonetically spelled text (see the facsimile reproduction). In presenting the text here in English translation, I have adopted the following conventions:

1. The text is printed without punctuation, as the author wished, but additional spaces and paragraph indentations have been added to mark the principal pauses in the flow of the prose. The infrequent periods and quotation marks in this edition faithfully reproduce those in Ménétra's manuscript.
2. The translator has tried to give an accurate and natural translation of Ménétra's French prose without seeking to invent an "eighteenth-century equivalent" in English. As Daniel Roche points out in his introduction, Ménétra's French is not always "correct" or elegant. The English version aims to be as faithful as possible yet still readable. There seemed to be no good reason to preserve, for example, the often dizzying combination of past and present tense in the French. I have tried, however, to avoid imposing order and logic where there is none. Historical linguists will of course wish to refer to the original French edition or, for Ménétra's phonetic orthography which even that edition does not preserve, to the original manuscript.
3. No attempt has been made in this translation to render certain peculiarities of Ménétra's French usage. For example, he uses *demander* (to ask) and *dire* (to say) interchangeably, as well as *que* (that, which) and *dont* (of which), *ou* (or) and *et* (and), *malgré* (despite) and *à cause* (because).
4. Added words are indicated by parentheses. As few words as possible have been added to facilitate understanding where the prose is elliptical (usually owing to missing personal or relative pronouns). Extraneous or erroneous words in the original manuscript, which were printed in square brackets in the French edition, have been deleted here.

The translation of the word *compagnon* warrants special comment. Normally it is rendered in English as "journeyman." But this is misleading, I think, for three reasons. First, the etymology of "journeyman" suggests payment by the day, which was not normally the case with the workers known as *compagnons* (cf. the French *journalier*). Second, to call a *compagnon* a journeyman is to domesticate the peculiarly French insitution of *compagnonnage,* which has no real English counterpart. And third, an important connotation of the word *compagnon* is that the compagnon and his master traditionally broke bread together (com-panion); to Jacques-Louis Ménétra, this was one of the distinguishing traits of the "good" master, or *bourgeois,* as he called him (and here translated, not without misgivings, as "boss"). In fact, when masters stopped eating with their companions, this was an ominous sign of social change. For these reasons, I have broken with traditional usage and translated *compagnon* as "companion."

The explanations given in the notes are translated from the editor's comments in the French edition, generally based on such well-known French dictionaries as those of the Academy, Trevoux, Furetière, the Encyclopedia, Littré, and Robert, with occasional translator's notes added.

Manuscript 678 of the Bibliothèque historique de la ville de Paris consists of two parts: a *Journal* with pages numbered 1 to 331, here translated, and a section of *Miscellaneous Writings* and poems.

A. G.

Journal of My Life

Introduction
The Autobiography of a Man of the People

This text has no history. We have no way of tracing its itinerary. What meager clues it contains lead nowhere: The manuscript comes from the library of F. A. Destouche, but no trace of this bibliographer has survived. It belongs to the Bibliothèque historique of the city of Paris, but the administrative records of that library do not reveal exactly when or where the manuscript was acquired. The historian soon finds himself going in circles trying to track down, as scholarly prudence requires, the whys and the wherefores of this manuscript and attempting to understand the no doubt unique destiny of the Parisian glazier Jacques-Louis Ménétra. The man did exist; traces of his life can be found, not without difficulties, in Paris archives. One day he decided to write this insolent memoir, this specimen of what a people's literature might have been. Many questions can be asked about the meaning of this authentic, first-person account of eighteenth-century life.

"The poor are mad," as Cesare Zavattini pointed out in 1936, ironically underscoring a fundamental truth about the way in which the language, physical circumstances, and ways of life of the poor conspire to create another world, a "culture of poverty," different from "high" culture and with a coherence all its own.[1] More serious, perhaps, from the point of view of the historian, the poor are silent; excluded from the normal channels of the official culture, they are usually forbidden to make their voices heard. Exceptional circumstances do sometimes enable us to hear these voices from another world. A family record might, for example, be expanded into a diary or chronicle. This was rare enough in the privileged classes and almost unheard of among the lower orders. Men who took up their pens were eager not so much to tell their own stories as to trace sudden changes in their family fortunes, to record the succession of the generations, the births and the deaths, the cycle of the seasons, the storing of the harvest, or the occurrence of some memorable event. Consider, for example, the sagathy weaver Pierre Ignace Chavatte of Lille, who from 1657 to 1693 kept a record of his life which today, thanks to Alain Lottin's exemplary research, is one of our rare direct sources of information about the artisans, the textile workers, the "simple folk" of the Flemish cities.[2] For the whole long reign of Louis XIV there is nothing else from all of France. Or consider the autobiography of Valentin Jamerey-Duval, a peasant who, after leaving home and contending with enormous difficulties, ultimately became librarian to the Grand Duke of Lorraine and one of the finest scholars of his time, and whose account of his life reveals what anguish could result from so remarkable a rise.[3] But for the entire reign on Louis XV that is all we have.

Within the next hundred years the industrial revoluton had altered traditional ways of living, the old urban civilization had begun to crumble, the political cauldron had come to a boil, and autobiographical writings by companions [i.e., *compagnons*, journeymen belonging to one of the mutual-aid societies known as *compagnonnages*; see introductory note for further comment on this translation—trans.] and workers had become a flourishing genre—a sign of irreversible social changes and of the development of new forms of alienation. The Provençal carpenter Agricol Perdiguier; Etienne Arnaud, citizen of Libourne, a companion baker; Pierre Moreau, locksmith of Château-Renault; the carpenter Joseph Voisin, known as Angoumois l'Ami; Auguste Batard, the harness maker of Mantes; the blacksmith Abel Boyer, born in Domme in the Perigord; Martin Nadaud, the Limousin mason; Toussaint Guillaumou, known as Carcassone le Bien-aimé, a companion cobbler; and many others noted by Roger Lecotte[4] began to talk and to write, breaking the centuries-old silence of the have-nots. They did so in part because their world was crumbling around them, and often too because personal commitment led them to seek avenues of self-expression, to debate and engage with their enemies. In forging their own identity they had to create for themselves a collective past.[5] Sociologists were quick to attempt to understand workers and peasants through biography, and scholars have ever since continued to make use of biographical source material. Thus biography can tell us about how journeyman artisans responded to the progress that was depriving them of their livlihoods, or about how peasants and workers today are reacting as the age-old story of expropriation is played out anew: "Tell me your life and I will tell you who you are." For anyone who hopes to imagine other possibilities for development, for anyone who believes that society can be understood only from within, this kind of knowledge is indispensable.

The very fact that Jacques-Louis Ménétra's text stands alone of its kind, a solitary beacon from another age, raises an important question: Was it possible in the eighteenth century for a man of the people to write an autobiography? By this I mean a true autobiography, a work centered on the individual, the "I," the strictly personal point of view, a work that sets forth the totality of a life and seeks to bestow upon that life a profound unity derived not from any external source but from within (the kind of view recently adumbrated in the work of certain historians and sociologists of popular culture, oral traditions, etc.).[6] Today as in the past, authentic biography[7] seeks to restore voices to people deprived of their opportunity to speak because "'I' happens to be nobody."[8]

In any case, it would be rather hasty to conclude that simply because no other workingmen's biographies have come to light, none existed: Chance played a part in determining what was preserved and what perished, and in any case, He who does not seek does not find. Every autobiography is, in a sense, an interpretation of the statement, "I became myself."[9] But what if historical circumstances are not such as to encourage self-understanding of this kind? Most people who spoke in their own names before Ménétra discovered who they were only by repudiating their origins, through a kind of self-imposed bastardy. Valentin Jamerey-Duval and Jean-Jacques Rousseau managed in their lifetimes to traverse the vast distance that separated, say, an out-of-the-way village in the *élection* of Tonnerre, or the shop of an ordinary Geneva watchmaker, from much-coveted status in the republic of letters.[10] Marmontel is another case in point.

Rousseau and Duval were continually torn between the desire to subscribe to dominant social values and the wish to be free and independent, a wish rooted in social difference. Both acquired a full measure of cultural capacity—of capacity, that is, to participate in the culutre of the official classes—and both refused in their way to trade the alienation of poverty for the alienation of culture. Both were aware, too, of their uniqueness. If the Genevan Protestant and the Burgundian Catholic differed in talent and renown, if the proud willfulness of Jean-Jacques, who could say "I constitute an undertaking that has no model and will have no imitator," contrasts sharply with the sincere modesty of the erudite Valentin, still both men invoked the imperative of knowledge to justify the candor of their self-revelation. How can a man establish his personality in the face of opposition? How does the world make us what we are? How is it that ordeals are always experienced as liberating? These were the questions they tried to answer. Thus both men are of the people but no longer see the people, i.e., the lower strata of society, from within: they are writer-observers, not workers indulging themselves in literary exercise. Their subject matter, their manner of treatment was in part given to them by what I may call the rhetoric of autobiography, which first appeared in European writing in the second half of the eighteenth century and whose possibilities each man explored in his own way. Both wrote for an au-dience prepared to understand what they had to say, for readers ready to recognize themselves in the candor of autobiography. Jacques-Louis Méné-tra is a writer of another breed.

His sense of his undertaking surely proves that the discovery that the personality has a history was not limited to cultivated circles. Ménétra's relationship to the past, his intention to give voice to his own history, is not unlike the relationship to the past of Rousseau or Duval. But he was also clearly aware of the difference between his project and theirs. Six introductory epistles (only one of which is reproduced in the present volume) and a concluding section of the text itself, all written, it seems likely, after the memoirs were complete and recopied, exhibit such numer-ous changes of mind, clumsy repetitions, and uncertainty of tone that we can only conclude that the author was unsure of himself, and uncertain of his purpose as a writer, to a degree that sets him apart from the ordinary eighteenth-century man of letters.

A relatively poor man, Ménétra attempted to justify his confusion by claiming that what he was doing was unprecedented in his social and cultural milieu. His tone is one of droll derision: tricks, pranks, mischief, nonsense, and folly are, as it were, the notes that fall within the natural range of a man who, unlike most writers of his day, cannot, in displaying his voice, make a great show of his learning or polished style. His vocabu-lary proves that he is familiar with the other culture—the culture of his betters—but that it does not suit him. The words that come to him natu-rally to describe his enterprise—memoirs, souvenirs, confessions, "Journal of My Life," history—only highlight the fact that his work does not fit any of the traditional definitions. Words and phrases such as "preface," "dedication," "epistle," and "profession of faith," common enough in liter-ary publications, crop up fairly frequently in Ménétra's writing, but while he knows the words he is not entirely in command of their meaning; his doubts justify his claim that, as a writer, he is less than a fully qualified journeyman. His writings are "scribblings," a mere "jumble." He is obsessed by the temptation to destroy what he has done: all his work, he says, is "good for throwing . . . into the fire . . . for renouncing . . . for erasing . . . for crossing out."

Why, then, does he persist in writing, and why does he preserve his finished work? Because he continues to believe in the deeper impulse that drove him to write, not simply for his own pleasure but in order to prove to himself that, despite all the changes wrought by the times and by the forces of history (and we shall see in what follows how important a part the Revolution played in his life), he has remained a fundamentally just and good man. The moral of this work, so alien to literary culture and so assiduously denied by its author, is to insist that the precept by which a free man ought to live is "To thine own self be true." This embarrassed attempt by a man of the people to justify his life offers the historian a broad view of the norms and values that were accepted, rejected, or modified by an entire social group or class.

The deliberate choice of a rather awkward and offhand style is a manifestation of class consciousness. Ménétra was surely intelligent enough to learn grammer and correct his spelling. That he did not do so illustrates his desire to express, through stylistic difference, his distance from the writing of the well-bred. The texture of the composition signifies its author's refusal to fully accept the dominant culture. Ménétra's style is what I might call partially alienated: he chooses to depart from commonly accepted practice and adopts his own rules. Written throughout in a clear and legible hand without any punctuation whatsoever, save for a few quotation marks to indicate dialogue, without breaks or divisions and therefore "without limits," spelled phonetically—which would not have been unusual in a routine business letter but which is unusual in a longer piece, intended for a wider audience—indifferent to distinctions of gender, jumping at will from the feminine to the masculine pronoun or from the singular to the plural, without erasure or "errata," the three hundred pages of Ménétra's manuscript attest to the possibility of "libertarian literature." The shadow of great literature does not eclipse this work, despite its frequent clumsiness and occasional confusion and repetitiousness, for its savor and the talent of its author show through in frequent insights and delightful quirks of style. What is more, the text offers an independent view of the world and the story of a unique individual who, though aware of the literary proprieties and conventions of the age, chooses not to subscribe to them.

It is possible that Ménétra read Rousseau, whom he knew and whose works were widely disseminated prior to 1789. In a letter he mentions the *Social Contract, Emile,* and *Héloise.* It is probable, given his wide-ranging curiosity, that he also read many other writers of the first and second rank. But his silence about whatever reading he may have done clearly indicates his distance from the accepted genres, from the Memoirs, Lives, and Histories of the day. He is a "poor scribbler" because he belongs to another social class. A commoner, without ancestors, his problem was not to explain how he had arrived at his station in life but on the contrary to make it quite clear that his destiny was to remain precisely what he had always been, and perhaps, too, to suggest how history was destroying the traditional ways of the people among whom he had been born. Writing his story enabled him to resolve the contradiction inherent in his writing at all; remembering the past was a way of asserting his ability to be himself, in spite of others and of the times in which he lived.

We do not know exactly when this text was written. Ménétra claims several times that he began writing on 9 August 1764, and the manuscript was completed on 25 Vendémiaire in the Year XI. It is doubtful that the writing took forty years, but there is evidence of some backtracking and pangs of conscience. In the first place the manuscript is in two parts. One contains the 331 pages of the Journal per se, and it is these pages that are reproduced in the present translation. The other includes various sketches and essays composed at different times between 1768 and 1802, some hundred-odd pages here referred to as "Miscellaneous Writings." Analysis of these writings has made it possible to date some of the events referred to by Ménétra in his Journal. Beyond that, the Miscellaneous Writings show that, even as his interests changed, Ménétra continued to evince a desire to write for an audience. He collected the entirety of his output: halting love poems, family epitaphs, acrostics, work songs written during his travels as an itinerant artisan (the first of which, probably composed in 1757, is not dated), verse plays concerning his dealings with the jury of The Paris glaziers' guild, political poems in honor of the son of Louis XVI, La Fayette, and Bonaparte, some fifteen erotic poems, several prose plays on the French Revolution and on various religious matters, and a so-called "Search for Truth."

The very heterogeneous character of this oeuvre recalls works by the inspired tinkerers of modern art, the architects of the ephemeral and the

Sunday painters. Like them, Ménétra frequently initialed his minor crea-tions, displaying his signature as though to take possession of the work—a little ostentatiously, perhaps—and thereby to reassert his identity. All of this indicates that Ménétra was very attached to what he wrote. He took the trouble to keep and later to recopy works composed at various points in his life. His manuscript is in some sense the monument he built in his own honor, to proclaim that a man of his station and his stamp could in his own way emulate his betters and stake his all on the possibility of commu-nicating with another generation. The children and nephews mentioned several times in the nervously inquisitive pages of the "Autobiographical Pact" would have been able, in any case, to profit from his example. The care taken with the calligraphy of the text, the attention devoted to page layout and presentation, and the meticulous preparation of a title page for each play suggest the habits of the Parisian artisan and pride in a job well done.

Densely set on the page, the text of the Journal contrasts with the loose, fragmentary composition of the notebooks of poetry and prose. Only the first few pages of the Journal exhibit the customary attention to visual matters; the rest evoke the labor of a copyist determined to allow no breaks or pauses in the flow of his script. That the manuscript is recopied from a text written earlier and revised in retirement, at the end of the Revolu-tion, is indicated by various pieces of internal evidence: a brief profession of faith at the end of the work is included in the introduction; the tragic events of the Terror, treated in detail in pages 303-328 of the Journal manuscript as well as in the Miscellaneous Writings ("My Reflections on the Revolution," pp. 69-78, "My Answers to the Invective," pp. 78-83, "My Response to the Caluminators," pp. 83-94), "On the Day of 9 Ther-midor," "On the Day of 13 Vendémiaire," pp. 94–101, and "On the Most Impressive Days of the Revolution," pp. 102-104), are referred to as early as the second page of the Journal manuscript as well as in the foreword or dedicatory epistle "To Myself" on page five. It is worth noting that all the names from the period 1789-1800 have been added in the margin, as though upon rereading, when there would have been nothing more to fear from the revolutionary commissars.[11] Certain events are adumbrated in the Journal before the occur, as on page 177 of the manuscript where Ménétra concludes the account of his adventure with the young governess Manon with the announcement of the rediscovery of the children, recounted on page 255.[12]

All things considered, it seems likely that Ménétra first conceived his

project in 1764, that he was able to write a version or fragments of the
Journal sometime thereafter, and that he probably recopied everything at
some point between the Year X (1802), which is the date given on page 4,
and the Year XI (1803), when page 331 was written. To complete the
project, miscellaneous works were collected and recopied from originals,
now lost, composed between 1757 and 1802. Proof that Ménétra's interest
in this work was rekindled can be seen in the binding, crude as it is, the
use of sheets of a single kind of paper, and the renumbering by double
pages from 1 to 251, added to a page-by-page numbering scheme that
contains errors in Ménétra's own hand (two series of pages 167, 168, 169,
for example).

All of this effort must have required considerable psychological stamina
in order to overcome the difficulties that surely would have confronted
any urban artisan engaging in what after all was a pursuit rather unusual
in this segment of society. Writing, as well as reading for that matter,
would have required a financial investment, which, though not enormous,
might well have given pause: paper had to be bought, along with goose-
feather quills, ink, sand, a writing desk, and perhaps books and brochures
that may have served as inspiration. Reading and writing both required
the right physical setting: one would have had to overcome the handicaps
of bad housing and lighting and the disturbances due to crowding in
shared rooms or back offices; beyond that, it took effort to write legibly
with instruments less easy to handle than the glassmaker's diamond, hammer, and plate of mastic. Last but not least, to write was to make a
deliberate choice, to break the habit of oral communication and to shun
common leisure activities. To write was to stay away, for a time at least,
from the cabaret, from the groups that gathered to gossip on a doorstep or
around the chimney, and to choose instead a solitary activity, to exhibit
qualities of introspection relatively uncommon in these circles and, when
one has read the Journal, quite surprising in a man like Ménétra.

The reader may find it useful to know something of the chronology of
Ménétra's life. What is obscure in the text of the Journal itself can be
clarified somewhat with the help of information from the archives.

Jacques-Louis Ménétra was baptized in Paris, in the Saint-Germain-
l'Auxerrois Church, on Sunday, 13 July 1738. He was the son of Jacques
Ménétra, a master glazier, and of Marie-Anne Marseau.[13] He spent his
childhood in Paris, leaving the city on 29 March 1757 to begin his "tour of
France." He apparently returned a short while later, because he mentions
a stay of three months in Orléans and says that he spent part of the winter

in the capital, from which he set out once more at an indeterminate date. The marriage license of the son of the man who employed him in Angers enables us to fix the date of his stay in Anjou as the summer of 1758[14] and of his arrival in Brittany as the autumn of that year, since it followed both the wedding and the battle (cited by Ménétra) of Saint-Cast, both of which took place on 11 September 1758. His stay in Bordeaux and departure from Guyenne can both be dated, very roughly, as having occurred in the summer of 1759: he was in Bordeaux during the earthquake that occurred on the night of 10 August 1759, and he left the city after the return of Marshal Richelieu on 18 September 1759.[15] He probably spent the fall and winter in Haut-Languedoc, moving between Agen, Auch, and Toulouse. He attended Holy Week services at Isle-Jourdain in 1760 and subsequently, in May or June, found work in Montpellier.[16] He states that he was then in his twentieth year. If his stay in Nîmes lasted approximately five months, then he must have arrived in Provence in 1761, around springtime. He was then obliged to spend Easter at Carpentras,[17] and he attended Corpus Christi ceremonies at Aix in the month of May.

Neither the Journal nor any other document gives us any precise information about his stay in Lyons or about his final return to Paris. A comparison of the text of the memoirs with the summary, in burlesque verse, that introduces the second part of Ménétra's works turns up certain discrepancies. In the memoirs there is a long and detailed account of certain events, including Ménétra's appointment as "first companion" in Lyons during his eleven months' stay in that city, which are said to have come after his return to Paris, his second stay in Nîmes, his slow journey northward, his work in Mâcon and Burgundy, the carnival of Bourg-en-Bresse, the trip to Geneva, and various events that take place in Paris. In the verse summary, however, the Lyons events are mentioned only briefly and are said to have occurred during the first return journey to Paris. The chronology becomes clearer if we accept Ménétra's assertion that he was in Paris for the inauguration of the statue of Louis XV on 22 June 1763. If this was indeed the case, then he must have stopped twice in Lyons, the first time for a longer period than he says, and some of the things that he claims happened during the second stay must in fact have occurred during the first.

A visit to Dijon during the snowy season suggests that Ménétra returned to Paris during the winter of 1762-63, with Saint Luke's day (18 October 1762) marking the high point of his stay in Lyons. Thus he would have begun his new life in Paris in the spring of 1763, only to depart again that summer, before returning home a second time in 1764, and some of the events ascribed to that time in the Journal must actually have taken place earlier, in 1762-63. Ménétra was probably in Bourg for the 1764 carnival, after which he visited Geneva and returned, by way of Sologne, to Paris during the summer of 1764. The date that Ménétra gives for the commence-ment of work on his Journal, 9 August 1764, may well be the date that he finally returned to Paris to stay.

Having attained his majority, the twenty-six-year-old Jacques-Louis Ménétra married in June of 1765, as we know from the marriage contract signed on the 28th of that month before the notary Sibire of the rue Saint-Denis.[18] With two-thirds of the manuscript recopied, almost forty years of life still remain to its author, who depicts his youth as hectic but his years after the age of thirty as a time of nostalgia passed in monotonous routine. There is very little chronological detail about the period 1765-89. A few facts are clear, however: Ménétra did witness the accident on the rue Royale on 30 May 1770. He was by then the father of two living children, a daughter, Marie-Madeleine, baptized in Saint-Sauveur parish on 9 May 1761[19] and a son, whose date of birth and first name we do not know. Ménétra is mentioned in the *Almanach du Commerce* of 1769. He sub-poenaed Sir Collet de Grandmaison to appear in court on 5 November 1771 for default of payment. He probably met Jean-Jacques Rousseau in his room on the rue Platrière in June 1771.[20] The Marseau-Oran wedding took place in 13 August 1773, and several verse plays illustrating Ménétra's disputes with the warden of the glaziers' guild date from 1776, shortly before Turgot's short-lived dissolution of the guilds. Ménétra's father died, according to his epitaph, in November of 1776, and his wife left him for the first time in 1778. He dwells at considerable length on the bankruptcy of his uncle Marseau, the glazier, whose petition for bankruptcy, dated 5 February 1778, has been found in the Archives of the Seine Department.

At the outbreak of the Revolution Ménétra was fifty-one years old.[21] His journal proceeds from this point in more or less chronological order. The last piece of evidence concerning his life is his daughter's marriage license, dated 20 Fructidor in the Year XI of the Republic.[22] The manuscript of the Journal ends on 25 Vendémiaire of the same year. Jacques-Louis Ménétra, having had his brush with history, then exits the scene.

It is impossible, after spending several years of one's life with a charac-ter like Ménétra, not to feel a pang at having his story end so abruptly. Ménétra was seductive by design. "I am vigorous and a little wild, I keep no venom in my heart, I try even harder not to get angry, I forget everything overnight; I love my children dearly and my wife the same way, I love the small and the great, I love any man who is benevolent and loving."[23] Behind the awkwardness of the poetry [the passage just cited rhymes in the original—trans.] A personality stands revealed, a need to conquer the hearts of others. We know that Ménétra was a seducer and a tease. We also know that he was a man of small stature—that is all we know about his physical appearance. He embodies the traits of the Parisian, as his "companion's name," Parisien le Bienvenue suggests (companions called one another by these chosen names; "le Bienvenue" is Ménétra's own unorthodox spelling—grammatically, the feminine final "e" clashes with the masculine article—trans.)

This son of the largest city in the western world has left, for our pleasure and edification, an incomparable, if occasionally histrionic, account of the lives of ordinary men and women during some sixty years of the Age of Enlightenment, men and women of the class that produced the *sans-culottes* of the French Revolution. He enables us, two centuries later, to gain a better understanding of how the culture of this group was created and what role it played in their lives. Delving into his five hundred pages enables the historian to get away from the usual procedures and categories of cultural history. An alternative to the statistical approach, the study of the Journal helps us to see how a social group coped with changing values and norms.

Ménétra's account is more than just picturesque; it restores the human dimension to the study of social conditions and brings flesh and blood to lifeless sociological categories. What we can finally see, with the help of these memoirs, is ordinary, everyday life.[24] Indispensable as quantitative social history is,[25] the Journal enables us to move beyond it to a more dynamic mode of inquiry that gives full weight to the way in which individuals help to shape the norms that govern their lives.[26] Unlike judicial records, Ménétra's Journal enables the historian to see how average men and women, people who never fell afoul of the police or the religious authorities, lived their lives.[27] Of course it is always possible to object that the story of a single individual is atypical. But what a biographical approach may sacrifice in breadth it gains in depth. It casts new light on the results of work based on police and church archives. For sources such as these must be approached in a particular way, a way that inevitably obscures certain aspects of life which a memoir like Ménétra's can brilliantly illuminate.

Ménétra's Journal is unequaled in its descriptions of private life, as is evident if one compares it with, say, Chavatte's memoir. It shows how individuality impinges upon society and how character and imagination influence the collective perception of mores. Misrepresentation, exaggeration, and error take on meaning, as do omissions and fantasies, for it is impossible to separate the two questions that lie at the root of any attempt at autobiography: Who am I for myself? and Who am I for others? The relationship of individual to society can be treated in ways other than those imposed on Rousseau by his feelings of guilt and on Valentin Jamerey-Duval by his bastard birth. An everyman's theory of the personality can be seen in the very incoherence of a first-person account filled with expressions of longing for freedom, social and sexual fantasies, and moral and religious dreams.

Ménétra's text enables us to inquire about the structure of collective feeling, but without losing the point of view of a specific class. Its truth is not to be found in some inaccessible reality but in the way it helps us to gauge the distance between individual and collective behavior. With a style, a language, a mental equipment all his own, Ménétra gives voice not so much to a mentality as to a culture. His Journal also contradicts the view that biography is a pedestrian historical genre: after all, doesn't every life begin with birth and end with death?[28] Biography sheds light on the way in which society actually works, for we see how all the various aspects of the social structure impinge upon the life of a single individual.[29] It begins to make sense to talk of the historical anthropology of the working classes of Paris in the eighteenth century.

Jacques-Louis Ménétra, Parisien le Bienvenue, was a child of one of the great capitals of modernity. He was born and died in a city that grew in population from between four and five hundred thousand to between seven and eight hundred thousand citizens and in size from 1,000 hectares in the time of Louis XIV to 3,000 hectares in the time of Louis XVI (when Verniquet prepared his map of the city). He was the child of a city that survived the ordered disorder of expansion and the unruly order of the Revolution. Born into the class of artisans which, along with workers and fringe groups made up three quarters of the population, he saw history from below and provides a complement to the familiar observations of such commentators as Rétif de la Bretonne, Mercier, and various physicians and travelers. In particular, when history intrudes upon his life in 1789, he shows that in every historical event there are many actors, and that the Revolution and the turmoil that surrounded it were compounded of a hundred different daily happenings, reflecting an equal number of individual lives. Banality is an ingredient of history too.

But something strange happened in the Paris of the Enlightenment and Revolution. What was unusual about the experience of Parisians was due, as I have shown elsewhere,[30] to an extraordinary accumulation of wealth and intelligence. In the upper reaches of society traditional values were on the decline even as the pace of change in material life was accelerating. This accelerating pace of change, visible in fashion and in the sphere of consumption generally, affected other spheres as well. These upheavals brought the possibility of personal freedom within reach; but the limits of change can be appreciated only if we look at society's lower strata. Ménétra's life spans the period from the reign of Louis XV to the coming of Napoleon; he shared the destiny of his fellows, and his life tells us much about the way in which obscure men and women responded day by day to the imperatives of history.

"The stew that I'm concocting here is nothing but a record of my life's attempts." These words of Paul Cazin might equally well be applied to Ménétra's Journal. The right way to approach the Journal is not by paraphrase but rather by patient exploration. Our purpose is to understand the decisive changes in the life of the common people from the seventeenth century to the present, the most important of which come together in Ménétra's Paris.

In establishing the text of the Journal I benefitted from the help and friendship of Frédérique Blanchot and Jean Colson, who also assisted in the checking of numerous facts.

My thanks also to Mme Verlet and the personnel of the Bibliothèque historique of the city of Paris; to Marie-E. Bénabou, Roger Chartier, Emile Ducoudray, Michel Feuillas, Maurice Garden, Dominique Julia, Marcel Lachiver, Nicole Lemaître, François Lebrun, Philippe Loupes, Jacques Maillard, Henri Michel, Raymonde Monnier, Jean Nicolas, Nicole Pellegrin, and Jean Vogt.

Sabine Juratic and Martine Sonnet helped me to locate certain essential documents, and I would like to single them out here for special thanks. Special thanks also to André Pézard for listening with the attentive and enthusiastic ear of the philologist.

Daniel Roche

Journal of My Life

To my mind

Made to stand, my mind, above all your scribbling
This will be a preface or at any rate a dedication
surely destined for the eyes of magistrates
or at very least some head of State
asking humbly for their suffrage
and making a show of pompous verbiage
and so, my mind, you're probably going to speak of your ancestors
and seek by your writings to make them known
and trace your origins to all those noble knights
and your nobility at least thirty-two quarters
so that your children and little nephews
will glory in their earliest forebears
But if you're going as I cannot believe
to bid farewell to the common class of men
I hope to see all these writings tossed into the fire
You must know my mind that man is born glorious
they will find rightly that there is no spelling or comma
much less any vowel, or consoles [sic] and many gaps
they will say that you are my mind a poor scribbler
that you show off your weaknesses and defects and errors
you see that your papers are filled with errata
Believe me tear it all up and burn this mess
This is Ménétra's idea

Journal of my life
written by me in the year 1764
Ménétra
entirely without ostentation or reflection
To write the truth as I see it means not to speak of arms or heraldry to forget about one's ancestors and not to embellish one's name with vain titles

I was born on 13 July 1738 a native of this great city My father belonged to the class usually called artisans His profession was that of glazier Hence it is with him that I begin my family tree and I shall say nothing about my ancestors My father married and set himself up at the same time and wed a virtuous girl who gave him four children three daughters and one boy myself all of whose little pranks I'm going to write about

My father became a widower when I was two years old I had been put out to nurse My grandmother who always loved me a great deal and even idolized me knowing that the nurse I was with had her milk gone bad came to get me and after curing me put me back out to nurse (where) I ended up with a pretty good woman who taught me early on the profession of begging She had for foster-child a mute whom people said I mimicked marvelously My mother[1] and my godfather when they came to see me and brought me a belt of the order of Saint Francis[2] for they had pledged me to all the saints found me in a church begging charity[3] They took me home and from then until the age of eleven I lived with my good grandmother My father wanted me back afraid that he would have to pay my board He put me to work in his trade even though several people tried to talk him out of it (but) he wouldn't listen to them I had a pretty good grandmother As she had several children she tried every way she could to expatriate me from the house which got my father hot and very excited

When a place as choirboy at Saint-Germain[4] came open I won the

---

[1] Ménétra uses the word "mother" interchangeably with "grandmother" and "good mother" (bonne mère) in referring to his maternal grandmother, Mme Marseau (née Boyer).

[2] The holy sash distributed by Franciscan monks and certain confraternities to their young charges. It was intended as a reminder of the sash that St. Francis gave to St. Dominic in 1227 or 1228, an angelic sash that recurs in Franciscan iconography and symbolizes devotion to the baby Jesus and the Nativity.

[3] Demandant la calistade, meaning begging. The term probably derives from the Italian carista or the Provençal carestié. Its use illustrates how foreign words were picked up by workers on the tour of France—Ménétra spent time in Provence.

[4] Ménétra's parish is one of the oldest in Paris. As the parish of the Louvre, its population

competition I stayed there around three or four months when I became sick with boredom from not seeing my grandmother It was in the days of those beautiful and miraculous and extraordinary miracles brought about by the malicious mischief and greed of a grocer in the faubourg Saint-Antoine during the procession on the Sunday of Corpus Christi known as Madame Lafosse's Sunday[5] The good mother of the baby Jesus stood at the corner of the rue de Lappe As she turned her head from the other side of the rue Saint-Antoine (on the day) at the moment when the procession passed suddenly men posted there began shouting Miracle! She was actually watching the procession pass by The scandalous story of the miracles showed plainly what the grocer was up to with another man a sculptor another crook of the same type The priests pretended to believe (and) the vulgar who love novelties particularly the Virgin who produced several children ran to see this miraculous miracle especially the good women and all the devout My good grandmother took me there during the neuvaine and I stayed like the others two hours on my knees listening to people mutter between their teeth and (one) burned a little candle in honor of the lady who had so nicely turned her head and her sweet little boy This little ruse made that swindler a fortune in the neighborhood (where he) was not much in the odor of sanctity because rumor had it that without this happy stratagem he would have gone bankrupt

This shows quite clearly that there have always been hypocrites who take advantage of the people's credulity and that when religion is involved the priests dive right in by reason of fanaticism and superstition Not very long ago my good grandmother was always telling me blue tales of the miracles of Monsieur Paris[6] and my mother found it very wrong that

---

included not only working people but also aristocrats after the Court's return to Paris in 1715. The parish church was a collegial until 1740–44. From then on the canonry joined that of the cathedral. The canons and curates of Saint-Germain had long maintained a choir school, which took in six pupils for training in music and Latin. Saint-Eustache and of course Notre-Dame also had choir schools. These institutions were part of the Paris school system. Ménétra may have attended classes at the parish school after leaving the choir school. See M. B. Aubry and J. Hillairet, *Saint-Germain-l'Auxerrois* (Paris, 1955), and R. Charter et al., *L'Education en France, XVIe–XVIII siècle* (Paris, 1976).

[5] A reference to the commemoration of the miraculous recovery of Mme Lafosse, the wife of a cabinet maker of the faubourg Saint-Antoine, during the Corpus Christi procession of 30 May 1725. The fraudulent miracle described by Ménétra probably dates from the period 1740–45.

[6] An allusion to the Jansenist beliefs of the populace aroused by miracles brought about by the intercession of François de Paris, a deacon and member of a family of magistrates in Parlement who was venerated for his holy life. These miracles were responsible for the

the *parlement* should have walled up the cemetery in which this would-be newly-made saint was buried

It was at about this time that one of my uncles who lived in the Ile Saint-Louis took me to Issy to a village one league outside of Paris to collect a hundred écus that were owed him for a building that he had glazed there The fellow received us quite handsomely served us a copious dinner and we stayed at table until quite late in the evening I had gone out to look for fruit in the garden Night fell and the gentleman of the house kept my uncle there and soused him with drink[7] and my uncle made no haste to depart At last the fellow saw us to the door and bid us good night and a pleasant journey Both my uncle and I had to relieve ourselves We went out he took me by the hand and without noticing we went backwards we turned our backs on Paris My uncle went on about his warm welcome and how well we were treated and what is more paid We walked the wine warmed us I found the route longer than it had been that morning my uncle teased me that I was unhappy about not being caressed by my grandmother Finally after walking for about two hours we see a light in the distance My uncle says to me Do you see the lanterns of the faubourg Saint-Germain and at that very moment the light disappears and the night goes blank We continue walking and come to a village It was frightfully dark everything was shrouded in sleep Through the slits of a door we spot that blessed light We knock we ask if we are far from Paris A voice answers that we are three leagues away My uncle begs that we be let in (for) we have lost our way and are in need of shelter A woman comes to the door We sit down I fall asleep from fatigue my uncle does the same

(He) wakes me up when he sees moonlight we make for the countryside To top off our good fortune nobody is home We suspect that my aunt has gone to my grandmother's by way of the rue aux Ours à la Vièrge[8] We see a lighted candle and two old women on their knees who rise at the sight of us One cries out it's my child and the other it's my

---

disturbances caused by the so-called convulsionists in the Saint-Médard cemetery (faubourg Saint-Marcel). Ménétra links these practices to the legends and fables contained in widely circulated publications printed by Troyes booksellers.

7 *Fluter*: to drink copiously, a Parisianism for "to intoxicate."

8 A miraculous statue which had been an object of popular devotion ever since a miracle in the fifteenth century, when a Swiss soldier struck it and made it bleed. The commemoration of the miracle on 3 July is mentioned by Rousseau, because it involved the burning in effigy of a Swiss soldier in which he saw a sign of his persecution.

husband and both say that it's for having invoked this piece of earth molded by the hand of man and want us to believe that it's a miracle when it was only our mistake and pure chance In the end all it cost us was our fatigue and a few Ave Marias

The youngest of my uncles worked at the abbey of Saint Denis[9] and brought me to spend six weeks with him The fathers liked to take me into the garden and make me sing I played a thousand tricks on them that made them laugh On days when the crypt was open for viewing I went downstairs with the brother and imitated him with his stick pointing out all the trinkets invented by fanaticism and perpetuated by superstition I don't mean the rare things but all those bones and skulls of saints about which one day the fathers argued among themselves whether it was the head of Saint Dionysius of Corinth or of Saint Dionysius the Areopagite that they had in the crypt brought there not (by) faith but by the igno-rance[10] and simplicity of our early ancestors and the bad faith of those who governed the peoples to keep them in harness

I became homesick for my grandmother When I felt a little better I went back to my usual ways which is to say that my father was always angry with me One night when I was lighting the way in a staircase where he was installing a casement and not mounting it the way he wanted with an angry kick (he) knocked out all my teeth When I got back home my mother took me to a dentist by the name of Ricie who put back the teeth that weren't broken and I went three weeks eating nothing but bouillon and soup

In those days it was rumored that they were taking young boys[11] and

---

[9] This Benedictine abbey is celebrated for its tombs of the French kings and for the relics in its crypt: a piece of the true cross, a nail of the Passion, and the bones of Saint Dionysius, the first bishop of Paris and martyr whose fantastic identification with one of the fathers of the Eastern Church had been the object of criticism ever since the sixteenth century. The monas-tery was rebuilt by Robert de Cotte shortly before Ménétra's uncle started work there.

[10] The French reads *qui apporta non (par) la foi mais bien par l'ignorance,* by which Ménétra probably meant *non pour la foi mais bien par l'ignorance* (as translated—trans.).

[11] On 22 and 23 May 1750 Paris was rocked by a popular uprising caused by a rumor that the police were kidnapping young children for the islands and colonies. Officers of the police had in fact made arrests in connection with a campaign against begging, and their actions may well have been interpreted as Ménétra suggests. Disturbances broke out at several points, including the area around the Pont-Neuf and the City and in Montmartre. The investigation ended with the execution of a junk dealer, a coalman, and a merchant (perhaps the bottle merchant mentioned) and with mild sentences meted out to a few police officers. The execu-tion in the place de Grève provoked incidents that were quelled by the watch. See M. Herlaut, *Revue historique* (1922); J. Nicolas, *L'Histoire* (1981); and, in the Bibliothèque nationale, Joly de Fleury MS. 1101–1102.

bleeding them and that they were lost forever and that their blood was used to bathe a princess suffering from a disease that could only be cured with human blood There was plenty of talk about that in Paris My father came to get me at school as many other fathers did along with seven big coopers armed with crowbars The rumor was so strong that the windows of the police station were broken and several poor guys were assaulted and one was even burned in the place de Grève because he looked like a police informer Children weren't allowed to go outside three poor wretches were hanged in the place de Grève to settle the matter and restore calm in Paris One of these poor victims lived in our house (and) was a dealer in bottles who was accused of fanning the flames[12] He was pitied and mourned because he was a pleasant young man

In our house lived a fellow by the name of Simon whose job was to put the dead of our parish into coffins As I was staying across the way with a cooper I heard a noise like a package falling on our sign It was nighttime and (I) couldn't see anything I tell my mother who runs down with a light and at that moment Simon's wife falls with the sign breaking the iron gibbet and falling dead in the street Her husband was found asleep and drunk as usual and we remembered that she often said she would hang herself rather than live with such a drunk

It was at this time that they had me take my first communion I may say that I couldn't believe that the son of God allowed himself to be fed to men just like that Since I went to catechism and had received several prizes and sometimes asked the priests questions that they answered in monosyllables either to shut my mouth or to shut me up (and) said to me emphatically These are mysteries I had had many doubts about their sincerity after serving at mass one day as choirboy I saw two devout women who wanted to take communion It was at the end I told the priest who told me to go find the sacristan whom he asked whether there were any hosts in the ciborium (The sacristan) answered that there were but that they were not consecrated This virtuous priest responded that it made no difference Because of that I never believed in their mysteries and particularly the words that this upright fellow allowed himself to utter blessing chastity and decency So I never wanted to be with these hyp-ocrites and have never liked their company

I liked to make a kind of fireworks commonly known as Chinese rock-

---

[12] *Apporter le feu*: to provoke revolutionary agitation, or more commonly to incite the people to riot.

ets Since these were invented not long ago (and since) I went to the house of a cousin of mine who was a fireworks maker (and) I went with my friends to play tricks on apple sellers and others by slipping (these firecrackers) under them and under their chairs which made them jump in the air with fear and in our opinion it was all for fun

So one day the sad sacks[13] pinched us and took us to the station house[14] and they sent for our fathers Luckily for me mine wasn't home and my mother came to claim me We got a speech from the commissaire as a result of which the only fun I had after that was learning how to swim But I got old man Jerome who was a fisherman mad by jumping on his gear[15] and taking his boat out on the river He liked me and he always said that he would tell my father but since he knew how quick my father was to get angry at me he didn't say anything

---

[13] Among the various epithets for the forces of law and order were the *tristes à pattes* used here, *pousse cul, parents de la pelle à feu,* and *lapins ferrés.* These terms were commonly used to designate the soldiers of the city guard and the watch. Under the authority of the *prévôt des marchands* and the *lieutenant général de police,* these forces numbered about a thousand men, some on horseback, the others on foot. The soldiers of the watch owned their offices, while the soldiers of the guard were employees of the police and for the most part army veterans. Both forces were commanded by the same man, the captain of the guard and inspector of the watch. During the period in question this post was held by Louis Duval (1733–45), who was succeeded by his son-in-law Louis Le Roy (1745–70). Both the guard and the watch maintained posts in each neighborhood, from which patrols went forth into the city.

[14] The *lieutenant général.de police,* a post established in March 1667, was solely responsible to the king for the Paris police. Under him served two *commissaires* in each of the city's twenty *quartiers.* They were responsible for receiving complaints and carrying out investigations. Some specialized in particular areas, such as morals, food supplies, etc. The eyes of the authorities, these men knew the streets and their inhabitants and played an important though ambiguous role in everyday life, preserving and protecting the population of Paris. As magistrates they were involved in both civil and criminal affairs. Owners of their offices, their reputations varied greatly. By the end of the Ancien Régime they were widely criticized for venality and lack of impartiality. They were aided in their work by inspectors of police (in theory one for each *quartier*), responsible for keeping an eye on suspicious people and places and reporting them to the *commissaires* and the *lieutenant général.* The inspectors also specialized, some in plays, others in prostitution, gambling, morals, horse markets, booksellers, and criminal affairs (to which three inspectors were assigned until 1750, and four thereafter—these were the forerunners of the present-day Sûreté). See A. Williams, *The Police of Paris* (London, 1979), and A. Farge, *Vivre dans la rue au XVIIIe siècle* (Paris, 1979). The *commissaire* who kept an eye on Ménétra was probably Chenon of the rue Saint-Honoré. See Jèze, *Etat de Paris,* and the *Almanachs royaux 1730–1789.*

[15] *Bascules,* literally, swings: a device for catching and preserving fish used by Master Jérôme, a member of a guild of some one hundred "mechanized" fishermen and sixty others who fished with ordinary lines or "rods." *Bascule* was commonly used as a synonym for a type of boat in which freshly caught fish were preserved.

I sought despite my mischief to make myself useful to my father I worked hard but none of that counted in my favor In his nightly rages my father kicked me out of the house I was forced when my poor grand-mother couldn't let me in to sleep in the boats or on a rock that I had adopted below the Pont Royal toward the Tuileries (and) that I still look at And there I spent many a night I had chosen that spot because the watch didn't like to go that way So if I've become what I am it's the Eternal One who protected me because I fell in with a bad lot as a result of my father's imprudence but what little good sense I have stopped me short of the crimes that my friends and neighbors and others that I knew because I hung out with them got involved in and were punished for

One night my father put a gash in my leg My good grandmother came for me and had me carried in a chair to her house where I stayed for six weeks When I was better the master of the choirboys[16] wanted to take me to Notre-Dame where he had just taken up his duties My parents couldn't persuade me to go anywhere except Saint-Eustache because I wanted to be able to see my grandmother I went back to work and my father used my mother's money to pay for me and one of my uncles and a cousin to be accepted as masters[17]

I began to become one of the leading mischief-makers in my neighbor-hood While I was spending my time under the Pont-Neuf people daily told my father stories about my little pranks One day when he wanted to give me what he called a thrashing the trap door to the cellar was open because the cesspool cleaners had removed the rock that covered the opening and in fleeing my father I stumbled down the stairs and fell into the cesspool People came to help but no one dared to touch me my father and some friends took me to the nearest watering trough and gave me a thorough washing People said that I would be happy and that this was a sign of happiness

---

[16] The Notre-Dame choir school was the largest of the institutions in which choir boys were raised free of charge by the Parisian clergy. The cathedral school had twelve pupils, and after puberty many of them received an ecclesiastical benefice and could pursue careers in the Church or in music. See also n. 4.

[17] In the Paris guilds the order of ranks from lowest to highest was apprentice, companion, master. In the glaziers' guild apprenticeship lasted four years and companionship six, unless one completed the tour of France. A master's certificate cost 1,000 livres, except for the sons-in-laws of masters and companions who married a master's widow. All were required to prove their skill by passing an examination or submitting a masterpiece, which was simply a check on a man's professional competence. Ménétra obtained a master's certificate. See A. Franklin, *Dictionnaire historique des arts, métiers et professions, exercés à Paris depuis le XIIIe siècle*, 2 vols. (Paris, 1905–06), as well as ch. 3 of the commentary to the present work.

Around this time my stepmother died My father wanted to give her a good funeral She deserved it She was not just a stepmother but actually a mother to us because she loved me she said because I was naughty I missed her and with her death lost a great deal because she headed off many of my father's rages at me On the day of the burial my father told me to pay close attention to see that the priest was there and that whole candles were placed around the body[18] I did exactly as I was told The candles had been used before I reported this to my father The next day he took me to see the priest and gave him such a talking–to that I got a good laugh out of it telling him that when he didn't work he wasn't paid so that since he hadn't said his prayers he didn't intend to pay for them and got back the six francs the priest had been paid for his presence I remember pushing my father to this extremity to show up the ambition of the priests

As for me my father couldn't control himself and hit me all the time I was not one to endure such things and used to run off to play in my old neighborhood One day I was swimming at the place known as the Sands[19] below Henri IV when I suddenly noticed my father up on the Pont-Neuf with a rope in his hand Immediately I snatched up my things as best I could and crossed over to the Jardin de l'Infante side of the river where I heard my father calling me and promising not to say anything because all the old women were giving him a hard time

A few days later it was Sunday and I was playing hide and seek[20] on the banks below the arches of the Pont-Neuf when one of my friends by the name of Cadet came after me with a whip that got tangled up in his legs

---

[18] An allusion to the practices of the parish clergy, who reused old wax for which worshippers paid as much as new candles. We know that this actually occurred because of a conflict between the parishioners and the clergy of Saint-Germain-l'Auxerrois in 1745, which led to intervention by the archbishop and the *procureur* of Parlement. See the Decree of Mgr de Vintimille, deliberation of the church council of Saint-Germain-l'Auxerrois, 16 May 1745, and the memorandum to the *procureur général* of the Parlement of Paris, BN 4oZ Lesenne 1023. This case is revealing of the clash between Jansenist and Ultramontane sensibilities then occurring in the parishes of Paris.

[19] The river then was less well channeled than it is today, and a number of sandy inlets formed under the quays and along the banks. At the foot of the Pont-Neuf, upstream from the Louvre and on the opposite bank, there were two beaches known as Les Sables and Le Jardin de l'Infante, where Ménétra and his friends liked to go.

[20] Ménétra writes *à la cligne misète*, meaning *jeux de crismisete pour cligne musette*, sometimes known as *cline mizette*, or hide-and-seek. The word occurs in Rabelais: see J. Boulanger, *De Ludis privatis* (Lyons, 1627). It probably comes from the fact that one person closed (or blinked: *clignoter*) his eyes while the others hid (*se mussent*).

and he fell into the river I and several of my friends ran after him and we pulled him in below the Samaritaine The next day as a sign of joy I made some firecrackers and we put them in slits in the rocks A guy named Cadet Lapierre tried to blow on one and lost half his nose and everybody said it was always me who played these kinds of tricks

Finally I went home to my father after making many promises few of which I kept One day I was working at the home of a woman of quality who made a bargain with me that each time her chambermaid would show herself to me she would give six francs and I would keep it a secret It was this charming maid who received my first blushes also with her money I had a ball Since it happened often I learned quite a bit I couldn't hold on to such a fortune Then an incident occurred that repelled me One night the chambermaid invited me into a room (and) brought a bottle saying that her husband was going to bring a brioche or canary-bread Nobody showed up (They) made me spend the night freezing to death and not daring to make any noise And the next day around noon somebody came to tell me that my beauty had been obliged to leave and that she would come back as soon as she could (and) that she felt sick and had decided to go see her husband and his mother had not left her[21]

That led to other relations And I remember the first prostitute who asked me up to her place since I had heard that that sort of woman robs you I had taken the trouble to put my money in one of my shoes When I saw how well she behaved I gave her double what she asked and this woman became one of my closest friends These interludes were so pleas-ant that every day I tried to make new conquests In the end my reward was what you might well imagine and that made me a little wiser

In these days my father drank all the time and was always throwing me out of the house I made up my mind I remember that several times when he said he was going after the watch he lost or dropped the silver buckles of his shoes or garters and I was careful to pick (them) up and take them the next day to M Peze Several times he put his money in the pockets of his apron and afraid he would lose it I took it upon myself to put it away As a result the dear man remained calm and quiet for a time One Sunday night he came home angry and full of wine threw himself on my sister and started to mistreat her I wanted to help her but even worse befell me In a rage he threw himself on me my sister tried to close a glass door (and)

[21] Ménétra's use of pronouns is unusual. Here he uses *dont* where one would have expected *que*.

caught my hand Cry as I did she didn't want to hear anything I was
forced to break one of the panes My father shouted that I was trying to
stab him My hand was all bloody and since he was yelling so loud I made
the mistake of drawing my knife to hide it and he was shameless enough to
tell everyone that I had tried to murder him and my dear sister to please
him (though she) knew the truth let people believe it

Then my relatives and my good grandmother who knew my father
inside out and knew what he was capable of told me and forced me to
leave him I left Paris the first time on the day after Damiens' torture[22] I
packed my bag Accompanied by some friends sons of merchants of the
Pont-Neuf to one of whom I sold a silver buckle I therefore left Paris by
way of Hell's Gate I often looked back and it seemed to me that the people
I passed were saying that I was afraid to leave my village steeple So I
hastened my step in the direction of Orléans

In a town near Orléans where I'd stopped to refresh myself a horse-
dealer who had two horses asked me if I wanted to ride since he saw that
I looked tired I accepted Then he met one of his compatriots and at some
village along the way stopped for a drink with his friend He gave me his
horse's bridle and told me to go slow and he would catch up But after a
while one of his horses took the bit in his teeth I couldn't restrain him I
lost the bridle and the horse escaped into the woods I chased him and
after covering quite a distance saw a man by a thicket in the middle of the
forest I asked him if he'd seen a horse He told me to get down and we
would look for the horse together He tied the horse to a tree and told me
to follow him Since he had a rifle I realized he was not a hunter but a
poacher But I was wrong he was an out and out thief

With the butt of his rifle he lifted up some brush and more or less forced
me down into a cave where I saw before my eyes two women blackened
by a lamp that was burning there I stayed there for nearly six weeks He
had a friend and didn't let my presence embarrass him with these two
women and while I was in slavery I ate very well

Finally the fear of being discovered made him say to one of these women

[22] King Louis XV was attacked and slightly wounded by Damiens on 5 January 1757.
Fearing a conspiracy, the police clamped down, and the would-be regicide was executed in
spectacular fashion in the place de Grève. Barbier, a lawyer, and Casanova have left accounts
of this terrifying scene, which attracted thousands of spectators. Under the Ancien Régime
regicide was the most unpardonable of crimes, for it struck at God's sacred representative on
earth and cast doubt on the paternal relationship of the monarch to his subjects. Ménétra
attended the execution (see II Fol.3.).

who took the most care of me and whom he called the Black to send me on my way unless she wanted him to change my name Catching only half of what he said I immediately asked this woman to let me go But after a while she kissed me in tears and wished me well and told me to flee as fast as I could

When I saw the light I felt suffocated and set off with long strides I came to a big highway I saw a peasant When I asked him which way to Orléans he said he would go with me Because he saw me all covered with black I was foolish enough to tell what had happened to me He took me to a constable who took me to jail even though I mentioned the name of a master glazier who worked for my mother After a week they heard from Paris and having been careful not to mention my father but only my grandmother and having been identified by Mister Michenaut the master glazier they took me into the forest of Cercotte with an escort of men armed with axes and pitchforks and at each thicket they made me get down for I was riding double with a trooper Our search was in vain and I always suspected I hadn't noticed the spot I remembered the poor girl who had saved me

We returned to Orléans where I stayed for a while and (I) returned to Paris where my poor grandmother was most impatient to see me And I went to work with my uncles where with my grandmother's help I got myself some clothes

One day a companion who worked with me asked me to go with him to a fortune teller in a narrow street behind Saint-Merry She looked at his hands and told him that he was a Judas that he would not die in his country and that he would be a language teacher What she predicted came true He died in Italy and was a teacher of French and was Judas in the Supper that the king[23] makes on Holy Thursday As for me she predicted that I would be happy particularly with women and that I would fall ill at the age of sixty and that I would live past the age of seventy-five On the way down my friend said that if she had predicted anything horrible for him he would have stabbed her I didn't want to have anything to do with him after that

---

[23] Probably an allusion to a pageant staged on Holy Thursday by the parish clergy of Saint-Germain-l'Auxerrois and paid for by a royal endowment, commemorating the Last Supper of Christ and the Twelve Apostles, including Judas. I have been unable to find any trace of this custom in either the histories of the parish or those of the Paris theater. Perhaps it was a school exercise.

Meanwhile my grandmother proposed that I go back to my father In the end he made a lot of promises and didn't pressure me and (I) went back to work for him As was to be expected I made the acquaintance of a niece who lived next door to my father and I behaved in my usual way with her She was embarrassed and I did all I could to keep things secret That didn't stop me from running around there was talk and I had to do it I made acquaintances of all sorts and kinds with that monster Du-hamel[24] and others four of whom were hanged in the place de Grève and especially the Giroux woman whose first favors I enjoyed was hanged in the Grève But Providence was watching over me and I was never one of them because they never made me part of their action

One Sunday one of my cousins told me that he would like to see the devil that one of his cousins had the Little Albert and (with) me if I decided to do it all three of us would go to rue de la Huchette and eat a dead sparrow[25] We went up to a room and burned a stick and I began reading at the place where the devil was supposed to come We had prepared a glass of wine and a piece of bread When all of a sudden we hear a great noise above our heads my two worthies take off and I try to do the same with the wizard's book in my hand and holding on to the door The fear that had gotten into me and my cousin subsided and we went back into the room and our friend I don't know if the devil took him I never saw him again

In those days one of my cousins had built a country house at Vertus which the peasants called la Vicara One day we had a bad fight with the peasants some of whose skulls got bashed in My cousin's son and I rarely missed with out stones But this fellow by the name of Debray smashed in the fronts of those brutes' skulls with a pitchfork on account of the care-lessness of a guy named Grandin who was a tough little guy (and) who we couldn't stand Before that I had played a few tricks on him along the river bank Standing on a board I had thrown him in the water and at the first opening[26] the ferrymen grabbed him he was whistling because he was in

---

[24] These people actually existed, but they have been transformed in Ménétra's imagination. For further discussion, see chapter 2 of the commentary.

[25] "To eat a dead sparrow" (*manger un moineau mort*), an expression used several times by Ménétra, seems to refer to nothing more than eating a common cabaret dish, some sort of roast bird. But there may also be a hidden joke, because the variety of sparrow that would have been familiar to the Parisian, a bird with brown plumage and black stripes, bears a name, *moineau*, that derives from monk, *moine*, owing to the color of its dress; hence Ménétra's expres-sion may mean something like, "Let's eat a nice fat monk."

[26] The entryways to the Louvre on the quays and neighboring streets.

the middle of the river and when they fished him out the boatmen baptized him profusely So his mother eventually went to see the schoolmaster
to have me punished I had foreseen this move So when the teacher told
me to go behind the door after thinking it over I made up my mind I grab
the key I close the door and turn the lock twice I take the stairs four at a
time despite the teacher's shouts My poor grandmother was obliged after
a while to go let him out This fellow had a nasty soul he had insinuated
that I was responsible for the death of my two brothers by making them
jump over woodpiles in the Jardin de l'Infante So I was always playing
tricks on him to make him pay

To get back to my story I put glass in the house at Vertus for my cousin
One day he said to me Jacques we are going your father and I to the
house here is a cod tail you cook and we'll have supper together and we'll
go down to the village Meanwhile I cook the cod In a cupboard I find
some flour I make a sauce He arrives (and) was about to begin eating
when he asks me where I found the flour I showed him the cupboard He
started shouting that I was poisoned that this was arsenic for killing rats
My father is asking me if I didn't taste the sauce My cousin is shouting
that I need to be given an antidote They took me dumbfounded to the
village (and) asked the people there to bring as much milk as possible (and)
force me to drink I never felt anything but unfortunately there was a dog
who was a guzzler who ate (some) and who died for when we returned
home he was stretched out dead on the ground

Since I was friends with the son of this cousin who had just made a trip
to England (and) had left his pistols in their holsters (we) took them out
for fun He took one and to tease me said that he was going to kill me and
I replied by taking aim with the other But he says no it isn't you I'm
going to kill but Nanette who was the cook The shot rings out the poor
girl falls on her back He and I both shout she was gone The constable
comes they question us They send me home and keep my unfortunate
cousin who gets sent off to the Islands[27] There was nothing to be done
about the tragedy This unfortunate young man was decent and likeable
and I am convinced he did it inadvertently because after all I was the one
who was supposed to be the victim but neither of us thought that it was
loaded

---

[27] An allusion to the practice of the police and government authorities, who round up
prostitutes, beggars, and petty criminals to be sent to the American colonies, as in the case of
Manon Lescaut.

In spite of my mischief I was still working for my father Then one day in a bad mood he happened to hit me I was all in a lather about it on the quai de la Ferraille when I ran into one of my Charpentra cousins who was a recruiting officer for the Auvergne regiment I told him I wanted to join up He gave me a cockade (and) had me sign the recruitment papers while we drank a last bottle and a penny's worth of bread and three pennies' worth of cervelat He told me to go home pack my bags and come back to meet him I go home My father wants to hit me I tell him I don't belong to you any more but to the King Then and there I take the cockade out of my pocket and put it on my hat My father is struck speechless and leaves without saying a word I pack my things The companion says he wants to leave with me when my father arrives with his cousin who says to me Jacques you've just done a foolish thing your father promises not to hit you any more (and) I promise to hold him to it After a lot of discussion I went to find the recruiter and brought him to my father to whom he handed over my enlistment So for a mug of wine a penny's worth of bread and three penny's worth of cervelat cousin to cousin it wound up costing my father eighteen francs And the whole thing was related to one of my female cousins who had the vapors and for whose suffering I was responsible

One day below the Samaritaine[28] it froze and I went with my father's companion and others to skate on the ice And I told my friend repeatedly not to go too far out Then suddenly he vanished from sight After that I was more on my guard My father (did not change) toward me even though I tried to behave and he saw that it was winter and I asked him for clothes Add to that the neighbor's niece who tormented me because her time was coming and my cousin with vapors who frequently vented her bad moods on me And then I scored with a little affair and laid low in a friend's room where I spent two weeks

Finally in spite of my grandmother I left to make my tour of France She and one of my uncles took me out to the Versailles road because there was a master there who needed a companion I left my relatives not without misgivings but that was the last time I was afraid to leave home I arrived

---

[28] Common parlance for the building constructed in 1608 to house the pumps that supplied water to the Tuileries and Right Bank. It was decorated with a bronze bas-relief showing Christ and the Samaritan at Jacob's well. Redone in 1714 by Robert de Cotte, the building had three stories and an apartment for the guard. There is a good illustration in J. B. Raguenet, *La Samaritaine et le Pont-Neuf* (Musée Nissim de Camondo, Paris).

in Versailles and I was met by a companion who was a friend of mine and who worked for the King's glazier I worked with him for around three months and I wrote to my grandmother

From there I took the road to Orléans where I went to see my old landlord and (he) told me to go to Vendôme to a widow whose husband had died six weeks before He was named Pasquier and I enjoyed a very warm welcome Despite my youth she had confidence in me There were four of us companions and all went by name Since I was having a good time and always enjoy myself with companions of every trade I made a name for myself Besides which my mother sent me money fairly often so I had a wonderful time In the town next to where the widow lived there was a game of quoits[29] It was not so much for the game as for the lady there who was most attentive to me So our little business got on very well

One day after I'd been out drinking the curate of a village came to tell the mistress that she could put glass in the window above the main altar So I went with the curate to take the measurements When I came back I went into the storehouse and behind some boards saw the new panels that the late glazier had made for this church Since I had sworn on my honor that it would be ready and in place for Saturday (that) enabled me to go off and have a good time The good widow begged me and then shouted at me and I said it would be done and installed

Later that night I went in and told my comrades to go to sleep I brought all the panels I cleaned them well In the shop I made so much noise that the night was completely shattered When I heard the widow opening the judas that gave onto the shop I burned pine resin When my fussing was done I went to sleep and in the morning I let my comrades come down and they were surprised to see the panels all ready I went down quietly I heard the mistress saying that it was supernatural that I'd had the devils for helpers and that there had been fire in the shop all night I made my appearance I told her to prepare us lunch and I started packing up the work and loading it on the horse my comrades practically didn't dare touch it The lady prayed to God I pretended to swear

When we arrived the curate fixed us a fine meal and everything went smoothly When I reached Vendôme my companions said that everything was installed but that they were afraid it wouldn't last very long She told them The next day at the raising of God[30] the whole window [would]

---

[29] *Jeu de bagues.*
[30] Ménétra says *Lever-Dieu* for the elevation of the mass.

crash to the ground A certain Gascon from Condom who played the hypocrite and flatterer told her and often repeated that I had a devil for a helper for he had heard me talking to myself several times and thought he heard me calling the devil that I did whatever I wanted to and that I cast a spell over good folks with my words and deeds that recently I had wanted to show them the devil and that recently I had turned white water black when he wanted to wash up and his face and hands were all black and that I played tricks that according to him were supernatural

This devout woman believed all these stories and waited with much impatience A young man knew whether the window had fallen out at the elevation Imagine her surprise when he came to tell her that everything was properly installed and the curate and parishioners were content

After dinner she took me aside and said Parisian it is very unfortunate for a young man like you not to believe in God and to have made a pact with the devil for it was quite impossible that the job that I had done by myself in one night could have been done in four or five days and that she had it on good authority that I was inspired by the devil that all the tricks I played were supernatural that I had caused all the dogs in one village to run after a peasant who had it in for me that I had by uttering some magic words changed the water so that it ran black when the Gascon wanted to shave That you wanted to show the other fellows the devil That she had talked it over with the curate and that he had urged her to pay me off and send me on my way

I had a good laugh over all this nonsense I began to get angry when she mentioned the curate and paying me off I told her that I would take it that I would not leave the city and that I would go work for another master that as for her curate he was an idiot and that the tricks I played for my own amusement were a lot like his mysteries At that point the curate arrived with a man who respected me and who had good sense After the initial compliments we started in on explanations and I in-formed them in a teasing way that everything they thought was super-natural was as clear as day So the curate and this hearty parishioner had a good laugh when they found out it was all a tease So the Gascon put up with all my jibes against him and all my jokes

It was about six months earlier while out for a stroll that I tried to jump over a ditch the way I used to do in the Champs-Elysées[31] and broke a

---

[31] Term applied to a section of the Grand Cours that was developed some time after 1670 in the marshy, wooded area west of the Tuileries. When the Duc d'Antin had a bridge built over

little bone and went forty days without doing anything to heal the break I went with one of my comrades to do work in a number of villages on behalf of the widow I was in a place called Mondoubleau working in the church above the main altar I was at the top of a scaffolding made of several ladders lashed together and set above the altar when the prior entered and asked me how the work was going He went to touch his hand to his hat letting go the ladder which fell step by step with me on top (I) grabbed the Eternal Father by the beard and ripped off his entire face The Holy Ghost that was a little lower down (I) tore off entirely along with the angels and the crucifix underneath I broke an arm After that the good people of the village greeted me by saying that I had exterminated the Holy Trinity

As soon as I saw that I had broken my leg [sic] I began to curse more than any priest or bishop had ever done The prior ordered that a wagon be made ready to carry me to Vendôme Unfortunately the bailiff did not agree Since I insisted he said to me Have no fear it is because of the prior's carelessness that you fell he's the one and we shall see who will pay the damages I gathered that a clergyman provided it didn't cost him anything didn't care a fig for a poor wretch who had been injured by his fault and that made me see their avarice So I was taken care of at his expense and I stayed seventy-five days and I had twenty-four francs to put me back on my feet I was with a good woman the widow Raluc who took good care of me at low cost and who wanted me to stay another two weeks without paying

I returned to Vendôme The widow's sisters pressed me to keep the promise that I had (made) partly for laughs and partly for keeps Since I had made enough promises and kept few of them I set out for Tours

On the way I had a delightful adventure It was on the road to Langeais I saw a woman in a wagon I asked her politely if she wanted me to climb in She was willing As we talked she told me that she had just driven her husband to Paris and that she was returning home and that if I wanted to spend a few days I would be the master of the house I accepted the offer with pleasure seeing it as an appealing prospect even[32] with a

---

the great sewer that still severed the promenade in two, the elm-lined walk was extended to the vicinity of the Etoile. In the second half of the century, as the city grew, great hôtels and gardens began to encroach on the northern side of the Champs-Elysées. Here people went to play tennis or *boules* and to relax in cafés. Not very safe at night, it was frequented by prostitutes and thieves, as police and morgue records show.

[32] An instance of Ménétra's habit of using an adverb of time, *encore*, where one would have expected an adverb of gradation, *même*.

farmer's wife She joked with me that he was going to meet Parisian women in Paris and on my way I've met a Parisian man for she had taken the trouble to ask me where I was from

Since she was traveling with a young peasant boy who was sleeping heavily when she woke him she said This gentleman here is a traveling companion and he got out of the wagon he said to amuse himself and he wasn't amusing me at all

We got to a sleeping place where we were quite reserved but on the road it was different She told me she lived near Tours in a place called Luynes Upon reaching Tours I bid her farewell and promised to visit soon And every time I went to see her I was always welcome

I went to the mother of companions[33] who gave me a warm welcome and sent me to a nice shop in town where the shopkeeper's wife had a sister I drove crazy It was a very good place Alongside my shop was a widow who had a young daughter She liked me to tell her stories and I talked a good line to the daughter So the shopkeeper's lovely sister told this widow it was a fine thing that I talked that way to her daughter

I was accepted as a *compagnon du Devoir*[34] and the companions made

---

[33] On the tour of France companions went from inn to inn. These inns were kept by women to whom the men referred as "mothers." By extension, the word "mother" also referred to the inn itself. In large cities there were several mothers, one for each society of companions and each different trade. The mother was an important figure, who, as the text shows, helped to maintain communication between cities. Her husband was known as the "father of companions."

[34] This was one of the three main clandestine workers' associations that grew up in the sixteenth century to protect the interests of companions of the various trades and guilds against the guild masters. The Enfants de maître Jacques (or of the Devoir, also known as Dévorant or Dévoirant) traced their origins to the mythical figure of Maître Jacques, a companion who was murdered for refusing to reveal the secret of the *compagnonnage*. They also prided themselves on various group mysteries and rituals, which distinguished them from the Enfants de maître Soubise (said by members of the organization to be a descendant of one of Jacque's killers, Jacques and Soubise both having been employed as masons in the construc-tion of Solomon's temple) and the Enfants de Salomon (who claimed that their group had been founded by Adoniram, the architect of the temple). The Enfants de maître Jacques were known by various names depending on their particular trade: the Loups (wolves), Loups garous (werewolves), and Compagnons passants (passing companions), were mainly stonecut-ters, while the Dévorants (devourers) included carpenters, locksmiths, blacksmiths, and glaziers, as well as cobblers and tailors. The Enfants de maître Soubise, who called themselves Bons drilles, were nearly all carpenters. The Enfants de Salomon also called themselves Loups, Gavots, and Compagnons du devoir de liberté. The Gavots and Dévorants probably separated during the religious wars of the sixteenth century, the former having sided with the Protestants, the latter with the Catholics. By the eighteenth century, these were no longer really clandestine organizations, for they were watched by the police and enjoyed de facto toleration by the authorities. The rivalry among the various groups led to disputes on the job

me recopy the entire role or what is called Master Jacques or the Devoir and (I) was named Parisien le Bienvenue

My boss was doing work for the abbey of Beaumont-lès-Tours Working in the refectory with a fellow from Lyons I scraped my leg sliding down a ladder that my comrade had allowed to slip Since he was shouting louder than I was the abbess[35] who was the aunt of the Prince de Condé came to see what the noise was all about and I told her it was nothing Since the ladder had flipped over it was my comrade who needed help But when they noticed that my stockings were dripping blood the abbess dressed my wounds herself and ordered me to do nothing for two weeks gave me twelve francs and severely scolded the guy from Lyons who never came back

A short while later I was in the garden with this fellow from Rennes messing around as usual we began to sing all the little nuns came [every day] to listen to us when suddenly we were quite surprised that nobody came to visit any more When the boss arrived he showed us a letter that went something like this "Sir send us two other companions be sure they have good trousers" We were not well trousered and apparently the truth was [that] the good sisters had caught a glimpse of what they had at heart The boss went to the superior and told her that he couldn't get any other workers that the simplest thing was that if we displeased them so much they should give us decent trousers to wear This was done they brought us each a pair of new leather trousers and the little nuns came to see us again as usual

Companions in all the city's trades wanted to have a *Te Deum*[36] said for the health of His Majesty and since they wanted the backing of the princess and knew that she had some affection for me they proposed that I go deliver the request She said to me in a friendly tone I shall be delighted to you are Parisian but I do not know your companion's name you

---

and often quite violent riots. The word *Devoir* is virtually undefinable [and untranslatable], for it refers to both the *compagnonnage* and its rites. See E. Cornaert, *Les Compagnonnages en France* (Paris, 1966), and Barret and Gurgand, *Ils voyageaient la France* (Paris, 1980).

[35] A reference to the abbess of the Benedictine abbey of Beaumont-lès-Tours, Henriette Louise Marie Françoise de Bourbon-Condé, eighth child of Louis III, prince de Condé, known as Mademoiselle de Vermandois. Named abbess in 1733, she was a great builder who completed, sometime after 1757, the major projects begun subsequent to the fire that ravaged the convent in 1680.

[36] No trace has been found of this service of thanksgiving for the health of Louis XV, though many such services were offered in 1757 and 1758 to thank heaven for having spared the king's life.

haven't put it on the document you gave me I am Madame called by the companions Parisien le Bienvenue [welcome] Well then she answered be welcome

We all assembled and counted 875 companions of every trade It cost (each of us) around twelve and a half *sols* We were accompanied by drums and oboes and were all lined up with our ribbons in the streets of the city and of the abbey of Baumont where the abbess in her princess' garb received on a silver platter that I presented to her the blessed bread and a brief compliment that had been given to me She put four louis on the plate and said to me I am very satisfied with the blessed bread I have just received and with the compliment of my little glazier

I was friends with the son of the mother of companions who was a saddle maker by trade and had his boss's wife for a mistress He left town and I basically took his place The husband wasn't at all displeased She was charming He was all right and had a small house in the country where I had a gay old time with the wife I also went occasionally to visit my good farmer's wife who cooked me fine meals

When it came time to leave Tours the companions gave me an escort of violins and oboes and afterwards led me back to town and wouldn't let me leave until they'd accepted me as a full-fledged companion[37] and the next day I went looking for my charming saddle-maker's wife in her country house where we said our farewells with many regrets I also went to say goodbye to my good farmer's wife who made me eat many fresh eggs I missed that charming town were I had been so well treated by my boss and boss's wife and all the good people who loved me

Finally I left for Angers in the company of a fellow from Rennes On the way I had a stroke of good luck upon entering a small forest I spotted a little shepherd and a young shepherd girl in action I crept up as quietly as I could (and) when I was close I made a noise The boy took off without his clothes and the girl tried to cover herself My comrade took off after

---

37 There were three degrees of *compagnonnage*: aspirant, *compagnon reçu, et initié* (received and initiated companion), and *compagnon fini*, finished or full-fledged companion. Ménétra was both received and made a full-fledged companion in Tours. The full-fledged companions were also referred as seniors (*anciens*). The senior companions, familiar with the customs of the organization, were entitled to preside over the reception of new members as well as to serve as "first companion," the official who, elected by the seniors, was in charge of the society in a particular city. Ménétra was first companion in Rochefort, Bordeaux, and Lyons. In larger cities there might be a first companion for each trade or *vacation*. The first companion played an important role in hiring and discipline.

the boy but I amused myself with the girl half willingly the rest by force But I had second thoughts because my comrade didn't try to take advantage of the situation I retraced my steps and stopped a second time and as I was a good Christian and had heard that a sin paid for was half pardoned I gave the girl three coins of two sols and continued on my way

I arrived in Angers In that charming town I was well received by the masters and companions I worked for a good fellow who had a son he was going to marry and a young girl ready and ripe for marriage I tried in every way to please him by insinuating that I was master of Paris and would settle in his area Around that time the militia[38] came recruiting By showing my master's letter that my good grandmother had sent me occasionally she also sent me something to have a good time on I was excused

I had for a friend the son of the master locksmith of the king at Versailles who received at least five or six louis a month We spent the money together for I was always one of the gang Around that time my boss's son married a girl from the town of Ponts-de-Cée He invited me to the wedding[39] I promised him that I would leave early in the morning when a young girl of the house asked me if I wanted to accompany her and in my bedroom since I was still lying on a trunk started to put on a pair of white silk stockings so I could see if they looked good on her I took advantage of her imprudence and went to find my friend the locksmith to take him with me as we had promised He told me after we had drunk some white wine that he wouldn't be coming until afternoon So then I took my bride and we had a good time along the road we arrived just in time to sit down for dinner where the groom who was a real sly fellow looked at me occasionally smiling and chewing his fingers The groom's sister pouted at me and my new conquest looked at me on the sly After the meal toasts to your

[38] Care should be taken not to confuse the bourgeois militias that preserved law and order and helped to defend certain cities with the provincial militias that were organized during the wars that marked the reign of Louis XIV. The ordinance of 1728 ordered that 60,000 men be drawn by lot for six years' service from among unmarried men and widowers between the ages of 16 and 40. Cities ceased to be exempt after 1742. Drawing of lots for the militia often created disturbances, which grew more widespread after 1750, owing to repeated recruitment for the War of the Austrian Succession and the Seven Years' War. Masters holding Parisian certificates (*maîtres par lettres de Paris*) were exempt.

[39] Ménétra attended the wedding of René Changeon, master glazier and son of René Changeon, also master glazier, in the Saint-Maurille parish of Angers; the younger Changeon married Louise Merlet, age 20, daughter of Louis Merlet, roofer, on 11 September 1758 in the Saint-Aubin parish of Ponts-de-Cée (AD Maine et Loire, GE. Ponts-de-Cée).

health[40] That pleased the guests but my boss's daughter started scolding and I started in dancing and teasing The wedding lasted three days Afterwards we had to return to Angers

I went with my boss to do a job in a castle I'll never forget the name of the place la Sablière where I got into some mischief The boss warned me not to climb a certain small staircase near where I was working Curiosity got the better of me no sooner was his back turned than I started up Soon I heard somebody going down alongside me but I couldn't see any' one I went down and I heard someone go back up Fear took hold of me and I went back into the room Seeing me struck dumb the boss told me it was only an echo from the stairs

A few days later an old servant asked me Do you want to know why you heard footsteps going up and down the stairs Good heavens I said I certainly do Well then listen to what I have to say Here is what he said The son of the lord of this castle had a tutor who was very strict and was always reprimanding the boy for not learning his Latin properly because with the pack of priests you're not worth much if you don't know that dead language One night the boy made a pact with the devil in the very room you're sleeping in He wrote out a note and signed it in blood The devil came and took the note and the room was all engulfed in flames When the tutor saw thick smoke pouring through the lock he had the door broken down and we found the young man dead and stretched out on his bed and it was by this staircase that he last went up to his room

After hearing these words which were supposed to reassure me I said to my boss You can stay but as for me I'm leaving And I was off that very moment Even though the servant protested that he was only teasing my mind was made up The master followed me

I walked four leagues without saying a word Finally we passed by a village and the dear man asked me if I wanted some refreshment I went in I heard a man who spoke rather well and I recovered the use of my tongue and my boss started talking to me Ah Parisian it's four long leagues we've come and I haven't been able to get a word out of you I answered that I couldn't get over what I had heard He tried his best to talk me out of it but I wasn't having any of it The Lord's wife came on purpose to Angers but she couldn't get anything out of me either

It took me a while to leave that town my two fine girlfriends began to

---

[40] *Salut chanté,* an Italianism, from *à la salute:* Toasts drunk at the end of the meal and accompanied by song.

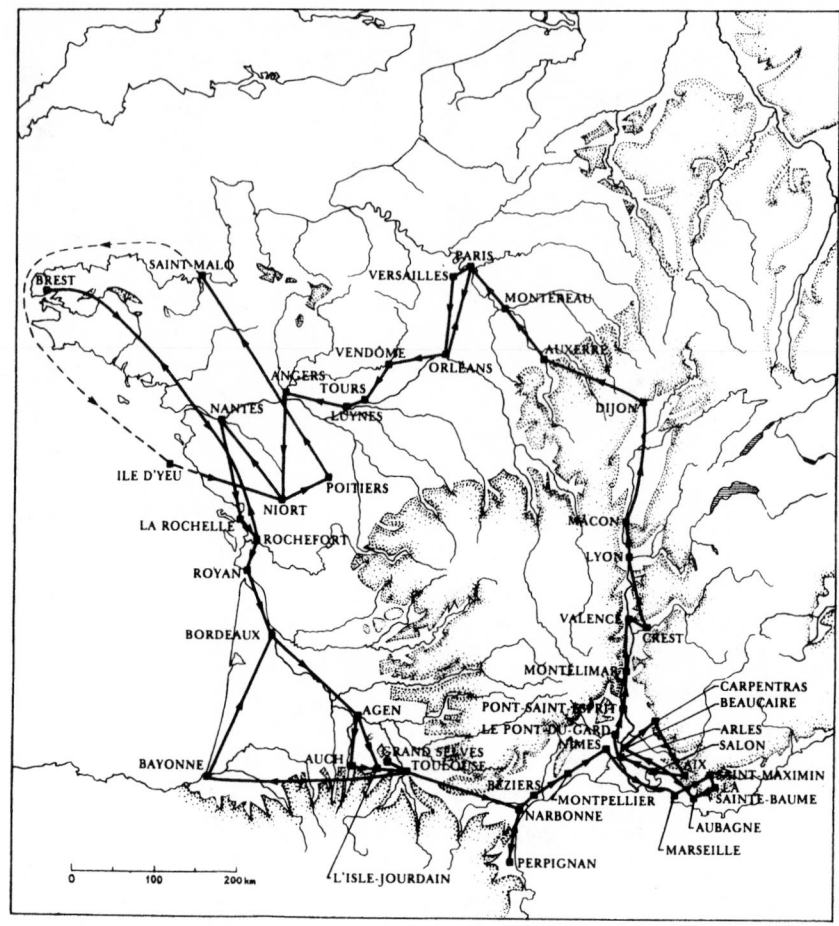

First Journey: 1757–1763

see that petticoats fetter a man more than usual Each of them tormented me They had been inseparable friends and became enemies despite my precautions

But an event[41] occurred in Angers that served me as pretext What

---

[41] No trace of this great battle survives in the city archives or parish registers. The date, Saint Bartholomew's Day or August 24, is surely a mistake if Ménétra fled the city on 11 September, the confirmed date of the wedding. That such an incident occurred is not beyond the realm of possibility, though it was probably less epic in scope than Ménétra would have it. Companions took care of their own wounded and sometimes hid the dead to avoid prosecution. Court records for this period have disappeared. Similar riots were recorded in 1730 at La Crau and in 1733 at Châlons.

happened was that on the eve of a feast of (the) Virgin a companion locksmith on his way to a tailor for a suit of clothes encountered a couple of Gavots [see n. 34 above] who grabbed and beat him He complained to the mother of companions at the same time [a] number of companions went off to the mother of these Gavots to get his things back but they weren't handed over until hard words had been exchanged on both sides From that day on whenever there was a meeting it turned into a fight Finally it was decided to have a real battle which was set for Saint Bartholomew's Day

The companions were not the stronger party given that the shoemakers and men of other occupations (who) were either friends or countrymen of the Gavots had gotten together not knowing anything of the mischief that had been done We wrote to several little towns nearby particularly a little village named Saint-Georges where there were about thirty-seven companion carpenters who didn't want to make any promises but who were too much for the poor unfortunate shoemakers and their followers

On our side we counted only five hundred companions and on their side there were more than seven hundred fifty On the appointed day we formed up in three ranks In the front rank were the big men canes in hand including one companion glazier from Rennes who was in command because he had been a sergeant of grenadiers The second rank was armed with rocks and stones and I was the third in command The third rank was supposed to pick up loose canes and headgear and rush the weakest spot

When we saw that multitude arrive we thought we were lost but we believed in our valor and in our good cause The whole bourgeoisie had taken up arms but dared not move and remained neutral When the signal was given the leaders of the shoemakers and some others asked for an explanation and (wanted) to know why they were about to fight They signaled that they wanted to talk and nine of us leaders from the other side approached We gave them satisfaction The leader of the shoemakers and the others went back to their lines to talk Anybody who wants to fight fight for us the Gavots were in the wrong we're pulling out A large group followed them

A hundred and thirty-three companion carpenters on whom we had not counted (and who) had posted themselves clandestinely behind a hedge thought the enemy had been defeated and was fleeing (They) had clubs and at three quarters swept down on those poor wretches There were seven killed and seventeen seriously wounded and around forty others hurt I just missed being killed by one strong Gavot but I fended off the blow and did to him what he thought he was going to do to me because he fell over backwards He was one of their leaders a fellow by the name of Flamand la Gambille a stout and powerful man Warrants were issued for our arrest and some sixty of us fled across the Maine on a kind of raft whose cable we cut for we had crossed without the sailors and the constables of the marshalsea were after us

We walked all night and at a farm took several sheep that we skinned and ate halfcooked We split up I went to work at DonayenAnjou [from which] I returned clandestinely to Angers in the hope of seeing my boss's daughter But (I saw) quite the opposite the other girl Since the companions were going to escort me by night to go to Poitou behind a slate quarry as I had just come to say my farewells what a meeting It was my little Angevin girlfriend who wanted to stab me and then herself or so she said if I didn't give back what I had taken Hearing some noise the companions fortunately rushed in and got rid of her I since learned that she had for her reward a pretty little girl and my boss's daughter had a nice baby boy

I went to work at Niort in Poitou where I stayed with good people who treated me like their child and made me the most beautiful promises in the world I stayed there around three months [when] I wanted to go to Poitiers to see my friends It cost me plenty

I arrived one Sunday morning and was hired to work the next day After dinner I was with my comrades on a kind of esplanade playing leapfrog[42] I went home to sleep peacefully at my master's house When I went to (work) the next morning two town constables[43] asked me if I wasn't the Parisian I answered yes They invited me to follow them and put me in jail After an hour I saw a group of my comrades brought in and they imprisoned all the foreign companions

We stayed about six days rather well fed by the masters of the town We were seated on the witness bench (*sellette*) and interrogated one after another like criminals the judges had it in for me in particular because they said I was from Paris and looked like I knew what was what and

[42] In French, *jouant à coupetête:* "Ils sautent tout en criant coupetête, l'un par sus l'autre, estce pas jeu honnête" (Rabelais).

[43] A reference to the four sergeants of police who served under the *lieutenant criminel et de police* and were responsible for patrolling the streets. The latter official, a member of the *présidial,* one of the regular courts, was probably the one who interrogated Ménétra. This incident sheds light on the authorities' suspicion of the *compagnonnages* and on the rivalry between soldiers and civilians. See P. Boissonade, "La Police municipale de Poitiers au XVIIe siècle," in *Bulletin de la Société des Antiquités de l'Ouest,* 2e série (1895–1897) 7:564–567.

answered them (more skillfully) than the others We were accused me in particular of having cut down the young trees that stood on the esplanade We stayed almost thirty days (when) someone came to tell us we were free My comrades in misfortune made me write and demand reparations The only answer we got was that we were free and justice had been done that the cadets of the regiment had been demoted and that it was they who had done the damage

When I saw that I went to my mother's house to get my bag and without saying good-bye to anyone started on my way and falling in with an Angevin companion tinsmith and a Langrennois [see n. 49 below] cutler who had been mixed up in the whole wretched mess we decided to head for Saint-Malo and sign on as sailors We had heard that some of our comrades had earned as much as eight hundred francs in three months the idea was to get back on our feet But what happened was the opposite and I sank into misery

We arrived at Saint-Malo where we found a corsair named Sainte-Marie and signed on to go after the English[44] They paid us twenty-seven francs a month and a share in the booty But while waiting for the ship to sail I worked in Dinan for a bourgeois who was sergeant of the bourgeoisie and since they were making him sign up everyone from the town and the surrounding area because they were sure the English were about to attack my boss fell ill (and) I took his place after agreeing that he would give me fifteen sols a day plus board That was the beginning of my military exploits

They gave me seven men to guard a small canon located on high ground near Dinan The fellow on guard fell asleep and was taken by surprise (he) was the reason I was busted to the rank of ordinary rifleman They had us maneuver with three soldiers between two riflemen and we practiced firing I returned to Saint-Malo when the English were beaten at Saint-Cast[45] Then the duc d'Aiguillon gave them quarter because if he had wanted none of them would have returned to England

[44] This episode took place during the war between France and England known as the Seven Years' War (1756–1763), which in Europe saw the French and their Austrian allies pitted against the English and the Prussians and on the seas and in the colonies saw the clash of the French and English navies. Colonial rivalry and the problem of maintaining the balance of power in Europe were the main causes.

[45] Ménétra arrived in Brittany after the battle of 11 September 1758 at the bay of Saint-Cast, where the duc d'Aiguillon repelled an English landing. The following period was one of feverish military activity, including mobilization of the bourgeois militias and impressment of

So then I sailed[46] with my two comrades They armed each of us with a musketoon two pistols a scimitar and a hatchet (*hache d'ababort*) We stayed at sea hugging the shore for about five months One Saturday after dinner we spotted three sail that gave us chase (and) that were flying the Dutch flag but were in fact English We flew the master flag (?) They each fired a canon We replied and ran up the French flag We were forced to flee and gained a small port where we took on water and the enemy ships didn't dare approach We went back out to sea

We spotted a small coaster that was hovering around us We fired a canon and it hove to There were eleven Englishmen on board and (we) sent the boat to the bottom Then we saw the three sail that had given us chase In broad daylight we figured we were trapped Our captain made a really pathetic speech that we were going to fight for God for our King (and) for his interests We also got double rations he had several bundles broken open and we each got a pair of stockings and shoes and (he) ordered us to take to our stations and to do our duty

Fortunately the wind came up That kept us from falling into their hands When we came upon the French coast the captain ordered that the eleven Englishmen be put ashore and I was ordered to escort them A ship's lieutenant who respected me ordered me to take six men with me I didn't miss the opportunity to take my two comrades with me

We entered the port of the isle of Yeu where the governor invited our lieutenant to come to the fort to refresh himself and ordered me to wait for him to return I spotted a tavern where wine was sold We went in and drank (and) ate soft bread I told my comrades that I wanted to take off and (they) took me at my word I told them to make a good show of it because people were watching The minute we were out of sight we threw our musketoons behind some hedges and went our separate ways

I set out for Poitou and went at least several leagues with twenty sols in my pocket (and) without having made like a crucifix[47] It was the month

<hr />

sailors for the navy. Since Dinan is 33 kilometers from Saint-Cast, Ménétra must have been assigned to coastal patrol duty and probably participated in training exercises with forces that were maintained on a war footing from the end of 1758 until 1760 for fear that the British would return.

[46] The activities of the corsair Sainte-Marie of Saint Malo should be seen in the context of the naval operations of the fall of 1759 after the French defeat off the coast of Quiberon in August. Ménétra exaggerates his length of service on board the corsair: it does not take five months to go from Saint Malo to the isle of Yeu.

[47] In French Ménétra writes *faire le crucifix*, by extension from the popular expression

of October I slept most of the time in the brush I was almost naked and full of vermin One night I had a stroke of good luck I heard barking I went toward the sound I saw a nice-looking farm I asked if I might not spend the night in the barn With the dog still barking I saw a friendly-looking fellow who bade me enter a low room in which several persons were seated at a table (he) sat me down and gave me something to eat and drink asked me where I was from I told him what happened to me (he) ordered that I be shown to bed The next day I went to thank him (he) gave me a twenty-four sol piece (and) a good lunch filled my pockets and wished me a good journey

One day while I was passing by a farm a dog ran after me and bit me in the leg and ripped my poor clothes The mistress was at her door I begged her to call off her dog but her response was to look at me disdainfully and say he was doing his duty With that I drew my pistol and made him bite the dust She started yelling and all the farm hands armed with pitchforks and clubs came running after me but I held them off by saying that if they made the mistake of coming near me I'd do the same to them

Finally I came to Niort It was night The master was quite surprised to see me and in such a state (He) promptly sent for his wife I was shown up to a bedroom they changed all my clothes and the boss's wife threw my rags into the fire and by the next day I hadn't a thought on my mind I wrote my grandmother who sent something to help with my resupply[48] I tried to find out what had become of the ship I couldn't find out anything until I got back to Paris after my tour of France [and] I went to the marine bureau and they looked through the registers they thought it had perished for more than six years nobody had heard of it [and there had been no news] I saw that Providence was looking out for me

After recovering and without regrets I left my boss and his wife who had always wished me well and who wanted me to stay longer but I couldn't stay in one town for such a long time

I went to work in a small town called Montreuil-Bellay because there was a fellow from Rennes there I stayed for a while with him He became jealous because his young wife liked the stories I told her I received a letter from Nantes from one Guépin[49] letting me know that if I wanted to

---

faire le demi-crucifix, "to make like a half crucifix," from the action of extending one arm to beg for alms.

[48] *Ravitailler,* naval term for repairs and reprovisioning.

[49] Possibly the surname of a companion, though generally companions were known by the

stay with a widow he had told her a lot of good things and he would send me twelve francs in the mail

I left my old comrade and set out on the road to Nantes where in a big field I ran into two Gavots who tried take my bag I defended myself and didn't want to use my weapon unless I had to By chance two companion hat makers happened by and gave them what they deserved I arrived in Nantes where the companions were expecting me and hired on with a widow who seemed charmed to have me and I was enchanted to stay with her because in my opinion she was a charming woman I hadn't been with my good widow three weeks when one Sunday she gave me four louis to buy a suit because she'd heard me say that I liked a gray color that I saw a young fellow wearing I refused but the gift was so kindly offered that I accepted

I stayed for nearly eleven months with my widow because the town was proscribed[50] so that there were only three companions there We drove the masters wild and had many different ones One day the first warden of the guild came to make a pact to get the companions to come back After some amiable talk we got angry and even abused one another Without help from my comrades I threw him out the window And I was obliged because there had been so much noise to jump myself into the manure heap where I didn't hurt myself After that we didn't want to hear any more talk Finally other masters came looking for us and we wrote to bring the companions back in That was a great treat for me because all the masters entertained us

I was in my widow's good graces We sat together at table after the companions had had their meal and we amused ourselves drinking good wines and my widow was captivated She told me one day that she had let herself fall so that I could pick her up the way I picked up one of my mistresses That's what I did So I found myself the master of the house nothing could be done without my consent Sometimes there was trouble because of my negligence

I had made the acquaintance of one of my neighbors who healed certain diseases As I'd caught a trifle she undertook to treat me and to make

name of their native city or province, with some distortions introduced by Ménétra's spelling, as above, Langrennois for Langrois.

50 In other words, the city was boycotted by the companion glaziers of the Devoir because they were dissatisfied with the pay or working conditions. In reading about this episode, the reader should keep in mind the major construction work that began in Nantes in 1755.

something out of it to boot[51] But she had a pretty cook who was anything but cruel to me (So) after a while I quarreled with both of them one out of jealousy the other out of ill humor Though in that house I was as welcome as my companion's surname would suggest (I) left without saying good-bye

Then came the celebration of Twelfth Night The mother of companions invited all the companions of every trade to pass round the cake There were well near a hundred and eighty of us My friends and I (were afraid) that one of us would catch the bean because the rule was that the bean king and his comrades were obliged to treat With this apprehension in our minds the bean fell to me They decorated me with ribbons I asked to speak Everyone listened I said My countrymen you know that the glaziers' trade has the fewest companions We cannot treat you as you deserve I beg you to elect another king in my place and I willingly give up my royalty And with one voice they all said Every man will pay his share only the king will be exempt

So for the holidays I forgot my comrades and upon returning home at eleven o'clock at night found my good widow waiting for me to pass round the cake there were five or six of us and once again I was bean king I went to see my surgeoness the next morning I don't know but that chance made the bean fall to me I went to reclaim my royalty at the mother's place where there was a big meal A group of companions came to escort me as they had done the night before in great pomp and ceremony My widow was invited to the ball as well as my surgeoness and her young cook whom I sent someone to invite and fetch on the sly And I did the honors and everyone was happy because a lot of the companions had brought their bosses' wives and daughters

I missed a great opportunity This widow sold glass wholesale to all the masters in towns for twenty leagues around and made shipments to the Isles I was the one who did all this business and wrote all her letters and counterfeited her signature so well that no one could tell the difference Everything passed through me and I couldn't keep still I always needed something new and was always on the run

In the forest of M de la Chapelle I was out walking one Sunday over by the Exchange side while my widow stayed over by the Graveyard (I was) with two comrades who challenged me to go kiss the girl who served drinks Since I was properly turned out I introduced myself and politely

---

[51] In French, *en avoir les gants,* literally, to have the gloves from.

asked her permission which she granted Imagine my surprise when a little guy with a sword put himself in my way [because] you find people like that in such places as well as in Paris He gave me a rude shove I did the same He drew his sword I disarmed him Others of his ilk drew their swords and I was on them so fast that all three were injured I ran like the wind hearing shouts of Stop Police they got me But luckily for me Sergeant Gaborie was a master glazier who let me escape I went to my good widow's and she hid me in her sheets But the next day the inspector paid a call she said I hadn't come back After that since I was not safe I sent to the mother's and more than sixty companions showed up to escort me to the Pirmil bridges[52] And the next day my good widow bade me farewell with tears in her eyes she gave me money and sent my strongbox to La Rochelle I promised that I would come back And to seal my pledge (I) gave her a beautiful diamond that she returned to one of my cousins when he passed through Nantes

I went straight to a master who had a big shipment of window panes to cut for the Isles This fellow had heard of me that I cut big glass well (so) I stayed two weeks and got a nice compliment and (then I) was sent to Rochefort and worked for the King's Hospital where I was fixed up With my comrades I installed glass in three of the king's ships the Foudroyant the Tonnant and the Vavie One day we found an open keg of powder and I filled a coco[53] with it telling everybody I would make some fireworks My comrades filled their pockets (with powder) and at night in our room we had a good time putting a candle to it I told my comrades to have done with it and watch out they wouldn't listen I was in bed Two of them were over by the window All the powder went up and the front of the house collapsed My comrades (were) blinded and I let out a shout people rushed over to help I told them how my friends had been careless It cost the boss forty écus for the damage and repairs and my two friends were in the hospital for six weeks and (they) went more than a month without being able to see clearly One of them will be marked for the rest of his days people nicknamed him Quercy le Mal-savonné [the ill-scrubbed]

All the companion glaziers were assembled to draw for the chance to glaze the king's vessels in Brest Three of us were taken They gave us a green cockade and fifteen francs to travel sixty leagues through terrible

[52] Bridges over the Loire built in 1563 and renowned for their length.
[53] A hollowed-out coconut shell or gourd brought back by sailors from the coast of Africa or America.

country on bad roads escorted by marshals from brigade to brigade all for fear we'd wander off The day they were ready to be masted they asked us if we wanted to go to sea Me with my memories and because I had been flogged wouldn't hear of it I had this comrade and friend by the name of Saint-Germain who wanted to go see the ships at anchor and asked us to get them to take him on board Then they fired the canon (and) in spite of himself he said his good-byes and we teased him from a distance about his curiosity And this poor unfortunate young man perished in the first clash

We returned to Rochefort where I was named first companion All my comrades had fever because this is a very swampy region (but) I didn't catch it I left for Bordeaux I boarded a ship at Royan There were three of us We had taken some supplies I was on deck some well-dressed passengers asked me where I was from When I told them I was from Paris (they) wouldn't let me leave and invited me to a sumptuous dinner which put my traveling companions out of sorts The next morning they pointed out Bordeaux and upon our arrival they invited me to go see them and (said) it would give them pleasure and (I) thanked them as they deserved One of them told me his name was M de Radix[54] and I found out he was one of the big merchants in Bordeaux

I had been in Bordeaux around three months when an earthquake hit[55] It was around ten at night and the first shock knocked me against my boss and the second caused him to fall back on top of me The noise was terrible everybody was shouting everything was crumbling The father and mother were in bed and called to their son at the top of their lungs He was named Bordas When we got up not without fear that the house would come crashing down despite the fear I couldn't keep myself from laughing at the sight of a man and woman in the street with the bed on the ground and completely naked The woman on top and showing a gigantic buttocks because they were both very stout We picked them up and were out running in the fields all night long you saw nothing but men and women draped in sheets as in paintings of the last judgment The fear evaporated with the daylight and the whole thing gave the priests plenty of nonsense to listen to because there are idiots (here) just like anywhere else

[54] Probably a phonetic spelling of Gradis, who was one of the leading Bordeaux merchants. See M. Butel, *Négoce et négociants bordelais au XVIIIe siècle* (Paris, 1978).

[55] The Bordeaux earthquake took place on 10 August 1759 some time after eight in the evening.

One day me and this fellow from La Rochelle wanted to see if we could find any female game We went to the moats around the Trompette castle[56] When we found what we were looking for by agreement I was first by the way then the Rochelais took his turn I spotted the old soldiers coming after us to take us by surprise I yelled to the Rochelais to run for it Either he was hot at it or thought I was joking or didn't look in the right direction because he was blind in one eye he got himself caught and was taken off to the Blue Dial[57] with his jumper dragging

The next day I went to see him with several companions and he gave me a royal tongue-lashing and I teased him about letting himself get nabbed[58] and about not using his good eye We took good care of him the whole time he was in the Blue Dial because he was very well fed and (we) rewarded him as we did any companion who fell ill or got put in prison on companion business (and) to whom we were obliged to give five sols per day and all the companions took turns visiting him and bringing him what he needed

In the meantime a great misfortune befell a companion stonecutter who was not put to death because he had killed a Loup [see n. 34] stonecutter[59] All the first (companions) in the city worked to get him pardoned It did no good The day of the execution the shops were closed and all the companions were ready When the moment of execution arrived a hundred and some armed companions snatched him from the hands of the executioner and took him and put him on a boat for the Médoc where he died six weeks later of the fright he had had in those few moments

While out for a stroll along the paths at Tourny this local swell came up to us looking for a fight especially with me I pummeled him with my walking stick They took us off to headquarters I defended myself so well that he came off as being in the wrong That taught him not to mess with the companions

---

[56] Fortress that dominated the western access to the city, between the walls and the faubourg des Chartrons. Built between 1654 and 1680, it symbolized royal control of the city. In short, it was a financial drain, a political affront, and a major problem in planning the western part of Bordeaux in the eighteenth century. Its poorly maintained bastions and filthy moats and keeps made it a hangout for loose women and idle men. Disabled army veterans acted as guards and turned their victims over to the city authorities.

[57] Probably the prison.

[58] Ménétra's French is odd here. The translation is based on the editor's suggestion about how it ought to be read.

[59] The incident has left no trace in the city archives (*juridiction de la jurade*). Ménétra's French is barely comprehensible. Again, the translation follow's the editor's suggestion.

During all this time our one-eyed Rochelais was still in the clink and he told the companions who went to see him that he would avenge himself as as a matter of fact we fought after he got out Another deal that didn't come off so well for him[60] because I hurt him and he was laid up on his side for more than six weeks and all as the companions said because he didn't have good eyes We made it up because (I've) never been one to hold venom or rancor

An order from the court came down to Bordeaux to recruit for the militia Although I was exempt being a master of Paris in my capacity as first companion I had to be part of the group along with the others Since the intendant was protecting the local boys who had all paid him off his intention was to recruit only strangers and exempt all those who had made him presents which we knew nothing about

All the companions assembled[61] behind the fort of the Hâ on a big field where there were more than four thousand of us of every occupation and trade (and) where we set up a camp repeating all the time that we were obeying the laws because the strangers in Bordeaux had never had to draw lots before We resolved and were all of the same opinion that we wouldn't draw our lots unless the local boys did So after several representations that we made to the intendant[62] who refused to back down we picked a

---

[60] Literally, the expression used is *il ne fut pas bon marchand,* literally, he was not a good merchant, a popular expression meaning he found himself in difficulties, whether in business or elsewhere.

[61] This second Bordeaux incident has left no record, despite the detail of the narrative and its general agreement with the situation in Bordeaux. In the opinion of M. J. Cavaignac, it has to do with a series of incidents that saw the companions of the city pitted against the authorities. For example, in November and December of 1759, the bakers were involved, and the construction workers were mixed up in several other episodes. The latter were particularly upset about the requirement that all hiring be done through a hiring office controlled by the guild masters. Several of these conflicts resulted in the "massing of forces" outside the city. All the facts are plausible, but Ménétra is infatuated with himself, especially in any situation where he sees himself as dealing with powerful men on a footing of equality. For the same reason the figure 4,000 is no doubt exaggerated.

[62] As intendant, the great Tourny saw to it that militia recruitment operated smoothly. He reduced the number of exemptions and required the guilds to supply contingents. At the same time he made use of his right to grant exemptions, and whenever there was trouble he cracked down. See M. L'Héritier, L.-A. *Tourny, intendant de Bordeaux* (Paris, 1920). His son, who succeeded him in 1757, must have adopted a similar policy during the war, but the archives of the intendancy are not complete. The period in which Ménétra's story is situated is known to have been one during which there was hostility to militia recruitment in Bordeaux and its surrounding area. In any case, the incidents, which posed a threat to all the urban authorities, fell within the jurisdiction of the intendant responsible for recruiting militiamen. He was obliged to take account of rivalry among the various powers: the city (*Jurade*), parlement, and the intendancy.

council of thirty companions strong-willed men of resolve One of the men
picked was a Guyennois from my group The council wanted a man who
could write the Guyennois came looking for me and I was the thirty-first
companion

So then I made the regulations and took the count of my companions
Food came to the camp from all over Everybody chipped in There was a
general treasury (and) everyone was written down for the amount they
contributed because the masters who had no children were delighted with
our decision and contributed funds to each companion No companion
could leave camp without authorization of the council Every two hours a
hundred companions armed with walking sticks were sent out to guard
the camp and another hundred returned As a result no one could enter or
leave without an order And we all had tents since the weather was good
this didn't bother anyone

On the third or fourth day two gentlemen on horses came on behalf of
M. l'Intendant the hundred-man advance guard brought them to the
council All thirty-one of us were gathered in a circle with me in the
middle seated on a rock and holding quill and paper in my hand And they
explained themselves like this We are sent by Monseigneur l'Intendant
[that] if you don't do as he wishes he is going to order the soldiers to fire
the canon at the fort of Hâ and elsewhere

They were ushered out and after a conference it was decided that I
would make them an answer They came back into the circle and I said to
them Messieurs all the companions will always submit to the wishes of
the King and of M. l'Intendant on condition that the local boys be subject
to recruitment into the militia just like us We beg you to communicate
this to M. l'Intendant for this is the intention of all the companions They
came back several times to say the same thing Same answer (The intendant) asked us to send twenty companions to confer with him but we
avoided the trap and kept calm

We had been camped for eight days when a gentleman arrived on behalf
of M. the premier Président[63] who said that his master wished to come to
the camp and that he would come after dinner It was answered that he

---

[63] André-François Le Berthon, chevalier, seigneur d'Aiguilhe, vicomte de Virelade et de
Castillon, a friend of Montesquieu and member of the Academy. The parlement was at this
time opposed to royal policy on the edicts of finance and to the policies of Messrs Tourny
Senior and Junior concerning the beautification of the city and compulsory labor requirements.
Ménétra's perception of local rivalries is accurate.

would be most welcome It was decided that two hundred men would go to receive him and that I and another Parisian carpenter whose companion's surname was La Brèche would make him a compliment that we learned by heart and that at the same time we would present him with the list of local boys from whom the intendant had received presents and of those whom he wished to exempt

My fellow Parisian took the right with a hundred men each armed with a walking stick and (wearing) our liveries[64] and I took the left with a similar escort we were a quarter of a league from the camp and at four o'clock we saw approaching a coach with six horses and two others behind with two squires When they saw us marching up and me and the (other) Parisian (make) three deep bows they opened the doors of the coach The premier président had looked up in my direction I saw tht my companion hesitated to speak I began my compliment When two domestics led me over to the right alongside M. le Président it caused a bit of a stir because the hundred companions I had with me wanted to follow me into the camp

Each group of companions stood in front of its tent walking sticks in hand and looking firm The président asked me which group was which and I answered by naming them all He seemed quite pleased When he had toured the camp I made the sign we had agreed on if he approved our conduct with one voice all shouted Long live M. le premier Président he seemed quite pleased by that and when we escorted him out he said these words to us Is everything that is written true I answered him Yes Monsieur we don't want to impose And he answered me Hold firm stay calm and I will support you After bowing to take our leave he let me know that his wife would come to see us the next day I answered him that we would be honored to receive her as he had been received The next day more than twenty coaches arrived We had doubled our train and all the ladies were quite pleased to have such a fine escort This time my countryman made the compliment and afterward we allowed to enter only the masters we knew supported us

The président sent us a message informing us of the arrival of M. de Richelieu[65] who was to make his way down the Garonne We agreed that

---

[64] *Livrées*, meaning the exterior signs of certain estates and trades, not necessarily implying service as a domestic.

[65] The maréchal duc de Richelieu, governor of Guyenne, appointed by the king in December of 1755, made a solemn entry on 4 June 1758. Spendthrift, libertine, and authoritarian, he

we would meet his boat and that three or four hundred men would be left to guard the camp and that the thirty-one first companions would present him with a petition and that if he did not approve each man would go his own way On the other hand (if he approved) the first companions would raise their canes in the air and shout three times Long live the King and M. le duc de Richelieu

The day arrived all properly turned out canes in hand and decorated with our ribbons we went to the landing The bourgeoisie was in arms We placed ourselves in front of them (which) they didn't like at all He [Richelieu] was received by the leaders of the city under [sic] a dais and (when) one of our companions presented him with the petition in spite of the efforts of the intendant He said Strangers have never drawn for the militia and they should be left alone All at once we thirty companions raised our canes It made quite a noise to hear all those voices shout three times Long live the King and the duc de Richelieu (and) the firing of the canon

We had a ball and returned to the city each to his master's house I left town and the companions escorted me out to the sound of violins And (I) went off to Agen I did two leagues that were equal to more than ten regular leagues from Port-Sainte-Marie to Agen (?)

The master took me to a convent where I was welcome I stayed there about six weeks At first the little nuns hid from me as (though) I were the anti-Christ They had given me a bell that I was supposed to ring whenever I went into the dormitories Since I went there often and didn't want to make a nuisance of myself so they got used to it particularly two good sisters who were happy together and went about arm in arm And they knitted me some [illegible] stockings and had the other sisters knit for me too

When there was something to do in their cell since they had a voice in the chapter they always found something for me to do and nothing had ever been so well done as by the Parisian So my boss got suspicious I left

---

made skillful use of his authority over the *parlementaires* and *jurats*. He left Bordeaux for Bayonne in April 1759 and returned on 18 September: it is this return that Ménétra describes. He was in fact welcomed by the *jurats*, but the minutes (AM, BB. 126.18.09.1759) do not mention any participation or submission of a petition by the companions. It is unlikely that such an occurrence would have gone unnoticed, but it may have been considered best to omit from the minutes any account of a conflict that was embarrassing to all concerned, in which the governor would have been empowered to intervene on account of his military functions.

this convent and those good sisters with much regret and went to work in the country house of the bishop who is lord and count of Agen[66]

Once I was at this castle my boss told me to do as little as possible an order that I followed to the letter having made friends with the major-domo and valets who fed me well and treating me as a countryman invited me to join in all their celebrations

In this place I saw a lot of fanatical peasants who brought the bishop partridges and pheasants every day and when he went out in his carriage with six horses and a mounted chaplain in front holding a cross the way they carry flags all those wretches left their fields to run up to the road and lie down prostrate in order to receive a wave from Monseigneur and offer him a thousand blessings for the one of his

I left Agen after having a good time there I met a countryman of mine by the name of Cordier son of the Swiss of Saint-Germain-(l'Auxerrois) who sold small hardware with a tart at a market known as Saint-Caprais two leagues from Agen We spent several days fooling around Since there was all kinds of game around I wanted a piece and once again I got what I deserved for my trouble

I left him and went to work in Auch capital of Gascony with the boss who did work for the cathedral where there are glass paintings more beautiful than any other The canons are so jealous of these that they take turns standing guard Whenever I worked on the glass in this church they were always present and never left me or my boss alone The lower forms represent the creation of Adam to the death of Christ the best joints I ever worked on

I was in communication with my boss's wife who was absolutely trust-worthy also she was always making me presents and her husband was not exempt from these Since he was enjoying himself with her he confessed to me that he had caught something and since he figured I knew what I was talking about I gave him to understand that it might be the aftereffects of an old illness since I had a little recipe for corns[67] on the feet he used some and gave some to his wife And to me in private he suggested he had played around too much with her he was good enough to tell me that it

---

[66] Joseph-Gaspard de Chabannes (1702–1770), anointed in 1736. He was a powerful and prestigious man, but virtually nothing is known of his episcopacy.

[67] *Maladie des cors aux pieds,* literally, corns, Ménétra's private term for syphilis. We gather that he caught a dose at Saint-Caprais ("I paid for it once again") and passed it on to his *bourgeoise.*

was doing a lot of good for the two of them so all three of us were cured
He never mentioned it to me (again) and I figure he never even suspected
that it was me who gave them such a fine present He saw me off in the
friendliest way and I headed for the highway to Toulouse where I ran into
a fellow with whom I traveled as far as Montauban As we talked along
the way (he) told me that he knew how to cure fever I wanted to know
too I had to ply him with drink and he told me his secret and even gave
me the powder

After leaving him I passed a place known as Moissac Point Since the
weather was bad I stopped at an inn where I saw next to the fire the
daughter of the house who was complaining that she had the fevers I
offered to cure her The father and mother were delighted I made her
take some (of the powder) in some wine and gave her another dose (for)
when the fever came on again But no one wanted me to leave The next
day my powder did its job and the people from the town and roundabout
came and (I) cured them Since I wasn't selling my powder I stayed in
this charming place four or five days enjoying myself and nobody charged
me a thing

I left this place with plenty of blessings from those good folks who were
mostly Protestants and arrived in Toulouse where I was hired by a good
widow one of the biggest shops in the city The first thing the widow said
to me was that she had been hearing about me for a long time and that she
was delighted that I was working for her I answered and she was quite
pleased There were four companions in the shop including my old pal the
one-eyed Rochelais on whom I still enjoyed playing tricks I met my
countryman Cordier and we enjoyed ourselves in the rue Gourmande and
(I) bade him farewell because he told me he was returning to Paris this
unfortunate friend died cruelly and in dire poverty for when I got to Paris
I was surprised to find him when I went to clean myself up at the Petit-
Chatel(et) bridge (and) put my foot on the stool (?) I wanted to get away
but he spoke to me thus "there is no stupid work there are only stupid
people" So I let myself be had I gave him nothing except a bottle of wine
(He) went back to work as writer below the charnel house of the Innocents where I saw him One day while out drinking with me and his
friends he felt ill and went to sleep under the Pont-Neuf on the side of the
quai de la Ferraille Asleep on the parapet he died and went stiff

But to get back to my story I was in Toulouse one Sunday while I was
walking outside the city over by the faubourg Saint-Michel I ran into a
woman who came up to me and asked me if I wasn't the fellow who had

asked her the previous Sunday to see the devil I answered no and said I'd rather see a pretty woman She apologized to me she said that if that was what I wanted she'd show me a real charmer I went with her without fear that I was going with the devil (We) came to a nicely furnished room and found nobody there I told her I had not come to her place for nothing and she seemed pretty nice to me and incidentally (she) was She told me that if I wanted to see this young person I should come back after dinner but that I mustn't say anything about what had happened between the two of us I went there after dinner and found a charming young person who told me that her husband was in service and I should come see her I returned there and found no one and (I) found the detour charming be- cause instead of seeing the devil I had spent some pleasant moments with a respectable woman and without interest (?)

I went with one of my comrades to work for a few days in the country at Muret Upon returning I went to the mother's but my comrade went straight to the shop and (I) arrived late The companions and the cook were asleep The only person waiting was my widow We had supper together and afterwards she wanted me to sleep in her bed giving me for a reason that she had asthma and would spend the night in an armchair I accepted this fine proposition and spent the night as one should in such cases There was an Angoumois an old companion glazier whom I of- fended and who had pretensions I tried to reason with him but the widow on the contrary tried to annoy him

Fortunately for him there came a Gascon lord who had a small castle called Savenes four leagues from Toulouse (He) came to ask my widow for a companion saying that everything was ready to go to work The widow insisted on giving him the Rochelais After asking where I was from and (as much because of) signs from the Angoumois as because of the widow's carrying on I went off with this good lord In eight days' time I earned twenty-one écus from my work and all he said was that if I continued in this way I would end up richer than he was

Since it was the edge of winter he secured me work at the abbey of Grandselves[68] where the brother who did the glazing had died some six months earlier Since they had heard of me because I had taken lodging in a place called Aucamville and worked for several lords and curates in the

---

[68] Benedictine monastery in the commune of Bouillac, nearly 40 kilometers from Toulouse. Fewer than twenty monks lived there. See Dom Cottineau, *Répertoire topo bibliographique* (Paris, 1939), p. 1,330.

area I was very well received It was on a Sunday when I made my entry
into this convent followed by the lord for we were both on horseback and
(I) rode ahead of him (because) inferiors ride in front of superiors this
being the fashion in this region We passed by a forest where thirty or so
wolves followed us at some distance I made friends with the brothers and
especially with the keeper of the stores Since their only pleasure was to
play cards and my shop was out of the way every night they drank (there)
and played until matins

It was in this abbey that I made a name for myself curing fevers Since
my cures were free people came from all around The brothers and I ate
some good chickens and I was most welcome in all the nearby towns
especially one place known as Bouillac I had cured the count of the place
who had had the fevers for six years and since on the eves of holidays and
Sundays I did not sleep in the convent I came to this house where I was
very well received The fathers and brothers pulled out all the stops to get
me to stay with them suggesting that I become a brother but I never liked
to be fenced in and liked even less losing my freedom

One day I went off to Toulouse to buy myself a suit of clothes when I
was forced to stop a league from the city by a heavy storm I went into an
inn and asked for a drink Two well-dressed men were playing with some
shells and a pea The point of the game was to figure out which of the
three shells the pea was under At first I won twelve francs (but) went
back to my village somewhat crestfallen after losing eighteen francs I
realized that there were fellows out there sharper than I was

I went back to the convent on occasion (but) no longer enjoyed myself
since I had learned and even seen with some brothers what these fathers
were capable of doing I persuaded a brother carpenter to quit work and
went to buy him a suit of clothes in Toulouse and he threw his habit in the
nettles and (we) went off to have a good time in Toulouse Earlier I had
sold to the brother keeper of the stores some of my powder for twenty-four
francs and spent one night making some for him and (I) gave all my tools
and everything that was left to me to a poor man who carried my glass
when I went to work in towns and villages and who went to Toulouse to
fetch whatever I needed I made him into a wretched painter and a poor
glazier

The good people of Aucamville escorted me out of town with tears and
drums beating and to several of them (I) gave some of my powder for I
was well liked and (I) gambled with the best people in town and every
day was invited to eat with somebody or other There were plenty of

people who wished me well and who did me good turns I went to say my farewells to a good hermit who had received me and the banker and the millers and farmers with kindness (when) we had gone to the hermitage which was a league and a half from Aucamville (and) known as Notre-Dame de Tourville I went to see my old lord who told me that if I wanted to come to Paris that he was going there to serve for a quarter as brigadier of the body guard (and) he had the cross of Saint-Louis[69] He promised to go see my father and he kept his word

Since I was in money and in Toulouse I conceived a desire to go to Saint-Jacques [i.e. Santiago da Compostella] A group of three of us set out in spite of my widow and all the reasonable things she had to say on the subject and (I) left my bag and (we) headed off we went to Bayonne passing through all of Biscaye As we were as well as I can remember leaving Saint-Jean-Pied-de-Port or Saint-Jean-de-Luz to enter Spanish Biscaye we spotted some companions on their way back who were in a miserable state I asked the Angevin and the Agenais who were my traveling companions the one a tinsmith and the other a cutler not to go any further and (we) returned to Bayonne where I saw justice being meted out to whores on the Bridge of the Holy-Spirit or penaco[70] They had been put in an iron cage and were naked (or) in gowns and by means of a swinging arm they were dunked into the river So I asked the whores in these parts if they didn't want to be cleaned up

I left Bayonne alone after finding no work there my traveling companions did find work and they escorted me out of town Once on my way I could not decide whether to go to Toulouse or Bordeaux because there was a fork in the main road and when a postilion asked me where I was going I told him I didn't know which road to take He told me that he was going to Bordeaux and said that if I wished he would get me a ride on a carriage that he was leading (and) that was coming shortly and that he would take me as far as Paris if I wished since I had told him in a few words that I was from Paris and he told me that he was my countryman I accepted the

---

[69] Cross of the order instituted in 1693 as a reward for military valor, worn with a flame-colored ribbon. Chevaliers and officers received a pension of from 800 to 6,000 livres. The person in question is probably M. de Varagne de Gardouche, marquis, seigneur de Belestat, born 10 June 1725 and a member of the king's musketeers, not a bodyguard as Ménétra suggests. In 1757 he was only *mestre de camp* and not *brigadier.*

[70] Mistral's "Trésor du Félibrige" suggests that *penaco* derives from *pena + quieu − co,* or *peine-cul,* literally, pain-(in the)-ass. Today in Bayonne people refer to the bridge of Pannecau, translated locally as "passage" but without any precise philological justification.

offer And the next day I found myself in Bordeaux without having put hand in pocket because at every post along the way my countryman had paid and we said good-bye to each other and see you again

I went back to work for about two weeks in Bordeaux and (then I) set out again with five companion stonecutters When we reached Port-Sainte-Marie we had walked three good hours for five hours of road because there are no villages or houses along the way (but) they didn't want to believe me (We) met a man from the area and asked him if it was a long way from where we were to Agen He answered half a league[71] I took him at his word and said we would give him five sols He was bleeding from the nose My companions forced him to walk He walked at least two and a half hours with us and we were still very far from Agen when we told him to turn back and that the next time he saw some companions passing by to tell them the truth

I left my companions and went to Gascony to a place known as Isle-Jourdain where I knew a companion who was established there (and) where I stayed for a while to rest Since it was holy week (and) the vicar of the place knew my friend he asked me to sing the lamentations of Jeremiah which I had in the book that my good grandmother had sent me Which gave pleasure to the inhabitants of the place that I sang in their church but on the day of Easter since the vicar liked whatever might please the parishioners he asked me for my book in order to sing the *Filiae* telling them that he was going to sing them the joyful song that was sung in Paris but in the refrain I started singing *Alleluia* which he didn't think was sung Because of that the whole congregation sang *Alleluia* out loud At the end of the service they thanked me and were quite content and invited (me) to sing for the whole two weeks of Easter and (I) made them many copies

I set out again for Toulouse since my funds were greatly diminished I was down to seven or eight sols One night I went into an inn and asked for a bed and two soft-boiled eggs saying that I wasn't hungry and the daughter remarked to the mistress that I spoke French well She asked where I was from When I said that I was from Paris she wouldn't hear of my going to bed because she said her son had been in Paris and that he was out hunting and would be back before long and that he would very

---

[71] *Laigue* for the more usual *lieue* or its Bordeaux form, *legue*. The Gascon league was equal to six kilometers. The same anecdote occurs in A. Perdiguier, *Mémoires* (Paris, 1980), pp. 172–73.

pleased to see a young man from Paris I saw a dead sparrow on the spit and I said (to myself) They'll be saying that I'll want to eat it but then I thought of my purse

Finally my man arrived We made acquaintance He enjoyed asking me about the Pont-Neuf Henri Quatre the Samaritaine the place des Victoires and about everything that was remarkable in Paris All the folks who had come to drink and had never seen anything but their own village steeple listened and opened their eyes wide My young man enjoyed himself and meanwhile I was thinking the whole time about my pocket Drink revived my good spirits Supper was served and I did the honors The mistress poured the first *pega*[72] and the son the second at the third she said to me Well Parisian it's your turn Which I took and went to sleep nice and warm But the next morning upon arriving I had said I'd be leaving early and it was nearly nine o'clock and I was (still) mulling things over How was I going to get out of there When the young man came into my room and said that they were expecting me for lunch I made up my mind After lunch I asked how much I owed Nothing but what you want to give the girl I generously gave her four sols and congratulated myself for coming from Paris I said my good-byes and thanked my wonderful hosts

I reached Toulouse My widow had made up her mind and told me that you couldn't trust the word of a Parisian that I was too flighty that she had given her word to the Angoumois I pretended to be angry for a bit and inwardly I was charmed

Since I had left behind a pretty good bag I got rid of what I didn't need and set out for Narbonne From Carcassonne to Narbonne I was accompanied by a big German companion breeches maker who made me a pair of leather breeches all festooned with flowers While sitting under an olive tree I heard a woman shouting and calling to us The German wanted to get on and told me to forget it but I was always ripe for an interesing encounter so we went to see what was what What did we see A woman who had just given birth She gave us her purse and said she was going to die asking us to take care of her child The German had a gourd full of wine we made her take several swallows and I put the child in one of my shirts for she had no pack hers being in the coach She had gotten off for some things she needed and the coach had gone on its way

---

[72] *Pega*, a pitcher of wine, a measure possibly derived from *pega* (meaning pitch), from which *péga, pégal*.

Since we couldn't see any village ahead of us or the coach either we decided to carry her to the town where we had eaten (and) where they took care of her I carried the child and the German who was extremely strong carried her all the way The child was baptized that very night The German was the godfather I learned from the woman herself when she passed through Narbonne that her child was doing well and that she was going to rejoin her husband who was a sergeant in the regiment of Flanders

So I arrived in Narbonne and went to work for the widow Estève where I was quite happy One of my countrymen arrived a fellow by the name of Oran whose very name I should have forgotten but since my family made a bad marriage with his and they have insulted me I will say what it is This delightful young man asked me to get him a job where I was working I had him hired on even though there wasn't enough work to keep us busy I asked him (why) after having been in so many towns he had not been received as a companion and since he was in bad shape I gave him what I could And he told me that since Lyons he had not worked (and) not having found work and having heard from the companions that I was in Narbonne (?) All of it was a pack of lies

Since our widow had left for a farm or small house in the country we set about (doing the glass) melting While I went down to the cellar to look for wine to start the fire in the fireplace my countryman put in a lot of kindling although I had told him not to The upshot was that the whole chimney and the house caught fire Me and this carpenter did all we could and we managed to put it out I hadn't seen any sign of my countryman I looked for him I went to our room but he had taken the precaution of removing my bag and was in bed at the mother of companions' place where I went to find him and dealt with him as he deserved and took back my bag They told me that he was in desperate shape unfortunately for him that was nothing

The following Sunday while out walking I saw four companion lock-smiths arrive walking sticks in hand who had come from Béziers on pur-pose to give my dear countryman a beating And (they) would have left him for dead on the square if I had not stopped them by telling them that they shouldn't beat up an aspirant and that I was a companion We went to the mother's where they showed me a letter from the companions of Montpellier who didn't know that I was in Narbonne (reporting) that he had stolen a diamond some shirts and some silk stockings and (that) they

had invited them to give him a thrashing[73] I went back to look for him
and to ask him to return the diamond but he had cleared out (He) had
asked the widow to give him three livres for me had stolen from me a pair
of plush trousers a brand new pair of stockings and some yellow pumps
that people wear in Languedoc I never saw him again but I heard plenty
about him

Before that I had left Narbonne [to go] to Perpignan with some companions on a pleasure trip When we got to the mother's and the companions
found out I was Parisian they paid me a fine tribute because about a
month before there had been a Parisian glazier who gave the blessing with
his feet[74] for a theft committed in Spanish territory three leagues form
Perpignan

After returning to Narbonne I stayed there a while longer and gave up
my place to a friend of mine from Rennes who needed a job I left with a
fellow from Saint-Germain who had been a captain of the Gavots in Avignon and who had been received as a carpenter *compagnon du Devoir*
Three-quarters of a league from Béziers I almost ended my days because
there were eight big Gavots waiting for us in ambush I spotted them and
told the Saint-Germain to look tough He wanted to run I cocked my
pistol which I carried on the road in a bandolier and hidden in the folds of
my clothing When they saw me armed and because they wanted to jump
us they told me that it wasn't me they were after but my comrade I said to
the Saint-Germain to hold tight and they wouldn't dare take a step Some
people happened by so all we had out of it was a scare but my escape
almost did me in because when we got to town the carpenter invited me to
go with him to the mother of companions' place where he was expecting
somebody

I asked for the mother of carpenters and somebody took me to the
mother of Gavots instead The minute I entered I saw I was in for it
because of my mistake The Gavots had come back and asked me what I
wanted from them and said that either I drank to their health or they were
going to blow me to kingdom come I answered them firmly They wanted
to insult me but their father arrived who told them as I had been telling

---

[73] *Passade*, from the Occitan *passado, passa*. The passage apparently means that the companions of Montpellier wrote to their comrades in Narbonne to urge them to give Oran a
thrashing. This is one of the meanings of *passado*, the other being to give alms.

[74] To be hanged.

them that at our mother's place they wouldn't be insulted They stood me to a drink and told me I was a good fellow I went to the mother's where the companions were gathering to rescue me from the Gavots and we went looking for the Saint-Germain whom we carried through the town in triumph

In Béziers I received a letter sent to me from Montpellier by a master glassblower who had contracted to make six-hundred lanterns and (he) sent me twelve livres for my trip I left with a sergeant from the Béarn regiment and we stopped in a convent known as Labadie where we gave alms[75] to strangers He wanted me to stay and so did the brothers of the convent But since I wanted to get to Montpellier early and couldn't avoid the misfortune that was to befall me I continued on my way and stopped to sleep at an inn four leagues from Montpellier

While eating supper I heard a wagon stop and some men saying We'll be in Montpellier before five o'clock Since it was a fine moonlit night I asked if they would accept some money to let me ride in their wagon There were some sacks of grain I put my bag in with my walking stick and went to sleep I was rudely awakened and asked if we had arrived No but get down I saw myself surrounded by thieves who were looking me up and down I saw my bag thrown down and one of the brigands cut it in two with a large knife They asked me for my money and made me undo my trousers which were new and made of black hide and I had to trade pants with one of the thieves As I was buttoning up my pants they told me to turn around

I didn't dare draw my pistol which was fortunately hidden in the folds of my clothing (and) to keep it from swinging I had attached it with a large pin Looking in my bag they found powder and a brush they threw the powder in my face and said a lot of stupid things and then they told me brusquely to clear out I was still afraid that they would make me get undressed (so they could take my clothes) but they saw a stain on the front of my shirt which was only wet because I had had some eau de vie that the wagoneer had in a gourd before going to sleep Because they would have blown my brains out with my gun

I walked almost two leagues without shoes and arrived with my wretched crew in Montpellier When I got to the mother's the companions upon learning of the misfortune that had befallen me loaned me everything that I needed And I was lucky that they didn't search my vest

[75] *Donner la passade:* see n. 73.

pocket where I had my diamond and that they didn't find my walking stick All I lost was my kit The boss who took me on didn't advance me anything

And then I went to work in the city hall where I made three lanterns pretty much like the ones in Paris (and) the last of which was received by the provost and aldermen to whom I presented it in company of my boss who was a glassblower[76] The master glaziers made me many propositions [objections?] I told them that I was master of Paris that they couldn't stop me The companions wanted to take a hand in the dispute I told them that it was the fault of the masters who had not presented themselves and that it was basically their own fault I took with me a fellow from Lorraine and another from Burgundy and we worked in the city hall I settled with the boss for fifteen francs per months and six francs for every hundred lanterns and plenty of food and twelve francs that the gentlemen of the city gave me to begin and twelve additional francs at the end of the job They kept their word

After about three months the job was just about done and (I) stayed on only to make sixty additional lanterns that they called spares in case one got broken or otherwise and when I wasn't thinking about it at all I caught the smallpox I was at the mother's drinking when I felt a headache from the blanquette or the muscat wine Finally I had to lie down without knowning what malady I might have the companions took me to the Saint Eligius hospital[77] mounted on a donkey with a cover over my back two companions on either side holding me and another holding the bridle and several following which made a nice cavalcade

Since I was recommended by the gentlemen of the city I was very well received particularly by two gray sisters who were from Paris and who took good care of their countryman One morning I felt that my face was on fire The nurses ran for the good sisters shouting The Parisian has the

---

[76] The first lanterns in Montpellier date from 1697. The city modernized and repaired its lighting beginning in 1754. After much deliberation a contract for the supply and repair of 600 lanterns was awarded to Sieur Rigaudin, coppersmith, for 2,400 livres per year. Ménétra was hired to install glass in the lanterns and then to repair any that were broken (AM, DD. 304, BB. 1757, 1759, 1760, and DD. 310 bis, 19, for the submission of the contract).

[77] The city hospital, it grew extensively in the seventeenth and eighteenth centuries (and today is the rectorate of Montpellier). All sorts of diseases were treated, and in the period 1750–1760 the hospital could hangle 150 to 200 patients. The staff included four surgeons, six apprentice surgeons, three physicians, six male nurses, and sixteen *soeurs grises* (gray sisters) or servants of the poor, i.e., charity patients. See L. Dulieu, *Essai historique sur l'hôpital Saint-Eloi* (Montpellier, 1953).

picotte[78] I gnawed a crust of bread and it was that that saved me for I
was eight days without seeing clearly and I couldn't swallow anything
except consommés because I had smallpox pustules in my throat and those
good sisters told me that the crust of bread that I had eaten saved my life

It was something of a phenomenon in those parts for a young man of
twenty-one to have smallpox so when the surgeon or one of his assistants
came to visit there were students piled up as high as the bed canopy I was
alone in a small room I ate *petits pieds*[79]

The companions wanted me to cut cards with them again (but) the
sisters didn't want me to leave them so quickly Finally I wanted to leave
and I almost did myself down because in hastening to dress I put the
hospital cap and hankerchief in my pocket What a surprise I got when
the Swiss guard asked me if I had anything of the hospital's on me I said
no When he found these things in my possession my protests that I'd
taken them by mistake were in vain the misers said that they would have
to make an example of me because they were robbed every day In the end
the good sisters came and found me with all the gentlemen assembled and
saw that I was being taken for a criminal they went to find the superior
and had me released

I stayed for a few days at the mother's where it happened that when I
went to sleep in a room a young fellow who was a gardener (with) whom
(I) had slept and eaten the next day I wanted to wake him up saying
Friend let's go drink some white wine He never answered me I remembered clearly that he had spoken to me during the night but it was to say
adieu I went to see my good sisters to whom I gave a small glass chest
along with a writing table that I gave to the mother superior In exchange
I got a beautiful brown suit of calendered cloth[80] that I had tailored to fit

---

[78] *Picotte*, the Occitanian term for smallpox, rather rare in a twenty-year-old but devastat-
ing to the infant population. The main symptoms mentioned in the text could well have been
consequences of this disease, normally accompanied by fever and rash: 8–15 day incubation
period, temperature of 102–105 degrees, headache, sore throat, and of course a suppurating
rash followed by desiccation. The scabs drop off after twenty days. Numerous complications
killed many patients, who were highly contagious and therefore kept in isolation. The bread-
crust treatment is not attested in any of the traditional sources. It demonstrates the medical
imagination of Ménétra, who survived by chance. Inoculation considerably reduced mortality from smallpox in the second half of the eighteenth century. See C. Rollet, *Cahiers
d'histoire* (1978), p. 418.

[79] An allusion to the southern dish known as *pieds et paquets,* a sort of stew of sheep's
hooves and tripe.

[80] An allusion to the practice of calendering, a process for giving a luster to cloth using a

My boss made a deal with me that I would clean the lanterns the price was set at five sols each I cleaned as many as twenty-five or thirty a day When he saw that I was going so fast I left everything Around this time a fellow from Quercy came with a girl disguised as a boy tailor and he was a companion cutler who brought her from Toulouse At night we ate together but I realized that this was men's merchandise and I wasn't wrong The first night they slept together in the room we shared The next day the Quercy fellow went to work and came back at night to drink with us and went to sleep at his boss's I took his place that night half by force half with her consent The next day she told her lover what had happened but since several of us slept in the same room he couldn't tell which one to go after He took each of us aside and we all had a good laugh at their expense because all the companions joined in the teasing The two individuals were forced to leave town and everybody including the mother said nobody but the Parisian could play a trick like that but I flatly denied everything

At this time one of my countrymen a tailor who shared our lodgings[81] died The tailors invited the companions and especially me who marched first behind the body with crepe in my hat afterward we had a big meal where I was toasted for being a countryman of the deceased

There was a big fight one night while we were walking on the esplanade at the end of the place du Pérou I was struck in the right leg by a tailor who threw a wood seam-presser at me He paid for it all right Then I went to see the good sisters who thought it was the large pox[82] and (I) stayed in the hospital until I was fully recovered since I was well treated Since the companions came to visit me one patient a heavy tobacco user was always bothering me to get the companions to bring him some I had them do it but I fixed it with very fine dry (powder) He found it so good that I couldn't keep him supplied he gave it to the other patients who all wanted some That made me see that all these tobacco gourmets are easily

---

calendering machine. Also refers to clothes bought second-hand and given a new shine by calendering.

[81] Probably a companion who shared the same room in the inn run by the mother of companions.

[82] *Gros grain*, an unusual expression that may refer to another fever with rash similar to smallpox, whence the pun. *Petit grain* was used for scarlet fever and measles, which did not leave permanent scars like smallpox. Littré's dictionary records the expression *grain de petite vérole*.

taken in The surgeons to whom I told the whole story laughed themselves silly over it

I left my good sisters and traveled through a charming countryside to Nîmes I went to work for a kindly widow by the name of Fricot I stayed with this widow for about five months I thought of settling in since I was welcome and (since she) resembled my good widow of Nantes in every way I promised her that I would finish my tour of France quickly and that I would stay in Paris just long enough to have my relatives' consent that as for property I had none that I had only my master's certificate which authorized me to establish myself anywhere She was enchanted She promised me everything accompanied me for two leagues with the handsomest of promises We said tender farewells to each other with the hope of joining our lives in marriage

But when I reached Marseilles I wrote to her that I was going to stay there for two weeks and that I would go to Lyons directly She sent me a charming response and twenty-four francs asking that as a token of my friendship I send her my master's certificate which I had shown to her which I did not do because I saw that she was puffed up She was Protestant and her late husband was Catholic and had left her ten thousand livres on condition that she marry only a Catholic

I didn't answer her and stayed only a short while in Marseilles For when I arrived (we) went into a cabaret they brought us four glasses and an equal number of pipes of tobacco and (I) saw two broads come in and (we) quickly made their acquaintance But since I knew their wiles I was only teasing and I knew that seventeen companions from my group had become infatuated So I got out of there as fast as I could lest I become the eighteenth

I went to see Sainte-Baume[83] and spent six hours climbing (I) went by way of Saint-Maximin and returned via Aubagne and went to see the famous Beaucaire fair where I found a worthy fellow who had just bought glass to glaze the *sanitat*[84] of Carpentras We went to work for this chap

---

[83] The place to which, as tradition had it, Maître Jacques went after returning from the East, before he was murdered. It was also supposed to have been the refuge of Mary Magdelene, the converted sinner. The pilgrimage—still practiced today—took companions to a cave in the side of the mountain. In the nineteenth century a register of pilgrims was found there, together with souvenirs of early visitors.

[84] *Sanitat*, or *sanital*, the hospital of Carpentras, established some time after 1750 with a bequest from Monseigneur d'Inguimbert, was barely finished when Ménétra arrived on the scene. The building cost more than 500,000 livres.

where I told stories about Sainte-Baume to one of his daughters who was pretty as a picture (and) who was called Norade I stayed for a while particularly as it was the time of a jubilee[85] All strangers had to take communion or else (they were) forced to leave town[86] I decided to do it partly because I didn't care and partly because I was in love I was ready for the occasion After me and my comrades had fortified our consciences our boss found us a Dominican who had big sleeves For me he made the sign of the square[87] very easily It didn't go so well with my comrade who was put off for a week Since we had told each other all the little tricks that we had played I said to him But then you've committed enormous crimes if he won't do for you the same as he did for me Later during the night I thought about it since I had taken it right after his siesta Then I went back and when he saw me he said that he had heard everything Then I could finish off the affair and get everyting that was coming to me that my boss's daughter was willing to give

All over the city they were putting up artistically made iron crosses There were a lot of locksmiths and we were always going off on drinking bouts One night I made up a song about the city of Carpentras The next day all the companions stayed away from work violins and oboes were brought in and everybody had a bottle and a glass in hand and a companion locksmith (who) had the song written on his back in big letters with white chalk on an apron and we sang it over and over (which) greatly please the residents who followed us from corner to corner through the town

In those days I went to Jew town[88] to play tricks on those unfortunate

---

[85] Jubilees were held every twenty-five years. The last one was in 1750–51, so Ménétra is confused about the date. The anecdote probably dates from Easter time, when communion was still compulsory.

[86] *Battre aux champs*, roughly, beat the bush, meaning, to leave town.

[87] *Le trait carré*, literally, sign of the square, for sign of the cross, and, by extension, to receive absolution. The meaning of the sentence is rather obscure.

[88] Jews in the Comtat were truly second-class citizens. Papal laws afforded them protection but imposed many restrictions on their activities: they were required to wear yellow hats (and, for women, yellow marks as well), they could not sleep outside the city walls or engage in any business other than usury, secondhand clothing, and secondhand furniture. Jews and Christians were strictly segregated, mixed marriages were prohibited, and contacts between the two communities were watched. The various Jewish communities in the Comtat prospered during the eighteenth century. In 1755 the Carpentras ghetto had barely 1,000 inhabitants out of a total population of 10,000, and that of Avignon only 300 Jews in a total population of 25,000, but both grew in size in later years. The gap between the economic prosperity of the ghettos and their legal status made things difficult, and the Jewish commu-

Jews Then I met one of the wealthiest Jewesses in the synagogue (she was) nice and believed what I told her that if she wanted to become a Christian I would marry her and take her to Paris Since her father was a widow and the laws in this territory are very strict for Jews he would have been obliged if his daughter were baptized to give her half her property She often came to my shop to let me know her intentions she gave me wrapped in paper some unleavened bread which I said I liked and in the paper on which I wrote to her I wrapped pastilles and other tidbits which she gladly accepted My boss lent a hand but her nurse who was Christian and didn't leave her gave the game away and ruined all my plans

The bishop of Carpentras[89] had ordered a glass coat of arms to be placed over the gate of the *sanitat* promising to pay us for work My comrade and I worked on this job for several Sundays and when the arms were in place he showed us his Italian-style generosity[90] He gave me twenty-four sols Since he had hidden the money as he handed it to me I figured it was a gold louis but when I showed it to my comrade he took it out of my hands and went to give it back to the bishop

All of us companions were desperate to learn how to handle the espadon and the walking stick In tours I had taken some lessons (and) we practiced at the mother's and I demonstrated to the others which led to drinking afterward so the mother didn't care And one day three or four of us were in the fields we met a Jew who didn't have his yellow hat and who was carrying two fine chickens We took them from him and ate them He had us brought before the consuls for (that) but he was still in the wrong because he didn't have his yellow hat

I had my eye on a cute little button seller across from my shop but since she was smarter than I was she asked me to take her walking outside the town For my little Norade did not leave her mother and went with a bashful lover who made her suffer and didn't make me angry so as not to embarrass me although in love I have always acted as I wished (?)

---

nity was held together by outside pressures. The archives provide abundant confirmation of what Ménétra has to say. Although there was never a pogrom in the Comtat, there were innumerable minor incidents, crude jokes, conversion campaigns, and daily humiliation, as was inevitable given the traditional image of the Jew to which Christians of the time subscribed. See R. Moulinas, *Les Juifs du Comtat au 18e siècle* (Toulouse, 1982).

[89] A reference to the successor of Monseigneur d'Inguimbert, Joseph de Vignoli (1758–1778), born in Camerino and bishop of San Severino. His coat of arms is no longer displayed above the hospital entrance.

[90] Probably an allusion to the avarice of the Italian prelate and an expression of traditional hostility to the ultramontane clergy.

She had (another) lover to whom I brought good luck he married the little button seller and I had caused him to come from Paris I promised her that I would take her walking on Sunday at a place called Pernes I told this to my boss (who told me) that I'd better keep my eyes open that she wanted to trap me that when we came back into town together she would have me arrested by the pope's soldiers for seducing her and that no matter what I said or did I would be obliged to marry her[91] I went walking I promised her everything she wanted and a quarter of a league from town at a moment when she was least expecting it I ran and returned by another gate When she saw that I had trapped her in this way she went the next Sunday with her (second) lover and on purpose made sure they were taken prisoner and they were married When she was where they put the girls I saw her through the bars she told me that I was the author [of her child presumably—Trans.] but she was always thinking of me

When she was in Paris she was always very polite to me and decent and sometimes she asked Do you remember the walk at Pernes we were very young One day I said to her That day is as old as your daughter She smiled at me and squeezed my hand As for the fellow for whose happiness I was responsible and to whom I wrote when I was in Paris where he was a pasta maker[92] he was (not) grateful even though he had made his fortune And when he met me (he) was polite but he always had that recent trip to Pernes on his mind

[91] The procedures for illegitimate pregnancy in the Comtat are not appreciably different from those stipulated in French law, which required young women to declare their pregnancies in order to avoid the presumption of infanticide (edict of 1556, renewed in 1708). The texts do not indicate to whom these declarations were to be made, however, nor under what conditions. Here we see that they were made at the consulate and resulted in a period of imprisonment. Ménétra could have been prosecuted on a simple charge of failure to acknowledge paternity but would not necessarily have been imprisoned. This story shows us what was a rather common affair in the cities, that of a young woman duped by a promise of marriage and abandoned. Ménétra's Comtadine comes out of it better than most, for she has an accommodating fiancé. The details of this case cannot be checked, since the consular court's archives for the first trimester of 1761 have disappeared. BM, Carpentras FF. 60 (9–43).

[92] Italian pasta was introduced into Parisian cooking in the second half of the eighteenth century. This was in part the result of a campaign by physicians, who advised people with fragile stomachs to eat pasta, and in part the work of the pasta makers who held a monopoly on the manufacture and sale of pasta in Paris. So to the names of the good Doctor Malouin of the Académiie des Sciences and Sap, the pasta maker of the rue des Prouvaires, we must add that of Ménétra if we wish to understand the popularization of spaghetti, lasagna, and macaroni.

When I wrote my widow in Nîmes she sent me an answer filled with love and kindness and whenever I wrote to her I found reasons why we could not continue on our way My travelling companion said that since we had good reason to get moving we should go to Aix to see the procession[93] which really shows you the fanaticism and superstition that the priests have always done their utmost to fob off on people

The decision made we asked for what we were owed The boss said many prayers but when he saw that all we wanted was to get on our way we were forced to take him before the consuls who obliged him to pay us And (they said) that we were free to go as he was free to pay us off which he didn't hear at all repeating that the work that we had undertaken was not done But since we were paid by the month he lost his case because I answered firmly before the consuls that we had made no promises and that in France people are free What I said went over very well because they had just been annexed to France[94] along with the Comtat of Avignon

So that he paid us off and to avenge himself despite being a good fellow paid us in small coins of which it takes seven to make one sol of the pope's money and six to make one sol of the king's Since he owed the two of us around thrity-three livres we were really weighed down The good lord of Venasque changed the money for us and the day of our departure he asked me to dine with him That good old man had taken a liking to me and sent for me to come talk to him about Paris He servants liked me too and had often given me good meals He had a gourd filled with his best wine for me He and his whole household bade me the most tender farewells My boss came looking for me and said he didn't want me to leave feeling bitter I went to say good-bye to the boss's wife and daughters but the charming Norade absolutely refused to come out

It was on a Sunday that I left that delightful city accompanied by

---

[93] Ménétra also refers to this as the Foux d'Aix. Corpus Christi, celebrated after the octave of Pentecost, reveals a popular devotion to the Eucharist. It became firmly established under Pope John XXII. In Aix, starting in 1461, it became the occasion of one of the most celebrated festivities of modern Provence. Pageants stretching over two days depicted pagan deities such as Diana, Mercury, Pan, Bacchus, and Pluto, biblical characters including Moses and other Jews, and scenes from the life of Christ. The ceremony ended with a procession of notables, followed by the grim reaper wailing and swinging his scythe.

[94] Ménétra is mistaken. In 1761 the Comtat Venaissin was still under the authority of the pope, though it had been under the control of France economically and for customs purposes since 1734. Conflicts with the court of Rome led to the occupation of the Comtat from 1768 to 1774. See P. Charpenne, *Histoire des réunions temporaires d'Avignon et du Comtat Venaissin à la France* (Paris, 1886).

almost all the companions of every trade each with a glass and a bottle in hand we did our duty a companion stepped on my gourd and broke it which broke my heart it [the gourd] was charming

In this part of the world fanaticism and superstition are at their height (and) the unfortunate Jew[95] cannot go out without a yellow hat his wife without a yellow ribbon on her bonnet Saturdays they have to listen to the exhortations of monks most of which make no sense If they're unlucky enough to respond or to look distracted they are immediately [illegible] with bulls' pizzles Ah the Christian religion which they say is tolerant (How) can you ministers of the alter act with so much cruelty that they [the Jews] are forced to hide in doors and alleyways When you go through the city making a procession and carrying about what you impose on the people your most secret mysteries you order the man who is carrying the figure that you call our Savior to beat them freely with this sign of our redemption You don't think that they are our brothers and that they are equal to us in the eyes of the Eternal Yes they are our fathers It is from their remote ancestors who are also our ancestors that we all derive our existence And you men filled with ambition it is from their religion that you derive all your dogmas and ceremonies

We went down to Avignon and I started singing the refrain of that old song of my godfather's of whose death I had learned and who had tenderly raised me with my good grandmother "I am on the bridge of Avignon" Try as I might to sing it well he always told me I wasn't getting it and he was right And this time I got it right because I was standing on the bridge as I sang

We went for a walk to look at the Jews passing in front of a glazier's shop I looked in to see if by chance he had any masterpieces since I kept a notebook of them that I working on during my off hours But I've lost it since I lent it to a cousin and was never able to get it back While I was staring at the shop and pointing it out to my friend from Rennes the boss came out to ask us politely if we were glaziers (I) answered yes He asked us to come in gave us refreshment His wife a friendly woman gave us a good welcome and asked where we were from We were really welcome

[95] Preaching intended to convert the Jews and street incidents during processions and festivals are recorded in the court records of the Comtat. Jews were forbidden to enter the holy places and to go outside on Sundays and holidays; they were advised to avoid the passage of the Holy Sacrament and were required to salute the cross during Holy Week. See Moulinas, *Les Juifs.*

there The boss told us that in a town he called Bédoin at the foot of a mountain in Provence named Mont Ventoux he had a brother who had left the day before and had asked him to send down some companions to repair a church damaged by a storm that he was going to pass through Carpentras where there were two companions he would try to persuade to quit but that if any (others) happened by he should send them down I answered that He couldn't persuade us to quit we had quit on our own He invited us to go down to Bédoin

The companion came We identified ourselves he took us to the mother's We told him that we did not want to work in town The companions came we declared ourselves out of work The master came to invite us to go work it would only be for two weeks he would go with us we made him beg us He told us he would pay for our trip and would give each of us six francs We made up our minds we promised him on our word as companions that we would leave in two days

We had a good time we tried to forget our mistresses in the arms of other women for there was no lack of them in those parts or anywhere else I forgot the masterpieces that I wanted to draw I went to see all the sights of the city I went to the mother of locksmiths I found my old countryman We didn't want to part he was angry that I had agreed to go to Bédoin when we could have finished our tour of France together I promised him to come back for him He escorted us along with many other companions

So we hit the road with the boss he put us up with a Provençal lord for whom he had worked in a pretty castle This good lord had us dine with him at his table and was as polite as could be He knew I was from Paris he liked to have us tell him about our pranks and everything we had done on the tour of France I told a few stories The lord and his wife laughed so hard they were crying a priest who served them as chaplain but who had nothing of the hypocrite about his stifled a laugh by putting his handkerchief or napkin in front of his mouth (and) the mistress couldn't take any more The master told her to come back the next day to hear me In thanking him he said to him Master when you come to work in the castle bring me a worker like the Parisian and (we) said our good-byes

We came to Bédoin (a) charming little town and we were warmly welcomed All the promises we had been made were faithfully executed We set to work We were with good gentle and friendly people All the good people of this area are I think the best I have ever seen the fanaticism nearby but also they are on the pope's land

Since we were in the season when it is possible to climb to the top of that mountain[96] which is out of reach the rest of the year several of us climbed up taking provisions with us and it took us nearly five hours On top (we) found charming greenery and very sweet air a lake about a quarter of a league long We had a lot more fun going down than we had had going up One day my boss asked me if I wanted to go with him to the castle of Crillon[97] He told his wife not to wait for us since the job could not (be) done in one day We came to an old castle at the foot of a hill of the sort they describe in romances Above the gate was an inscription that ran like this "Fear God and the arm of the brave Crillon" I looked at what had to be done There were around sixty panes to set I watched the boss take out a spatula a flat tool for puttying I said to him Go see the caretaker and let me do that I didn't like his awkwardness His way it would have taken the two of us two days In the wink of an eye the job was done and when he came back he was surprised And (we) went back to town The boss's wife found the story incredible she couldn't get over it and he kept telling her The Parisian did it all alone

Since I had given him some powder for curing fevers and he had taken some (and) was cured this good woman hit on the idea that I was a magician because I was always singing and happy but (also) because I don't like priests because they act like hypocrites (and) because I played tricks So there was my boss's wife back from Vendôme (?) because I was telling jokes to the girls and stories to the women I straightened her out and the Rennais too

When the two weeks were up I wanted to leave The Rennais tried to get me to stay We were with such good people (and) besides the boss's wife saw that my powder was begining to catch on because it is in Crillon that the powders of Aillaud[98] are made I gave her some as a gift and she gave me six francs which I accepted (I) set off and left the Rennais and

---

[96] Mont Ventoux drew many curious climbers: Petrarch in the fourteenth century (see his letter to Father Denis dated 9 May 1331), Thomas Platter Jr. in the fifteenth century, and Peiresc on two occasions in the seventeenth century. In 1701 Father Laval began an era of astronomical and botanical observations, and in 1778 he was followed by Darluc. See G. Brun, *Le Mont Ventoux* (Carpentras, 1969), and P. Pansier, "Les Ascensions du Ventoux," *Annales d'Avignon et du Comtat Venaissin* (1932), pp. 117–130.

[97] Louis de Berton de Crillon, companion of Henri IV (1541–1615), warrior, and one of the great figures of the sixteenth century, whose popular biography should be treated with caution. The château de Crillon was altered many times between the fifteenth and nineteenth centuries. (Musée Calvet, Avignon, MS. 2385. Fol. 86.)

[98] A reference to the all-purpose specific developed and sold by Dr. Jean Aillaud (or

went to find my countryman who was waiting for me at the mother's in Avignon where we celebrated the feast of Saint Ann with the companion carpenters who invited me (and) to which my old countryman Parisien La Breche belonged

We had a good time for several days and went to see the beautiful Jewish quarter and (we) wanted to see the vice-legate[99] who had just acted in the most atrocious way toward an unfortunate woman from this area who had a dispute with a woman she knew In the course of this quarrel she had thrown a stone which unfortunately had broken the glass of the carriage in which the vice-legate happened to be passing by And (he) ordered that she be given three turns of the rope which dislocated all her limbs She was carried to the *sanitat* she died in pain Everybody in Avignon was horrified I asked myself Is it possible that men who are supposed to set an example of humanity and love for their neighbor and who call themselves the ministers on earth of a kind and benevolent God that such men know nothing but ambition and vengeance So the people of Avignon were happy to have shaken off the rule of the Italians and to have placed themselves under the protection of France

We left The companions escorted us Since my countryman was a generous fellow and could afford to be liberal he stood the mother of the escort and twenty companions of his trade to a meal and (we) went to sleep The next day we set out for Orange The weather was fair Suddenly there blew up one of the worst storms I've ever seen the thunder rumbled the rain came down in buckets I took shelter under an olive tree I called my countryman who was under another tree he hesitated finally he came At that moment the heavens opened the thunder cracked and the tree my countryman had just abandoned fell to the ground in ashes We threw ourselves down on the ground The first thing I did was to thank the Eternal for sparing us and we prayed to the Providence that had saved us in the end When the storm had passed we went over to examine (the tree) all that was left was the stump We stopped at the first place we got over our fear and continued on our way because we wanted to see the fountain of Vaucluse

---

Ailhaud) of Lourmian in Provence. This scammony-based purgative powder was tested in Cadenet and dispensed, with much publicity, throughout the kingdom. After Aillaud died in 1756 his son continued dispensing his preparation. Both were *docteurs-régents* of Aix.

[99] G. A. Salviati was the vice-legate representing the pope in Avignon from 1760 to 1766. He is not to be confused with the archbishop of Avignon, F. M. Manzi (1756–1774), who succeeded him as legate. The vice-legate was responsible for temporal and political affairs.

The next day we set out again we met two monks My countryman greeted them and I did the same they looked at us with disdain I said to my countryman Look at those pious lay-abouts how hypocritical they seem with their rosary at their side those humbugs surely take us for robbers we might well be let's scare them follow them Let's not go too fast we've passed them They looked down We asked them since they knew the area if it was a long way to the next village and we walked along with them They kept a sharp eye on us I told them that I had stayed in a convent of Bernardines and that their order was supposed to be benevolent was supposed to give to the poor and try to do good and not to be too hard on their fellow man

Since we were going backwards backtracking so to speak I refrained from writing to my widow Along the way we found ourselves on the bank of a small river (and) without a bridge or boat in sight but there was a sturdy fellow who carried me on his shoulders My comrade wanted to cross (by himself and) after removing his shoes and stockings (he) took another path (and) would have drunk a mouthful if this worthy chap hadn't fished him out

So we went to see the real Aix Fair and stayed only two days I also wanted to see Salon to see all that people say about Nostradamus[100] In the middle of a church against the wall we saw this tomb [i.e., of Nostradamus] about which so many stories are told with a portrait under glass and a stone on top My comrade passed his knife through the slits in the tomb and did not die as they try to make the vulgar believe

(We) went over to Arles to see its beautiful boat bridges and then went in the direction of the Cévennes and decided to head for Dauphiné[101] We stopped at an inn (and) as we arrived somewhat late they put us in a room in which a man had died They had put him in a sheet and laid him in the street That night my comrade got up to get some things he needed Imagine his fright to discover that he was stepping on a human body He woke

[100] Michel de Notre-Dame (born in Saint-Rémy-de-Provence in 1503, died in Salon in 1566), physician and member of a family of physicians, was known for his work during the plague of 1525–1529. He settled in Salon in 1545 and became celebrated for his research in astronomy and astrology. His predictions enjoyed immediate success. He was buried in Salon in the convent church of the Friars Minor. Ménétra's text adds a detail to the popular legend surrounding Nostradamus, according to which he continued writing his prophecies inside his tomb.

[101] The translation follows the editor's interpretation of Ménétra's peculiar French. He went to Valence to visit members of his mother's family, but his story is set on the right bank of the Rhône, which he crossed again at Pont-Saint-Esprit.

me up (and) I thought that men had been stationed to murder us We woke up the whole house and they explained what had happened and (we) left even though it was not yet dawn Also for the trouble they caused us we took two nice ducks We gave one to the first inn we came to in exchange for having them cook the other

That night (we) came at sunset to the home of a worthy fellow and had supper with him since hardly any strangers travel in these parts he was enchanted with our conversation When I told him that I was going to see my family and that they hadn't seen me for almost seven years tears streamed from his eyes and he told me I hope that what happened to my wife doesn't happen to your grandmother I told him to bring us some wine and to tell us what made him so sad After watering his tears with a few glasses of wine he told this story I had a child who went off at the age of thirteen and we went several years without any news of him One night a fellow came by riding a good horse and asked to have supper with us After supper he asked us if we had any children I told him that we had had a good-for-nothing boy who had left without saying a word and that for twelve or thirteen (years) we had had no news He asked my wife Would you recognize your son Oh yes she said in ten thousand for he has a mark in the middle of his head from a burn where no hair can grow At that very moment he removed his hat My wife dropped dead from joy without speaking (another) word My wretched son while I was trying to find help for my wife with the servant and the maid saddled his horse and for six weeks now I haven't heard a word about him All that he told me was that he was an officer in a regiment and that is all (I) know

I promised myself not to tell my grandmother when I arrived and I hoped although she would be delighted to see me that she wouldn't do what that good woman had one that she wouldn't die of pleasure I consoled that good fellow and told him I hoped he would hear news of his son

And we arrived at Pont-Saint-Esprit where a lot of Loup [see n. 34] stone-cutters were working who wanted to pick a fight with us over nothing I told them that if they were game we would wait for them on the outskirts of town for a fair fight with walking sticks They accepted our challenge We waited for almost two hours and saw no one coming because they wanted our walking sticks (and) since they had seen me armed they hadn't dared come near for they preferred to take the walking sticks from passing companions when they had the upper hand

(We) continued on our way and went to see the beautiful bridge over the Gard which ignorant and superstitious people believe was built with the help of devils (We) went to Montélimar where the companions of the town had heard what had happened at Pont-Saint-Esprit (they) received us warmly and showed us a good time and the next day escorted me out of town because my comrade wanted to stay and work being tired of the long journey we had made together

And (I) went straight to Valence thinking that I would find a brother of my grandmother by the name of Boyer since my mother had recommended him to me I went to Crest where his widow had retired on some property and (saw) that she was from that area When I arrived it was almost night When I told her that I had come on behalf of Madame Marseau she threw her arms around me saying that I was her little nephew because I resembled her dead husband (she) kept me for several days in spite of myself fed me good meals and wanted me to eat salad made with nut oil (She) made me her heir took me to the notary Since my late uncle had left her his property and since I was the first relative who had come and since I would be coming back to Nîmes because I told her that I hoped to establish myself there (she) declared me her heir but when I went to Paris and my mother heard about the death of her brother my uncles carried on so that I gave this gift to her which was then lost and I never spoke of it again

I left this good aunt and went to what the people around there call the donkey-post[102] to get myself a mount Since I was with several companions and I spurred my donkey on to reach the village of Lapalud before anybody else the donkey tossed me into a ditch and I had no choice but to arrive in Lapalud all rumpled the companions teased me and gave me the surname Lapalud

I went down to Lyons where I wrote to my widow (informing her of) my arrival I told her some jokes and said I would stay in Lyons until I heard from her which she quickly sent me along with reproaches that were so well written that you couldn't get angry about them I was hired by a swell master by the name of Simon When I was introduced to him I warned him that I only wanted to stay two weeks He asked me where I was from When I told him that I was Parisian he immediately called his daughter and said to her You see this companion does he suit you better than the Berrichon and the Comtois he is from Paris and he is finishing up

---

[102] Ironic term for a place where one could rent an ass on the road, as opposed to the Royal Post Houses, which rented horses and carriages.

his tour of France She answered with a smile and he said to her You're a clever one I'm sure that you like him better than the other ones That smile and that look did not lie and I chalked them up in my favor She had an old Cerberus of a maid who kept a close watch on her because my new boss was a widower

I was in Lyons at the time when they put on that delightful farce for the hunchbacks who were summoned one night to a house over by Fourvières on orders of the nephew of the duc de Villeroy[103] or by invitation they got there and had to wait at least two hours When the lights were turned on there were hunchbacks everybody all around was a hunchback One of the guests who was a notary noticed that they were all hunchbacks he didn't want to taste the refreshments and they all wanted to get out of there But the lighting was from torches held by hunchbacks and the music was played by musicians made up as hunchbacks who made the air re-sound with the hunchbacks' song It was said that some hunchbacks had insulted the nephew of the governor of Lyons That caused a bit of a stir but eventually people got over their bad feeling and laughed about it and sang the song which was heard all over town

One night out walking alone on the place Bellecourt I was looking for excitement I met a woman a little on the old side but quite radiant I asked her if she wanted me to go with her to her place She accepted my proposition but I was forced to speak quite loudly I saw that she was hard of hearing When I got to her door she said good-bye and told me that if I wanted to stay for a little while I should come back the next day at precisely eight o'clock when she would be alone that for the time being her husband was at home She had seen a light in their bedroom The next day I was on time I found her alone but she played the prude and wanted to have a royal love affair I brought things to a head and since I had to in order to make myself heard I raised my voice and took her by force I extinguished the light and went at it

We were pretty happy with each other I was about to begin a third time when I heard a knock It was the husband I dressed she opened the door I was behind it a stroke of luck She held the candlestick in her hand and said she would go down to look for a candle I shook her hand I went up one flight I went down I couldn't figure out how to open the

---

[103] Gabriel-François de Neufville, duc de Villeroy, peer of France and maréchal de camp. The government of Lyons had been in his family since the seventeenth century. I have been unable to verify the facts of the story concerning the farce.

door I cursed I grew desperate Finally I knocked at the door What luck it was my hard-of-hearing lover who came down to let me out

I went to my boss's they had eaten supper They teased me I told something of my adventure but when I mentioned that the woman was hard-of-hearing I saw my boss change color and ask me nervously the name of the street I named another street and he said to his daughter I don't think it can be your aunt that the Parisian accompanied home for I walked your uncle right up to his door So I didn't finish my story but I saw clearly that I was one of the family

My boss took me and a comrade to the convent of the Recollects[104] At dinner they gave us soup with oil Then I went to work and the fathers and brothers came and asked where I was from They asked me if I knew the ones from Paris They asked me a lot of questions I answered them but in a teasing way I told them that in Paris people called them oil lamps All at once they undid their belts and started running after me I jumped into a ditch in the garden A young brother who tried to do the same broke his leg I doubled back They put him in his cell Before the convent surgeon arrived I cut up some linen and told everyone that I had broken my leg twice I patched him up with the help of the fathers and brothers The surgeon arrived He looked (at what I had done and) approved and I learned later that he was not put out So being the cause of an ill I instantly offered my services to put it right

The next Sunday after dinner the boss asked me if I wanted to see the île Sainte-Barbe on the Saône that he would go (there) with his brother I had to worry that this was some kind of trap he was laying for me having to do with my hard-of-hearing lady I accepted promising myself to be on my guard We left My boss told his daughter and the cook to go get their aunt and we would find his brother I showed no sign of surprise it was indeed my elderly conquest We went to that delightful island where we had a Lyonnaise-style snack while walking My competitor took me by the arm and said So Parisian you're going to leave us and abandon the girls and women of Lyons With these words I figured the jig was up and kept my eyes open If he had looked at me he would have seen that I had changed color Instead of answering him I looked behind me and I saw that my boss was having a conversation that looked serious to me with the

---

[104] Convent of Reformed Franciscan monks located in the Saint-Barthélemy hills on the left bank of the Saône: *Histoire et description de la ville de Lyon* (1761), p. 197. The joke about the oil candle is difficult to understand. It may refer to the monks' diet or other customs.

woman who looked at me with what seemed a friendly eye I answered my man that I had given my word of honor and if I didn't keep it even he would find me in the wrong

He heartily approved and said But if you stay here a year or two my brother would sell you the shop and with your charm I could get my niece to marry you When I saw that that was all he had on his mind I regained my powers of speech and thanked him as he deserved I answered him negatively that it was a long time since I'd seen my family and that I wanted to know their wishes As for the proposal he'd just made this was an honor I had not expected and it would remain always engraved in my heart We all joined up again and (I) took my young lady by the arm I would have liked to take the aunt to find out what she said and my boss talked about but I heard that nothing would ever come of those plans because she died while I was in Paris and so did the niece

Since it was extremely hot we went one night over toward the Ainay chains[105] for a swim One fellow lost his footing The current carried him away he disappeared Without thinking of the danger (I) promptly ran after him in spite of everything pulled him over to the bank When the young man came to everybody kissed me professed friendship didn't want to leave me wanted to make my acquaintance The next day (they) came to my boss's place to take us over to the young man's father's house (He) gave us a good lunch and told me not to forget them My boss was delighted that I had saved the life of the son of an important man in town (he) made me offers I left for Paris (he) lent me two écus of six francs excorted me out of town and wished me a good journey and said I should come back whenever I wanted But during my stay (in Paris first) he died and then his sister and daughter (died after him)

I thanked my companions It cost me the twelve francs that my boss had lent me They gave me a grand escort to the music of violins At the escort mother's place where many companions had assembled to wish me farewell the four most senior companions in the town ran after me at nightfall to bring me back to town where they gave me a supper All the companion glaziers were there (they) invited my boss and (we) spent the night and in the morning some of my comrades including my friend from Rennes escorted me (out of town)

And (I) took the direct route toward Dijon on the Mâcon road I saw

---

[105] Which used to be stretched across the Saône to prevent access to the city via the river.

Mandrin's advance guard[106] of twenty men and a half hour later I saw him leading his troops I saluted him he returned my salute And all the inhabitants of this area had nothing but good to say about him And (I) went to sleep in the town known as Maison Neuve and slept in what I was told afterwards was the bed where Mandrin had slept I continued on my way the whole town was in an uproar because of Mandrin's visit during which he had asked for a stirrup cup or what they call in these parts the wine of honor Which is given to the kings of France by the provosts and aldermen on bended knee and in a cup of gold That was one of the most serious charges and (something to do with) a poor unfortunate pregnant woman who was killed at Autun when the inhabitants closed their doors to him Everywhere I went people said nothing but good about him and even spoke of his good deeds

I arrived in Dijon Imagine my pleasant surprise when by chance I met one of my old friends and countrymen by the name of Du Tillet whose father was in business across from my father He was an officer in the kitchens of Monsieur le premier président and wanted to stay by my side (He) kept me (with him) for eight days in spite of myself

Finally I left and while I was on the road to Auxerre [since] I was in company I suddenly felt a pain in my foot which became swollen Unable to go any farther I asked (my traveling companion) to pass by the mother's and send me a mount to carry me into town Which really got me riled because it didn't get there for at least three hours Riding on an ass I made my entry into Auxerre where I stayed four days I was given a warm welcome by the companions and I wrote them a song because they were very happy in the town

Since that had cleaned out my purse I tried to make up some time At the first inn I found myself at the guest's table where I spent more than

---

[106] Louis Mandrin (1725–1755), a celebrated bandit chieftain and smuggler born in Saint-Etienne-de-Saint-Geoirs in Dauphiné near Saint-Marcellin, whose exploits in 1754 and 1755 struck many as nothing less than a war on the *ferme générale*, which collected indirect taxes and customs duties. He visited Burgundy several times. Ménétra is probably describing the taking of Cluny in October 1754, though with some details borrowed from the capture of Beaune in December 1754 or of Autun in the same month. He was arrested by French troops in the territory of Savoy in May 1755 and executed in Valence after a trial under so-called extraordinary procedures. Mandrin is remembered favorably in popular legend and indeed gave rise to a whole literary genre, the *mandrinades*. Ménétra could not of course have run into him in 1762, when he had been dead for seven years, but he may have encountered an irregular group of bandits who claimed to be Mandrin's followers. Both the police and the public used the term *mandrins* as a generic appelation for bandits.

usual as I was getting up to leave the innkeeper's daughter who was a plump and delectable broad asked me if I was the one who had come calling on her As she was holding a candle in her hand I blew it out and took advantage of the situation Somebody called her but we had a different answer ready She wished me a good journey and I wished her a lot of children and (I) arrived in Montereau with an empty purse

Since I had no bag having sent my kit ahead I couldn't visit which wasn't necessary (?) In my confusion upon entering the city I spotted a glazier's shop and asked the master if he had any work for me He answered that if I wanted a job I could go to work right away He gave me a gauge for cutting what is called a boundary panel I took my diamond but I had broken the handle so I asked for a piece of wood He immediately went over to a tavern across the way and said to his friends Here's a companion who seems just like the two others I've got

I went about my business I went into a room I found the mistress and told her that what the boss had given me was done and what should I do next She went in secret to look for him I told him I was waiting for you Oh says he that's enough for today comrade come have a drink with my friends That was where he told me what he had said to them I didn't want to stay more than three or four days but he and his wife were both so nice about it that I spent two weeks making him around eighty panels We parted good friends He accompanied me to the ferry paid me well and gave me provisions for the journey

And I arrived in Paris (and) got off the boat at port Saint-Paul and went straight to my good grandmother's I told her I'd been at Dijon and (after) she had thanked me profusely since it was a Sunday and there was nobody but her I wanted to kiss her Try as I did to explain that I was her (grand)son she wouldn't believe me Then one of my cousins arrived And showing her the letters that she had written me she said I would die happy I have the pleasure of kissing you She told me to go right away to my father's and not to say that I had seen her first I came to my father's There was only a girl there who said Your father is with his friends He gave me a warm welcome he told me he wanted me to stay with him Even though that was not really what I wanted I abided by my grandmother's wishes I went to fetch my kit Imagine their surprise when they saw me dressed in new clothes and very properly and with a watch made of similor[107] which they took to be pure gold silver shoe-buckles and garters and a hatband I had had made in Lyons

---

[107] An alloy of zinc and copper, of fairly dark yellow color; the term occurs in the En-cylopédie.

I went to see my sister who had married the companion who had worked with my father when I was still there and who had sent me in Vendôme and elsewhere some of that powder to drive my comrades crazy which gave me the reputation of being a magician I began working for my father after telling him that I would be leaving at any moment for Nîmes He did all he could to talk me out of it my mother did the same and little by little I forgot the whole thing

Paris was for me so attractive that I gave myself up entirely to my passions The following Sunday there was a kind of dance in my father's neighborhood I was invited There were some elegantly dressed wig-makers wearing swords at their sides which looked really sharp I saw a lot of my old friends After the dance we went to this muscat wine tavern on the rue de l'Arbre-Sec where we found some blue-ribbon hurdy-gurdy players[108] I wanted to have a good time with them as much as anybody else and after a week I saw that I had lost more than I won With my receipt and some quiet that was soon forgotten

One night I was drinking a bottle with a friend when I heard someone drink to my health I said thanks adding that I couldn't place the person or the voice Imagine my surprise when I heard whispered in my ear I am Giroux I asked her why she was wearing a disguise she answered me that that was her affair But two days later I learned that she had been arrested and that four members of her gang were going to be tried who were from the neighborhood and old acquaintances of mine including that monster Duhamel who had murdered his mistress and had had the cruelty to grill her heart and then eat it He was bold enough to tell the police lieutenant during his interrogation Monsieur if you tasted it once you wouldn't be able to get enough

One of these poor chaps was the son of a café keeper The night that they were supposed to be broken on the wheel and the Giroux woman hanged (somebody) sent for my father While we were eating three men arrived in a cab and knocked at the door asking for M Ménétra I asked if it was the father or the son They said It's the father My father left frozen with fear I followed the carriage My father appeared The fellow asked him Do you recognize me My (father) said yes He begged pardon saying that about seven years ago I used to play with your son and I was the one who took that silver mug for which you so abused your boy And

---

[108] The hurdy-gurdy, a stringed instrument in which the bow is replaced by a wheel, was commonly found in the cabarets and streets of Paris. But here the word seems to be part of a rather obscure play on words intended to refer to a prostitute.

by the way I also took your son's cover The clerk asked if that was all he had to say He answered yes that he was very glad to have seen him They brought my father back home and all the neighbors came to congratulate him and console him for what had just happened

I was afraid that the poor Giroux women would send for me since I had had her first favors I went with one of my cousins to see them igno-miniously end their days She was hanged last at the stroke of five in the morning and the four others were broken on the wheel These poor people had a room in the rue des Fossés-Saint-Germain They hid themselves in the closets and she went out picking people up While the victims were with her she would grab them around the waist and those monsters with eelskins filled with lead would murder them and then throw them into the river by night The Giroux woman's mother was a fruit seller and hawker (she) sold their judgment and sentence and (I) bought the document on purpose because she was hawking it all over the neighborhood

Since Taconnet[109] (the) harlequin who had lived with my grandmother was staying with Nicolet[110] I went to see him I stayed for the show He had for comrade a fellow named Gaudon[111] a very good harlequin who looked upon me as a friend In those days there was a show every night at eleven and they invited me to come to their show and I got to be known One day a young man came up to me and said that he knew me I asked him how and his name since he was with a very beautiful woman at the show he said to me My name is Mongeaux and I am staying at your grandmother's in the rue de la Grande-Truanderie

He invited me to the café He asked me to invite Taconnet and Gaudon We had a good time Gaudon said to me There is a charming woman They invited her to come back often We learned that she was the wife of a man named Lescombart When I went to my (grand)mother's I went to see

---

[109] Toussaint, Gaspard Taconnet (1730–1774), playwright, stagehand, prompter, harlequin, and actor. He was known mainly for his vulgar plays, which were staged by Nicolet's troupe. In 1760 he lived with Nicolet in the impasse des Quatre-Vents (AN, Y. 54).

[110] Jean-Baptiste Nicolet (1728–1796), son of Guillaume, a celebrated impressario of the itinerant theater and puppeteer. He ran a puppet show in the Saint-Germain fair and in 1759 established a theater in the boulevard du Temple. His staging of major repertoire pieces caused him difficulties with the leading theaters, but he had powerful protectors and was able to continue his activities up to the time of the Revolution.

[111] Pierre Gourlin, known as Gaudon (1733–?), painter and later theater impressario and actor. His tightrope dance spectacles were held in the boulevard du Temple or in front of the colonnade of the Louvre. He was a strange and restless character who was involved in numer-ous scrapes with the police.

Mongeaux We had a few parties together me dressed up as a Harlequin I was crazy enough to buy the costume and he came as Pierrot Fortunately we lost touch because he got the punishment he deserved along with his mistress but I was no longer in Paris I went to see him at the Châtelet[112] (when) he was still being held only on suspicion but (to) one of his friends who came to see him as we were drinking having brought a fellow named Veron with me he asked what they were saying about him in Paris He told him in sign language that I thought boded no good and (I) didn't go to see him any more after telling him that I didn't think he was guilty of such a dark crime

My father had promised me eighteen francs per month for my upkeep but he avoided paying I got almost nothing out of him so without hurting him I figured out how to get out of the deal A fellow named Lenoir an old comrade of mine said to me I want to treat you to a dead sparrow with a beautiful woman from the neighborhood who would like to make your acquaintance Since he had a grill and was a good fellow I accepted the offer To know a pretty woman the whole thing was attractive At the appointed time I saw a pretty woman come in accompanied by another who was pretty old but very affable Saying that she had things to do (she) left us and said she hoped we'd have a good time Seeing that we were beginning to get on my friend said he would have to leave us The two of us stayed and we soon became intimate She said if I wanted she would make me supper i told her that I accepted and that I would sleep over It was all agreed and we had a good supper and afterwards she took me to her room behind the abbey of Penthemont[113] I spent the night with an extremely passionate young woman We had lunch together She didn't want to let me go but she was imprudent enough to say Go my dear friend your Rosalie has had a delightful night and has had more pleasure than she ever had with your father I looked at her with astonishment and left almost without saying a word

One Sunday while walking with my young sister on the boulevards[114]

---

[112] This vast building, which was a prison, courthouse, and passageway all in one, stood at the end of the rue Saint-Denis at the entry to the Pont-au-Change. It was the seat of the *prévôté* of Paris and the court of the *lieutenant général de police*. This was the court of first instance for all civil and criminal cases for Paris and its suburbs.

[113] A well-known thirteenth-century abbey maintained by the Bernardines and specializing in educating aristocrats and providing them with a place of retreat. It was located in the faubourg Saint-Germain, rue de Grenelle and rue de Bellechasse.

[114] Developed after 1705, the boulevards were the great promenades of eighteenth-century

waiting for the moment when we could go in to see the show of my friend
Gaudon I noticed a waiting carriage and realised from the livery that it
could be Mme de Gardouche seigneuresse of Belpec in Gascony for whom
I had worked and who had given me a very warm welcome The chambermaid said with astonishment Madame there is your glazier who worked in
your castle The door was opened and I was told to climb into the carriage
with my sister After asking me questions and saying many friendly things
(she) invited me to come see her in two days which was a holiday to come
in the morning and that I would spend the day with her chambermaid and
we would go walking with her husband

For some time I had been ogling a pretty laundress who lived in our
house and whom I wanted to launder myself pretty badly Whenever I
ran into her I told her that I adored her and said what young men usually
say in such encounters She listened all right We began meeting but I had
a rival or should I say a competitor who thought he was pretty hot stuff
being a corporal of the watch Whenever he saw me talking to that lovely
girl he tried to lord it over me I showed him my teeth He told me he had
long arms

On the appointed day I went to see Mme de Gardouche[115] I came to the
house I asked the Swiss if I could speak to Madame I was announced
The chambermaid showed me into a dressing room I saw Madame's bosom
more or less in the way they paint Venus She pretended not to notice I
couldn't restrain myself the chambermaid found a pretext to leave us
And I became you've got to be there to feel it Madame rang for her
lunch It was brought in an order was given I shared the lunch and
became again the god of pleasures Satisfied she was I was invited to
come back using the utmost discretion saying that I was a relative of the
chambermaid as if I had a Gascon accent So still another cousin was
added to my family Madame was obliged to dine out Nevertheless they
gave me a very good dinner and I went walking with my new male cousin
and my dear female cousin We went to Ménilmontant where I was well
treated

And then (I) went back to my father's house and he vented his bad
mood on me telling me that I was corrupting the neighborhood girls and

---

Paris. Five rows of trees were planted along their borders, and new houses, booths, and theaters
lined their north sides.

[115] This episode is not improbable. As we know, Ménétra had a distinct predilection for
women of high birth and low virtue.

that he knew more than he cared to say He got angry I asked him if it was from his Rosalie from a prostitute that he had heard all that His rage got the better of him He told me that he had met Fleury [apparently the corporal of the watch mentioned above—trans.] and that he would be sending (me) to a place on his orders and that it wouldn't be long

I left the house swearing I'd never return My sister said she would tell me everything that happened and I was off Who did I meet in the street Rosalie who upon seeing the state I was in I told her that she had made my father angry with me She asked for an explanation We went into a café She didn't want me to go and prevailed upon me to take her home but that night was not like the first she used all her wiles and everything she had Finally believing that I was avenging myself for my father's unpleasantness I promised everything and stayed with Rosalie for about a month until the day of my departure and she took every possible precaution and swore not to tell anyone where I was working what she knew about my business with Fleury

I went back to the neighborhood that morning My father was not home in spite of my sister I carried out my trunk with the help of my friend Lenoir who spotted my father some distance away coming toward us (and) enticed him into a tavern Another friend named Lapierre helped carry my trunk And it was good-bye neighborhood I was on my way My little laundress was at the window I signaled to her she came down We went to the Saint-Germain cloister I told her what had happened to me She told me about Fleury's impertinences and all the oaths and threats of vengeance that he said my father had authorized We parted with many promises and I said I was going to expatriate myself from the neighborhood and that I would let her know where I was working She cried saying that if I had so much trouble it was her fault I let her think so and we said our farewells

My friends came looking for me my trunk was at the home of one of them The one who had entertained my father rejoined us in a tavern called Les Trois Maures Rosalie came I got angry and said to her in a low voice tonight early in the room I didn't realize how true these words would prove

The four of us set off for the Pont-Neuf and ran into Fleury with a fellow named Robert a recruiter He tried to insult me I told him I despise you and respect your company for a fellow by the name of Charpentra a recruiter had joined us And I did well he wanted to patch things up between us but Fleury in his haughty way (set) conditions that I not speak to the laundress again I shot back that he had the Lagué woman and that if I had wanted to press my point I would have taken her He sputtered with rage He tried to slap me I hit back I took the bottle and said to him Get out of here this isn't the way I want to avenge myself but a soldier like you I'm scarcely afraid of You have your sword to end every discussion here is my cousin Charpentra he will lend me his and we'll go see if you're as brave as all your bluster would make people think He tried to brush me off with contempt Charpentra who was the one who had taken eighteen francs from my father for my de-enlistment said Ménétra is not one to be treated with such contempt big as you are he is capable of giving you a run for your money He said to me Cousin have you got any money I have some if you need it I said to him I guess you only lend with strings attached No my friend said he someone has to make amends for your father

They went to look for a wagon[116] and one of us the loser would pay for it After a lot of excuses[117] on his part and (because) there were many young fellows from the neighborhood around he made up his mind and said Robert will be my second I answered I won't ask you again My friends my fate is in your hands A fellow by the name of Givet said I'll be your second

Six of us got in and went to a place behind the walls of the house known as Père La Chaise's[118] He parried my first thrusts with apprarent scorn I pressed him I hit him on the side of the belly I told him he was wounded I backed off he threw himself on me like a madman I parried I wounded him in the arm his weapon fell He swore like a lunatic I heard Robert telling me I was a brave fellow As he had picked up his weapon I put myself on guard Since I was hot I said to him It's your funeral He took his épée and put it back in its scabbard Charpentra Givet and Lapierre came with me

I went to the faubourg Saint-Antoine to my brother's house I told him

---

[116] *Roulant*, a sort of chair on wheels or horse-cart. In 1760 there were some thirty stations set aside for hackney carriages commonly known as *fiacres*. See Jèze, *Tableau de Paris* (Paris, 1755–60), p. 339.

[117] *Défaites*, used here to mean pretexts or excuses.

[118] At the place known as Folie Regnault: in the seventeenth century this was a hill outside the walls where the Jesuits owned an estate. Père Lachaise, confessor of Louis XIV, had his private residence there. The estate was divided up after the expulsion of the Jesuits in 1763, and in 1771 rue Saint-André was cut through to the boulevard. The cemetery known as Père Lachaise was established by the city around 1804.

part of the adventure He offered me a job in a factory on the rue de Charenton I accepted I left my friends after downing a couple of bottles of wine My brother-in-law wanted me to sleep at his place I remembered my words to Rosalie and wanted to find out what she might have heard about me By night I entered the faubourg Saint-Germain It was almost eleven o'clock I found a good supper She knew that I had fought with Fleury and that he wanted to teach me a lesson at my father's behest having to do with a neighborhood woman She claimed all the glory for herself promised me never to love anyone but me and said she would do everything she could to please me and that her house was my house

The next day I left against her will I went to a writing shop I asked for a sheet of paper I wrote to my widow after a few irrelevancies to find out if she would send me what I needed for my trip I went back to Rosalie's We spent the day at Vaugirard The next day she went back to the neighborhood and her wretched trade She told me that my father had just joined forces with Fleury's father to have me banished

The next day I went to find my brother-in-law and at night I returned to Rosalie's My father was breathing fire because of me I was informed of everything I went to find my friend who was holding all my worldly possessions I told him about my departure He approved At the end of the month I had a letter from my good widow along with sixty francs I went to say my good-byes to my grandmother she was bedridden and my aunts claimed that I was responsible and didn't want to let me say good-bye I brought matters to a head I forced my way in I entered I threw myself headlong on my poor mother saying It's Ménétra At the repeated sound of my name she made an effort and coughed up all sorts of dreadful things into a bowl and regained consciousness For two days she didn't say another word and we didn't expect anything more I stayed a few days more and saw her a little better So I said my good-byes promising that in a few years I'd come back to Paris with my charming widow

But it was written that I should not bring back the one and that I would not see the other again for my good mother survived nearly eighteen months after making a good recovery from her illness and (I) wrote her often Having taken my vengeance and measured my worth I left Paris though not without saying good-bye to my charming laundress who made me many oaths And (we) finally had a secret conversation in which she poured our her heart but for me (it was) as usual

To show my widow in Nîmes that I was acting in good faith I sent her a trunk with all my belongings The day I left my friends and some cousins my brother-in-law and my grandmother came to escort me Since I had concealed my departure from Rosalie I wrote to her and gave her back the key to the room thanking her affectionately for she had acted faithfully almost more than if she had been my wife I was afraid they would escort me too far My little laundress was waiting on the road where we parted content with one another

I was on the road for two weeks traveling by wagon from time to time occasionally amusing myself with inn girls and all to pass the time I went to a small farmhouse of my widow's two leagues from Nîmes and was warmly welcomed and (I) sent her an express as she had indicated in her letter She arrived the next day with two female relatives Our interview was quite pleasant after a few well-deserved reproaches for (I had been gone) nearly nine months whereas I had only asked for three to finish my tour of France After many petty explanations I reclaimed my rights as usual and everything was in tune when jealousy that wretched malady took hold of me

Since she had been raised in the so-called reformed religion [as Protestantism was then known—trans.] priests were drawn to her for as they said they were always afraid that she would return to her first faith Besides that they knew me to be someone who put little store in their mystery and we often argued about all their fine imagining I went often with my widow to her little place in the country which was a very pleasant spot and to evade the watchdogs who were always harassing us Since I had played the jealous husband to the point where I looked like one my widow withdrew somewhat and gave me the cold shoulder

I tried to make her jealous (of) the daughter of a good Protesant man who was big in business and who put up with me and gave me a warm welcome in his house and told me about all the mortifications that the Catholics forced them to endure because of their beliefs[119] I became more interested in seeing this fellow who was goodness personified and made pleasant conversation (and) whom I liked better than those fanatics who

---

[119] After the revocation of the Edict of Nantes in 1685, the reformed churches ceased to have any official existence in France. Ménétra describes the situation of Nîmois Protestants who appeared to have converted but actually continued to practice their religion in secret, persecuted by the religious and civil authorities. The preachers officiating at these services were often Swiss-trained. Bear in mind that this urban Protestantism, based as it was on private worship, was able to adapt more readily than rural Protestantism to the de facto situation. It was in this period that the link between rural Protestantism and the primitive "church of the Desert" first appeared.

gave me a headache with their priests and their superstitions and (I) gave no thought at all to his daughter who didn't play the prude the way the Catholic girls did

I went frequently to their prayer meetings which I found quite edifying even though they were forced to pray to God and to sing his praises in secret in out-of-the-way places because troops were sent out to stop them from meeting I thought it over and said to myself People are right to say these men adore and revere the same God (yet) they are more or less proscribed since they cannot hold any office So it is really true might makes right

One of the stiff-collars who came to the house most often playing all sorts of cleverly insinuating parts under the mask of religion tried being pretty smart with my woman whose confessor he was proud to be One day after dinner to which he had come without being invited this creature struck up a conversation with me (He) applauded everything I said and I said to myself Hypocrite you're saving me a pear for dessert And I was right the moment came and it happened

That morning my widow had said that she would ask a tailor to come make me a suit of clothes which I would need for she had taken the trouble to provide me with linen I promptly answered that there was no rush This (remark) had been reported to this abbot who had gotten into a discussion with me The widow was in an office in the shop which I had modeled after the offices in Paris shops (and) since I had decorated it she liked it a lot Since I had received a letter from my grandmother which said a lot of nice things about her after reading the letter myself I gave it to her She took it into her office and left the abbot and me at the table for my two comrades had left to go to work

He kept telling me tht M Fricot had been alderman of the town and that I who was supposed to succeed him I wasn't taking the same course since I did not attend church and liked to pray only with the Camisards [Protestants] and rather than set the widow an example of the duties of a good Catholic since I had come back I had tried to corrupt her in every way and he knew plenty about it To this whole tirade I responded Monsieur l'abbé I see that the confession that you preach so much has a great effect particularly on female minds Who tells you that I'm not a good Christian I'm a better Christian than those who moralize I love God I injure no one I do not seek to lead anyone astray What more do you want Just don't box my ears a second time And I said all that because one day he had allowed himself to talk to me about confession

He blushed and said that it was done out of esteem and friendship I said heatedly Your sacred hands must not touch anything profane Because one day I noticed that he tried in secret to put his hands on the widow's breasts with which she was tolerably well equipped You're mad (says he) I don't know says I in response which one of the two Evil spirits is leading you astray (says he in return) believe me return to the fold of the Church or you are lost Ah says I you don't know me very well I've never left it and nobody can make me change my belief

He calmed down but he didn't understand the meaning of my answer Well then my dear Parisian you will have to make a general confession I take it upon myself to hear you I told him I've just made it to you what is more I've already found my man (and) when the time comes I will do everything I'm supposed to do and what is more I'm not yet hitched All that I'm asking you Monsieur is to read your breviary not to come any more to lecture me and to stop your visits to Mme Fricot I uttered these last words forcefully and he withdrew Since there is no one more vindictive than a man of the Church I went to the office and warned my widow but she was obsessed with the mob of priests who were always coming to visit So I pretended to see nothing and hear nothing I had it on good authority that they proposed to hire the son of a master from Arles but she answered that she had set her sights on me and there should be no further discussion of the matter

One night I said to her I don't understand you Do you think that when we're finished you will still be obsessed with those lousy priests and that they will continue to have their way with you And that abbé Milet would still be after her and that if she refused to send them all packing my mind would soon be made up She answered me in a way I had never seen before in her that I was the master and should do as I pleased

I went out without thinking I filled my trunk with my belongings One of my comrades came up and was surprised I said to him Bourguignon not a word of this let's carry my trunk to the shipping office (They) checked it to Lyons The next morning before the town awakened (I had) a draft for thirty-five francs drawn and cashed by a good Protestant stocking merchant (He) gave me thirty francs and two pair of floss-silk stockings it was all done in a moment and I set out on my way with my walking stick and apron worn as a bandolier

I walked for part of the day without thinking about what I had just done I wrote to the widow and have had no news of her since except that she had sold her shop and retired to her pretty country place where we had spent many happy moments promising ourselves that we would love each other forever with one of her relatives On several occasions I was tempted to write but I had left her so suddenly that I forgot her as I had forgotten the others because I knew love only in pleasures and not in perfect friendship I had in any case found in this charming woman what I had never found in the others tact in her dealings her affection her love for me which was not equivocal All her perfections and all her good deeds had attached me to her I was truly sad about leaving and I never forgot her

I crossed the Cévennes Night was falling when I arrived in a village whose name I've forgotten all in a turmoil When I went into an inn I was told that at an inn on the road the man and woman had murdered their child I asked for an explanation They told me this story At the other end of the village is another inn They had two sons One of them is a curate (who lives) a league and a half from here The other enlisted and for twenty years had been in the service and had not returned home Yesterday he arrived at his brother's (so that they could go together) to his parents' The curate said You will go tonight and they won't know you I will come tomorrow morning and will gently break the news to our father and mother The officer climbed back on his horse asked for supper at the inn gave his mother who didn't recognize him his purse and went to bed During the night they murdered him In the morning the curate arrived and asked where is the officer who stopped here last night They became agitated They said they hadn't seen any guests He went to the stable found the horse and asked them what they had done with his brother They let out a cry you have killed your son That is clear They've been digging Several bodies have already been found and later the courts found out all the crimes committed by this shameful family

I left the next day and went to Saint-Hippolyte in the Cévennes where I worked with a good Protestant who told me tales of the cruelties that the missionaries had perpetrated in this unfortunate region with their conversion by dragooning I went to work one day with the son of my boss who was on pins and needles waiting for us to come back They took me to an inn where as soon as I entered they said There is a papist I told them that if I was I would pride myself on it that there were decent men in both houses But one said to me You believe in your Saint Jerome and Saint Augustine they are good-for-nothings Without thinking what I was saying I answered that he didn't know what he was talking about After a good argument he finally said to me that those who change religion

are good-for-nothings I answered that Luther and Calvin changed religions that one was a canon at Noyon and the other an Augustinian and
that he had been whipped and branded in the place de Grève He leapt at
me and several of those madmen wanted to kill me said they would have
my life I challenged them one after another The marshals arrived and
snatched me from their hands I knew their name(s) The fiscal prosecutor[120] wanted me to denounce them and said he'd know what to do with
people who insult Catholics and what is more who'd fired a pistol at me
He took me into his safekeeping

My boss came the next day to take me away making a lot of excuses but
his nephew argued that they had done the right thing My boss's sons
slapped him I have him a cold look I asked to be paid off despite the
protestations of friendship and (asked too) that they repent of the foolish
things (they'd said) and that it was the wine and everything must be
forgotten if we want the Eternal to forget our sins

Having received a letter from the mother of companions who invited me
to come as soon as possible because I was expected (I) said good-bye to
these good people The son wanted to escort me and (we) walked five
leagues together (He) took me to a relative's where I was received
warmly and treated well

In these cantons there's a lot of wolf country There are plenty of woods
and bad roads but since I passed through during the good season it didn't
seem unpleasant to me except for the length of the route One day in the
middle of the forest I heard some wolves cry I saw a legion of them I
drew my pistol I fired I saw with pleasure that they all took flight At
that moment I heard a strange noise I thought that other wolves were
coming to eat me It was the marshals on the trail of some robbers They
stopped me and asked me where I was coming from and who I was (They)
took my weapon my walking stick and asked for my papers I answered
them I showed them my master's certificate (They) gave me back my
things said to me that the woods were full of robbers and smugglers (and)
that I would arrive at sunset

One of them offered to let me ride double I agreed We stopped at an
inn I took care of my needs I heard the hostess reproaching them for not
taking care of their prisoner The whole village wanted to see me the girls
the women pitied me each person told his tale I asked for wine I stood

---

[120] In seigneurial jurisdictions the *procureur fiscal* was the representative of authority (and
in particular of *le fisc*, the tax collector). He was the most important figure in the minor courts
and worked hand in hand with local lords.

the guards to drinks I wanted to kiss the young ladies They pretended to try to stop me I heard someone say What a shame he doesn't look like a thief I answered You mustn't judge a man by his looks a scoundrel often resembles an honest man Somebody said I spoke well the men wanted to have a look at me The tavern did a good business I deliberately refrained from drinking with the marshals I told some stories and those good folks looked at me with compassion When the guards wanted to leave I drank with them and said good-bye and they wished me a good journey All those good people with joy in their faces looked happy Then I kissed girls women and everybody was happy and satisifed

The next day I left accompanied by several itinerant merchants who were headed for Lyons and I made the journey with those good fellows We saw a pack of wolves I fired I caught one of them I broke its thigh It was the seond shot I had killed a dog and wounded a wolf That made me think of the time when I was working at M de Gardouche's castle and his game warden gave me a young wolf that I kept for around eight months and that followed me everywhere I was obliged to muzzle it because it was beginning to bite children It slept at the foot of my bed It (be)came strong and carnivorous People advised me to get rid of it that even though it knew me it might do something unfortunate I took it to the entrance of the Verdun woods and the game warden who had given it to me shot it with a rifle

I arrived in Lyons on a Sunday and on the way I had slept in the company of a fellow who told me that he was going to Paris and who wore a wig and said he was on his way from Marseilles to claim an inheritance I gave him a letter for my grandmother in which I explained to her why I had been obliged to leave Nîmes and she never received it I took him to the mother's and escorted him on his way promising to come back and see us soon and several of us accompanied (him) and bade him farewell

On Monday I invited several companions to have a glass and I told them not to mind if I didn't hire on with them that in any case I would be working some time in Lyons that they should know that having (been) dismissed upon my departure I could no longer do the Devoir with them (?) but that I would in any case consider it an honor to spend my time with them My friend from Rennes was in Lyons and the first companion was there with the others who said that they would not stand for it that I had taken my turn bravely and that they would be happy to have me join their ranks I agreed and (they) went to have me hired by Sieur Michel rue de la Brèche Saint-Jean where I stayed eleven months

A large number (of those) who had known me had decided the night before to invite me to go back with them and we took the day off We had a good time telling one another about all the crazy things we had done My friend from Rennes talked about Carpentras and the little wafer he had swallowed me for love and he to stay with me I told him that he had to be a highwayman and murderer if the Dominican Father made him wait a week after me before giving him the square to swallow (He said) that he knew I had had two brides of the baby Jesus in a convent in Gascony and that was enough to send me to the big oven and that I must not be afraid of roasting I asked about my old master Simon and his family Somebody said that the girl was dead and that the father who was a jolly fellow had followed her and his shop had been sold

I went to work but on Saturday the first companion came together with the secretary to bid me farewell since he was leaving town the next day all the companions were obliged to escort him out of town Imagine my surprise when they gave me the position of first companion I objected they forced me I accepted and held on to the post from then on with the consent of the masters and companions The son of my old boss from Saint-Hippolyte came to work and to be accepted as a companion but being of the Protestant religion and professing as much he could not be accepted[121] In any case I took him on with me and my boss was quite pleased and he observed all our holidays

The first Sunday of every month all the companions were obliged to go to mass together and in ranks as they were told and had to go to the offertory in order of seniority starting with the first companion

In such a large city I had business almost every day with the arrival and departure of companions or with letters from cities on the tour of France having to do with disputes of the sort that can arise between masters and companions One day a Bourguignon who was in the Hôtel-Dieu passed away We went to fetch him and had him buried at our expense with a big funeral to which we invited the companions of other trades

The cousin of my friend from Saint-Hippolyte came to the mother's place I was immediately summoned he figured on being received the way I had received his cousin Though I held no bitterness I asked him if he might not be coming to insult me again and to tell me that Saint Augustine

---

[121] After the revocation of the Edict of Nantes (n. 119), Protestants were excluded from membership in various guilds. The Enfants de maître Jacques ceased to accept companions belonging to the reformed church.

and Saint Jerome were good-for-nothings I told him Tomorrow is Sunday and I will find out if there's work for you in the city The next day I wanted to take my vengeance not out of malice but to teach him not to insult people When we were all assembled I ordered that he be brought in He saw us standing around a table in deep silence every man in his place and all with hats off except for me I was the only one with my hat on my head and an inkwell and paper in front of me and (I was) sitting down I said to him Saint-Hippolyte you come looking for work in this city but your wicked dealings with me your religion be that as it may we respect the foundations but you have insulted the memory of two fathers of the Church you are required right this very moment to make your repentance and beg pardon and you must never again insult another companion

Without saying a word he went down on his knee to beg my pardon Get up man is not made to humble himself before another man but only before God It is not me you have offended but all who share my faith and all companions Leave us now we are going to decide if you shall work in Lyons We decided that he would given work I asked that his cousin be brought in so that he could see the orderly way we conducted our meet-ings When he was brought in I said to him Saint-Hippolyte it is thanks to your good and quiet behavior that your cousin will work in this city go tell him

Since we were close to Saint Luke's day[122] the glazier's holiday I said to them I should like my comrades to have a superb feast we already have seventeen aspirants who are waiting to be received we do not know how many the companions of nearby towns will bring You know that I get three livres for each one and thirty sols to the other two first companions and we shall make the sacrifice We have a hundred thirty-some livres in the treasury We can add twice that amount if each of us gives six francs We shall have a great mass sung with music we shall have a holy bread baked and supported by four *dauphins* [apprentices as is clear from subse-quent text—trans.] a plaque bearing the arms of the glaziers which the Rennais and I shall take it upon ourslves to make will be carried on a cart by four apprentices Since almost all of us have gray white suits we shall go in uniform We shall all wear white stockings our hair in curls and tied up with a white ribbon each of us with walking stick in hand with a blue and

---

[122] Saint Luke, the evangelist and patron of the glaziers' confraternity in Lyons, had his feast day on 18 October. In Paris the patron of the glaziers was Saint Mark.

green ribbon white gloves and a bouquet We shall go the night before to decorate with flowers the shops of the masters who have companions we shall have violins and oboes two city guards by day with four drums and each with our liveries alongside We shall invite the two first companions of each trade we shall give a meal and a dance we shall request the day off The second day each man will retire when he wishes

All my comrades approved I said to them Here are the Angevin and the Rennais who have been around a lot we have been together in cities where we staged celebrations they will be in charge when I am absent They said to me But chief you cannot go on foot to oversee the preparations or to invite the companions we shall pay for a sedan chair and the first shop to be decorated will be yours I accepted We got everything ready Former companion glaziers who no longer saw much of the companions came looking for me knowing the celebration we were going to prepare as did the two fellows from Saint-Hippolyte to contribute just like companions After thinking it over I told them that I would let them know but that in any case they should come on the day of the celebration and consider themselves invited guests but as for allowing them to contribute to the treasury neither I nor the companions would allow it but they could in any case come to the dinner and the dance They thanked me and were very happy

Finally on the eve of the celebration (I was) well dressed (with) my hair done up in curls (when) the sedan chair arrived I gave the (bearers) the list of (places) I had to go in the neighborhood People looked My boss and his wife were pleased they were invited to the dance in addition their shop was decorated to the sound of violins and oboes (which) accompanied me on my way Every shop that I entered to oversee the preparations offered me refreshment They were enchanted (and) gave my horses [i.e. bearers] so much to drink that when they were about to cross the Saint Vincent bridge (they) turned me over As I was followed by many companion stonecutters (they) carried me put ribbons in their caps others waved bouquets The woman giving out bouquets spotted me and gave me one because she realized that I was the one who had given her the order [illegible]

Finally I was given a warm welcome everywhere bottles and glasses were on the workbenches I went to visit the duc de Villeroy who granted permission for the dance the next day to run all night I came to the mother's Come night I went with my comrades to decorate the shops all the masters were ecstatic The violins and oboes played wine flowed I

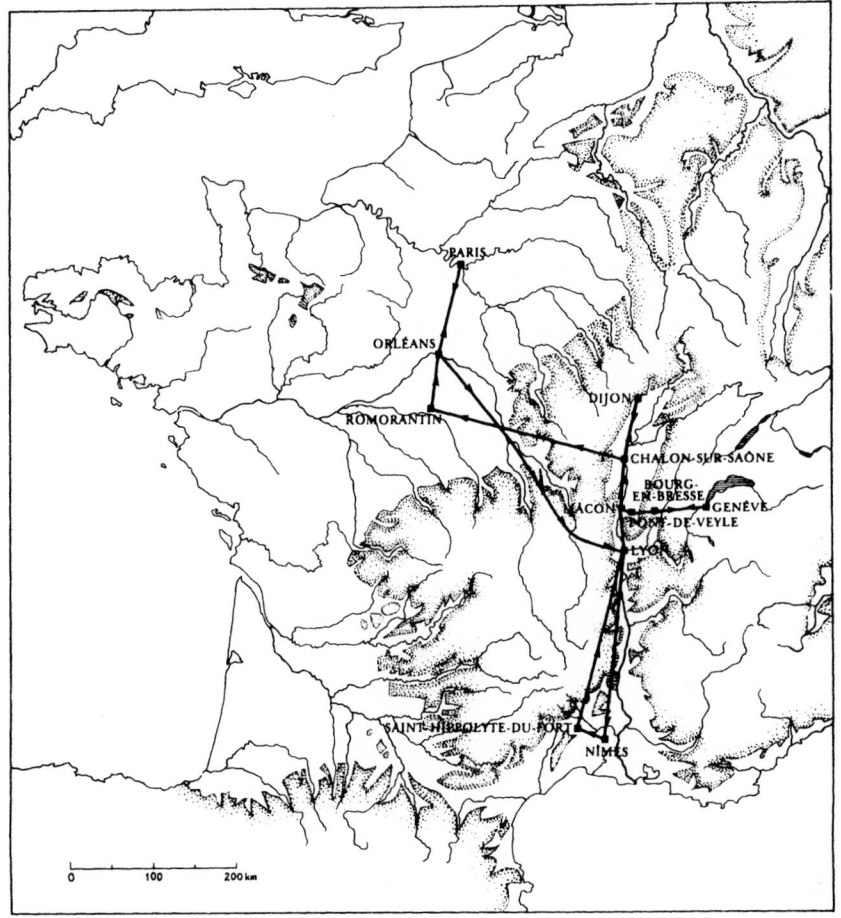

Second Journey: 1763–1764

stayed with one master (who) gave me and several comrades a good supper We returned to the mother's between midnight and one o'clock We
received twenty-one companions Everyone returned to their bosses' and
(it was said) that every companion should dress as prescribed that he
should arrive at the mother's precisely at ten that those who were under
the influence of wine would be fined and that we would take lunch
standing up and each companion would have only his half bottle

It was a day of pomp and ceremony such a splendid feast had never
been seen All Lyons turned out to see us march in twos myself in the lead
with two ribbons in the third buttonhole the father of companions on my

right A holy bread of enormously great size was carried by four apprentices the feast and dinner went off triumphantly Each companion went to
fetch either his boss's wife or daughter all other women being excluded
unless they were decent Many masters came (and) received a warm welcome That night everything went off with the greatest of harmony I
opened the dance with the mother The refreshments everything was in
order The fellow glaziers of the city who had joined in the meal reiterated
their offer to pay their share I turned them down They invited us to a
dinner that they wanted to give over by Guillotière for fifteen of the first
companions We accepted We went to rest after telling all the companions
that they were free to enjoy themselves as they wished The companions
of the other trades wanted to give a lunch to the three first companions
and to others whom they knew We accepted for the following Sunday

Everyone who wanted to come for lunch (and) eat what was left over
came back at two o'clock We rode in a carriage and went to find the
fellows from the city and the two from Saint-Hippolyte who were waiting
for us there were more than thirty of us at table They wanted to toast me
as had been done the night before I said to them But my friends today we
are all comrades together and are proceeding in unison We drank and ate
well and sang until midnight when everyone went home We continued
the following day and found ourselves in debt to master Jacques for only
thirty-some livres all expenses included which (debt) was soon paid off

About a month after the feast I ran into a Comtois who had been a
companion and he was in the Lyons regiment He had been dismissed from
our midst for unsavory dealings He offered me a drink I refused He said
that I was acting proud because I was the first companion of the city
Well says I to prove to you that you're wrong let's go in I was holding
two pieces of red and blue glass in my hand and we sat down at a table
After the first few glasses of wine he picked a quarrel with me on the
subject of the feast (saying) that he had presented himself that the Rennais had come and said something in my ear (that) I had forbidden him
(toenter) because he was wearing the king's unform He insulted me I
answered him The tavern keeper spoke up in my behalf He got angry
smashed his fist down on my two pieces of glass and broke them in pieces

I said to him Comtois what you have just done is not the act of a brave
soldier it's not me you've wronged but my boss You have your weapon I
went to look for one to settle the affair I ran In the wardrobe where I
hung my clothes was a sword belonging to my boss who was sergeant of
the bourgeoisie I put on something that I could slip the sword under-

neath We went behind the Ainay chains I laid him on the ground I took off.

I wanted to go to the home of a young woman whom I knew On the way I ran into one of my comrades I told him what had just happened to me I went into his shop he alerted the companions That night they hid me in a place where the devil and all his minions couldn't have found me I wanted for nothing They made inquiries it was for the good of the companions

The Comtois was taken to the hospital he said where I lived and they came and took the fellow from Saint-Hippolyte instead of me He was put in prison He was released only three days later after proving his innocence All the companions took an interest in my case The authorities wanted me dead or alive Finally I made up my mind to go The companions were opposed and tried to keep me from leaving Finally the mother received a letter from a master in Mâcon asking for three companions to glaze a small church named Pont-de-Veyle I persuaded the companions to let me leave

I went to my boss He figured my account I owed him seventeen francs He said to me My friend Parisian you've been in the house around eleven months and you have twenty-four days of drinking sprees I don't count them I'm very happy with you here are twelve francs so you can drink to my health I wanted to try to set you up in business in Lyons The widow Saintongeois was not indifferent to you I think that she's going to come to say good-bye and to make arrangements with you so that when the storm has blown over you can return to these parts if (you) haven't forgotten us As he said this to me tears streamed from his eyes his wife looked at me sadly his young boy said to him Papa the Parisian won't be telling you any more that you were at Malines because I teased the father sometimes about not puttying well and said that he made lace The other child fretted and reproached me because I was leaving and because he had not seen me for a long time The comrades who had escorted me were dumbfounded Finally the widow arrived and found me changed I said to her If I am changed Madame I have not changed in your regard and I shall always be proud of having won your respect After affectionate words on both sides and after I had kissed her and told myself that we could see each other again some day without fear I saw that she was asking (the boss's wife) if I had what I needed to travel She answered her My husband has supplied him

I left them in tears over their generous behavior toward me and a group

of companions escorted me along the road to Mâcon And on top of Bar-
mont mountain (I) met the two companions who were supposed to come
with me and there I said my final farewells to the city of Lyons where I
had had such a good time

And (we) came to Mâcon where after a good rest we went to Pont-de-
Veyle where we were put to work And I behaved and worked so well
that all those good villagers were content We were at it for nearly three
months and enjoyed ourselves because the meat days [Sunday Monday
and Tuesday before Ash Wednesday—trans.] were starting and (I) was on
the lookout for female companionship as usual The companions from
Bourg-en-Bresse invited us to spend the meat days with them We left on
Saturday and when we stopped on the way to eat a calve's head at a place
called Maison-Neuve we saw Mandrin's sister[123] pass on horseback accompanied by at least a hundred and twenty men armed to the teeth and
all sitting astride sacks and led by a fellow named Broc who asked us who
we were since we were standing at the crossroads to watch them pass We
told him that we were companions of the Devoir He saluted us and said
Shake then We told him that we were going to drink to his health He said
he would come up and drink with us Which he did in fine style promising
us that he would avenge the death of his friend But in this region people
didn't approve of him as much as they had of Mandrin

When we arrived in Bourg-en-Bresse we were required to make a deposition and from there (we) went to meet the companions with whom we
had a good time This is a real land of Cockaigne The next day we walked
around the city and that night there was a dance where we were well
treated as we were throughout the rest of our stay

One morning I woke up to the sound of a female voice gently asking me
where the door was I had paid no attention to the people sleeping in our
room (which) had several beds Since I was on the side of the crossing I
looked out Light dotted the sky the object was charming I took advantage of it Ah the finest pleasures are the unexpected ones I asked a
Burgundian beside me if he didn't want to enjoy it too He responded that
I had gotten her too hot I opened the door and went to lie down The
next day while pretending to sleep I saw two females arrive It was not

---

[123] Ménétra's second meeting with the Mandrins is interesting for what it tells us about the
popular legend. Louis Mandrin had four sisters: Marie, Marianne, Anne, and Cécile. Although we know a great deal about Louis's brothers' participation in his exploits, we know
nothing about what his sisters did.

yet morning It occurred to me that it was the mother and daughter My conjectures were not wrong Later I watched the day slowly dawning I saw someone go out I thought that like the night before it was the mother who had just left I got up I went to the bed I set about my duty Someone cried out I fled I ran into a pile of glasses on the table together with the woman's cries they made a dreadful racket My two other comrades woke up The head of the household came up with a light saw a woman in the middle of the room and shouted that his honor had been insulted Then the master of the household said that the woman was an inveterate sleepwalker and everything was all right and she should be allowed to finish her dream and she must pay the damages His daughter came up and opened the curtains I saw clearly that I had made a galling mistake but since she was found at the scene she paid for the glasses despite her protestations She was abused and molested[124] her daughter broken (?) and she paid for the glasses

Since I was on the road to Geneva I wanted to go see that rival of proud Rome Upon arriving in the city I was taken before the king's resident After asking me my country my occupation and my religion he told me that I could not work and gave me twenty-four hours to see the city He asked me if I had what I needed for my journey if not he would supply me I thanked him and turned around and went to work in Mâcon

Since I had thanked the companions the first time and was finished there I enjoyed myself with two of my countrymen one of whom was a tapestry maker and the other a brick maker[125] that is a sculptor-mason and since there was no Devoir for that estate I imagined one and gave my friends the name companion of the loaf

Since all it cost to be received into this group was a bottle of wine and since I was quite well known all the companions of every trade wanted to become companions of the loaf It was just a joke the whole thing was just to drink and break bread together and laugh and have a good time For nearly three months we received innumerable companions and all over France people wanted to join the loaf

I received a letter that had made its tour of France and was signed by all the first companions of all the trades who begged me to give up the Devoir

---

[124] *Maniée*, meaning that she was slapped around and molested.

[125] In French Ménétra writes *gibier*, an unusual term in this context, unless he is misspelling *gibleur*, a derivative of *gibler*, to cook bricks. The meaning is still rather remote from mason-sculptor.

of the loaf and not to accept any more members because the companions
were neglecting the Devoir I answered them in more or less these terms
To you my countrymen and all honest comrades The idea of the society of
the loaf is a pure amusement and should not prevent a worthy companion
from doing his duty [Devoir] Here are the details I have thanked the
companions of my trade and am working at Pont-de-Veyle You know why
I was obliged to leave Lyons for the honor of the *compagnonnage* I am
isolated I have two companions with me who in their trade have no
Devoir (and) several young Protestants of various trades who cannot belong to any Devoir because of their religion (and) who might spend their
time with the Gavots Loups Renards and Arpaillants[126] and all those
who abhor the Devoir This is what's involved Reception into the loaf
involves no oath other than drinking and breaking bread and paying for
two or three bottles That's what it consists of The secret is a pure joke it
goes like this "Are you a companion (of) the loaf" : "yes ready to drink
and break bread" Say: "The spring brings the flowers and fair weather
brings the colors" : Say the rest of the oath of the loaf: "The autumn makes
the grape grow and fair weather makes good wine" and all for the glory of
the loaf So my countrymen you can know the truth from the companions
who belong to the loaf As for myself I shall return home and shall always
take pride in having been companion of the Devoir and it will be deeply
engraved in my heart as in yours and (I) am my countrymen and all my
comrades Parisien le Bienvenue

This institution of the loaf had a remarkable effect Everybody wanted
to belong to the loaf for laughs and a good time as a result I was invited to
all the feasts and all the parties in that place A godfather and godmother
invite to the baptisms as many people as they want boys and girls each
man takes his lady by the arm and goes to church A dinner is laid and the
guests return it and people get to know one another A companion friend
of mine by the name of Mâcon la Demoiselle who had returned home and
who was a carpenter by trade invited me We had a good time I made a
pretty acquaintance I was welcomed into the house The father was a
good master carpenter I ended up as I had with the others

Staying with me was a fellow from Champagne who was so stupid that
when I wanted to have a good time he said I was a sorcerer One Sunday

---

[126] Among the adversaries of the Devoir Ménétra lists the Gavots, the Loups, the Renards,
and the Arpaillants (about whom the bibliography of *compagnonnage* gives us no information). See also n. 34 above.

morning he left his silver cufflinks on the chimney I exchanged them for
mine which were nearly identical but made of pewter That afternoon
after doing a few tricks I said that I had the power to change silver to
lead He challenged me I said that all I had to do was touch a thing the
wager was one meal I touched them He said they hadn't changed To
find out the truth we took them to the goldsmith It was lead He treated
(and) begged me to restore them to their natural condition I evaded him
saying that one of these days he would buy me lunch Nobody wanted to
let me touch their buckles and (I) told him that I wanted to make him see
the devil He agreed on condition that his cufflinks be made silver again I
told him that he had to lend me his hat and his cufflinks and that they
would be changed I went into a dark room I put some lampblack in his
hat and in dim light I told him to put his cufflinks on the table I exchanged them and I told him to take his hat and to do as I did and knock
the inside of the hat against his forehead and to repeat that gesture thrice
times three I told him to take back his cufflinks We went in he was all
black I put him in front of a mirror and I said there is the devil who gave
you back your buttons He felt ill They said there is another of the
Parisian's tricks They wanted to see the cufflinks I bet that they were
silver They put them to the test They showed them around I won and
had a good laugh on them

Finally I left to return to Paris I arrived in Dijon I asked about my
friend du Tillet He was in Paris I was leaving but that night on the
boulevards I met a young girl I asked her what she was doing She told
me that she was waiting for someone She cursed she grumbled because
the person was making her wait I pressed my point she and I sat down
on a bench in spite of the bad weather It was snowing and there I was
still once I got started I walked the little lady back but when we reached
a streetcorner she left me suddenly and started running I ran she went
into a tobacco shop I looked in and saw her at the counter I went in and
asked for a half ounce of tobacco I gave it to her and went away mulling it
all over

The next day on the main road a rather well-dressed man carrying a
small bag over his shoulder came up to me and asked me if I was going to
Chalon and (said) he was going farther I said yes He asked if he could
walk with me but said he had to stop for a couple of hours in Chalon We
traveled as friends we didn't miss a single village along the way each one
paid his share and we arrived in Chalon My traveling companion left me
gave me his word (that we'd meet again) at the town gate I went to the

mother of companions The companions wanted me to stay to rest They told me that there was an execution in the town and that we would go to watch it Imagine my surprise (when) I saw my traveling companion standing beside the victim and I thought I recognized the thief of the forest of Cercotte who had kept me prisoner in a cave I was not at the meeting place and stayed a few days to rest

I left with a young fellow from Narbonne who was going to establish himself at Romorantin in the Sologne I made a detour and worked for two weeks for a good fellow who was going to marry a young girl from Chateauvieux a small town four leagues from (where I was working) we stayed there around ten days She was the daughter of a good farm woman she like me the young man acted jealous I set him straight I was having fun at his expense I passed for a magician A fellow from the village got angry because in doing a trick I slapped him I promised him that the next day the village dogs would run after him and in fact the dogs did piss on his legs on his clothes while in church The more he hit them the more they came He begged my pardon I told him (that) I had cast a spell on his shoes He wanted to throw them into the fire

I was having a good time People were telling me ghost stories In this area they're extreme fanatics They tried to get me to believe that where there is a cross on the road there are always ghosts We went out one night and on the road right by a cross I spotted something existing A donkey we had brought with us started neighing and refused to go any further the young fellow with me did likewise in a real quandary I finally made up my mind I charged the cross club in hand while swearing loudly I saw a man club in hand We fought he shouted for mercy I was past all hearing I kept on hitting The young fellow and his mount fled My man shouted murderer I left him and followed my road

I came to a small bridge I thought I saw some men with their arms raised waiting to club me to death I tried shouting Who goes there but it did no good I had to pass I went forward What did I see Willows that had been cut and had indeed frightened me and (also) the anger that I had felt against that man at whom I had shouted and who refused to answer but the blows of the club had loosened his tongue All that had taken my wind away

I arrived and to get me back on my feet the boss's wife gave me a soup made with herrings that I didn't want to eat The son said to the father that I had killed a ghost and that I had made it cry out The next day we found out and the rumor spread all over town that a man had just missed being killed by thieves I asked to see him and I went and asked him if he would recognize those who had put him in such a fine fix He said no that there had been three or four of them and that he'd defended himself well I said to him That will teach you to be out at ungodly hours alongside a cross and I think it was you who played the thief You see it was either you or me because it was with me alone that you fought and you are an impostor My boss's son passed by as we were fighting It wasn't the donkey it was me alone and if they dealt with all these fanatics the way I dealt with you they would celebrate but believe me you better not say that you just missed being killed by thieves because you were doing a fine job of trying to kill me

The magistrate sent for us and (I) made a deposition He sent for the ghost who didn't mind being brought in by two guards and around here he didn't pass for being too [illegible] The magistrate admonished him not to go out any more on the main road at night and that he better not tell people that it was thieves who nearly killed him when it was really a Parisian who had rubbed his nose in the dirt I said my farewells to the good folk of Romorantin and the son wanted to escort me as far as Chateau-vieux jealousy having taken hold of me in regard to his young mistress who was quite nice (and) with whom I could have made do very nicely

There were two roofers who wanted to accompany me We had worked together in a convent of Bernardines one day while they were in the choir singing their matins I was up above and the stone chain gave way while I was in a basket and one of the stones fell along with a section of stair I tumbled down amid the debris[127] They ran for their lives and left all their prayers The next day out fooling around in the garden which is bordered by a small river the Cher one of the roofers wanted to show off how well he could run Since there were rocks and open fields[128] all around he slipped and fell into the river We tried to run after him We found a boat I jumped right in the current carried us Having no hook or stick all three of us tried to catch him the boat capsized and all of us wound up in the river the river known as the Cher which is very deep and swift We grabbed the branches of trees and our young man made it back to the boat

---

127 *Dégravonner*, a word apparently made up by Ménétra to mean "tumble into rubble" (*dégringoler parmi les gravats*).

128 *Sols*: in the area of Berry around Romorantin, a *sol* is a park, and perhaps by extension a flat area unencumbered by rocks; or in this case it may be a misspelling of *sole*, meaning sole plate, the base of a stud-wall framework.

which was floating away We shouted for help nobody heard us The boat and the fellow in it continued on its way I gripped some kind of branches and pulled myself out of the water but I lost sight of my comrades I called to the fellow in the boat who had not come back about the danger he'd been in I threw him a branch I climbed into the frail little skiff (and) with great difficulty we made it back to our two friends We had trouble getting them in and getting back to the convent We arrived all four of us wet and chilled to the bone and we left town

It was at Chateauvieux that I did the Devoir for the last time There were several carpenters and locksmiths who escorted me and (I) passed Orléans where I went to see M Michonneau but he had died Since more than three months had passed since I had sent my chest to my grandmother's (and) I had heard no news I was worried But my friend from Rennes who had left me en route at the house of a friend in Etampes came to meet me and tell me of my (grand)mother's death What pain I suffered I lost a (grand)mother who had loved me so tenderly

I went to my brother-in-law's who gave me a warm welcome and the next day went to see my aunt thinking that she had taken care of my trunk I asked her to give me back the letter since she had not wanted to accept it Wasted effort she told me she had lost it I left in a funk (and) I had a devil of a time getting it back My father having heard that I was in Paris wanted me to go see him So I went He kissed me and gave me a warm welcome asked me when I was coming back home told me that he had in his possession what was coming to me from my grandmother's inheritance that I should forget all that had passed between us I said to him Father a son should not have anything against his father and I have always respected you Your rages against me were extreme I should show indulgence toward my father's feelings just give me permission to come have the honor of seeing you occasionally As for what you have in your possession keep it for the time being I don't need it and I left I paid no attention to all his fine promises and accepted none of his conditions for I knew all too well how my father controlled himself

I went looking for work and went to see M Vilmont One morning when I went to work I was sent to a cabaret I saw a tall man who said he was a master glazier and that he needed two good companions who knew how to set in lead that he had undertaken to install the stained-glass windows in the cloister of the Petits-Pères[129] on the place des Victoires

---

[129] A monastery belonging to the Order of Discalced Augustinians, also known as the "little black fathers."

and that he had heard of me Since the job was interesting I gave him my promise for the following Sunday He told me his name was Elophe and that he would be delighted if I could find him another companion like me I went to see one of my friends I found a comrade from the tour of France La Brie

I was glad to leave old man Vilmont I agreed on thirty-five sols per day plus six livres per window We set up at the Petits-Pères I drew a window with its border it suited the boss (but) the Brie fellow wanted the border done differently I drew it on the ground in the cloister with white chalk I made some remarks to him he erased part of what I had just drawn I shoved him he shoved me back and there we were going at it when several fathers arrived along with our boss They pulled us apart I showed what I had done It was approved One father said they ought to get two other companions M Elophe said that we were the companions most skilled at this kind of work I said Anybody who wants to do it can do it since the father said that I'm leaving The fathers stopped me The boss begged me They reconciled the two of us me who like my comrade had no rancor but a quick temper

The father procuror gave us twelve francs for drink and Elophe took us to drink a bottle The job was done I made the acquaintance of a pretty flower girl every night we went to Magny's or the Cadet Buteux Along with my comrade I took some of (my) meals at Taillefer's opposite Saint-Eustache where you can get a very good meal for five sols (and) where I had been several times before returning to Languedoc When the job was done I stayed with Elophe for a time Then I left him and went to work for M Jerome

One day while working a cook asked me to come measure a pane I went in I saw a pretty woman who showed me the broken pane and told me to come back soon When I came back to set the glass she said that I was always in a good mood and always singing that she watched me from her balcony I teased her She said that I must have a mistress I told her that since coming to Paris I hadn't met any girls She asked me if I liked to dance I said that I didn't know how but that I could jump around She poured me a drink and asked if I wanted to take her dancing along with the chambermaid I said with pleasure She told me they would be ready at exactly five o'clock that I should wait for them with a carriage on the rue du Roule

When the time came I asked the boss's wife for six livres She only wanted to give me three claiming that I wasn't going to work the next day I went to my wigmaker's I put on a suit I saw that my new lady friend was standing at the window watching everything I did I hired a cab My two ladies got in and we made our way out to Magny's When we got there we danced Even though we were drinking the mistress repeated several times that we would have to eat something I played deaf I pretended to pay no attention my funds were greatly diminished Somebody noticed While the chambermaid was dancing somebody with a faint knock passed me secretly under the table twelve francs My tongue was loosened I ordered a nice chicken and a salad I went up to the dance girl and asked her for some tickets[130] to make her happy I saw my flower girl arrive I told her that I was with one of my sisters and a cousin and she believed me (and) went away

We spent the evening in pleasure and amusement That unexpected hand underneath the table it seemed that everything around me was coming together those twelve francs given with so much tact All that a woman with a servant and a delightful conversation When it came time to leave I sent someone to look for a carriage we came to the door She said her good-byes saying see you again I made it clear that I didn't want to say good-bye at the door but in the apartment They said it was impossible They objected that it was late and that I must go I insisted I won my case there I was in the apartment I wanted to stay They raised a lot of objections I came out of it the way any good boy should come out for the first step is the hardest

They gave me a good lunch which I ate with my lovely companion They said the door would always be open for me and I took that as an invitation I went often to visit I made inquiries I found out that the lady was kept by a blue ribbon[131] Our relations lasted a good long time and would have lasted even longer if I had not turned a deaf ear to marriage The father and the mother pushed her to call it quits with what she had A lover arrived on the scene a clerk in the king's (tax) farms I bowed out and put her out of my mind and instead of Mlle de Beaufort she took the name of Madame B. . . We lost track of each other

I went every night to the Cadet Buteux or Magny's with my charming flower girl who was like a lot of other women of her ilk and like me not very faithful We lived without embarrassment that was my nature My

---

[130] Ménétra probably wants the band to play dance music, which one could request by buying tickets known as *cachets*. *Cachets* were also used to pay a dance teacher for lessons.

[131] Chevalier of the Order of the Holy Spirit, from the blue ribbon attached to this honorific decoration, established by Henri III in 1578 and awarded to one hundred noble recruits.

friend Elophe came to persuade me to quit my job and go to work for him (he) offered me twenty-four francs a month and good eats But I didn't want to leave my boss right away I asked for two weeks during that time I took my bearings One night on the way back from the faubourg Saint-Germain I ran into my old girlfriend Rosalie We drank a bottle The time passed she wanted me to go home with her I made her some empty promises I left her

I was stopped in the rue Dauphine by the cops[132] Since I was carrying a lantern[133] like the street lanterns they thought I was a lantern thief They surrounded me and took me to headquarters Try as I might to explain myself the black beast wouldn't listen to me it did no good to say I was coming from the residence of M le duc de Nivernais[134] They went looking for several master glaziers who vouched for me The guards accompanied me to M Jerome's place but the lantern was completely broken He grumbled a bit That's what I was waiting for and I loudly demanded to be paid off

I went back to work for Elophe his niece took a liking to me Since I had had my fun and a few scrapes she advanced me what I needed for clothes and to get myself in shape I had a small room in a back street in the faubourg Saint-Jacques behind the Sorbonne She paid two rents and as a reward she was with me master and mistress of the room where we went to have our fun The poor girl was a little touched in the head but she had a pretty young niece who liked nothing but pleasure I got to know her So I named my room the place of conquests because all kinds of women came up to see me

One night on my way to my room all alone and on the lookout for a willing partner I spotted some game I offered my hospitality She refused me with sharp words I gave her the old in and out The sad sacks[135] came

---

[132] See n. 13.

[133] Paris lighting was much improved in the late seventeenth century, when the lieutenant of police, La Reynie, distributed 6,500 lanterns. Each lantern, equipped with a candle, was suspended by a rope at second-floor level; residents were responsible for lighting the candles, under the supervision of the *commissaires*. Around 1763, lieutenant of police Sartine experimented in the rue Dauphine with the first reflector lanterns, which were installed in the rest of the city starting in 1769. Laterns were manufactured, under contract from the city, by lantern makers and tinsmiths, with glaziers employed to do the glass.

[134] Louis Jules Mancini Mazarini, duc de Nivernais (b. 1716), soldier and diplomat. The duke was a man of opulence and intellect (elected a member of the Académie française in 1743 and of the Académie des Inscriptions et Belles Lettres in 1744). His residence was located in the rue de Tournon.

[135] *Tristes à pattes*, an appelation attested in a "decree concerning soldiers of the Paris guard known as *triste à patte*," Paris, 1789 (BN, LB 39 7313). See n. 13.

running I ducked out of sight The sergeant and his men didn't spot me but the corporal hurled himself at me As he tried to grab my collar I gave him a punch the street not being very wide he fell on his rifle and made a hash of it (They) surrounded me put the cuffs on and took me to headquarters The corporal made a deposition I contradicted him in every particular and why hadn't they brought the girl in to make a deposition and that he was drunk and that he fell on the ground And in fact he was liquored up The inspector ordered me released At the gate they jumped me and took me to inspector Laporte whom they woke up (and) who ordered me put into the stockade[136]

I arrived The guards at the gate asked me what it was all about I told them It's nothing you look like a good guy you'll stay with us (tonight) tomorrow you'll go to the white room[137] I took twenty-four sols out of my pocket (we) drank a drop or two Come morning I was with a bunch of revelers (who) kept feeding me drinks I saw a companion glazier by the name of Martin who had come to visit a fellow in the clink I told him to go fetch one of my cousins a hardware dealer An hour later he arrived (with) a leg of lamb a four-pound loaf and a jug of wine I asked him not to tell anybody I told him just to alert my boss

There are plenty of women around and they're all giving out drinks The wife or rather the mistress of my cousin came to visit me (She) came with a charming blonde who seemed to take a great interest in me and said she'd use her connections And (they) came often to bring me dinner which we ate together A nice-looking brunette with a lot of flesh on her whose brother and I had shared a bed took it upon herself to carry messages for me and let me know that she didn't hate me

Robert (the) recruiter came one day to see if anyone was willing (to join up) While drinking with him I told him my story and asked him not to tell my father No sooner does he get outside than he runs to tell my father My father comes and wants to lecture me Some of my friends arrive and we lecture him with a bottle The next day which is Corpus Christi I go to the chapel where they are about to say mass What do I see The chaplain is the brother of a woman who used to have an eye for me I got down on

---

[136] *Mettre en canton*, a familiar expression for prison attested in the *Rat. du Châtelet* (Paris, 1790), by an anonymous author; possibly derived from *cantonner*, to place under surveillance.

[137] No document exists to enlighten us about the meaning of this expression, which may refer to lighted rooms in the Châtelet prison where jailers put prisoners who paid them bribes to be taken out of the darker dungeons.

my knees on the steps of the altar and responded to part of the mass He stared at me When the mass was over he had me brought to the clerk's office and asked what the story was I told him He asked the clerk to check the records They said I was a free man He gave me a little lecture particularly not to see his sister for fear of breaking up her happy home

I went to say good-bye to the guard and begged him to excuse me if I didn't wait for the people who were coming to have dinner with me My father came and said that his friends were working on getting me out My little brunette arrived at that moment and I told her that we were going to leave together I said good-bye at the gate to my father who got angry that I was about to give him yet another new daughter-in-law

We went on our way We went to Vaugirard and all to keep the wolves at bay That night I took her to my room After a lot of nonsense about what will her father say and what will her mother say we got down to business and spent a good night That morning as she was leaving the mistress of the house called her a corrupter of young men and turned her back on her I kept my mouth shut Finally I went down this woman bawled me out I told her I was the master in my own house and I didn't owe her anything She said it had nothing to do with that it was just that she saw a new face every day I said that I hadn't set foot in the house for eleven days She called her husband who assured me that at least eight or ten women had come at different times of the day and that if he had known where I worked he would have sent them to me I laughed he was a good fellow we went off to drink a bottle and he said to me The thing is my wife would like to see you settle down and you could establish yourself in this neighborhood with a widow who lives on the mont de Sainte-Geneviève (and) who has a very nice shop I told him that that might suit me just fine some day

While working for M de Laborde[138] as I was making some kites for his children which earned me some nice tips his butler said Monsieur would like to speak to me I went into his office He said My friend I would like to have a glazier on my staff I've noticed you you would eat with the servants and I shall pay twenty-five sols per day not counting the small

---

[138] The family was one of the most important involved in the operation of the *ferme générale*. The reference here may be to Jean Joseph de Laborde, court banker, whose *hôtel* was located in 1765 in the rue des Blancs-Manteaux and in 1770 in the rue d'Artois; or it may be to Benjamin de Laborde, like his relative a *fermier général*, first valet of the king's bedchamber, and correspondent of Voltaire; in 1765 his *hôtel* was located in the rue Grange-Batelière.

bonus that I may offer I shall give you a week to decide And (I) thanked him That night after supper I said to M Elophe You are going to lose M de Laborde's business he made me an offer he gave me a week and since I wouldn't think of cheating you I'm letting you know and to keep things right I won't come back to work He thanked me and said he would be grateful

His niece told me that the next day her uncle would be eating out and that I should come to dinner since she would be alone I arrived at the appointed time As soon as the door was closed I sat down at table on which there was a fricasee I was taking a chicken off the spit to take it apart when the master and the mistress walked in And (they) saw a sumptuous table and me in intimate conversation with their niece They asked me to stay but I didn't dine as I had planned

After dinner they took me for a walk We went into a tavern we had a talk He asked me if I intended to set myself up in business that he owed eight hundred francs to his niece and he would give them to me besides which she had twelve hundred francs of her father's property I agreed He said he would look for an empty shop Empty words One day when he was talking to me about all those things we were carrying on our shoulders a casement of sixteen large panes he tripped Since he was wearing nothing but a wig his head went through the panes he was caught The pieces of glass tore at his collar the slightest movement caused him intense pain I finally got him out after a lot of trouble but his poor wig was lost and he had cuts all over his face and neck During this operation I couldn't keep from laughing and telling him that he ought to wear a hat

Since he was working for the duc de Ballainvilliers[139] and since the duchess was there (when) he arrived he mistook her for a chambermaid he wanted some laughs he put his hand on his throat and said many sweet things to her I signaled him He thought I was encouraging him to press his point and Madame was quite angry I was forced to say out loud That is Madame la duchesse because he was hugging her very tightly She called her servants Elophe is the smallest of men He got down on his knees and being a fine talker he humbled himself He was told to get out and never to set foot in the house again He waited for me We drank

---

[139] The title should be marquis rather than duke. The personage in question was Simon Charles de Bernard de Ballainvilliers (1721–1767), who was named intendant of Auvergne in 1757. His *hôtel* was located in the rue des Saints-Pères.

several bottles with the Swiss[140] (He) begged me to say nothing to his wife about what had happened

Since I saw that all his fine promises were merely words that the niece (and) the daughter were both after me I left without saying anything and took a job along with a young man whom I had taken on as apprentice working for a fellow by the name of Langlois an old friend of mine who had once sold me a used Harlequin's costume But before going to work I went to spend two weeks in a castle called Montigny belonging to M Trudaine[141] where my friend Du Tillet and his wife had taken work he as majordomo and his wife to take charge of the linen I left that charming place where I played open-air tennis[142] and received a warm welcome

My friend Langlois worked for the nuns (of) Saint Thomas[143] restoring the lead in their leaded glass windows We spent two months on that job When everything was done the mother superior asked me if with my boss's approval I would be interested in working inside the convent that I would be well fed and that I wouldn't start until eight in the morning and would quit at six and that I would receive in addition twelve sols per day I accepted the offer (and) observed the rule which was (that) when I went into the dormitories or left to take my meals I carried a small bell in my hand And those smart sisters when they heard the sound of my bell liked to watch me underneath their black veils and I had the pleasure of looking at a lot of death's heads And so after eating a good supper in my

[140] The Swiss porters of noble and royal households enjoyed the privilege of selling wine over the counter, whence the expression "*boire en suisse.*" See R. Dion, *Le Vin et la vigne en France* (Paris, 1964).

[141] Jean Charles Philibert Trudaine (1733–1777), conseiller d'état and intendant de finances, succeeded his father as director of Ponts et Chaussées (the department of bridges and roads). A member of the Académie des sciences, he was one of the most prominent officials of the French monarchy in the eighteenth century (see his eulogy by Condorcet). He owned the château de Chatillon as well as that of Montigny in the Yonne. His *hôtel* was in the rue des Vieilles-Haudriettes.

[142] Played in the open air in a large court, according to the Encyclopédie. Each team had three, four, or five players equipped with *battoirs*, a kind of racket, either round or square, made of wood covered with very durable parchment and equipped with a long handle for chasing balls. A match consisted of five or six games. It was important "in this game to have a good server who could serve the ball hard enough so that the other side could not catch it." Each missed ball cost fifteen points.

[143] Convent of Dominican nuns founded in the seventeenth century and enlarged in about 1765 as far as the rue Feydeau. The place is known mainly as the scene of Mme Doublet's salon, from which came the *Mémoires secrets* of Bachaumont.

convent with the twelve sols I was paid every day before leaving I went to the Cadet Buteux to look at faces and my little flower girl met me there

I left my apartment and took another on the seventh floor of the Saint-Germain cloister where during my hours of leisure when I had any I fixed up my little attic with mirrors all around (so that) I saw myself on all sides when I slept So when I left that pretty alcove the landlord gave me thirty francs

Since I started working in the convent I'd become weak I wanted to sleep all the time I told my friend Langlois that I thought that somebody was putting something in my food because I was no longer vigorous and had no feeling I didn't want to go back to work Langlois came up to my apartment because the Mother procuress had sent him to find out why I was absent He told her what was going on She said that she had nothing to do with it that if I came back she would put everything in order and I would get twenty-four sols every day for drink I went back

One day I was alone with Mother Saint Ursula and was in her cell which looked out on the garden of the Petits-Pères She said to me Mister glazier if I had been a woman of the world[144] I wouldn't have wanted to have relations with those men pointing to the petits-Pères I forgot myself in that moment I became once more the rival of the baby Jesus She was charming plump lots of flesh Oh what pleasure for a mortal to have one of those pretty brides he leaves mouldering in his seraglio That one reminded me of the two in Agen They had done nothing but knit me some socks This one gave me something quite different with which I was very pleased

But there was always something to be done I painted their cell The Mother procuress liked my work and since she was the only one allowed to take me into the cells the others being obliged to cover themselves and avoid looking at me (it) came to pass that we ate and drank all sorts of treats together and got on so well (that) all the beds of the mothers and sisters served as our sofas and heard our sighs And that got me back on track again Unfortunately it all came to an end and (I) only went back two or three more times reclaiming my rights each time

Since I had bought myself a small boat which had cost me forty-two livres Chenier one of my cousins told me that he wanted to have an outing on the water and that we would go to the islands above Charenton and that there would be four men and each one would bring a girl I told him that I had none at my disposal for the time being He answered Don't be

---

[144] *Femme du monde*, at this time a common synonym for prostitute or loose woman.

embarrassed my mistress will bring you the one who came to see when you were in the stockade

I got things ready and all seven (of them) arrived with food and (we) set out We had a good time Each fellow entertained his girl in those islands filled with willows that protect you from the sun and prying eyes I made a conquest she gave me her address (and) told me to come see her whenever I liked That was what I needed

We were retuning home by night enjoying the cool moonlight when we saw somebody shouting and I spotted a young man who was drowning I picked up my boathook I was lucky to catch him under the arm we got him into the boat My friends took him by the head and the foot and he threw up all the water he had swallowed We passed under the bridges even though the guards were shouting for us to bring him over to the bank

Since I knew that you were supposed to leave a drowned man in the water[145] until the inspector arrived and if he's dead the men who pick him up get six francs Otherwise if they fish him out living (they) get only what the victim is willing to pay Since this was contrary to all human feeling we went downstream toward the Invalides where some of his friends came to take him bringing him clothes and putting him in a wagon since I had given them the address the next day the father and the mother and his brother came looking for me at my friend Langlois's (They) came to thank me with offers of money which I didn't want to accept because I had acted as I did out of humanity and I would do the same for any person in similar circumstances They thanked me and three weeks later my young man came to visit me and called me his savior although I had been to his father's house and he didn't know what to serve me

My new conquest really enjoyed these outings in the boat and with my cousin we went out at night in two couples I knew the son of the Samari-taine ferryman who was a good sort and he guided our boat We were

---

[145] This is confirmed by the work of Philippe Nicolas Pia, alderman of Paris and hospital administrator who specialized in this area. In 1772 he set up an establishment for drowned persons, which he discussed in a series of brochures published between 1773 and 1789. There he denounced the "lamentable prejudice" that forbade anyone to touch a drowned person or to pull the body out of the water until a *commissaire* had been called. Popular beliefs were here more powerful than the law, which did not prohibit pulling drowned people out of the water and did not require waiting for the arrival of a *commissaire*. The popular attitude no doubt had to do with ignorance of the methods of resuscitation. Beyond that, however, was a deep-seated hostility to water, which deprives the body of heat and therefore of life and is thus a harmful element, coupled with boundless exaltation of air and fire, which were thought to be beneficial and healthful elements.

careful to fill his belly with drink One night on my way to my beauty's I was accosted by a well-dressed fellow wearing a sword (He) asked me if I wasn't so-and-so I answered yes This little lord then raised the ante and said that if I went to see the Dupré woman any more he would make me regret it I answered that there was (no) living soul who could stop me He said he would stop me and that he would let me have it with the flat of his sword I challenged him He drew his weapon A trip and a rabbit punch was what he got in return He tumbled over I grabbed his sword and broke the blade in two and threw it in his face I took the handle and went to an alley near the Oratoire where some hefty friends of mine were drinking in a tavern They told me the hilt was silver damascened with gold I said I was going to give it back They followed me I found my man in the midst of a crowd of people wiping himself off Some said he was in the right others that he was in the wrong I went over to him I said to him I'm a nice fellow Here's your hilt and when you want to give somebody the flat of your sword I'm your man and remember don't throw your weight around without thinking because you're likely to meet your match He told me he'd like to make my acquaintance Willingly We went down to the Muscat Wine Cellar in the rue de l'Arbre-Sec He told me what he had done for the Dupré woman He poured out his woes he adored her he couldn't live without her I laughed I've never felt that I think you can love without all that trouble

He told me I was a good fellow and he wanted to be my friend I was wary I gave him a false address I knew he was the son of the comte de Verthamont[146] I went to Chenier's mistress's place I found the Dupré woman there[147] She said she loved me more I let her go her own way But Sundays and holidays we took outings on the water at Saint-Cloud or Sèvres Langlois gave me an address in the rue Feydeau of a woman by the

---

[146] The reference is probably to Jacques Martial de Verthamont, councillor in the Bordeaux parlement, who had three sons, Jean-Baptiste, François, and Cyprien, among whom it is hard to identity the chevalier challenged by Ménétra.

[147] The Dupré woman, like Rosalie and Beaufort, is hard to identify, because prostitutes used common professional names. According to M. E. Benabou, there was a dancer by the name of Pelagie Dupré, who was sumptuously kept around 1755, and several other Dupré women arrested by the police between 1760 and 1765. As for the names chosen by prostitutes, there were fashions and traditions, for certain names had a nice ring and were adopted repeatedly. A celebrated *fille* attracted many imitators. What is more, it was useful for a prostitute to be able to vanish into anonymity, hence many changed their names often to elude the police. In the brothels, moreover, madames changed their girls' names to suit themselves.

name of Denongrais[148] who kept one of the leading bordellos in Paris (I
was supposed) to do some repairs When I went in they took me to talk to
the mistress We recognized each other It was Rosalie's old madam The
first words out of her mouth were to ask me for news of Rosalie I think
she's got her own place I told her that I didn't know what had become of
her that I have always been grateful but I didn't know what I had in me
toward her and that disgusted me since she admitted she had known my
father

She asked me if I had a mistress I gave her reason to doubt it She said
to me Hold tight and I'll soon find you a nice one With these words she
pointed out fifteen or so who were in a large salon some in front of a
mirror others putting on their garters still others playing cards She said
to me Tell me you wouldn't be able to make up for Rosalie's absence with
one of those young ladies there I burst out laughing she said Here is a
handsome glazier if one of you girls wants him for a lover I'll let you have
him They looked at me and looked at one another and I felt ashamed
because they began staring me up and down from head to toe She said to
me Do your job and come have dinner with me and my old sergeant Her
pimp was a sergeant of guards And you can bet (I) came

The following Sunday she said to me for there were twenty of us at
table I know that you like blondes sit down next to that one I was a bit
tongue-tied but I saw young men who were girls' lovers and who flirted
with them I did the same and I found out later that she allowed this
liberty only on Sundays and holidays and after the girls had gone back to
their rooms I promised to come back during the week I had noticed that
when these young men came to visit they brought bouquets I adopted this
custom and had some good times because my little blonde went at it with
obvious pleasure and she had a lot of spirit

Meanwhile my cousin decided to marry his mistress I wanted him to
think it over he wouldn't listen to me Neither his father nor mine showed

---

[148] Denongrais (also spelled Dehongrais) was an "abbess" (the common term) well known
to the police. Her "convent" (as brothels were called) was located in the rue Feydeau in the
Montmartre section. This was a fairly high-class establishment though not, as Ménétra suggests, one of the best in Paris, like the brothels of La Gourdan or La Paris. Denongrais was a
veteran of the profession who had been in trade for some time by 1757 when La Payen
denounced her to the lieutenant of police: "Monsieur Marais sometimes dines at Madame
Denongrais's" (then in the rue du Coq). R. Héron de Villefosse, *Histoire et géographie galante
de Paris* (Paris, 1957), p. 154. In any case, to have a sergeant of the guard as pimp was such a
commonplace occurrence that it became proverbial.

up He said to me Well cousin you will take care of everything We went
to rue Mouffetard to ask for her hand. He [i.e., the girl's father—trans.]
was a very rich man who called himself a paper dealer[149] (and) who bought
from all the people who pick up scrap with little hooks Our entry and the
proposal were most unusual Counting Chenier there were three of us we
entered a large courtyard We saw a tall man wearing an apron with
pockets with two men beside him who followed his orders using some kind
of rake and a lot of linen drapers with small hooks We greeted him He
indicated with his hand that we should enter a fairly decently decorated
room I saw a somewhat older woman well dressed a beautiful gold chain
at her side[150] big gold earrings (and) an enormous gold chain and cross
(around her neck) We greeted her respectfully I kissed her I saw my
would-be cousin-in-law who had already come in (with) a very friendly
sister who started giving me the eye They asked us to sit down they served
us drinks in old silver goblets that had been made in the time of Henri IV

The father came in hadsome with a vest trimmed with gold that went
down to his knees a wig with six rows of large curls cuffs that reached to
his fingertips I made the proposal with my hat off He told me to put my
hat back on He answered that he had only two daughters and for the time
being he had made up his mind to give each one (only) six thousand francs
not counting their trousseau and that he would pay the wedding expenses
provided that both daughters were taken off his hands I ansered affirma-
tively speaking in their favor The younger daughter winked at me I said
that I was eligible for marriage The conversation became general We were
served a bite to eat everything was going along wonderfully I sat down
beside the younger sister I squeezed the mama's hands while asking for permission to visit her home which was granted to me with all the ceremonies
of the faubourg Saint-Marceau

We said our good-byes and (I) kissed the younger sister and took the
prospective bride who was living with my cousin by the arm She told me
that she was going to tell the Dupré woman about the proposal I had made
for her sister and that her mother had asked her my estate and that if I
wasn't kidding we could double the family I said to her I know you're
too cautious but when all that gets out doesn't she have her cavalier who

<hr>

[149] The reference is probably to Jacques Bernard, the only paper and scrap dealer in the rue
Mouffetard, faubourg Saint-Marcel, who is mentioned in the 1760 *Almanach du commerce*.
  [150] *Clavier*: a string of small chains worn by women, generally on the side of the belt, and
sometimes used as a keychain.

importunes her What is more with me she has nothing to gain You're not kidding then she says to me I say You wouldn't want me for a brother-in-law In response she took my hand and kissed me

For the wedding Dupré gave a pair of silk stockings as a present and a beautiful shirt and I gave her a bouquet as was customary She told me not to get angry that her cavalier would come at night to dance and I told her likewise if I was often at the side of the bride's sister she shouldn't pay any attention if I spoke to her sister it would only be because the occasion required But she was too sharp to be fooled She sulked (and) irritated the cavalier and (as) that didn't bother me at all I went about my business We separated and (I) went to spend the rest of the night with other fellows from the wedding party and didn't return to Dupré's house until the day after her arrest The cavalier's father had had her seized and locked up in the Madelonnettes[151] It was a long time before I found out what happened Her daughter wanted me to claim her furniture and belongings but a brother-in-law of hers took possession of everything and when the poor woman got out she had nothing and nowhere to turn

I went as usual to Denongrais's place One day after dinner she said she had something to say to me We went into her room (and) after sitting down she said Menetra tell me is there something wrong with you young men run around and sometimes they don't know what they've got because Josephine which was my mistress's *nom de guerre* is complaining and she is sick I immediately brought out my weapon and said have a look After the minutest of examinations everything proved to be all right Button up she said I'm happy We'll I'm not Since Jake here is holding his head high I told her he wouldn't go back in the way he came out So there was nothing for it but to take the plunge and we were both content and I promised I would be faithful I risked nothing by promising I had often made the same promise to others

Elophe felt he had to avenge himself against me for quitting him and abandoning his niece He strong-armed me[152] to go work for old man

---

[151] A convent founded in the seventeenth century in the rue Fontaines-du-Temple, which received wayward girls in forced or voluntary detention. The house required payment of board and Dupré's presence there would suggest that she was a woman of some quality. No entry records exist.

[152] *Octonner*, an unusual word, which may be a distortion of *hortonner*, known to have been pronounced in Lyons as *heurtonné* (see Nizier de Puits Pelu, *Le littré de la grande côte*), which means to knock around, slap about (*urtoner* in fourteenth-century Italian), and by extension, a person subject to violent abuse.

Gerard the king's glazier in Versailles And I was forced to go but before leaving I figured I'd play a few tricks on him While staying at his house I had painted in large letters over the shop entrance the words Glass Shop There was a fellow named Bussie whom he had also had picked up who came and joined me We agreed to persuade all three companions he had with him to quit and to take them with us to Versailles Before five in the morning I got a ladder and wrote the word Broken in front of the words Glass Shop in exactly the same style of lettering since I had done both When the deed was done we went to a cabaret to wait for the companions to leave When they arrived I invited them to come in They did We drank some white wine We took it easy my comrade and I had lunch They joined us I persuaded one to quit the others were in no condition to work One was a French Guard the other the nephew of Ramponeau[153] and a real *ramponeau* [type of tumbling doll—trans.]

The fellow who left with us had the keys to an apartment in M Darvelay's house He wanted to drop them off I wouldn't let him He didn't know how to write I wrote to Elophe for him in these terms "Here are the keys I am leaving with the two companions you strong-armed and I'm the third" I told my two comrades to wait I went to see my flower girl I went to see Denongrais Since I had become the friend of the house I was told that she would come to Versailles to see me on Sunday I promised to come she objected for fear I would tire myself She gave me a change of linen and promised that more would be sent and we parted with everybody else in the house still in the dark except one girl who served as a messenger That was as it should be

When we reached Versailles M Gérard recognized me since I had worked for him about nine or ten years before The companions were friendly to me There were about thirty-five of us in the anterooms of the palace At night we climbed up on the tables and pretended to fence The footmen (and) the hundred Swiss (guards)[154] looked on with amusement

---

[153] Cabaret keeper celebrated from La Courtille to Belleville. He ran the Tambour Royal, which was successful enough to draw buyers and to earn Ramponeau an offer to play himself on stage at the Gourlin Theater. A lawsuit resulted when the wine seller withdrew. The episode was commented on by Voltaire. In 1772 Ramponeau established himself in Nouvelle France, where he purchased the cabaret of Magny (spelled Magnie by Ménétra), A la Grande Pinte, frequented by a large clientele and numerous prostitutes.

[154] An elite corps of the king's household guards, recruited from the Swiss cantons since 1516. Armed with halberd and épée, they were responsible for guarding Versailles.

The *enfants de France*[155] were brought in to watch our antics The boss was delighted he reminisced at dinner he told the story of how I had once convinced a companion to spend the night in the deer park by telling him he would be able to catch badgers[156] and (that) the skin was worth three livres and he was arrested by the marshals who hauled that idiot off to jail and that I was the one who played the deer and all the companions ran after me and the nobles amused themselves watching our hunt And one day in the hall of mirrors playing hangman there was a fellow who tripped me and I broke my nose and the nobles who were there scolded him because I set free several at once And I was given twelve francs which I spent the next day with my comrades

Since I saw that this pleased the boss his wife and his sons and daugh-ters the next day when there were only five or six of us fencing I said that since our shop was on a little square we could get six barrels and with our benches make a little theater We had eight or ten lights and (I) announced that we were going to do the Parade du Savetier People wanted to throw us money we wouldn't take it and every night as long as Bussie and I were there we had a good time

The Denongrais woman wrote me that she couldn't come that some business had come up but (she) sent me white linen and two écus of six francs wrapped in a collar with a pretty little note that I should let her know the day I was leaving and she would come to meet me in Passy Our quarantine was over we were supposed to leave on Sunday morning and we were owed six francs three livres for the arrival and three for the departure when we went to the inspector he asked which of us were Parisien and Manceau He told us that he had orders for us to stay and work for a fellow by the name of Petit who was the glazier of the king's stables where all the panes had to be reset in lead

Well I had around a hundred and twenty street lanterns to make for Langlois not to mention my acquaintances and I knew the flower girl was waiting for me in Sèvres and the Denongrais woman in Passy I came up

---

[155] The king's grandsons and the children of the dauphin, Louis, and his wife, Marie-Joséphe of Saxony, three boys (the Duke of Berry, later to become Louis XVI, born in 1754, the Count of Provence, later Louis XVIII, born in 1755, and the Count of Artois, later Charles X, born in 1757) and two girls (Clothilde and Elisabeth). See P. Girault de Coursac, *L'Education d'un roi* (Paris, 1972).

[156] In a section of Versailles that had once been a deer park, Louis XV kept a house for his clandestine love affairs. Ménétra apparently entered the adjoining garden.

with a stratagem that worked When I went back for my pack M Gérard greeted me (said to me) that I should stay in Versailles and that after the job was done I should come back to work for him as one of his four companions and as far as he was concerned I should go with Manceau and talk to Sieur Petit (and) he would go with us I gave him an honest excuse

I gave my pack to Bussie and told him to tell the flower girl that I was forced to remain in Versailles Since he had a woman too both of them were waiting for us at Sèvres I took with me Manceau and the companion I had lured away from Elophe we went to Sieur Petit's the companions congratulated me that I was about to join them I asked them if Sieur Petit was there They said only his wife was that was just what I needed I went in and said Madame I've brought you the two companions that your husband asked for She accepted them without saying a word (and) even though the companions were waiting for me to have a drink with them I hightailed it across the fields without fanfare

I went and met Denongrais who was waiting for me with a nice fish stew and (we) returned to Paris in a carriage for Madame never traveled by any other means The next day I went to my friend Langlois's and Bussie and I deliberately walked back and forth in front of Elophe's shop Elophe said he would have us arrested We showed him the cockades we had on our hats and took his two remaining companions on a binge

The French guard had had a dispute with his mistress whom I too had taken to bed and (he) spent seventeen days in the abbey[157] People told me to hide because the master of Versailles wanted me on account of the swindle I'd pulled seeing as how the companion I had given him in my place wasn't up to the job

I therefore went to work in Mont-Saint-Hilaire[158] for a master who had a job resetting the windows of a college in lead I stayed for about a month without giving my name He gave me twenty-four francs a month and plenty of food I visited Denongrais often One Saturday night after supper the master had a bottle brought in and said Let's drink to the health of M Ménétra I saw that for several days he had been telling me that he

---

[157] *Abbaye*: the use of the word to mean "prison" is not confirmed by the usual sources. This usage may have been peculiar to the Paris working class, to denote a prison for delinquent young men. Or it may have to do with a quirk of style in a text that was probably recopied after the Revolution, during which the abbey of Saint-Germain-des-Prés was converted into a prison.

[158] There is no *collège* at Mont-Saint-Hilaire near Etampes, but there was a priory and by extension a collegial.

would sell his shop if he found someone who wanted to stay with him for a couple of years and (I) hadn't paid much attention I thanked him for his honesty and went to work as usual when Langlois came looking for me Since several days were owed me he told me to quit and not to worry about it and then (I) went to work making lanterns at so much apiece

Although I was earning pretty good money I was spending it at a good clip too I had a friend whose countrywoman worked as a cook for the mistress of Christophe de Beaumont[159] She lived behind the Louvre he took me there one day The mistress had gone to the theater we were given a warm reception the servant kept us company that made even couples I ingratiated myself I noticed we were losing our inhibitions and we let ourselves go a bit They told me that whenever I came I would be warmly welcomed I went all the time and took them to Gaudon's or Nicolet's where I often had tickets and they told me that their mistress kept company with Carlin[160] Samson[161] and Christophe de Beaumont I couldn't help thinking about that motley mix The three leading Harlequins of France one did his acting at Notre-Dame the other at the Comédie Italienne and the other in the place de Grève I wanted to make sure of the truth I saw them and was completely convinced I kept up this relationship for a while but since I never liked being tied down and still less the petty attentions (that romance requires) even though she was quite passionate as I had business elsewhere and occasionally saw a tall

---

[159] Christophe de Beaumont (1703–1781), named archbishop of Paris in 1746, adversary of the Jansenists and the *philosophes*, a rigorist and zealot. He was no libertine.

[160] Carlino Bertinazzi (1710–1783): one of the greatest harlequins of the eighteenth century and the third great harlequin of the Italian comedy.

[161] Henri Samson, executioner of Paris (1740–1793), one of the most extraordinary men of his age. Born into the family of Paris executioners, he received an excellent education. He was fifteen when he unofficially replaced his father in 1754 but did not come to hold his post officially until 1778. Along with his son he was executioner during the Revolution. Gentle, pious, and studiously elegant (Parisian men wore clothes of "Samson green"), Monsieur Henri was a scholar who lived in a bourgeois manner. He owned a large house with a garden in the Nouvelle France section, at the corner of the rue des Poissonniers and the rue d'Enfer, which he sold in 1778 to move to the rue neuve Saint-Jean (now the rue du Château d'Eau). His walks might well have taken him to the rue Pavée. Like all executioners, Monsieur Henri played an important role in popular mythology: he performed his duties before a large audience in the place de Grève (where executions were held) and on Saint John's day. He had a large income from customary fees, tickets sold to the curious, and sale of victims' anatomical parts. He enjoyed a reputation as a healer in an age when people believed that human fat could cure rheumatism, and that a specific made from lichen that adhered to skulls could cure gall and kidney stones and apoplexy. Like his father before him, Henri Samson surely had a good knowledge of human anatomy; both men set fractures and were students of botany.

cousin of mine we gradually lost touch I often thought of my three
Harlequins That men of such different estate by character and rank were
linked together and all for a woman that made me see clearly that all men
have their weakness

Langlois and his wife took it in mind to get me married and sell me their
shop since they had become wealthy thanks to the benefactions of M de
Boulogne[162] The woman had not been ungrateful as I had ample opportunity to observe For I had seen her many many times go to the back of
the shop ever since a certain corpulent individual had decided to take her
up the back stairs and worked so hard at climbing that he had been forced
to rest being unable to continue either up or down But Langlois coveting
his neighbor's property called me to help this individual who without our
assistance would have croaked because we had a devil of a time getting
him out of there (not) without having a good laugh and making some sarcas-
tic remarks[163] at Langlois's expense who was scarcely embarrassed at all

His wife therefore wanted to fix me up with one of the alleged female
relatives of this M de Boulogne who had eight hundred livres in rent and
said they would pay for equipping the shop After the interview I agreed
I had already seen this girl at the house when Sieur de Boulogne was
there They pointed out that since M de Boulogne had many poor relations
and especially daughters he came to see his relatives at Madame Langlois's
rather than have them go to his house so that they wouldn't be seen or
recognized by the servants Monsieur was supposed to give her a little
dowry and we were supposed to meet to make an agreement in the presence of the dear relative The person was charming a gold watch was
offered to me they had two of them They were not totally dismayed unless
it was underneath Langlois told me that I would be happy in acting as he
did

But this M de Boulogne this family to pass for a hats-on type [i.e., a
noble] All that didn't fit at all with my character Langlois and his wife
took us out walking I was taciturn they criticized my behavior Finally I
made up my mind I went to see my friend Du Tillet who was still with M
Trudaine I told him how things stood he saw the situation the same way

---

[162] Jean Tavernier de Boullongue (and not Boulogne, as Ménétra would have it)
(1726–1787), a councillor in Parlement, maître des requêtes and intendant des finances, was
the son of a contrôleur général des finances. A member of a wealthy and powerful family, his
hôtel was in the rue Saint-Honoré opposite the monastery of the Jacobins.

[163] *Donner des lardons*: to lampoon, gibe, hurl sarcasms, also used by Voltaire in a letter to
d'Argental dated 1 February 1762.

I did I told him that I didn't know how to get out of it It's simple I'll get you hired here Monsieur has a nice house in Châtillon and has some greenhouses that need glazing What is more (he) would like to have a permanent glazier for his country estates I'll introduce you I was accepted

I left Langlois and all the rest I said and spread the word that I had left for the country and in fact I went to Châtillon I was given thirty-five sols a day and fifty whenever I had to go to an estate called Montigny over by Sens I was given board When Monsieur visited his country estates it could hardly be otherwise since Du Tillet was his majordomo I passed the time agreeably I went occasionally to Fontenay-aux-Roses I made friends with the glaziers in the area I helped them out None of it was very interesting I made the acquaintance of a lady friend that kept me busy

I went to Paris to see Denongrais Madame la Police had been interfering with business she made up her mind to sell her property and to retire with her cuckold of a husband to her native village for she'd put by quite a bit in the course of her work I was all for it She said to me I see clearly from what you've just said that you never loved me She was right for never had a woman touched my heart except for sensual pleasure and nothing else I promised her to come say my farewells and they've yet to be said

Since it was the good season we went to Champigny and went with some friends of mine to what are called *guinguettes* [open-air cafés with music and dancing—trans.] Sundays and holidays we went to dance in front of the castle and other days usually with the people from the *guinguette* we played tennis or went visiting the local festivals One holiday in a village one league from Montigny people were playing tennis on the square when Du Tillet showed up accompanied by the lord the magistrate or sheriff and the priest I heard somebody say That's the Parisian over there I wondered what this was all about It's because they know you're good at tennis said my friend they're going to propose a match In fact six young men came and politely gave each of us a racket My friend said no since he didn't know how to play but he said But as for my friend he'll give you a good show I declined They insisted the lord the sheriff and the priest joined in I played applause hands were heard to clap They took us to the castle (and) gave us refreshment

I was greatly applauded I promised again that the fellows from Montigny and I would be waiting for them next Sunday People came from all around I was all over the court and we had a good time we won and whatever else they were well entertained My friend went all out because

M Trudaine had wanted to see me play and when I passed in front of him he and the people around him said to me Courage So I answered that that was one thing I wasn't lacking

One day I followed the game warden Since I had no rifle I let him run all over the fields and went to a village where I had seen the curate pay his respects to M Trudaine who recognized me and said I was pretty nimble at tennis and took me to his presbytery for a drink

After some idle talk we finally got onto the subject of religion We talked about the mysteries of the sacraments I told him about the Protestants of the Cévennes I spoke passionately about the sufferings that had been inflicted on men who worshipped the same God except for a few matters of opinion And (I said that) the Roman religion should be tolerant if it followed the maxims of its lawgiver that because of its mysteries it was absurd and that all mysteries were in my opinion nothing but lies And that so long as they sold indulgences and gave remission for sins in exchange for money fear of hell which was like purgatory just an invention of the first impostors that Jesus had never spoken of purgatory And that all those sacraments were nothing but pure inventions to make money and impress the vulgar And that he himself who was a very intelligent man was not capable of making his God chewing him and then swallowing him That we mistreated those peoples who did not share our belief (and who) according to the Church should have been damned because all the priests went around saying Outside the Church there is no salvation And that we accused those who worship idols of being idolators when we prostrate ourselves before statues We even worship a piece of dough which we eat in the firm belief that it is God And those idolators only worship all those things to keep from being hurt by them and other things in the hope of getting some good out of them while we on the other hand we were real man-eaters After praying to him and worshipping him in order to satisfy him we've got to eat him too

He answered me with objections as many others had answered me His one and only response was to say to me All these mysteries must be believed because the Church believes them he said to me My friend you are enlightened It is necessary that for the sake of government nations live always in ignorance and credulity I answered him So be it

That night upon reaching the castle I told the game warden that if I had had a rifle I would have gone hunting with him that if he wanted I would go with him that if I killed a hare or a rabbit I would spend an écu or two We set a date for the next day and as we entered a thicket he said

to me There's one Parisien I took aim The dog ran he took off after it
put it [i.e., the prey] in his game bag and we went off to have a meal at my
expense He surely put one over on me because I hadn't had the presence
of mind to touch (the animal) to see if it was warm But he paid me back by
way of certain card tricks I pulled on him and others that he wanted to
know and that I taught him later

We had a good time in these parts I ran around with the servant of the
priest with whom I had had the conversation and with whom I conversed
whenever we met I went often to his house on the pretext of borrowing
books One day when I thought he was at the castle I ran over to the presbytery After a little discussion with the governess just as I was embracing
her I heard him coming I ran over to the fireplace and sat down in the
alcove buttoning up with one hand holding a book with the other and
red as coral and the girl standing around doing nothing For I am convinced that if he had asked her either she would have confessed or he
would have paid no attention or he was preoccupied with other things
All I got out of it was a good scare and I said to myself that the next time
I would turn the lock two turns

A man who finds himself in such a spot feels really stupid when he has
to button up with one hand and a priest in front of him a trembling girl
Oh what a rough moment a cold sweat broke out over my whole body and
still it did not want to settle back down to normal All I got out of it was a
good scare

We returned to Châtillon and (I) went to Paris to see the inauguration
of the equestrian statue on the place Louis XV[164] The next day I went to
the town house looking for the business secretary who gave me thirty-six
francs I bought myself a pair of dancing shoes and a pair of stockings and
went to see my father We went out for a bottle Since he had already been
drinking two fellows from Provence said Look he's drunk I told them
they were out of line my father chased them away They tried to slap my
father We went at them a trip and a rabbit punch was all it took A friend
of mine named Lenoir held the other one who was trying to jump me The
one on the ground had lost some change in the gutter I was gentleman
enough to pick it up He shouted that I had taken his money I went for

---

[164] Construction work in the square, known today as the place de la Concorde, began in
1757 and ended in about 1772, but the statue was inaugurated on 20 June 1763. *Le peuple* and
la ville were amused by the following lines, first heard on that day: "Oh, the beautiful statue,
oh the handsome pedestal, the virtues go on foot and vice on horseback."

his collar I knocked him down saying he was a lowlife The cops arrived
My father in his drunkenness kept saying that if I was guilty I must be
punished I showed my money Those creeps said that it was theirs that I
had found in the street

The cops took us to see the inspector They maintained that it was their
money I tried to deny it but it did no good my father kept saying I must
be punished I pointed out that I had just been paid thirty-six francs by M
Trudaine's secretary that I had bought some shoes and stockings and that
I had spent with my father and a friend twenty-four sols the amounts
tallied Those two scoundrels maintained that the four écus belonged to
them My father insulted me I told the inspector to send someone out to
check with the secretary Providence arranged that he would be home He
came down he testified to the truth The two Provençaux were taken to
the Châtelet The inspector gave my father a complicated dressing-down
saying that he didn't have any compassion for his children The secretary
joined in and told him that he was not worthy to have such a son and that
it was plain that he was a father in name only All the people at the gate
threw stones at him and (he) turned around confused because I said I see
clearly that you don't have a father's compassion and that you only made
me for your own pleasure

With these words I left him I found old Jerome sometime fisherman
and friend of my father who didn't want me to leave him without extract-
ing a promise to come see him at La Ville de La Rochelle in the rue Saint-
Lazare He cried for joy when I told him the story and couldn't stop telling
people that he had seen me born that I was mischievous but incapable of
treachery and that he wasn't surprised about my father that he had always acted toward me in this way

I forgot everything and went back to Châtillon I had been there for a
while when M Trudaine sent for me one morning and said My friend since
I receive many people M de Margastaud[165] has brought it to my attention
that you go in and out of all the apartments opening and closing the
windows and shutters and that an unknown person could easily enter the
house in your stead I am going to have a livery made for you and you will
wear it in the house I answered him Monsieur I have never been in

---

[165] Among the Gascon nobility there is a family of this name, ennobled by the *capitoulat*
(or board of city magistrates) of Toulouse in 1684 and 1714. Perhaps the person described by
Ménétra came to see Trudaine in the hope of obtaining his recommendation for a lawsuit or a
purchase of woodland.

livery and never intend to be hence Monsieur it is my honor to resign from your employ He said to me My friend I shall give you a week to think it over I said to him I have thought it over and I am your servant

It was a miserable Gascon nobleman who was responsible for my leaving my friends He came to buy a forest which he said bordered his land and brought in little income But when I went to take leave of the secretary I pointed out to him that this forest where I had often gone bordered on the forests of the abbey of Grandselves known as the woods of Verdun and that they were important I found out that he was turned away by the secretary who passed this information on to M Trudaine and so I had my vengeance even though I didn't know it (at the time)

On leaving Châtillon I passed the rue de la Harpe and saw M Bellé who was on his doorstep and in joking around I told him that I was for hire He said if I wanted to work for him he had plenty to keep me busy and (I) was willing I worked there for a while where I drove his wife's sister wild I told her that if she wanted I would show her heaven and hell and the devil She told this to her sister who took me literally but that wasn't what I meant finally I kept my word While they were both seated in front of an open window in the downstairs hall I went into a house where I had seen a black cat I put it in the pocket of my apron Since it was almost dusk I said to them You asked to see the devil you will see him I made some grimaces and contortions and uttered a few words and I asked them if they wanted to see him as a man or as an animal They answered me as a cat I tapped my apron which was made of leather I turned part way around the cat escaped ran between the sister's legs and jumped through the window Both women cried out (they) could not contain their surprise To all and sundry they repeated that I had made them see the devil that is very true I led them to believe that if they had asked to see him in another form it would have been all the same to me They didn't want me to show them anything else Although I really wanted to show the sister something else she was always on the defensive

I made the acquaintance of a charming young girl who was a governess in a house on the rue des Mathurins I went there quite often It belonged to a widower One night we persuaded ourselves that the porter had not seen me come in and I proposed keeping her company for the night She agreed She told me to go ahead and to speak softly I went into her room we were in a conversation of the most earnest kind in which mortals engage and (I) thought I was among the Gods and in such moments we believe ourselves to be their equals

So I was in a state of sweet rapture when suddenly I heard via the swinging stairway the voice of a servant telling the master Monsieur we haven't seen the glazier leave The master said Let's go make sure I grabbed my togs and in great haste climbed up to a hayloft I crouched in a corner I spotted a small window that served as a skylight I pulled myself through and emerged on the roof I listened The girl's room was inspected She pretended to be asleep What do I see but two lights the master with a sword[166] in hand If he had been alone I wouldn't have been afraid but there were three of them I gently pulled the trap door closed and they searched the loft again and with the sword did what the customs officers do at the barricades[167] Lucky for me I had climbed through the window

What a sad night it turned out to be after such a good beginning I didn't expect it to turn out that way A good time to think things over A man in a rage me naked but for a nightshirt couldn't they easily run me through I was defenseless the honor and position of the young lady gone If I tried to escape over the roofs I could slip and fall into the street Then a storm came that I was lucky to live through I crept as quietly as possible back into the loft I cleaned myself up giving my love to all the devils (?) I looked around the loft all the bales of hay and straw had been moved I lost a silk stocking and again it was one of the silk stockings that Dupré had given me as a gift That reminded me that in those days I took my pleasure in comfort anyway I was always sure of finishing with the lady

All my reflections came to nought I had to get out without being seen I made up my mind I listened at the door of the room I pushed it open Everything was closed up I went downstairs on tiptoe and in the dim light it was almost impossible to see I crossed the courtyard and came to the gate that marked the end of my troubles I felt my way fortunately the big lock was not closed There was only the bolt but the bars were closed

---

[166] *Flamberge*: the name ascribed to Roland's sword and, later, to the sword of Renaud, eldest of Aymon's four sons. By extension, the term denoted a sword, possibly ironically.

[167] *Commis aux barrières*: employees of the *ferme générale* responsible for collecting duties and excise taxes known as *octroi* and *aides* at city gates. The *commis des aides*, as they were known, were involved in extensive tax collection activities in the countryside, the territories subject to the *taille*, and cities subject to entry duties: they monitored trade, investigated fraud, conducted searches, and kept an eye on cabarets. Detested by the common people (though many of them were of common birth), they were organized into brigades, each brigade being assigned to one of the major *barrières*, where a *receveur* and a *contrôleur* were stationed permanently. Their job was made easier by the construction of the so-called wall of the *fermiers généraux* in 1785, but in 1788 and 1789 they were attacked by large mobs.

I pushed them They screeched I was afraid of being taken by surprise
Finally I took the bull by the horns and made it to the street

I went to my room I cooled off or rather warmed up because I had a
cold sweat all over my body at Caplain's house To top it all off I didn't
have my skeleton key I walked on the quays with one shoe on and the
other foot bare I promised myself not to get into any more such fixes

Since I had undertaken to make lanterns for the city and they were
needed quickly in spite of my bad night I went to work Between ten and
eleven the servant arrived who laughed and asked me if I had slept well I
saw that he had my stocking in his hand I changed color and suggested
we go have a drink together He accepted he told me that he had seen me
go up and that it was the coachman who had given me away and that the
master had really raked him over the coals that he didn't understand how
I had been able to escape from right under his nose that he had been on
watch all night but that he had agreed with the porter to let me escape
that as for my stocking he had found it in the stairway and that this was
lucky because he was the last one to go there and that he had immediately
stuffed it into his pocket

I thanked him and promised myself not to get into such a fix but to
bring them home to my place where I had no fear of being run through So
I said good-bye but apparently it was written that we would meet again
and that in the end it would be where love would force me to endure his
tyranny He had caught me late but he had made me feel it and I finally
understood that all mortals must be governed by laws

I left Bellé and amused myself with my flower girl and ate what I had
At the end of January I made the acquaintance of a fellow by the name of
Gombeaut a well-known tippler and a man good with a weapon skilled at
everything and acquainted with everybody in Paris and I was initiated
into the fraternity of revelers We spent the night at the market in all the
bars[168] or Du Rocher[169] came to make his rounds He paid me a great
compliment he looked me over more than once

One day while joking around the table we saw two apprentice wig-
makers come in one pretty good sized the other quite small Since my
friend and I were with two nice-looking but unusual girls and I was

---

[168] *Rogomistes,* from *rogome,* alcohol, eau-de-vie, strong liquor, from which we get the
expressions *fioler la rogome* (to drink white spirits) and *voix de rogome* (hoarse from drink).

[169] A police inspector who lived in the rue Saint-Martin near the rue aux Ours. See Jèze,
Tableau de Paris, p. 108.

playing the fool they asked permission to sit down at our table and we joked around together and generously ordered a round of drinks Du Rocher's men arrived a sign that I saw being flashed to Du Rocher revealed that we were in good company After they left the barkeeper told us that Du Rocher had told him that they were the princes of Condé[170] and Conti And so I said They had a good laugh I had noticed their clothes (and) their linen but we thought they were just some of those rich wigmaker apprentices or masters

I took on one of the tarts who was called Aurora of (the) Night the other was called Aurora of (the) Day she was my friend's mistress I took her home with me and we became a couple Every night we had supper together and went to my place The two girls were inseparable As for trade their main place of business was the rue de la Monnaye and we were told that we would have to wait until the public was satisfied before we could have our satisfaction That was our understanding Now in my love affairs there was something wanting for my glory no woman had ever fought over me with a rival it finally happened One fine day my flower girl came to my room Aurora and I were going out It was two cocks fighting to the death I tried to stop it and calm them down they told me to mind my own business Bonnets in their pockets they went at it in the place du Louvre I stayed out of it Finally Aurora came to meet me in the alley of the Oratoire (she) claimed all the glory for herself but she didn't think (the other girl) looked very smart

My ties to her grew tighter She boasted of her exploit to her friend and that made me proud One night as my friend and I were going to meet our beauties as usual we spotted my mistress followed by a little man carrying a small bundle of sticks[171] under his arm We went up My heart was telling me it's my father We went in What do I see It was true He looked at me and after a few words my friend asked where his girlfriend was My father asked me what I was doing there I told him that this woman belonged to me My father went out grumbling as he went down the stairs

---

170 Louis Joseph de Bourbon, prince de Condé (1736–1818), father of Louis Henri Joseph (1756–1830), the last prince of Condé, and grandfather of the duc d'Enghien. Louis François Joseph de Bourbon, prince de Conti (1734–1814): in 1765 he was known as the comte de la Marche. His father was the protector of Rousseau and the spirit behind the society that "challenged" the Temple. These two young princes of the blood, heirs of the largest fortunes of their day (along with that of the Orléans), made quite free with their time and their manners.

171 *Cottret*: a medium-sized bundle of small twigs (usually spelled *cotret*).

We used the faggots to keep warm while waiting for the other girl We joked about what had just happened and that we got there just in time she would have been my stepmother None of this made me very agreeable toward my father but he was prudent enough never to mention it

(While I was) playing the bourgeois of Paris (and) scarcely working they tried to organize a new fire department[172] There was a fellow named Segrestier newly married who was a corporal and a cobbler by trade who put in my name and I was accepted on the spot when the chief found out I was a glazier So after that I wore a sword at my side most of the time

One day I went to Nouvelle France[173] for supper with Segrestier he was drunk We were alone with his wife and I had forgotten my skeleton key and there was a torch burning with the lady of the house It was close to midnight He offered me a place to sleep I agreed His wife would sleep next to the wall he in the middle and me on the outside We got into bed When the light went out my man began to snore quite loudly I reached my hand over his head I felt his wife's hand I squeezed it she responded She got up Slowly gently I pushed the husband aside he was over by the wall I was in the middle and the wife came to take my place We went to sleep

The next morning he woke me and I found myself alone in the bed He asked me to come have a glass of white wine he had something on his mind he asked me how it was that I wound up in the middle I told him

---

[172] Sartine, the lieutenant of police, reorganized the fire brigade around 1767 and placed it under M. de Morat; the brigade had been in existence since 1699. In the middle of the century it included sixty firemen organized in eight brigades. Most were cobblers and shoe-makers,along with a few locksmiths. De Morat increased the number of brigades to sixteen and the number of firemen to 160. Each fireman had to indicate that he was a member of the brigade by placing a sign and a bell on the front of his house. Firemen received 100 livres per year in 1750, increased to 200 by 1770. In 1716 pumps were stationed in all monasteries. By the end of the century Paris had twenty-five pumping stations and several water-wagon depots. The organization worked remarkably well (cf. BN.MS.FF. Joly de Fleury, 1325-103-106-245-247). As a brigadier, Ménétra may have received as much as 400 livres per year.

[173] The Nouvelle France section was situated beyond the customs barrier at the foot of the Montmartre hill and north of the barriére d'Enfer (along the current line of rue Lamartine). Along with Les Porcherons and La Courtille and all the outlying districts, it was filled with cabarets and *guinguettes*, to which the common people went to drink untaxed wine. The section earned its name in the period 1675–1680, when the police systematically rounded up people found in disreputable establishments and shipped them off to the colonies in America. Nouvelle France was divided into two parishes, Saint-Pierre-de-Montmartre and Saint-Laurent. The Sainte-Anne chapel was on the path north of the rue Saint-Lazare known as la chaussée de la Nouvelle France.

that he was the most restless of sleepers that he snored and pushed his wife who had fallen into the space between the bed and the wall He told me he thought I was too good a friend for that I got angry I asked him if he had doubts about my honesty and his wife's honor and said I would never return to his house He apologized and we both forgot all about it

I went to work with my brother-in-law We were going to paint or rather scrawl all over the beer and wine shops I excelled at making vine stems and flagons and beer glasses my brother-in-law excelled at portraits of Bacchus and Ramponeau

Meanwhile we made the acquaintance of a surgeon by the name of Baron a great lover of fireworks Since word of our painting exploits reached as far as the faubourg Saint-Antoine Charonne (and) Vincennes we made acquaintances all over consuming all that we earned by our endeavors Every Sunday and holiday in the morning we set up fireworks that we would set off at night outside the taverns in their gardens for anyone who would have us They'd put up signs that there was going to be a show people came running the tavernkeepers toasted us and almost every night we put on a show with the help of our friend Baron who threw himself wholeheartedly into the work

One day one of my fellow firemen came looking for me (and) to see our show we had supper in a large group I left him at his door in the rue Verdret promising to come with some other firemen for lunch at Demandeau's We waited for him in vain Someone went to look for him they knocked they looked through the keyhole They saw him stretched out on his bed I had my apron and my hammer I used it to pry off the hasp We went in he had poisoned himself He was a jewelry setter by trade On the chimney we saw a glass which still contained aqua fortis He had made a mistake His mouth had been eaten away[174] and he was buried with full military honors and (I) was quite angry because he was one of my good friends

I went to the faubourg Saint-Marceau one holiday to visit my cousin's father-in-law I was told that the family had gone to La Glacière I went there I was warmly received The young sister was dancing with a French guard[175] When she came back to the table she said There's our cousin I

---

[174] *Chantournée:* a term from carpentry meaning cut away (as by a bandsaw), here extended to describe the appearance of the dead man's lips, which had been eaten away by the acid.

[175] Responsible since 1563 for guarding the king, and marching ahead of the infantry, there were six battalions of guards, some thirty companies of 140 riflemen and three companies of

was flattering she pretended to listen to me I danced I noticed that she was making eyes at the French guard I teased

A fellow by the name of Véron one of my friends son of a starch-maker brother of one of my aunts came by to bid us good evening and have a drink as people will and he asked me to come over to his table I was with my friend Baron to whom I wanted to show off my new girlfriend The French guard came over to say good evening to the company I noticed an exchange of glances The evening wore on I went looking for Véron who said he wanted to talk to me We escorted the honorable family home Véron followed us we went into a café He asked me if it was true that I was seeing this girl and I ought to know that she belonged to the French guard and that in exchange for forty écus he would sell her to me that Chénier had been obliged to act that way and that was the way most of the girls of the faubourg were bought and sold I told him if that's how it is my friend no living person will ever get money out of me for a French guard's leftovers

We went to pass the night at the market Since I was wearing my sword Du Rocher arrested me Telling him that I was a deputy-brigadier fireman did no good in spite of everything they carted me off in a wagon and took me to Inspector Rochebrune[176] who gave me a tongue-lashing that a fireman should be brought to him at such an hour what if something happened And I went off but it caused me a lot of trouble and I had to run around to get my sword back It was on that fine evening that I saw and said farewell to that charming family for the last time

I continued going to the faubourg Saint-Antoine and doing fireworks and working with my brother-in-law but since I was getting nowhere and we were spending everything we earned I left him and went back to work for one of my former bosses a fellow by the name of Jerome One night on

---

110 grenadiers. Their blue jackets with red decorations and red trousers and stockings were a fixture of the Paris landscape, because the royal government used them to police the city. They were quartered on city residents until 1770. At that time work began on barracks at La Pépinière, Nouvelle France, Babylone, La Courtille, Brocas, Lorraine, Verte Penthièvre, and Popincourt. From guardhouse headquarters they patrolled day and night after 1765. The guards were largely responsible for maintaining order in the city, which they did with a heavy hand. Their tactics were governed by the doctrine of securing the bridges and the faubourgs. The guards became involved in numerous conflicts with the population of the city, conflicts immortalized in songs and posters. That they joined the Revolution in 1789 was due mainly to disaffection with their own officers and to the leadership of a few.

[176] Commissaire de police of the Saint-Paul section, rue Geoffroy-l'Asnier. See Jèze, *Tableau de Paris*, p. 107.

the way back from a celebration at Charonne with a quite nice young
widow I was taking back to my room on passing the rue Saint-Germain
we heard a vague noise We stopped It was a priest's cassock and under-
wear one of those hypocrites had debauched a tailor's wife Under the veil
of religion and confession those humbugs impress the weaker sex which
believes their words and all their chimeras The tailor having found his
wife in the arms of the god-carrier of Saint-Germain had thrashed them
both soundly and to give himself more room had thrown all their things
out the window He [i.e., the priest] was obliged to return home naked as
he deserved Since he lived in the cloister and was therefore one of my
neighbors a sympathetic fellow lent him a frock coat and in that sad state
he returned home He died three days later from the blows he had received
and from the shame of having been found out That gave me pause In the
rue des Mathurins too

But I was no longer afraid of anything I took my game to the chamber
of conquests Since I had no neighbors I enjoyed perfect freedom Some
time later I learned that my brother-in-law had left his shop and that my
sister had taken a position as chambermaid in a convent called La Roquette[177] We lost touch for a time (I) tried as usual to keep up relations
with all my girls at night I went for supper at the Cadet Buteux or at
Mother Chapon's in Nouvelle France or at the Faucheur I was very well
known and always in good company

One day while on the way up to Nouvelle France with some friends a
drunk who was passing alongside Saint Anne's Chapel picked up an iron
collar and put it around his neck saying What a nice necklace I picked up
a nail and drove it home with my hammer The fellow started shouting as
loud as he could we laughed and got out of there Nobody was willing to
take it off The guards arrived and refused to lay hands on it somebody
said it was a glazier (who did it) and who goes every day to Mother
Chapon's A detachment was sent By chance (I) happened to be in the
kitchen they came into the gardens saw Bussie with his glazier's apron and
took him away even though he had no idea what they were talking about
not having been with me He was forced to free the man from his collar

---

177 A convent of Sisters of Saint Joseph since 1690, La Roquette received guests in private
rooms for 400 livres as well as in dormitories. An institution serving old women, it was
transformed into a prison in the nineteenth century. The buildings were located in the area
bounded by the rue du Chemin-Vert, the rue de la Folie-Regnaut, the rue Mercœur, and the
rue Popincourt in the faubourg Saint-Antoine.

They took him to the inspector He defended himself he said it wasn't him his mistress had followed him I said to my friends Let's go somewhere else and a good thing too because since I had been fingered the cops came back looking for me on orders of the inspector

My sweet flower girl came looking for me They told her I had left She ran into Bussie's girl She told her what had happened All three of them went looking for us and found us at the Vache Noire in the rue Cadet He grumbled We were joking Since he was made of good stuff I said to him Go on my friend if anything like this ever happens to you I'll go in your place The women got hot went at each other argued they started swearing at each other We calmed them down I told them that on the same street where I'd pulled this trick there was a woman of stone (?) and that on the way back I'd show them that women in general are not worth much because this woman that they called the headless woman (?) she killed a drunk and that it was because of that that I put him [i.e., this other drunk] in the collar for fear that this woman although sleeping on the ground he would come caress her like the other one did that she killed and that she might have turned on him and that maybe I had prevented a great misfortune Finally our good spirts returned and (we) laughed about what happened and promised ourselves not to wear our hammers and aprons any more And on the way back (I) showed them the headless woman

One Sunday on the way to see Baron in the faubourg Saint-Antoine in the company of my friend Gombeaut we went all the way to the forest of Vincennes Upon making our way into the brush we found a human nest a young man and a young female really going at it He had taken the precaution of sticking his bare sword into the ground alongside him I said these words Be fruitful and multiply Since we had by chance interrupted him in this human activity he swore up and down at us Gombeaut was foolish enough to throw himself on his sword and we made him repent for his insolence because both of us hopped on the body of the young girl whom we didn't give any time to get herself together and the fool didn't dare come near us We made fun of him as we thanked the young lady for her cooperation and when we had gone off a little distance tossed him his sword because we looked out for each other

A few days earlier while drinking we said to each other We are great friends but we ought to be brothers But our funds were lacking We both sold our silver shoe buckles and moved in for the night with a woman Then we said to each other Now we're twins in the same family

Since I still had a boat that I lent to friends for fishing and outings a cousin of his by the name of Darthuy came to see me who was a glazier and worked on the king's fireworks (He) came to see me at my shop saying that if I wanted to make some money the police had thrown into the river opposite the first grating thirty-odd cases that had been in the water tower opposite the Palais-Royal and that a laborer working there had set fire to one which had broken half the windows on the rue Saint-Honoré I joked with him asking him if he wanted to make the (other) glaziers of Paris rich that in any case he should wait until I was established He told me that he had had a ball commanding in the field and that he went shooting in the park of Chantilly I told him we had to worry about the police but that we would pull them [i.e., the cases of gunpowder] out of the water at night and that one of my friends was discreet and a good diver so we went right off to look for him We found him it was my friend Lenoir we agreed on three livres for each of us

We chose a night when it was very dark Lenoir knew almost exactly where it was After diving for a while he found the spot With a rope and a hook we pulled them out of the water by the attached rings and I had a long crook that reached to the bottom where Lenoir raised himself up And we pulled out twenty-seven of them with great difficulty and a lot of worry about the police Finally before daybreak we brought my boat up under the Samaritaine and stayed until dawn pretending to be fishing Then the son of the guardian of the Samaritaine came looking for us And we asked him the secret and hid them until the following night so that we could unload them either at the Marion Arch[178] or else down at the Pont Royal At lunch Darthuy said he could only give us thirty sols apiece We told him that he was breaking his promise but in any case he could take them and we split up

We went to see a fellow named Lefebvre a fireworks dealer on the quai de la Ferraille and spoke to him about the boxes He told us that he would indeed pay three livres apiece and a good snack or lunch if we could fish them out and bring them to the port of Saint-Cloud We told him that we had them in our possession He told us to leave immediately and (we) brought them to Saint-Cloud with our friends and ate well and received

---

178 An arcade below the quai de la Mégisserie that gave access to the Seine and bore the name of a woman who kept a bathhouse and brothel in the sixteenth century. Water drained here from a horse trough and fountain used by water bearers, and the spot was a meeting ground and place of adventure.

our money which kept us amused and helped us to mock Darthuy whose plans were frustrated because he had not kept his word

We became friendly with the son of the guardian of the Samaritaine His father was one of those fellows who for a bottle of wine is your friend and since we were from the neighborhood we quickly got to know each other He had a daughter who had the reputation of being chaste and (I) took to seeing them and let them know that I planned to settle down I had the idea of going to my father to talk about it This young girl suited me well We went several times to Belleville or Ménilmontant accompanied by the father or the brother because her mother was dead

She had an aunt to whose home she said she often went to sleep This dear aunt lived in the rue Saint-Victor I had once been to her house with the young woman's brother Since I was in the neighborhood I went to the Maison-Blanche[179] after visiting the aunt who had not seen her for some time I found the young lady at table with some grenadiers of the guard I stationed myself at a table where I could see without being seen but from which I could hear a part of their conversation which I found not very amusing but quite instructive One of the grenadiers was telling her that he didn't care what she did that he had another lady friend and that he was going to spend the night with her that as for his comrades every man had his girl He didn't care what she did and all expressed in the grenadier manner and she had to pay her own share I was in a rage and didn't know what I might do when I heard them mention the little fireman without mincing their words

They went off leaving the young lady and ironically bidding her adieu I quickly finished my wine and as it was night I followed her closely and a good thing I did because she was feeling desperate She made a wide detour crossed the bridge at La Tournelle measured the heights of the bridges I followed her closely seeing that she made a gesture I went up to her I said Poor girl what are you going to do She recognized me she wanted to run I took her by the arm She told me that she wasn't worthy of my attention I reassured her I took her to a café

She wanted to keep back from me what I already knew She made her confession taking it slowly She told me that she had made the acquaintance of this grenadier when he was on guard duty at the Pont-Neuf that he took advantage of her that he took her to a room and she told people

---

[179] Hamlet on the road to Gentilly in Fontainebleau (beyond the present-day place d'Italie). It boasted a chapel and a way-station inn.

that she was sleeping at her aunt's that he was a monster and that the only thing to do because she saw clearly from everything I had said that I had heard everything and that the easiest way out was to throw herself into the water I consoled her I asked her if she was embarrassed She answered no and I said to her You're not the first woman to whom this has happened

I took her to my room We had supper together and I didn't have to pay forty écus to have the leftovers of a French guard but I did receive a gift that required me to put water in my wine[180] She was as submissive and apologetic as could be and we patched ourselves up with treatment provided by my friend Baron In spite of my other girlfriends I added her to my collection of sultanesses But the proverb is not false Can't stop at one drop he who has tasted of the forbidden fruit will taste again That's what happened to her She went back to her grenadier and so became the sort of woman who wants a lover of that ilk

Her brother one day while I was on my way to fetch my boat for an outing with Chenier whose wife had just gone and died from an excess of pleasure told me that I was responsible for his sister's dishonor I answered him angrily The father arrived They said they were going to throw me into the river I challenged them Our dukes went up and we were going at it when I said You and your father wouldn't dare go up against the French guard who debauched your sister while I kept her from drowning herself Chenier spoke up We agreed to go get her and snatch her back from the grenadier We went to the Maison-Blanche we didn't find her So we went to the Moulin de la Pointe[181] The first thing we see is Dulcinea he grabs hold of her The father insults the grenadier he takes her away We separate after I tell them that tomorrow I want an explanation with her present and we say good-bye

We went toward the Hospital expecting to find Gombeaut and our friends but fortune was against us Madame la Police broke up our household and forced us to separate He [Gombeaut?] came to tell me that the police lieutenant had taken an interest in our amours He was reeling

---

[180] Ménétra has caught another dose of syphilis, which he refers to earlier as "a gift." "Putting water in his wine" is his way of describing the course of treatment he follows, which involves keeping calm and avoiding excitement as well as taking various mercury-based remedies.

[181] On the road from Paris to Vaugirard, the mill marked the southern extremity of the region under the jurisdiction of the abbey of Sainte-Geneviève. At this time there were numerous mills in the environs of Paris, and many of the millers kept cabarets and *guinguettes*.

After drinking a few glasses of wine he left us despite our pleas We went looking for some little fish and when Chenier became lost in thought so did I Since love and friendship had never been my obsessions but only pleasure the bottle made me forget everything While we were sitting there three people arrived and asked to sit down at our table They were three *calotais*[182] from the Salpêtrière[183] two nice girls and a boy they called Balthazar all three brought up in the house Balthazar after drinking a few glasses went off as he was gravedigger for the house

We made eyes at (the girls) we struck up a conversation Chenier went to get four pigeons (and) some salad We bought them drinks The time passed the gate was closed They said that they had been out late before and that they slept at the home of a laundress in the rue de Lourcine Chenier said to me in argot that we should take them back to his place They couldn't walk any more they were out of their heads We took a cab quick coachman the Saint-Germain cloister When we got there we gave them food and drink we split up and each of us spent the night as he could When they woke up sober one girl called out to the other They answered each other they were dumbfounded We had lunch their fear subsided They talked about their house We told them that we were itinerant merchants and that they would tend our shop because Chenier had very good lodgings and in his front room there was a nice shop

He sent his apprentice to the shop which was in the passage Saint-Germain and meanwhile I went to look for provisions and to meet the boy from the Samaritaine He had put the girl in a place under the Pont-Neuf where he kept pigeons They went looking for her I made her confess that it was the grenadier who had debauched her and that I despite her faults had tried to dissuade her from doing anything rash after the scene she had with him at the Maison-Blanche that she had wanted to jump from the bridge of La Tournelle and that thinking to cure what her mistakes had caused I had had her treated by a surgeon friend of mine I held back the

---

[182] *Calotais*: the term is not used in police documents. It might be a misspelling of *calotins* (priests), but since it refers to two young girls and a boy it cannot mean the Salpêtrière clergy. In any case, only very young boys were admitted to the Salpêtrière.

[183] The Salpêtrière and the Hôpital were charitable institutions that accepted young girls for correction or imprisonment. Inmates wore gray frocks. In 1789 there were nearly 10,000 of them. Young boys abandoned by their parents or found begging were interned at La Pitié. There they received an elementary education and were put to work. The term "l'Hôpital" sometimes refers to the "general hospital," i.e., the administrative and religious organization that included, from 1656, La Pitié, La Salpêtrière, Bicêtre, and several other houses for which the headquarters was La Pitié. For Paris, this was the institution of the *grand renfermement*.

rest of the story because they were in such a lather that they might well
have forced me to take a drink from the reservoir I was sorry I had been
foolish enough to come alone I might well have paid for the grenadier
And I left on pretty good terms and never tried to see her again She ended
up the way any individual who goes with a soldier must end up She died
while taking the remedies[184] and that was a shame because she was nice
but she was defenseless and ripe for ravishing

I went back to Chenier's and found the two chicks playing the busybody
(and) making the beds that they and we had unmade during the night I
had run into my father who had seen me all dressed up (and) who asked
me if I wasn't working and (said) that he couldn't imagine that he saw me
every day in new clothes I didn't tell him that I sold my suit to get
another just as I did with a mistress

We spent the day and the night more familiarly but the next day they
got to be a burden and we decided to get rid of them I took the job upon
myself When night fell I told them that we would be going out for
supper Chenier went first after many detours I went into a fruitseller's
shop to buy some salad that one girl put in her apron to the other I gave a
four-pound loaf of bread and at the door of a cabaret I told them to go in
that my friend was waiting for us and that (I) was going to go look for a
dead sparrow And so I left them and offered them my final farewell and
(I) went to rejoin Chenier who was waiting for me in another place a long
way away and (we) never heard of those girls again because I had thoroughly confused them

I went to work for Jerome Since I was working by the day that didn't
bother me much and being a fireman we had made our arrangements
together While at work the members of the jury[185] came for an inspection

---

[184] Syphilis was treated at Bicêtre, which accepted sick prisoners, mainly women transferred from the Salpêtrière and voluntary patients admitted by the *bureau de l'hôpital* on
recommendation of the lieutenant of police. There were some 1,000 patients in 1765 and
2,000 in 1789. Treatments known as *grands remèdes* lasted six weeks to two months. These
included rest, a strict diet, bleeding and enemas, baths over a ten-day period, and rubdowns
with mercury compounds over the entire body which were intended to cause sweating and
salivation. These basic techniques of humoralist medicine were supplemented with religious
cures: weekly confession, masses, and sermons. A majority of patients left the hospital cured
after a suitable period of convalescence during which they received nourishing bouillon.
Many memoirs and reports attest to the bad reputation of this hospital for venereal diseases
and its staff.

[185] In each guild the masters elected wardens (*jurés* or *gardes*) responsible for overall
administration and for enforcement of guild statutes and regulations. The glaziers elected two

and said to me But Sir you are a master you owe your inspection fee I will give it to you They gave me a receipt I said to them Now you won't skip my turn Saint Mark's day is coming and if I don't take part in the nomination of the jury I'll have the election nullified because you've already skipped my turn They were annoyed that they'd asked me for the inspection fee so they didn't forget me and (I) was the dean of youth for the nomination of two jury members

I went to see my father and asked him for a hundred francs that he was holding from what my grandmother had left me He told me that he could not give me the money I told him that I wanted a new suit of clothes for the glazier's feast day He told me then that if I wanted to go to a tailor who owed him money that was all he could do and (I) took him at his word because I knew the old man So I got a gray suit that was all I got out of the property of my mother and my grandmother and I was lucky to get it because my father had always been tightfisted with me (although) with his daughters he was quite generous particularly the younger one

Gombeaut and I were practically inseparable and we were careful to send our nuns what they wanted While having lunch at pointe Saint-Eustache I saw the fellow who had traveled with me from the Cévennes to Lyons come in I called him by name He answered that that was indeed his last name but that he didn't know me and that he had never been in that part of the world Not being very subtle I insisted that I was not mistaken A glance from the person with whom he was drinking raised my suspicions I said that he was wearing a wig His comrade said he'd been wearing it for about two years He turned red As there were a lot people drinking in the room who were listening to what we were saying one of them who looked like a gay dog said I bet six francs worth of drink that

---

wardens every year on the day after Saint Mark's. Wardens were required to have ten years' experience as masters and to have been masters of the confraternity; in addition, "in order to avoid disorder, no *maître de lettre* may attend meetings or be named a warden, except those over sixty and other well-known senior masters (*anciens*)." This passage shows us clearly what Ménétra's status was: his only rights were to pay his dues and to vote for wardens. The wardens visited masters' shops ten times a year to see that the rules were being obeyed, and on each visit they collected six sols. Not only for Ménétra but also for liberal observers of the economic scene, the meddlesome wardens embodied the conservatism of the whole guild system. Ménétra's text is obscure, however, when it comes to the manner in which the glaziers' guild elected its wardens. His words cannot have meant that he expected to have a turn as a warden, given the statutes; perhaps he meant simply his turn to elect wardens. The position of "dean of youth" (*doyen des jeunes*) is not mentioned in the statutes or in such scattered remains of the guild archives as have survived. See also n. 17.

this guy is an escapee from Marseilles[186] and that he is branded with a stamp of the city His comrade also put up six francs for the sake of appearances and it was agreed that he would have to bare his shoulders But my man made himself scarce and by his carelessness he was recognized by all the old-clothes men as a fellow who had learned to write with a twenty-five foot pen and a bottomless inkwell And if he hadn't denied knowing me we would have had a drink and that would have been the end of it And he wouldn't have been found out

One Sunday with Gombeaut we went to Charonne to a cabaret called the Table de Pierre at the top of the avenue de Vincennes I saw my brother-in-law in the company of that young widow with whom I had lost touch She turned scarlet He said to me Brother I know you you don't hold it against me She got up and took me aside You know my misfortunes if we had stayed together I would be what I was in the past I told her that I was in no way the cause of her misfortunes and after a few comments about what she had just said I was finished One got up too soon the other too early let's drop it As for this widow (says he) I took her over because you'd stopped seeing her I told him You don't have to worry on that score you know me I've never been jealous in love but honest to a fault He told me he was waiting for Baron and they were starting to do fireworks again and that he had some already to fire off And I told him The only thing that bothers me is that in the family they're going to be saying it was me who procured the girl for you especially my sister whose character I know

I said good-bye to them when Baron and his wife arrived they were a bit surprised and obliged us to stay He said Bah we'll go have a good time tonight at the market I'll tell them I have a patient in town and we'll have a good time Anyway it was true that you saw all the revelers of Paris of boths sexes in all those cafés and every table was a show and he shared my taste for watching and listening

The evening went tolerably well The spectators found the fireworks superb but the tavern keepers were upset One flare had accidentally been

---

[186] The reference is to a man who has escaped from the prison galleys of Marseilles and who bears the tattoo applied to those sentenced to the galleys. The expression "learned to write with a twenty-five foot pen" means that he had learned to row, and the "bottomless inkwell" is of course the sea. Note that the escapee is recognized by dealers in secondhand goods, many of whom also received stolen goods and worked for the police as informers.

put under a canopy[187] it blew it away which made a very nice effect but then we saw the damages So I told the story of the bomb we had exploded at Notre-Dame-des-Vertus at cousin Chenier's for his wife's feast He'd had a canopy set up at the far end of the garden which cost him more than forty écus and through the carelessness of a fellow named Grandin who without orders set off some flares and firecrackers we had put aside the whole canopy was blown away

All present yelled bravo but seeing the damage I left unceremoniously Baron and Bourlier said they would never go back there and the tavern keeper got the tools that they left behind

We made a pact Baron came to meet us at the Grève and took all three of us by the arm while passing under the Port-Paris next to the iron bar in the middle I spotted a watch Since I was on the outside I picked it up They saw me only out of the corners of their eyes Gombeaut said You picked something up I stammered They want to see It's a watch We reveled until morning We sold it for forty-five livres We had lunch at the Veau qui Tète we met Chenier there with the two daughters of Pinard the pork butcher in my father's street We divided the spoils each of us had about fifteen francs left We split up with a promise to meet again that night at the Petit Charonne

I stayed with Chenier and his two companions who were restaurant whores We spent part of the day at the Veau qui Tète and the Pantoufle We went to the meeting we had a good time Chenier took his two tarts who never left his side especially the older one whom he hadn't altogether put down I saw little of him because he was too attached and he didn't see anything (?) I criticized him He got angry and (I) saw him only when he was in prison for debt (?) He let me know I ran over there He had that time to get away despite the surveillance of his watchdogs I hid him in my room A woman who did business on the quays was mixed up in his business with my help she got them out He couldn't stay in private keep[188] he wanted to go see his father-in-law to try to fulfill the dead woman's contract

---

[187] *Berceau* (literally, cradle) here refers to the vault of leaves formed by rows of trees that provided shade for people who came to drink in the cabarets.

[188] *En charte privée:* refers to a person held in detention in other than a public prison and not under the authority of the regular courts. The criminal ordinance of 1670 outlawed the practice. The reference here must be interpreted to mean a person held by the courts and threatened with imprisonment at the behest of his or her family.

Later we found four guys to go with us in case we ran into trouble At the first grating past the Louvre we spotted police game[189] We crossed the water We watched them take their department (?) some took the Pont-Neuf the others the pont Royal others got into skiffs We crossed and recrossed We got them all balled up mocking them and calling them stoolpigeons Seeing that they were still following us I went looking for my boat The kid from the Samaritaine came with me They all climbed in and it was good-bye coppers

Finally one day Pinard's daughter came to tell me that Chenier had been arrested at his house by order of the King that his father had obtained it and he was at Fort l'Evêque[190] I went to see him He told me that on the confinement order and the petition filed by his father he was described as a young man in need of correction who was to be sent for guard duty at the Château Gaillardin I went looking for my father who was a friend of his [i.e., of Chenier's father—trans.] A bottle got me the whole secret I had a petition drawn up in which I showed that the lieutenant of police had been deceived about his [i.e., Chenier's] age that his father had no further authority over him since he was married The police lieutenant gave old Chenier a tongue-lashing[191]

Through connections with a client of Jerome's we got him released He enlisted in the French guards he said to get back at his mother-in-law He sold everything and lived with this woman who was a merchant and in the end over my objections having lived with her he went ahead and married her We lost touch for three or four months He had repented but his time

[189] *Gibiers de la police*: refers here either to the guards or, more likely, to informers working for police inspectors. Recruited mainly from the jails and from Bicêtre and La Salpêtrière and modestly called "observers," some of them became under-inspectors; they were found at all levels of society. Here we see an example of the working man's irony: the hunter becomes the hunted, the "police game."

[190] A prison used by the episcopal courts until 1674, at which time Louis XIV abolished the private courts and it became a royal prison. It held prisoners incarcerated on the authority of a *lettre de cachet* as well as debtors arrested upon demand of their creditors. In the 1750s it held fewer than 250 inmates, 31 of them on orders of the king and 48 for debt. Fort l'Evêque also held actors interned on orders of the First Gentleman of the Bedchamber. The building, located between the rue Saint-Germain-l'Auxerrois and the quai de la Mégisserie, was demolished in 1783. The expression "château Gaillardin" is not confirmed by other sources; it may be a Parisianism for the old episcopal fortress. In the fifteenth century there was a château Gaillard which dominated the Seine from its Left Bank and constituted the fortified portion of the hôtel de Nesle, demolished in 1655. Perhaps the name was carried over to the Right Bank.

[191] *Donner une perruque*: literally, to give a wig, meant to scold someone roundly.

had run out It was written that he would be initiated like most of the bourgeois of Paris inscribed in the great register[192]

One day I was sent to a fire in the rue des Gravilliers opposite the rue des Vertus The fire had started in the third floor rear (and) had reached the stairway when a bourgeois said to me Save me in the front of my secretary are papers that contain my entire fortune You will find bags of silver they are yours but save my papers I went up even though the fire was in the staircase I broke through two fireplaces with a rope and an axe I said to my comrades if anybody wants to come with me Nobody followed I entered the room I knocked down the wall and threw the papers into the street two heavy sacks of silver followed Just in time because two minutes later the floor collapsed I had hooked my rope to the balcony and a good thing too and I slid down I told the inspector there was nothing more to worry about to turn on the pump to drown the two floors that had fallen one on top of the other.

A grocer came and took my arm to offer me refreshment and the fellow whose papers I had saved couldn't thank me enough gave me six louis which I shared with my comrades given that they were only cobblers and saddlers good for sewing up the hoses or pumping water or working the nozzles[193]

One morning while working with the glazier Jerome a woman came looking for me to measure a window pane I went in I took the measure-ment she told me to come back right away I came set the pane they asked me the price they said come get your money There was a woman on a bed When I came near her she grabbed me by the neck squeezed with all her might shouted kissed me bit me I tried to get out of there when three women who were looking on burst out laughing as loud as they could I heard another noise a small voice crying Gnet gnet I was released I fled and never had any desire to go back I came to the shop I told my story A woman brought me twenty-four sols for drink (she) couldn't keep from laughing nor could I promising myself never to be taken like that again

One evening Turkey Lenoir came to visit This was a nickname we gave him because not a week went by when he didn't make us eat one being a roaster by profession as when we were young little urchins our rallying

---

[192] *Inscrit sur le grand rôle:* can be taken as a joke, meaning all men are mortal or destined to deceit.

[193] *Flageolet.*

cry when we played police captain was crash! [*patatras*] by allusion to my name [i.e., Ménétra] Lenoir said to me My friend I'm in a position to win four louis I thought of you in connection with this plan The thing is I've got to hurl myself third into the river from the fourth arch I told him You can go look for somebody else You misunderstand he said it's to fish me out with your boat in case I don't drown myself (First) it will be my dog and then a log and after that I'll hurl myself I made this wager with some people of distinction

With that we left I took the son of the guardian of the Samaritaine and at five thirty we saw our man arrive We unmoored our boat and went out into the river He climbed out on the edge of the bridge he threw a log teased his dog and seeing that he hesitated pushed him in and he at the same moment holding himself stiff jumped feet first and not as I had supposed head first He was in front of us fished himself out and reached the flag of the Four Nations[194] as the river was very high At a tavern (he) was already drinking when a servant arrived and gave him the four louis and (we) went to use up part of it with a meal at the Gros Caillou we went back upstream in my boat (and) had a revel as long as the funds held out

And afterward (I) went back to work One day having lunch with Turkey at the Trois Maures at the carrefour des Trois Maries[195] I felt the urge to eat some salted fish Lenoir said I'll go get some He returned with old man Pinard who was very friendly to me who told me that he was unhappy with his daughters and that he was going to be forced to lock them up that the mother took their side and the elder one was running after Chenier and the younger one adopted the principles of the elder We parted good friends I ran into the younger Pinard girl We went into a place I told her briefly how things stood She promised to meet me in my room on Sunday morning She did not fail to keep her word and so she was initiated into my family with a promise to come at the same time every Sunday and holiday to visit me

I went to visit Gombeaut's mistress who was charming She lived in the rue Sainte-Croix-de-la-Bretonnerie I found her alone I played a thou-

---

[194] College founded by Mazarin in 1661 for selected students from the nobility of Italy, Alsace, Flanders, and Roussillon. The buildings, completed by Le Vau in 1683 on either side of a central chapel, comprised housing for resident students, libraries, etc. Now the home of the Institut.

[195] Opposite the end of the Pont-Neuf, this square was at the intersection of the old rue de la Monnalie, the quai de l'Ecole, and the quai de la Mégisserie.

sand tricks with her Gombeaut was at the door listening (he) knocked brusquely walked in said some hard words to me as well as to the young lady (and) hurled himself at me We scrapped and I left That made me see that jealousy is a disease that those who are afflicted by it forget their best friends He was so angry after beating the girl up that he enlisted So I wished him bon voyage and lots of bravery and docility when we parted without rancor And I saw him off

Since I was living with a master in the rue de Charenton who was not a master of Paris[196] he didn't dare work in the city and through me he undertook to do several buildings without risk of being caught That angered the jury which came one day to the corner of the rue des Deux-Ecus with the bailiff accompanied by the inspector to confiscate all the glass on the site I told the master to stay away and they paid for their naiveté because I let them think I was doing the job on my own account So he became more enterprising and I reaped the benefits

One holiday after dinner while walking at Courtille[197] with my boss we went into the Bois Fontaine where we found several companions who had known me Immediately we sat down A Vannois said to me Parisian a fellow from Bordeaux is coming who knows you quite well he says he made part of his tour of France with you hey there he is now After the first glasses of wine I told this Vannois and the Bayonnais to ask if he knew this Parisian that he had told them so much about He told them that he knew him very well and that he was not so great a worker as he would have people think that he had known him in Avignon and Lyons and (he)

---

[196] The faubourg Saint-Antoine was then, along with the cour du Temple, the enclosures of Saint-Germain-des-Prés and Saint-Martin-des-Champs, and several other places, a place where work was not subject to guild regulations. This immunity stemmed from the fact that labor regulations were originally seigneurial, promulgated in this case by the abbaye Saint-Antoine. The guilds of Paris naturally fought to limit these exemptions, taking it upon themselves to inspect shops in these areas—a right whose exercise sometimes proved dangerous. Ménétra is here playing a double game: his letters gave him the right to practice his trade in Paris, and he used this right to front for a colleague from the exempt faubourg, yet he did not set himself up in business in the faubourg, because doing so would have lost him the rights conferred by his master's certificate, as must have been the case with his brother-in-law.

[197] La Courtille was located on the slopes of Belleville, on either side of the village, beyond the customs gates. It was dotted with vineyards, gardens, fields, and copses, amid which *guinguettes* proliferated. Along with Les Porcherons, Nouvelle France, Petite Pologne, La Plaine de Grenelle, Le Moulin de Javel, Vaugirard, Gentilly, La Rapée, Charonne, Le Gros Caillou, Ménilmontant, and Pré Saint-Gervais, it was one of the high spots of popular recreation, both during the week and on weekends. During carnival time La Courtille was the scene of nonstop festivities.

said a lot of unpleasant things about me Then I said to him So you know this Parisian well do you my friends and I know him well You are from Bordeaux you are the son of Piton you pretend that your father is (a) rich man who goes around with a walking stick with a golden apple on top Listen friends he's bluffing you everything he's telling you is a lie So you see you're a liar there he is said the Vannois this Parisian go on he's doing well he doesn't recognize you and get out of here we don't want an impostor like you in our company And he left followed by a volley of catcalls And since then the companions have invited me to visit them and (said) they would always be pleased to have me join them and I went from time to time I was always welcome

One Monday on my way to meet them I saw at the first barrier five or six apprentice wine merchants accompanying a glazier whom I knew quite well One of these apprentices said to me Ménétra here's one of your colleagues whom we're going to turn over to the guard I pretended I didn't know him I asked him what it was all about He told me that he had four tin plates in the pocket of his apron I said to them What are you doing You're going to ruin a man who has a wife and children give him a few good kicks in the ass and beat him up a bit and let him go Some were willing Others wanted to turn him over to the police I pointed out that they would waste their whole day My arguments convinced them One of the guys who was holding him gave him a couple of punches that hit home They all gave him a few kicks in the ass He ran and my men were content We went into a grocer's I bought a round of drinks and was satisfied

I learned that Bussie was in the Grand Meudon[198] for battery I went to see him accompanied by three comrades We consoled him we drank we had a good time One of my friends who had never been in this place where the innocent mingle with the guilty asked me when we were above the yard who those people were down there I explained by putting my hand into one of my comrades' pockets A cousin of his[199] who saw me when I took out my handkerchief took it (and) put it in the pocket of his apron I forgot about it We went out onto the quai de la Ferraille holding

---

[198] Grand Meudon: there is nothing to explain the meaning of this phrase. For battery Bussie could only have been sent to the Grand Châtelet. There was, however, the hôpital des Petites Maisons for the insane in the rue de Sèvres or chemin de Meudon and Ménétra may have identified the two places, or perhaps he is amusing himself with a pun on château de Meudon, a royal estate.

[199] A cousin, in other words a pickpocket of the same sort as those imprisoned below. Ménétra spotted the pickpocket in the act.

my comrade by the arm I looked around to see which way we should go when I spotted my man who had gone up an alley and was trying to sell my handkerchief to a fence Anger took hold of me I grabbed the handkerchief and punched him so hard that there was blood all over his face Some guys I didn't know jumped me They wouldn't listen to reason they took me in spite of my resistance to police headquarters I explained my reasons The guy with the broken jaw had gotten away The inspector told me to restrain myself and said that I should have turned the fellow over to the police And (we) went to spend the rest of the day at Vaugirard where I knew the daughter of a dancing master and when we could find the time we danced together

I was on somewhat better terms with my father who was always asking me to come back to work for him my young sisters often asked me to And (I) always refused despite my father's repeated urgings that he was getting old and that I would take over the shop on terms that I didn't want to hear One Sunday my father invited me to lunch I went looking for salted fish I went to the Pinard woman She said to me Unless I'm mistaken it's Ménétra Her young daughter (who) was with her at the counter put a finger to her mouth Her father spotted it and said to me Believe me don't go hunting so close to home because I won't be as easy as my colleague Duru who was the pork butcher next door to my father (and) whose wife had been nice to me and whose brother was chaplain at the Châtelet I told him that he was always thinking like a man with horns and I left promising myself (to) keep it in mind because the mother was worth more than her two daughters

Time went by I had even almost forgotten when one Sunday on leaving my apartment I ran into old lady Pinard with a book under her arm She stared at me I said hello to her She told me she was going to mass I answered that I had received a good sermon from her husband She told me that I shouldn't pay any attention that she did as she pleased and was mistress of her desires So I said to her if that's the way it is would you like to go have a little something to drink in my room She made some objections as all women do but I was not fooled She came up We took care of things She was satisfied promised to come often to hear mass in the same way We agreed on the hour so there would be no mistake all for fear of running into her younger daughter whom she suspected of coming to visit me though I denied it as well as several of my other acquaintances

One day I went to buy a slice of ham and by chance found the older daughter behind the counter She asked for news of Chenier I told her that if she wanted to know how things were with him that in less than an hour I would be in my room and I would satisfy her She signaled yes she kept me waiting finally she arrived Since I knew she had a sweet tooth I served some biscuits and wine We talked I told her that Chenier had completely forgotten about her but that she could avenge herself After the usual fuss she acquiesced like her dear mother and her younger sister promising to come often for a good time especially on Sundays and holidays So each of the three had her appointed hour

Since my indulgence was not excessive Pinard generally kept a stone face One night passing in front of the shop I tapped the mother's arm with the tip of a cane I had not noticed that he was in the alley[200] opposite making water He saw me ran over like a madman took me by the collar I asked him if he was joking He answered no I tripped him and punched him We fell on top of one another A fellow named Patouflet separated us who was a wigmaker and neighbor (and) took me to drink at the Trois Maures He [i.e., Pinard] came in like a lion He said it was me who had turned his entire household upside down that not content to have debauched his daughters I had stolen his wife's honor and that for some time now she had behaved at home like a devil toward him and his daughters

During this diatribe I was laughing I teased him I offered him a glass of wine He said that if he accepted it would be to throw it in my face I told him I wouldn't allow that Lenoir arrived He tried to reconcile us but only made us more bitter He said he was going to club me I told him that when I was hit I hit back So I said to him Since you boast how fearsome you are you were a soldier Let's go Turkey said he would go find us two broom sticks I refused I wanted to fight with white arms [i.e., with fists—trans.] Finally I agreed and there we were alongside the river in the Jardin de l'Infante I defended myself because he was more muscular Suddenly he struck me a blow in the stomach with the tip of his stick Everyone watching shouted that this was a low blow At the same moment I struck him on the wrist and with equal agility on the arm I dislocated his wrist

---

[200] Alleys were important parts of Paris houses. Generally located on the side because house façades had only two or three bays of windows, but sometimes in the center, the alley led to the staircase and courtyard. It was a strategic spot, guarded by the principal (and often sole) tenant, the artisan or shopkeeper who lived on the ground floor. Alleys were locked at ten or eleven o'clock at night.

I threw away the broom stick and went off with Lenoir when the guard came to arrest us He [i.e., Pinard] had been scoundrel enough to denounce me to the police I was forced to sell my room and my boat and to hole up with one of my girlfriends who lived in the rue Verdret I wrote to Sieur Morat commander of the fire brigade about what had happened to me and (said) that I was going to lie low until things blew over

I got some things together The suit that had come to me from my grandmother's legacy and many other effects I put them into a chest and had them brought to the home of my friend Baron whom I went to see and (I) left for Sceaux-du-Maine to stay with a good man who had married the widow Morel I stayed with him part of the autumn and winter often going out with the good vine growers to work on their vines and frequently working in the surrounding region I went to Fontenay-aux-Roses where I had a friend the son of the butcher who was named Fleury who was a friendly young fellow He introduced me to a little brunette who carried fruits to Paris in her wagon and (I) often took advantage of the round-trip transportation to go to Paris

One day I met a fellow named Ferand a companion glazier who told me that M Vilmont had been asking for me but hadn't been able to find out where I was and that he heard that I was still on the tour of France that he had a hundred and twenty street lanterns to make and that if I wanted to go I would be warmly welcomed I went and he was very happy I went to work making lanterns for him at fifty sols apiece I ran into my brother-in-law who had fallen on hard times I told him to come work with me and gave him twenty sols per day and fed him and (I) took him every night to the *barrière Blanche*[201] where I had a young widow who sold wine and stew Every day dinner was waiting for me It was in this period that I liked to get my brother-in-law drunk and watch him spill his drink all the way home along a street that was not yet paved

M Vilmont had furnished a room for me in the rue Saint-Louis where the warehouse in which I made the lanterns was located and his shop was in the rue du Verbois I was completely free to entertain my girlfriends I made inquiries about the Pinard family It was a mess The mother had gone in one direction the daughters in another An infection had devel-

---

[201] A barrier at which the duty known as the *octroi* was collected; the building there was headquarters for the staff of the *ferme générale* who patrolled the road to Les Porcherons and Montmartre. The name (White Gate) came from old quarries in the area (now the boulevard de Clichy).

oped in his arm and they had cut it off and he had obtained the position of
police informer in which he was doing all right because the police lieutenant had gotten him admitted to the Invalides[202]

One night on my way home from supper with my widow having left my
brother-in-law as I was passing by the rue Montmartre I saw a man
coming out of an alley take a girl by the arm and with a threat throw her
into the street It was late I approached and found a girl in tears I
consoled her and told her that if she wished she could come with me in
complete safety She hesitated finally she made up her mind and I took my
chick home and added yet another member to my growing family This
little girl was well worth my attention she was charming Her father to
judge from what she told me was the spitting image of mine When he had
been drinking he sent her to stay with her mother's relatives as her mother
was dead After a good lunch she left for her relatives' house after promising that she would come back to see me which she did not fail to do She
was gentleness itself That showed me how much the drunkeness of fathers is responsible for the fall of their children Having written of my
escapades I have not written without ostentation without morals and
without reflection

By chance one morning while out walking on the boulevards I spotted
the Pinard woman the young one who was very friendly to me and (said
that she had) asked where I might be but that all her questioning had been
in vain She was stunningly well dressed she suggested that we go into a
place We started on an explanation Her father had sold the shop One
day while drunk he had broken the arm of which I had dislocated the
wrist It became infected (and he) went to the Hôtel-Dieu[203] But (she)
didn't want to tell me what base profession he was now practicing that
her mother was with a good farmer in the country that her sister had left
with a clockmaker named Jouannin for Lyons that as for herself she spent
time abroad with the man who kept her who was extremely wealthy I
wanted to acquaint her once more with what I used to know how to do

---

[202] Only army veterans were allowed into the Invalides. Pinard was probably granted a
place there and a pension in exchange for his services as an informer.

[203] Located in the heart of Paris, between La Cité and the Left Bank, the Hôtel-Dieu was a
complicated series of buildings, some of which dated back to the Middle Ages. Augustinian
nuns and monks from Saint-Victor, together with a large medical staff, took care of nearly
10,000 patients, who shared 2,000 beds. After a fire in 1772 numerous proposals were made to
move the Hôtel-Dieu, to no avail. All the hardship of Paris seemed concentrated here, and
nearly one-third of all patients died.

before I said my good-byes (so I) took her to my room which she accepted more gracefully And so (I) bade her farewell her and her amiable and distinguished family

I went to see M Morat commander of the fire brigade who received me warmly telling me that he was going to make a reform and establish the fire brigade on a more respectable footing and that each fireman should have a plaque above his door that would read in large letters King's Fire Guard I took up my old post with the same pay as before

My father received an invitation for himself and another one for me from one of my cousins from my mother's side who was going to say his first mass at Notre-Dame in the chapel (of) the Virgin having been a choirboy And (he) was named chaplain to Monseigneur the bishop of Lombes[204] Since we had enjoyed some gay times together I saw that there was more ambition than religion in him after all the nonsense we had talked about and (I knew) that he had no faith in all those mysteries and that he regarded (them) as pure figments of man's imagination the product of ignorance sustained by lies as articles of faith As I have not permitted myself in these writings to make reflections I shall say no more about it

All my relatives watched him officiate with veneration which bordered on adoration but I saw the whole business in a very different light I was never a fanatic and never (believed) and will never believe that any being on earth is capable of calling a God down to an altar at will and swallowing it nor of giving it to anybody who has a strong enough stomach to digest their God That strains the imagination of any (sensible) man So they are right always to have these words in their mouths Blessed are the poor in spirit the kingdom of heaven belongs to them

I went into the sacristy to pay my respects He smiled at me took me by the hand to invite me to dinner where I found myself sitting between a couple of fat priesties who were even jollier than we were I knew that he would return this visit He told me Cousin I didn't know where you were living after you left the Saint-Germain cloister that's why I sent it [i.e., the invitation] to your father and I'll see you again Which did not fail to happen

He came the following Sunday in the Bishop of Lombes's carriage I had told my young sister Prepare a little meal and we will be together again like old friends He explained to me that he had made this decision more

---

[204] The cousin obtained a position in the service of the bishop of Lombes, a muddy little bishopric of 1,100 inhabitants; the bishop in 1765 was Jacques Richier de Cerisy.

out of ambition than out of religion and for his peace of mind that he had had his fun and (now) I told him he was going to hear about other people's foolishness He said to me Cousin I've chosen the wisest course this is the way a man can live without difficulty and without the slightest worry I'll be going to Lombes at any moment I hope that you will do as I've done in any case in some other way by settling down I have no advice to give you let me offer you the same advice you sometimes gave me in spite of all our foolishness we have never strayed beyond the bounds of honor I hope you will be prosperous and get what you deserve As for your beliefs that's your own business You have always placed yourself above common prejudice you adore God you do no harm to your neighbor you are a friend to all men That's the real point We bade each other a tender and touching farewell which was our last because he died in Lombes ten months later

I promised myself that I would not tolerate any reflection I cannot stop myself A man like my cousin without burdens deliberately not work-ing drinking and eating well a good table with everything as he wanted it beloved by devout ladies receiving gifts loved cherished by his bishop this man died in the flower of his youth at the moment when he might have made a brilliant career when others of the same age are obliged to endure all of life's suffering to exist and live despite the fatigue and sorrow of which their lives are full

I looked all over for my girlfriends my absence had greatly confused them My little flower girl had married a companion harness maker for me that was one less thorn in my side The Pinard family had vanished from sight My laundress did not disturb me My governess I visited a few times very discreetly at one of her aunts My little brunette of the rue Mont-martre didn't trouble me at all Aurora was still plying her trade A chambermaid named Omphale who worked for the marquise de Lansedine was the girl I had with me most often and Elophe's pretty daughter who asked about me when I pretended to be away and who found me through her brother by meeting me at Gaudon's or Nicolet's where we always went to eat for she was a lot like her father in that regard she liked to grease the knife[205] My lesser acquaintances thinking I was still in the country left me in the greatest tranquillity There was only my widow (whom) I went to see every evening for supper and who did not allow me to sleep there

---

[205] *Graisser le couteau*: literally, to grease the knife, meaning to eat meat frequently and in large quantities.

because of her servants who thought more or less the same way she did that I was visiting her for honest reasons

As for my friends I was as I had always been toward them and I frequently made use of this principle Where there is discomfort there is no pleasure I thought about working I earned money and was no better off without being overly generous Finally my hundred and twenty lanterns were finished They ordered sixty more and (I) told old lady Vilmont that I wouldn't make them for less than three livres apiece because old Vilmont had fallen into his dotage

One night a fire broke out in the rue de Saintonge I ran over I had no fireman's equipment or uniform with me Nobody came I identified myself I grabbed a rope The fire had started on the fourth floor There was no rear entry The stairway was in front and was on fire I found a woman in an attic and a child both of them asleep I woke them up the smoke and fear suffocated them I fastened my rope to a beam I told the woman to grab the rope and to slide down as I did I took the child although it was naked I fastened it around my neck with my handkerchief No sooner said than done and I was down on the street People rushed toward me they took my burden from me The woman fortunately fell on straw and fainted My comrades from the fire brigade recognized me Everyone congratulated me for having saved a mother and child M. Morat arrived on horseback He asked to speak to me He introduced me to the inspector who inquired about the cause of the fire I gave my report and seeing that people wanted to compliment me I made my escape and ran to my widow's where I found my brother-in-law who was wondering what had become of me Never having been one to like congratulations much less respond to them I made my decision And this is what I've always done liking to do good and yet seeking to make myself known only very slightly This has always been one of my principles

I began getting some things together I took back my chest from my friend Baron whose wife had just persuaded him to leave Paris to practice his trade of surgery in a miserable town where he died of boredom

I went one day to say hello to my father who gave me an unsigned letter in which I recognized the handwriting of Aurora of (the) Night who informed me that she had been sentenced to two years in the Salpêtrière (and) that with some help from me she was planning to escape I obtained a permit under a false name and we agreed with Lenoir to help her escape I provided him with the means A dozen laundresses left the establishment twice a week for the wash boats each with a basket of dirty laundry

on her back Aurora had won over several of these women She let me
know this through a woman from the house who begged for alms in Saint-
Eustache On the appointed day I notified Lenoir and the boy from the
Samaritaine and before dawn we took our boat near the place where the
washerwomen's boat was anchored She spotted us and despite the screws
managed to escape by walking over the log rafts[206]

We had taken the precaution of bringing her a frock coat and a hat and
(I) took her to my room and went to get her things which she had left with
one of her friends And (she) gave her prison clothes to a woman I didn't
know to give to the woman who begged at the door of Saint-Eustache and
(I) started living with her again as I had done in the past Helping her
escape had made her devoted to me Her friendship was unequivocal and I
am sure that if I had not made it a point of honor I would have married
her She had been good and remained so She was therefore obliged to
start again and I had to get out of it as gently as I could seeing how attached she was

M Morat the commander of the fire brigade wrote asking me to come see
him because he had some business to discuss with me I therefore went at
his invitation He said many kind things about me and ordered me to find
him other young men like myself especially construction workers such as
roofers carpenters and others (for) he had in his brigade only shoemakers
and harnessmakers and these men weren't hardy enough for the job I
answered him that if he were willing to give me the stripes that signify a
corporal's rank I would get him several construction workers He gave me
to understand that there were members of the brigade with more seniority
than I but that he would give me my stripes any day Since I had been
thinking for some time about settling down this didn't sit well with me at
all and (I) demurred He talked to me at length about this subject and sent
me word through Segrestier and a fellow by the name of Dieu that he
would give me my stripes My mind was made up and I never showed up
again because they were beginning to organize as a brigade

One morning while out walking on the boulevards of the Temple waiting for Chaumont[207] a carriage was standing there and I walked around it

---

[206] Wood was supplied to Paris via the Seine. Log trains, formed on the Yonne and Marne
and their tributaries, were lashed to the bank until they could be pulled out of the water and
hauled to sawmills on the Left Bank from the quai Saint-Victor all the way to the hospital. By
walking over these moored logs one could reach the boats in the river: we know from reports
of numerous accidents that people actually did this.

[207] Antoine Dubuisson, known as Chaumont, an actor in Restier's company, which was
disbanded in 1762 after a fire in the Saint-Germain market.

I had heard someone call when a servant took my arm and asked me to come speak to his master I went over I saw a decorated gentleman whom the servant addressed as Monseigneur (and) who asked me if I was not a runner I answered no He proposed that I become his runner and asked me to get into his carriage I told him I hear you I run after women but nothing else good-bye And I laughed as I walked away Chaumont arrived I told him what had happened and we laughed about it That was the last time I drank with him as he died a few days later He was a very good Harlequin even though he could neither read nor write He had a great memory his wife taught him his parts He was missed and Carlin called him (his) colleague

One evening as I was returning to my room by way of the coach entrance so as not to go through the area in which I worked this house was occupied by a renter of carriages who had a pretty cook and who had seen the wolf as they say and did not play the prude She was standing in the doorway I joked We exchanged words that did the trick We made ourselves comfortable everybody returned home I took her found an open stable we went in We had reached the point where our souls were about to lose themselves in heaven when we heard a devil of a noise The mistress called her daughter a coachman worked the door handle Fortunately I remembered that I had turned the lock once The girl didn't lose her head shouted loudly that everything was all right that she was responsible that when she attempted to light her lamp with the stable lantern everything went black and instead of opening the door she had locked herself in that she was going up to the kitchen to look for a light Meanwhile I made my getaway The mistress was standing in the courtyard I played the brother[208] and fibbed and everything went off as planned So we had no further disturbance in our amorous occupations she came by my shop and from there into my room and everything went wonderfully in the morning as well as at night

When there was company in my room the door was shut and I could be seen every day because she often came with something to drink before dawn I made her think that my brother-in-law or some friends had come to stay with me although she was shrewd enough not to be taken in but I followed this maxim Where there is discomfort there is no pleasure she had to conform to this rule just like everyone else knowing that I was not

---

[208] *Je fais le frère:* perhaps this should be interpreted to mean, "I behaved hypocritically, like lay brothers and monks."

the only man to whom she offered her favors for her husband didn't sleep there So he [presumably Vilmont] said to me as a joke because he was a jovial fellow so you came to make lanterns for me and have a drink to- gether now and then we were more than friends and he had tried to do as I did at my age seeing that she always had plenty to do alongside my shop And I played dumb on this subject

My brother-in-law who had his contraband household (?) told me that he wanted to eat so I gave him thirty-five sols per day and never went back to my widow in the rue de Clichy and I gave her up altogether It was too uncomfortable for me You had to take too many dimensions (?) that didn't suit my nature and (I) never liked to make love *à l'espagnole* (?)

One Sunday night when I was with Aurora who was at that time the favorite sultaness at the porte Saint-Denis where all the revelers went at the sign of the Bois de Boulogne I ran into several of my girlfriends While I was sitting at my table somebody asked me to dance Upon returning to the table another woman whose feet she had stepped on let loose with a stream of nonsense and Aurora had to beg pardon for she was docile enough that she was quite polite This female kept on grumbling I said But come on I'm getting tired of this A fellow named Frémont drummer in the city guard came over and took sides I said to him Frémont we know each other He wanted to swagger a bit Angry words were spoken on both sides He said that he would show me a thing or two My friends and his squared off He told me to get out I left They followed us He insisted on having it out The only thing I have to say to you right now is to measure your distance It happened that the son of a beadle from Saint- Eustache was there with his sword he handed it to me The women got involved trying to stop us We were in the yard I told him Come over to the rue Basse They followed us His brother ran down as he was wounded in the hand as I had just told him He insisted They separated us The brother told me that he was my friend and that I was going to see the fuss he would make with this troublemaker We went back a couple of slaps and kicks in the ass and out the door put an end to the whole business He was only slightly wounded in the hand and we ended the evening together

My lantern business was going along when M Vanier inspector for lanterns[209] came to see me asking me if I wanted to make another hun-

---

[209] The lantern inspector was not an inspector of police. No police inspector had responsi- bility for lighting, and no one by this name is mentioned in the published lists of *commissaires* and *inspecteurs*. He was no doubt a city employee who oversaw the installation of the new reflector lanterns.

dred for the Marais being too far from one another and having the style (?) he wanted them to be made by me and wanted me to have everything I might need And so I took on the job and made them in old Vilmont's storehouse and his nice wife didn't even miss her appointment because she really liked to drink her drop That was a well-made woman

One day I ran into my old laundress who had married a companion har-nessmaker She was very friendly to me invited me to come up to her place in the rue des Gravilliers to she says see her apartment Her neighbor gave me a warm welcome when she said (This) is the fellow I've told you about We went in turned the lock twice we were involved in a most interesting conversation when we heard a knocking at the door It was the master returning home I had paid no attention to the wolf hound which had sniffed its master (and) stationed itself near the door barking He said to himself But my wife is in the room He called out No answer The neighbor opened her door (and) assured him that she had not seen her come in He insisted that she was in the room since his dog was there and he could feel that the door had been bolted that surely his wife had hurt herself The busybody neighbor advised him to go find a locksmith He kept on knocking Finally our unofficial protectress pointed out that there was a door in her room that opened into his (and) which was only fas-tened with nails and caulked shut Before he had knocked down his own door he agreed set about undoing this (other) door I opened and went out quietly not as I had come in She had the presence of mind to restrain the dog The door closed behind me and once again I had escaped from a tight situation

The next day I went to see the indulgent neighbor to ask how things had turned out It had all gone quite well she had been found in a chair unconscious and had played her part very well the husband had taken the thing well I thanked this charming neighbor who struck me as not at all indifferent to love and tried to worm my way into her place She confided in me that she was kept by a wine merchant also she had some good wines and I helped that good fellow drain his wine cellar without putting my harnessmaker's wife into a foul mood Since I have always been grateful I reminded her (?) of the tight situation that she (?) had helped us to escape from

One day my old friend Bussie came to see me having been sent by his boss to ask me if I wanted to make a lantern for the police station these lanterns being made of colored glass with designs on them I went with

him to P's We agreed on the price of thirty francs he having done the
design of one already His wife served us drinks and asked me where I was
working I told her and left A few days later I saw Bussie arrive accompanied by the boss's wife to see if I was making the lantern I showed her
the partially cut and greased pieces She seemed satisfied She was charming well dressed she had been a street parrot[210] She invited me to come
for a drink A glance from Bussie told me that they were intimate We had
lunch.

When we finished Bussie left us saying that he would be back Having
noticed in their conversation that he had not been greatly inhibited in
front of me when I was alone with her I said that I noticed that my friend
had his good graces in such a way that I made my intentions clear and
gently pressed my suit After some fine speeches from me she told me that
Bussie had told her about me that he had told her about some of my
pranks and said that I was fickle in love I answered that she ought to put
me to the test and that she would see that I was not as unsteady as people
said I was a little put out with Bussie and I hoped that Madame P would
be the victim She told me that she knew a woman who lived on this street
and that she would be very surprised if she saw her with two young men
like us and that she came to see her often I invited her to come see the
lantern She smiled at me and (I) squeezed her hand She responded to the
pressure

Bussie meanwhile arrived and I noticed that he looked worried Being a
man of the world I went out to let them say what they had to say to each
other I went back in I saw a nicely laid table I did the honors Our
spirits were high I sat beside the lady and from time to time squeezed her
knee She pretended not to notice When we parted she said that when
she came to see her friend she would inquire about the progress of the
lantern

I took that as I was meant to take it but the next day Bussie came to tell
me that his boss had paid him off because he had gone off on a spree I
asked him if he knew it was with his wife He told me he didn't know I
asked him what he'd had to say to the woman in private He hesitated
finally he told me that for the lunch that we'd had together he'd pawned
the lady's garnet necklace I got angry He told me that it wasn't the first
time and that it was really finished between them and that he saw plainly

---

[210] *Perroquet de toilette*: a synonym for prostitute, by allusion to the *marchandes à la
toilette*, women who sold clothing and linen and who were often procuresses.

that she had taken a fancy to me that she liked men like me of an amorous disposition that he was certain she would pay me a visit before long So I said to him Since you've just told me it's all over between you two I'll buy you a bottle and a salad He accepted my offer and we parted in the hope that we would soon be brothers since I didn't like spinning out the romance for too long

For eating this salad I had invited good old Férand a companion who worked for old man Vilmont and who had heard a part of our conversation which caused him to laugh until he cried And after listening to our pranks whatever he started in lecturing me saying that he couldn't imagine how a young fellow like me who knew my trade who had seen life who was moreover master of Paris wouldn't want to settle down (and) that he knew a nice good girl who had a little property

I think this was the first time that I thought seriously about tying the knot I asked him to make inquiries of the person about whom he had told me so many good things The inquiries were made The object pleased me and I was agreeable and we soon reached an accord There were at least six rivals and I won out over all the other aspirants I told her that I had been around that I had nothing few prospects but I could be the mainstay of a household I could set myself up being master of Paris that what I might earn would go to buy me clothes that I was going to make inquiries about buying a shop and that when my lantern job was done I would go back to my father's for form's sake and in part because of her family

That didn't stop the P woman from coming to see me I invited her in for a drink that was what she wanted In those moments Cupid that little god smiled on me We went into the office and had a most charming tête-à-tête People told me I was a little rogue and I didn't play around but anyway I did all right She had reason to be pleased because she said I was a Hercules of love So she got me where I was most vulnerable she flattered my self-esteem I outdid myself being in the arms of a charming woman who responded with the warmest expressions of rapture That day was one of the finest of my life for pleasure We promised each other to meet again and that if I wanted to take Bussie's place that she could devote herself fully to me and her husband would be delighted I answered all this in monosyllables and said I would think it over We parted and promised ourselves to see each other even more often to dupe her turkey of a husband about whom she complained bitterly since he couldn't perform the household chores being according to what she told me impotent So he looked like a real fat capon

One day after dinner we went for a walk on a slope over near Belleville We had eaten copiously We were as I was saying out of sight of the strollers when we sacrificed to Cupid[211] and were in sweet ecstasy one staring at the heavens and the other at the earth When all of a sudden two or three ruffians who had apparently heard our sighs appeared out of nowhere They put an abrupt end to the deep contemplation of nature in which we were engaged (and) hurled themselves upon us I tried to defend myself One grabbed my cane the other grabbed me around the neck the other seized my companion They took us to the fiscal prosecutor who gave us a lecture She just had a fright and I the annoyance of having been taken by surprise while making an offering to Cupid When we were released we promised ourselves to be more circumspect in our sacrifices to Cupid

That taught me a lesson and reminded me of the adventure in the woods of Vincennes That was enough to give her some reasonable excuses and try to get rid of her because she was beginning to be a burden to me being a very passionate woman Besides which I wanted to establish myself and as they say settle down and I was thinking of dropping all my girlfriends

I finished my work and was very well paid The first thing I did was to have a suit made by a tailor I knew in the rue Saint-Germain One day I went to see how the work was coming I found his wife in the midst of a group of neighbors and a little boy in the middle of the room as fat as a bushel basket who did nothing but fart in every direction You couldn't see his eyes or his nose He was completely deformed The mother was trying to find out what had happened by questioning him and his sister but to no avail when someone spotted a bellows in the middle of the room No doubt the sister had blown air into her brother's behind for she had surely seen her parents taking medicines by enema (and) I told such stories on this subject that nobody in the room could stop laughing about what had just happened

I went to see my father and told him what I was thinking about setting up a shop He tried to convince me that he would soon be giving up his shop once he had established my younger sister But as I had already heard everything my father had to say on this subject and as his way of thinking was incompatible with mine and as I knew he was talking through his hat I simply asked him if he would let me stay with him until I had estab-

---

[211] In *Monsieur Nicolas* Rétif de la Bretonne tells a very similar anecdote, which occurred during an outing in Belleville.

lished myself I knew that my father would like nothing better especially
since I didn't ask him for anything as he was very tightfisted I went to
see a fellow called Bruno who lived in the rue du Petit Lion who wanted
to sell his shop Since we had been friends the deal was quickly closed for
three hundred francs I went to my fiancée who advanced me the money
and (I took) her at once and entered into possession before I set foot in
this shop

One day while working at my father's I heard a revel in the street I
looked out What did I see The cops had just arrested M Laboureur
whom my father and I knew quite well My first thought was to snatch
him out of their hands I spotted a cart loaded with barrels I released the
winch the barrels blocked the passageway A crowd formed they could
not pass with their prey People shouted Hoo![212] They were forced to
release their captive me and my friends hid him in the stables and at night
we escorted him home He thanked me for my quick thinking And this
good man was going to be locked up for having answered for friends and
done them favors

Before leaving my father I had a stroke of luck and took advantage of it
A member of the academy ordered eight large cages of Bohemian glass
most glaziers had no idea how to do this kind of work because I was one of
the first to take it on I made them at his place and earned thirty-six livres
all expenses paid

It was around that time one day I couldn't stop laughing until I cried
despite the loss and damage my father had suffered I arrived on the scene
(and) what did I see My father and his companion had laid a number of
frames out in the street in order to pour water on them when all of a
sudden a bitch in heat came running down the street with a dog hanging
on to her and pursued by urchins and a pack of other dogs waiting to take
their turn they ran over the frames with their paws broke and smashed all
the panes of glass On one side my father chased after them with a broom
stick on the other side the companion clapped his hands to make them go
away people were shouting and laughing because they saw that the two
dogs having gotten themselves together couldn't get themselves apart
Never have I seen my father so embarrassed swearing shouting to the
devil with all the dogs and on top of that there was this fat boy called

---

[212] *L'on crie à la hou*, a familiar shout to show that one was chasing someone: "Hou-hou, je
te ferai devenir fou, je te ferai partout, hou-hou," writes Scarron. The same cry was used by
hunters to get their dogs excited.

Grésois who barked and threw himself on top of the dogs When I heard my father shouting I melted into the crowd and feigned surprise when he told me what had happened To console himself he went to the Tour d'Argent to find his friends and with wine he forgot his misfortune and me and my sister and the companion laughed ourselves silly

Opposite us there was a convent of mediocre virtue[213] which was on the third floor We heard moans and a few shouts The mother abbess being out a crowd gathered and the word went round that somebody was murdering one of those poor girls I went up accompanied by two apprentice barrel makers We knocked we heard moans we said with some wellchosen four-letter words that we were going to break down the door and the police were on their way Finally the door opened We saw a girl on the floor with blood on her hands We asked her what monster had done this to her She pointed and said it was the abbot who was behind the door We jumped him He had left his hat and coat and was trying to make his getaway when we noticed that under the coat there was a cat-o'-nine-tails with needles at the end of each branch Some people said he deserved to get a beating like the one he had just meted out He was on his knees he asked for pardon They kept it up

This hypocrite was reduced to the utmost humiliation feigned contrition and did many low things unworthy of his character Finally I said to him You have mistreated this poor girl what you've got to do now is pay her out of your pocket or else we're going to turn you over to the police As he was pulling his money by the hairs we heaped sarcasm on him I said to him You are a fine director you don't do a bad job directing your penitents If it's by flagellations it's not a bad imitation of our old anchorites who in all simplicity whipped themselves in order to gain access to the kingdom of heaven We gave him his hat and as for his coat I said that the girl could use it as an apron and that that would remind her of the good spanking she had received from the abbot He didn't ask for his other things and took off as if the devils were at his heels and he didn't have the slightest interest in exorcising them This taught me that those men have passions even more shameful than other men

Finally I moved into my shop which was completely bare everything had been taken out I had paid cash for some pieces of Alsatian glass (since) I was a newcomer in Paris and not yet known and (I) wanted to

213 See nn. 147–148.

make a reputation for myself In the meantime a fellow by the name of Damour a merchant who was an old friend of mine came looking for me one Saturday night to tell me that he too had decided to settle down and was about to marry and that he had been to see Father Basuel who was the priest who had given us our first communion and that he had told him that for penance he must go to Mount Valérien without eating and climb Mount Suresnes barefoot and what is more he must fill his pockets with stones while climbing I couldn't keep from laughing at this unusual penance and said You must have committed murder then or rape or something worse Since we had no secrets from each other I was just joking And just thinking about it I still laugh that men subject to the same passions and even unworthy to bear the name of men believe that because of their so-called character they can lord it over and subjugate others in the guise of religion at their whim

I promised him that as I was sleeping at my father's I would come as early as possible to escort him on this holy pilgrimage and edifying penance He was on time We left without eating but at the Neuilly bridge I fortified myself with a nice glass of ratafia and followed him while he did his penance After following him from point to point and doing all the stations we returned via Nanterre where we did another station of a different sort The little salt fish had done its job it needed watering and we watered it copiously My comrade had no more stones to carry but plenty of violet wine that made him forget all that morning's nonsense for we had plenty of discussion about all that idiocy We said to ourselves Is it possible that some men lord it over others by making them believe in chimeras and that we're dumb enough to believe in all their talk

A few days later since I was about to get married I went to see Father Basuel I needed a confession certificate which was absolutely indispensable I told him that I had come to make my peace with the Church not with God because I have always worshipped the Eternal but without having much faith in what the priests have to say about all their mysteries He answered that he didn't want to listen to me much less to hear me (confess) I begged him Wasted words I left He called me back I thought that as the saying goes he had put some water in his wine Not at all it was to tell me that he knew from my father that I was going to the Grand Penitentiary[214] I was ready to chuck him and all his ilk into the

---

[214] A church official who exercised the powers of the bishop in the area of penitential sacraments and who was authorized to hear certain confessions by priests and laymen in

river finally I repeated my request Don't waste your time he said to me
If you meet a water bearer send him to me but tell him that I will give him
only one sol By chance I ran into the water bearer for the house I told
him that if he wanted to play a trick I'd buy him a mug all he had to do
was dump a pail of water in his [the priest's] room He went up I followed
him He [Basuel] said You know I only give one sol The water bearer
pretended to pay no attention to what he was doing he tripped The
water was all over the room There was my confessor shouting at the top
of his lungs at the supposed clumsy fool he ran and I laughed at my
success I bought him a mug and told anybody who wanted to listen about
the trick I had just played on the holy man who came to see my father to
complain about it suspecting that I had had something to do with it

I told my father what day I wanted to sign the marriage contract He
told me Before that we have to go see old cousin Chenier senior We set a
date for Sunday morning In the meantime my fiancée made the acquaintance of or rather someone introduced her to a glazier named Deleus It
wasn't long before I heard about it I immediately grabbed a pen and
wrote in a few words that I was giving up the shop if she thought she was
better off with the new fellow who had been introduced to her and I had
no intention of standing in the way of anybody's inclinations She came
and told me that she had given me her word and even her heart that there
was nobody who could change her mind about me and we exchanged a kiss
of friendship

Sunday morning my cousin arrived My father took us to lunch at the
Veau qui Tète My cousin said to me Jacques you're going to get married
you're going to sign a contract tomorrow and your wedding is set for
Wednesday Your father will not give his consent unless you sign in the
presence of a notary (a paper saying) that you have nothing to ask of your
father from what might be coming from your late mother I wanted to
think it over and let it be known that I had received nothing He showed
me a document that my father had had drawn up to his advantage which
included my master's certificate which my good grandmother had often
told me she had provided to my father not wanting this to be known by

---

special cases. For repeated infractions of the laws of God and the Church, Ménétra could well
have been sent to the grand penitentiary, who dealt with cases of magic, blasphemy, apostasy,
perjury, assaults on parents, homicide, abortion, public concubinage, sexual offenses, etc. Cf.
Durand de Maillane, *Dictionnaire de droit canonique* (Lyons, 1770), 1:422–423, and
3:631–635.

my uncles as well as what it had cost when I broke my leg the first time in Vendôme and for a suit of clothes which was repeated twice in this solemn document

After trying to refute it my father said that no matter what I might charge he would hold firm Very well I said to him since it all hinges on that let's get to a notary and I shall prove to you that I'm disinterested and you won't have to remind me I signed what he wanted and immediately thereafter I put my affairs in order as my fiancée and I both wished

When the day came I asked my father to take the bride's hand as is usually done My father started making contortions that displeased not just me but both families I invited one of my uncles who was most delighted and who was grateful to me for it I gave a meal and my relatives asked me it it wasn't my father who had boasted that he would give the lunch I answered them that it was at my expense So for the supper they made him toss into the hat like everybody else And so ended my dealings with my father who behaved toward one of his own children less well than he would have done and acted toward a stranger

Before tying the knot and subjecting myself to the yoke of marriage I had to go to the trouble of getting that wretched confession certificate A person I knew got me one from a Recollect Father[215] in exchange for a few bottles and three livres That was all it took which shows that for wine and money the ministers of the altars will even sell indulgences and that anybody who gives them enough silver be he the greatest criminal who ever was the gates of paradise are open for him and closed forever to the poor and indigent Which shows the holiness of the Roman religion

The night of the betrothal[216] we arrived at Saint-Laurent a little late the Swiss had just closed the doors A coin of twenty-four sols got them opened again Immediately somebody went to look for a priest he couldn't come I went and told him that I would show my gratitude I rattled the

---

[215] The Recollect monastery in the faubourg Saint-Laurent sheltered some sixty friars in the 1760s. These Franciscans were rather popular in Paris and among soldiers in the army, which they often served as chaplains.

[216] In Christian doctrine marriage is a sacrament constituted by mutual consent of the spouses and, once consummated, forever indissoluble. It may be preceded by an exchange of "verba de futuro," the engagement or promises that create an obligation but are still subject to cancellation. After the Council of Trent canon law tended to downgrade the practice of engagement, with the engagement period being reduced to a few days or even a few hours prior to the marriage. Ménétra's engagement to his future wife involved a liturgy which including questioning as to absence of any impediment to marriage together with an exchange of promises by the affianced couple.

coins in my pocket That sound made him come running faster than all the bells of his church When he had done his job to punish him I thanked him and said in a friendly tone see you tomorrow

We went for a while without much business Finally we began to make some contacts and I worked hard and was quick and easy-going so that in a short while thanks to my good wife's frugality we paid off our debts I was happy I had dropped all my old girlfriends That didn't stop me however when I met a chick ready to lay from giving the old marriage contract a few healthy stabs all in secret That didn't prevent us from enjoying the closest of marriages

A neighbor named Sieur Ros called me and said My neighbor do you see those two pearl merchants' signs that cover up our own We must make a deposition on this subject I refused but I met by pure chance a man with whom I had a conversation on the subject I had absolutely no idea that he was a police inspector but thought he was or had been attached to the fire brigade he told me that he would take care of the matter So a few days later a police order was posted instructing that all signs must be placed against the walls of the buildings and the brackets that had held them must be removed[217] They were all dismayed especially Sieur Truchie whose sign cost more than a thousand écus

One day the father of Seiur Boucher a pearl merchant surnamed Jac-quin had me fix his windows and told me to go downstairs to his son who was blind to clean his window I knocked Nobody answered I looked through the keyhole Behind the door I saw something moving With the claw of my hammer I pried off the lock What did I see The younger Jacquin hanging behind his door I put the hasp back on turned the key

---

[217] Signs made of wood, metal, or stone often projected out into the street. Identifying homes and businesses, these signs used a picturesque symbolism based on mythology, chivalry, and even religious or irreligious themes; painted and carved images were mixed with slogans, letters, and puns. From the seventeenth century on, the police waged a continuing battle in an attempt to make the streets safer by limiting the size of signs. But they came into conflict with entrenched business custom and with an established system for making sense of the urban space. Ménétra's initiative is not improbable, but it does not accord with the chronology of the edicts concerning signs. In 1761 an ordinance specified the dimension and height of the sign bracket. Since this was not obeyed, it was reinforced by a second ordinance, dated 17 December 1761, which outlawed all signs that projected into the street and permitted only signs laid flat against the building wall. Sartine's successors attempted to enforce this law, and Sébastien Mercier shed tears at the sight of his city stripped of its signs. But after 1761 another system of advertising slowly took hold, though it did not finally become established until after the Revolution.

bolted the lock firmly closed the door and in great emotional turmoil notified the father that I could see something that was not right behind the door He told me to pry open the door he saw his unfortunate son hanging behind the door The inspector arrived and I served as witness

That reminded me that when I was quite young and staying with one of my uncles in the Ile Saint-Louis one Sunday morning while on the way to get some nails from a merchant at the corner of the rue Saint-Louis I went in by the alley door I saw the counter girl under the spigot of the fountain which was running into her mouth and her body was all twisted in contortions and the owner was in the corner of the room lying on the floor and foaming at the mouth I shouted for help I thought that they were possessed by the devil because of the cries they made and because of their contortions I was heard as the first who had seen them in that state They had poisoned themselves while having lunch together by taking coffee while the mistress and the cook were at mass and people in the neighborhood said that it was for love

One day while (I was) drawing a pail of water from the well the rope snapped The whole thing fell into the well Some time earlier the cover had fallen in along with another pail When a well cleaner asked six francs to go down into the well the boss who was a Gascon and a master carpenter by trade said to me But let's earn our money we'll have a good time I accepted the offer and with another rope descended into the well The well was underneath a shed and I equipped myself with a light and a rope and told him again and again to use another rope along with the one that was supporting me He answered that it would hold a hundred men my size and in truth it wasn't very heavily loaded I went down I attached everything that I found at the bottom to the rope I shouted for them to pull me back up My companion and (the other fellow) went to work I shouted to them not to pull in such a jerky manner I had almost reached the lip when all of a sudden the ill-fated rope snapped and I fell to the bottom of the well The light went out I shouted that I was not hurt but nobody answered me they left me to moulder in the well My companion had hurt himself They had taken him away When my wife told him that I was a goner the carpenter went up and threw himself on his bed I was abandoned Try as I did to call out no one answered Finally I heard an old priesty saying paternosters so I could breathe my last gasps and he said they couldn't try to pull me out of the well until the inspector got there

I tried calling out but to no avail He insisted that I was done for A good fellow by the name of Raoul came over and called to me I answered

that nobody could hear that doddering old fool and told him to go get a
rope and lower it down to me They wanted to pull up the other rope that
held the pails and the cover I objected with all my might It would have
crushed me senseless Finally the lifesaving rope arrived I attached myself
to it without any light and they pulled me up I saw the light I did not say
any Aves but I thanked the Eternal and the good folks who had saved me

I was completely soaked I was in a robe I ran across the street to a
good widow tavernkeeper who wished me well (She) gave me wine bouillon to drink I went back home I changed my clothes and went back to
work as usual I teased the people who had let me fall to the bottom of the
well They said they were injured when they fell over backward But
meanwhile vicious rumors spread their poison A colleague of mine put it
about that I wanted to do away with myself and that it was out of despair
I reviled him and avenged myself

It was around the time of that fatal marriage of the Dauphin[218] We
went my wife and a young person we found ourselves in the brawl in the
place Louis XV In trying to make our way to the boulevards we lost sight
of one another I looked around At the end of the rue Saint-Honoré I saw
some men carrying a woman dressed like my wife I hesitated It turned
out not to be her I went home Nobody I was really worried I saw
neighbors men and women arrived barefoot some of the women with their
ears torn off It was a night of celebration changed into a night of mourning Finally my wife returned home safe and sound and all we could do
was wail over that fatal celebration which was like a prelude to the
misfortune of the French

A merchant from the rue Saint-Denis Sieur Vatiende who had recently
traveled to the depths of Alsace invited me to his house to see six sheets of
glass that were just like Bohemian glass (and) said to me I thought of you
Since you have the intelligence and this is your trade this glass might sell

---

[218] On Wednesday, 30 May 1770, to honor the marriage of the duc de Berry, dauphin and
future Louis XVI, to Marie-Antoinette, the city staged a fireworks display near the river
below the place Louis XV. When the show was over, the large crowd could not find a way out
of the square, the rue Royale being clogged with carriages and fiacres belonging to people of
quality, who had watched the spectacle from stands set up along the walls of buildings
belonging to the crown (now the Ministry of the Navy). The ensuing shoving and riot left 132
dead and hundreds injured. This was followed by violent attacks on the authorities responsible for security: the city, the mounted guard, and the lieutenant of police. Their criticism of
one another underscored the inadequacy of the measures that had been taken and discredited
them still further (AN, Y. 15507, H. 1873, XI.8553).

in Paris I would introduce you and the people who run this glass works would trust you and you would keep a warehouse I told my wife about this offer and she rejected it out of hand It did no good for me to say it required no funds that they weren't even asking for security I couldn't make anything and I saw clearly that I was not the only one wearing trousers Realizing that I went to see a fellow named Lobjois who rented a warehouse and did a considerable business The glass works was called Baccarat

That got me down a bit[219] My shop and my trade began to be a burden to me I had two living children and as they say I had a king's desires[220] Two boys had died because of the carelessness of their nurse I was no longer the master the wife anticipated everything To have peace I overlooked things Getting ahead was her main passion and mine was to enjoy myself it was impossible to reconcile the two In the end I took up some of my old habits in spite of everything I took care of the house and despite the carrying on in secret and the arguments we prospered

My father wanted to quit his shop (and) came to see me about it as he wanted to sell to me because the companions wouldn't stay with him on account of his bad moods and quick temper I didn't agree to anything I knew my father his temperament was incompatible with mine I gave him a companion who became my brother-in-law by dint of intrigue who had received his last name as well as his first out of the baptismal font (and) who was clever enough to take all the property for himself and who together with his wife pulled the wool over good old papa's eyes

I was not invited to the marriage ceremony for good and just reason since I didn't want my father to become the slave of his children They promised him a great deal but they soon forgot their promise I knew everything even though they tried to keep it from me for fear that I would stand in their way But my dear sister Thérèse told me about it with a letter dated at eleven-thirty at night from La Roquette the same day with a kind of derision in the contents of the letter that was quite original and using the address to allude to the fact that I had no shop having written the address of my father only to cross it out to substitute my own I did not respond but I had my vengeance

But some time later one night at ten o'clock I heard knocking at the

---

219 *Dans la traverse.*
220 A proverbial way of saying that he wanted both a son and a daughter.

door I opened up It was my father They had thrown him out I said to him Father I don't know how your affairs have been arranged since it pleased you to keep them hidden from me but show that you're still the master of your own house and I will escort you there I gave him something to drink and then we went back to his door I knocked Somebody asked who had knocked I answered It is my father who is returning home and I said good-bye Nobody said a word I pretended not to know either of those two individuals My sister said Come in brother I didn't answer and pulled the door shut The wretches had thrown him into the shop onto a workbench and in falling he had lost an eye I asked after him often and spent a few moments with him He repented but I consoled him and tried in every way to make him forget his suffering

One of my dear cousins was to be married I was invited and we had a celebration There was a young girl there with whom I danced and to whom I brought many drinks and said some sweet things which I saw that she took to heart That night after the meal I went down into the garden I looked around for her I ran there I was in her arms We found a sort of shed in which barrels were stored next to the privies we started to play hide-and-seek with Peter[221] after the usual preliminaries for such occasions We were well hidden We saw somebody coming the bride accompanied by a fellow named Simon and both went into the privies The sighs prevented us from hearing anything We held each other tight Somebody came looking for the bride Simon ran hid himself on the other side of the barrels I left my young friend and pretended to look for her I brought her back and put my finger in my mouth and asked her and Simon for a talk She played dumb I explained myself Two hours later I took her to the hiding place where I sacrificed to Cupid and everything was all right

The next day the young lady came looking for me We played as we had done the night before we agreed to meet It lasted for some time Saint-Sauveur Saint-Eustache Saint-Leu were the places where we met Friends helped us out Our little affair lasted for some time but finally it came to an end her father and mother married her well to a pork butcher and (she) became a beautiful woman who I think did as many others have done dropped everything to live in more comfortable circumstances and in greater freedom

In our house lived a surgeon who told me he wanted to give me a

---

[221] *Jouer à cache-cache Nicolas*, a Parisianism for making love and its preliminaries.

remedy he had given my neighbor the carpenter I was working The cook seemed charming to me She was worthy of my attentions I explained myself She pretended to be shy finally I added her to my list When after a week I found myself afflicted with a little amorous illness I tried to get out of it When one Sunday two Gascons[222] asked me to go walking with them I agreed We stopped for a drink They put water in their wine I did the same They looked at one another smiled and said to me that this wasn't my custom I blushed and tried to persuade them that what they were thinking was wrong The surgeon told me [illegible] I am sure that you f . . . [ellipsis in original—trans.] Madame So-and-so's cook Well I said yes He answered by pointing to his countryman the carpenter And he did too And then he said And me too So I said well then we're three brothers and all three of us spoiled by the painful favors of this Circe who put up such a fuss The devil take her The surgeon made a few remarks and then said Well my brothers we'll all three of us patch ourselves up we shall follow the same course of treatment Ménétra is the only one who will have any real trouble because of his wife We fixed things up so well that we got used to it during the two weeks of our penance So the Gascon called me often and always had some business to talk over with me But it was to drown our sorrows and remember our intemperance So since then I've been very careful whenever I throw myself into the arms of one of those peasant wenches[223] since the only such compliments I've caught have been with those women and with girls who call themselves respectable

They came and knocked down the big wall alongside our house It was almost impossible to work on my jobs I took it in mind to make some small pieces in glass I was successful I sold them and set up a shop That made things easier I rented a shop in the rue Pavée Notwithstanding all my wife's objections I wanted to expand I succeeded in spite of all the obstacles that I had to overcome

---

222 Two Gascons: the Gascons were a relatively new group in Paris who enjoyed an image all their own, concocted out of a tradition that had elements of the literary and burlesque (dating from the time of the Gascon king, Henri IV), the military (from the musketeers), and the medical (many students of the Paris School of Surgery were recruited in Gascony). In reality there were relatively few Gascons, amounting to no more than one or two percent of all newcomers, but they stood out by dint of their customs, their speech, and their reputation for exaggeration.

223 *Cambrousses,* meaning peasant girl, a term of contempt for a recent newcomer to the city. The word comes from Provençal and was used in the seventeenth century to mean a chambermaid. By extension it referred to the countryside itself.

I fell ill They treated me for a disease of the nerves I was impotent in my entire body all I did was cry when I was forced to move They prescribed baths I saw no improvement in my condition I found out that the state executioner[224] had a room near the shop that he cured these kinds of diseases I had them set me down on my doorstep and waited until I saw him pass I called out to him I told him about my problem He told me that he would bring me what I needed I was waiting for him the way the Jews as the saying goes wait for the Messiah when all of a sudden I heard the proclamation of a judgment of the court of parlement imposing the death sentence on two boilermakers for having murdered their comrade I realized that my surgeon had gone to treat people less sick than I was to pay them a visit against their will The next day he came and told me that he was upset that unforeseen business had prevented him from coming (and) he advised me to take and to do exactly as he prescribed to eat not to take any baths and in two weeks I'd be on my feet again

This man took an interest in me His profession aside he was a gentle friendly kindly man One morning passing in front of the shop a chief clerk brought a print for me to frame representing the death of Abel He (the executioner) examined it he found a defect in the arm pointed it out most politely The person was delighted offered me a bottle of wine on condition that he would take his share I agreed He thanked me politely The person invited him He came On the way he asked me if I had said what he was I told him that it had not been necessary The fellow was delighted with his conversation He [i.e., the executioner] left first and paid the check The person could not praise him enough when I asked if he knew what kind of man he'd been drinking with when I told him I saw him change color and say Is it possible I see that he does know what he's talking about because he pointed out the defects in the print

There was a fellow called M Bertrand a button seller whom I met on the boulevards who had been after me for some time to join the confraternity of Saint-Prix which was attached to the church of Saint-Sauveur What variety there is in the religion of our fathers because in one church some are saved and others are duped You can see how simple they are from the fact that they combined two so-called saints so different by their names And (he) wanted to put my name up for nomination as a church-warden[225] of the Holy Sacrament on condition that we split the honorar-

---

[224] See n. 161.

[225] A member of the church council, which was responsible for the temporal administration of the parish, including the preparation of the budget, business dealings, supervision of

ium Never having been a pillar of the church and having very little faith in any churchmen and their religion I did not want to join and we drank a bottle and I paid

When we passed by the rue des Deux-Portes where there was a convent of prostitutes he told me to go up saying that I had treated him and now it was his turn to treat me The mother abbess thought she knew me We struck up a conversation (She) offered me her custom and for a joke I offered her mine We drank We each took a girl I took the mother abbess even though she was over the hill because of our old acquaintance She said the door was open for me and that I would always be welcome and I said good-bye and promised to come back soon

I had above my shop a stucco sculpture representing Henri IV with Sully which belonged to the Viscount de la Tour du Pin[226] Since a servant had broken his sword I had put it back together An Italian told me that if I wanted he would make a model and offered me twelve francs I accepted He made so many of them that everybody in Paris wanted one And I couldn't supply enough to fill all the glass cases that I made My good wife was clever enough to take all the profits and I in spite of everything I was always the fool for whatever we earned together she took upon herself to give to her nephews at the expense of me and my children It was around that time that three companion glaziers from Versailles came to see me and bought a glass secretary that I found out later was presented to the Dauphin I sold it to them for only eighteen livres knowing that every trade made a present of something related to their craft

I was working in the rue Platrièr for the hôtel du Saint-Esprit[227] which Madame de Bellegarde kept as a boarding house I was sent for and taken up to the third floor rear and shown a partition to be lined with paper I saw a man in a robe and a fur cap I hung the paper This man asked where

---

construction, and enforcement of regulations. The post carried no renumeration, and Ménétra's play on words (Saint Prix means Saint Price) was meant as a judgment on the venality of the church in general.

[226] Probably René Charles de la Tour du Pin, born in 1747, son of René François, comte de la Tour du Pin, baron de Plantiers (BN, LM. 3 1257).

[227] Ménétra adds his down-to-earth testimony to other accounts of Rousseau's last sojourn in Paris, when he lived in the rue Platrière in his old boarding house, kept by Madame de Bellegarde. He moved in in the fall, and the meeting with Ménétra occurred in June of 1770. All the details agree with, but add some new shading to, Rousseau's own sketch of his stay, particularly as regards his popularity and his feigned modesty. The promenades are described in *Rêveries du promeneur solitaire.* See also E. Foster, *Le Dernier Séjour de Jean-Jacques Rousseau à Paris* (Paris, 1911).

I was from I answered that I was from Paris He told me that I didn't
have the accent I told him that I had made my tour of France and had
returned by way of Lyons He asked me if I had gone to Geneva I told
him that I had spent only twenty-four hours there that the king's resident
prevented me from staying longer and looking around He seemed enchanted He asked about all the towns I had visited He questioned me
about my adventures and good fortune He sent for me often I asked who
this man was The mistress of the house told me that it was M Rousseau
and that this tall *brenne* (?) whom he called Thérèse was his wife and so
on

One Sunday in front of the house after dinner I saw M Rousseau pass
by I waved He shook my hand affectionately and asked if this was my
house I showed him around He asked me if I wanted to go for a walk I
said that I was going out He asked me which way I was headed I answered that I had thought of going to the Champs-Elysées to watch them
play tennis He said that if I wished he would like to accompany me   I
answered his civilities and we were on our way I saw a worried thought-
ful man he stopped to examine every tree and spoke to me very little

We watched the game we went home When we reached the rue Saint-
Honoré (he) asked me if I wanted to stop for something to drink I told
him that he had anticipated me and that I was about to propose the same
thing We went into the café de la Régence[228] He asked for a pitcher of
beer He asked me if I knew how to play chess I said no He asked me if I
knew how to play checkers I said a little He joked He said that was right
for my age We played I lost I listened and I heard people all around who
kept saying But that is Rousseau that's surely his brother In truth we
both wore gray suits and round wigs with three rows of curls The only
difference was that he carried his hat in his hand and my habit was always
to wear mine on my head Both of us had the same clothes but not at all
the same (breadth of) knowledge Between us (the difference) was like
night and day

---

[228] Among the seven or eight hundred cafés kept by members of the *corporation des limo-
nadiers*, the Café de la Régence had been one of the most famous since the Regency [following
the death of Louis XIV—trans.], from which it took its name in 1718. The vogue for this spot,
which was related to the vogue for chess (or "pushing wood," as it was called), is described by
Diderot in his *Neveu de Rameau*, and the *philosophe* continued to visit the café until his death
(see Madame de Vandeul, *Mémoires pour servir à l'histoire de la vie et des œuvres de Diderot*).
Ménétra's report is confirmed by the police archives, which tell us that the crowds of curious
onlookers who came to see Jean-Jacques forced the police to station guards at the entrance of
the café in the place du Palais-Royal, rue Saint-Thomas-du-Louvre.

The following Sunday we went for a walk over by the boulevards du Temple between the porte Saint-Martin and the barrière de la Courtille We enjoyed seeing the place called the Petit Pré Saint-Gervais which in those days was filled with trees and greenery quite a picturesque spot We sat down He told me about his difficulties with a number of men of intelligence one of whom had made a scene most unworthy of a gentleman and Christophe de Beaumont had excommunicated him but he didn't much care not being one of his flock I saw in him a good Protestant[229]

He said let's go and have a drink where we went last time and we shall find the person with whom I share my life We went in The mistress of the café told us courteously with the greatest of kindness that we could not stay the owner said the same I was quick to take offense and ask why They answered me that last Sunday several marble tables had been broken because such a crowd had come to see M Rousseau play that some people had climbed up on the tables He said to me My friend calm yourself let us go Several people followed us I was not happy I took it as an insult He calmed me The person with whom he had played came forward and eagerly agreed to accompany us to a café across from the entrance of Saint-Eustache where we went often (and) the owner of which knew me (and) urged me to bring him as often as possible so as to boost his business

I went to see him from time to time He liked to copy music[230] One day when I went in to see him I found his wife in a great rage who said to me Monsieur glazier what do you think of a man who has nothing who has just refused a purse full of money that M le duc d'Orléans[231] has sent him and acts the part of the philanthropist who opened the purse and gave some of the money to the servant and then handed him back the purse saying Monsieur the work that I presented to Monseigneur is not worth this much not even as much as it has been my privilege just now to give to

---

[229] Ménétra is referring here to the condemnation of *Emile* in 1762 by the Parlement of Paris, which was the cause of Rousseau's departure and exile until 1770. Rousseau launched a polemic with a letter to Christophe de Beaumont, archbishop of Paris, that remains famous today.

[230] When Jean-Jacques abandoned the usual practice of men of letters of living on gifts from private benefactors, he set himself to copying music for aristocratic clients. After his return, he kept records of his copying, which from 1772 to 1777 amounted to nearly 9,500 pages of elegant and artful calligraphy. In this way he was able to secure a modest income.

[231] In 1770 this was Louis Philippe d'Orléans (1725–1785), who had been duke since 1752 and retired from his military career in 1757. He divided his time between his castles at Saint-Cloud and Bagnolet. His son Louis Philippe Joseph was to join the Convention under the name Philippe-Egalité. The Orléans were the wealthiest family in the kingdom, after the king's family.

you Well Monsieur there you have it says she to me M Rousseau's noble generosity

He called me over Don't listen to that woman's raving and we discussed the affairs of the day and (he) invited me to go to the garden of the Palais-Royal at the Tree of Cracow[232] where they gave out the news true and false because he liked to listen to the reports (and) where this story was told in a thousand ways and (he) just laughed about it

I was with him one day in his office when the servant of a certain abbot who had lodgings in the same house came on behalf of his master to invite him to dinner He gave a singular response Go tell your master that I never dine with people of his robe and character but rather with men like you So my friend after you have served your master come dine with me and I will await you I could not keep from smiling His dear Thérèse kept saying Monsieur is that strong Madame (Bellegarde) asked me what had just happened I told her She answered me I was expecting that

And (I) am quite upset all the little notes[233] that he used to give me every morning to have lost them He was in the country[234] We lost touch He was away for a long time and (I) went to see him sometimes when he was living opposite the central post office

I was working for a convent maintained by the police and the mother abbess was not too hard on me Sometimes it cost me no more than a few panes of glass which somehow got broken when I went too long between visits One day I walked abruptly into the mama's room without announc-ing my presence Suddenly a person sitting there gave a shout hiked her skirts over her head and left like a shot The mistress and I were dumb-founded She said to me Today you cost me one of my best workers because she works here for free and it's all profit for me I wanted to know

---

[232] Owned by the Orléans family since 1673, the Palais-Royal was the palace built by Cardinal de Richelieu and reconstructed by the Regent. Its gardens and approaches were always crowded with *galants* and opinion-makers. The Tree of Cracow was so called because it was a gathering place for lovers of tall stories, called *craques*. The gardens of the Palais-Royal have been immortalized by Diderot, Mercier, and J.A. Dulaure.

[233] *Petits poulets*: literally, little chickens: kind and affectionate letters.

[234] Rousseau left for Ermenonville in May of 1778. Ménétra could have known the philoso-pher for a period of eight years, but it is highly unlikely that Rousseau's letters or reports by those who knew him would not have recorded some reference, however oblique, to such a lengthy relationship. It is more likely that their relations were brief, confined to the time when Rousseau was living in the rue Platrière and later, when he had moved to the fifth floor of a building opposite the post office in the same street, alongside a dealer in paintings—remember that glaziers often framed prints for art dealers.

who she might be I found out only long afterward thanks to her imprudence So she swore me to secrecy which I agreed to on condition that I could sample her wares like the others

One of my uncles got into a dispute with a glass dealer For the intendancy of Tours he needed thirteen hundred fifty pounds of Bohemian glass He came and asked me to do him a favor since I had been in Tours to put it about that it was a master of the place who had written me to send him this shipment I agreed He gave me a hundred écus in gold I went I chose Simon Le Brave Simon was given the word The invoice was prepared I had to sign a note for fifteen hundred livres payable in four and a half months That was the first and the last although I did a fair amount of business I didn't want any more contracts

At that time my wife and my uncles and cousins were plotting against me to have me locked up for a quarter at Saint-Lazare[235] they said to make me drop my girlfriends The petition was prepared by a cousin in the rue de la Grande Truanderie who left it for safekeeping with one of his aunts who was good enough to warm me all they were waiting for was my father's sign to finish this great and fine affair I went directly to my father's house I told him he'd better be sure not to sign I went to see someone I knew who was associated with the police I also saw Chenier I didn't sleep He gave me a pistol I swore I'd make good use of it not much trusting my father knowing that for a bottle of wine they could make him go against my interests

I arrived at ten at night rage in my heart I saw the traitress I told what I knew I said that I wanted a separate bed right away and if she got up at night to open the door I'd blow out the brains of the first person to enter I got into bed put my gun under the head of the bed and did not sleep The wife totally intimidated stayed on a chair When morning came (she) ran to the rue de la Grande Truanderie and told them that I had discovered the plot I followed her I watched her come back She was

---

[235] A religious establishment at number 107, rue du faubourg Saint-Denis. From 1632 on it was a convent, a seminary, a house of correction, and a hospital all rolled into one and run by the *lazaristes* of Saint-Vincent-de-Paul. The house of correction held delinquent children and scions of well-to-do families, whose relatives obtained *lettres de cachet* to have their children committed for libertinage or debt. In 1771 the prison held fifty-six prisoners. Ménétra was threatened with imprisonment after he made the mistake of signing a bill for his uncle without receivables to back the debt. Unable to pay, he was subject to prosecution; but the important point here is to note the fears to which a rather unscrupulous man of free and easy ways was subject if his family denounced him to the authorities.

terribly frightened she thought I might be violent with her I simply told
her You're returning from your council meeting go back to the house

I went to see Chenier who said to me Cousin I prowled around last
night with Givet who was like him in the French Guards and my behavior
toward you was only by way of reprisal I thanked him He wanted to go
shake up Marseau who knew him and was afraid of him I stopped him
and told him (?) but he told me to stay on my guard So I closed the door
when I returned home and put the key under the head of my bed Since
that time I have never been the same and I have never been able to forget
such a trick and such black treachery both by my wife and by my relatives

I had some time earlier renewed my acquaintance with my young governess who prided herself on working in lace Our friendship grew I had
never known what it was to love all the obstacles introduced me to love I
used to joke with those who claimed to be affected by this malady and
I felt obliged to offer this tribute to love I had never been and believed I
never would be afflicted since of all the passions I had known until then
all had been [illegible] In spite of everything I continued to see her and
sized things up so well that I overcame the plot against me and I pretended not to give any thought to the fact that it had come from my
relatives

One day somebody asked for me at the cabaret I went to see who
wanted me It was the Marseau boys I come said one of them from the Ile
Saint-Louis to inform you of the marriage of your cousin to Sieur Oran
Then I asked them why they hadn't come to the house he told me it had
to do with my wife I knew what to think about that He went on that his
son had told him that I knew what went on with the Oran family I told
him that on that score he knew as much as I did They forced me to
explain what I meant I said Well then here are the facts One of his
brothers was hanged in Spain near Perpignan the uncle you know was
whipped and branded and was arrested again and (he) is now in La
Bicêtre

With those words my dear uncle repeated the words of the Regent All
men have five fingers they're not all alike I told him As far as that one is
concerned it's your affair not mine and they left for I had been very cold to
them and would never have believed that I could contain myself but I had
very good reasons

He married his daughter sent me an invitation but not to the dinner I
asked if Marseau had received one (and) he showed me where the dinner
invitation was written I resealed the letter with a double louis and wrote
these words "You should have forgotten me altogether since I never

brought dishonor on my family and by your marriage you are going to dishonor it" When my uncle received this letter I found out from one of the companions he lost his grip on himself and said that he deserved it because he had done a foolish thing to me and that he would never listen to anybody (again) and that I had soul that in my place he would have done the same thing

Finally the day of this charming assembly they had a royal brawl and the cuckold from Picardy (?) was one of the most soundly thrashed I found this out from his wife whom I sometimes saw in secret and Marseau of the rue des Petis-Champs who was a member of the jury was beaten to a pulp So I wrote something on this subject which Renier had copied and sent to a good number of masters in the community so that the Marseaus were made to look ridiculous

Finally the due date of this note arrived The night before I told my wife that I had signed a note to the master of the Saint-Quirin glass works for fifteen hundred livres and that to pay it they would put me not in Saint-Lazare but in the Châtelet She couldn't get over thinking that it was for Marseau of the rue Saint-Avoye She said these words to me He wanted to ruin us And it was true If they had been able to put me in a cage It was supposed (that) since I had no acknowledgment (of debt) they would have said that I had illegally spent the money then they would have sold everything and my wife would herself have paid the price for the foolish thing she had started Being sequestered I would not have had the right to explain myself and all the wrongs would have been on my side and the worthy Marseau would never have opened his mouth

I can say that the three other Marseaus may have been led astray and they were no part of the fraud arranged by the one for whom I had signed the note That doesn't alter the fact that they were contemptible for having signed (the petition) against me They came to see me to say that they had had no part in this affair I wanted to believe them and I told them my feelings on the subject and (said that I) didn't want to see them any more or to have anything to do with them

Finally to get back to my note I went to see him the night before and as the saying goes faced bad fortune with a stout heart I pointed out that the bill came due the next day He pretended to be surprised he told me that he was to receive a bag of twelve hundred francs from M Joly de Fleury[236]

---

[236] Guillaume Joly de Fleury (1710–1787), named procureur général of the Parlement of Paris in 1740, is typical of the Parisian *noblesse de robe*: hard-working, cultivated, and a shrewd observer of his surroundings. See P. Bisson, *L'Activité d'un procureur général au*

at eight in the morning and that he would bring me the sum I told him
that I would come for the money that we would go together The next
day at six I was at the corner of rue Grenier-Saint-Lazare waiting for my
man Around eight I saw him go out and walk up the rue de Braque I
headed him off by taking the rue du Grand-Chantier He told me that he
was going to get the cash that I should wait for him in a cabaret at the
corner of the old rue du Temple I ordered a mug I sat myself down by a
window that looked out on the door of the house [where the money was to
be received] I paid and set myself to watch He came out overheated told
me that he had been paid that we should go for lunch at his house I
answered him that he should count out my share I put it in my hat He
told me to pour him a drink I told him that he wasn't good enough to
drink with me and that if he weren't my mother's brother I would break
the bottle over his head and that he and the other Marseaus had tried to
ruin me and that he had tried to lead my wife astray and that they would
die all four of them like the criminals they were and I left him and went
straight to pay off my bill

Though I'm no prophet what I predicted did come to pass They had
taken a dislike to me because I aped them and made good deals despite my
little mishaps They were jealous when they saw me prosper Marseau
from the Ile was stupid enough on the subject of the frequentation of a
countess (to tell me) that if I had been a Marseau he would have given her
to me being in my quarter (?) I answered him very positively that I was
more Marseau than their children and pointed out the obvious truth of the
matter I told him Even if my mother had cheated on her husband I
would still be of Marseau stock And if their wives made them cuckolds
(their children) would only be intruders transplanted into the family And
he didn't know what to say

My wretched father was blind He had his old governess named Fan-
chon (who) in spite of everything did not leave him and sometimes took
him out walking He suffered a thousand indignities at the hands of his
beloved daughter and he was in the most miserable state and quite sick
when one day I sent a wine merchant's boy for news of him and he came
back with word that my father was very ill I went there I asked to see

---

parlement de Paris, à la fin de l'Ancien Régime: Les Joly de Fleury (Paris, 1964). The family
residence was on the Left Bank, however (in the rue Saint-Guillaume until 1775, then in the
rue de la Planche). Hence Ménétra must have the wrong person. He may be talking about a
business agent who paid the debts of his clients and who had his offices in the Marais.

my father The man and the woman promised me that they were going to take good care of him and in case he died they would bury him honorably That I said to them is what you owe him in any case

I sent my wife She found him under his bed without care of any kind on their part She picked him up went to see him often I returned I asked to see my father They told me he was sleeping I took that well (and then) the next day I received a letter from my sister Thérèse telling me that they had taken my father to the Hôtel-Dieu I sent my wife there at once I went to see him He recognized me shook my hand begged my pardon and said that his children were trash I consoled him I told him My father a father shouldn't beg pardon from his children but should give his blessing He asked me to kiss him and asked that when he was a little better I should have him brought to my house and he would live with us I left him took my leave with a heavy heart My wife went to see him He was approaching the end and yet was still sipping mightily from a glass of Alicante wine My sister Thérèse sent word that it was all over

I went to see her I made up my mind to have it out with that ferocious woman I informed them (?) of the death I told her that she had no more father I reminded her of their promise [to pay for the old man's burial—trans.] She told me that it was impossible for them to keep it I insisted that they keep their word I stated my case vigorously That unnatural monster his beloved (daughter) said these words to me which I shall never forget Let the devil bury him if he wants I was no longer in possession of my senses I asked where his things were and for the silver cover that he had kept They said that it had been pawned I flew into a rage He said he would borrow some money I took it and wished that this unworthy woman who called herself my sister might suffer the same pains that she had made our wretched father endure that she would be bitten beaten scratched by her little daughter (and) he couldn't even protect himself since he couldn't see clearly

I went from there directly to my other sister who was not on speaking terms with me in part because of her charming sister whom she was proud of having raised And (we) went therefore to identify the body and bury it in the cemetery of the Innocents[237] which was on a very remarkable Saint

---

[237] The largest cemetery in Paris from the tenth to the eighteenth century, located between the rue Saint-Denis, the rue aux Fers, and the rue de la Ferronnerie. Dead from nearby parishes and from the Hôtel-Dieu were buried there until 1780. Its common graves received their daily ration of bodies, and its charnel houses sheltered public writers, small merchants, and spectators. The cemetery was closed because of complaints from neighbors about the

Martin's Day I took my little boy So ended the author of my days who with the money he had saved should have enjoyed an easier end

As I was crossing the Saint-Michel bridge on business I ran into cousin Chenier who asked me if I wanted to treat him to a drink and I told him that I had gone out without taking any money and that I was in a hurry He answered that he was in a hurry too but if I came back that way he would buy me lunch in the rue de la Huchette I promised to look for him on my way back It was the day of the drawing for the French Royal Lottery[238] I had twenty-four sols and to show him that I was not a liar I went to the bottom of the bridge and took the last ticket from the hands of a child I went looking for Chenier who was waiting for me Upon leaving for home I passed by the office I saw the list I looked I had two numbers I went in I told Chenier to wait I turned in my ticket They immediately counted out forty-seven livres I explained to Chenier that I had twenty-four sols and before going to meet him so as not to be taken for a liar I had bought this ticket We took a cab Drive quickly to La Glacière for dinner and (I) returned home again with around thirty-six livres That kept the wife from getting angry since money was all she knew

Some time later Mary full of grace took it into her head to leave me She took our daughter and everything she could carry with her including the silverware and went back where she came from (She) was gone for two or three months During that period I passed the time rather well thanks to[239] my governess who came often to keep me company since my wife had left home the way she did having packed her bags as they say

I didn't lose heart and while she was gone I kept up the business And

---

stench, as well as because a grave collapsed and a campaign was launched to expel the cemeteries from the city. A market was built on the site: commerce supplanted death, an allegory of the times.

238 The lottery was introduced into France by Italians in the sixteenth century, and despite the ban on games of chance it met with tremendous success, in part because of the good works it made possible: in 1658 there was a lottery for the general hospital, in 1701 for fire pumps, in 1754 for foundlings, and in 1757 for the military school. The royal lottery was established in 1776, in part to attract the money that bettors were losing to other lotteries. One could purchase one or more numbers, alone or in combination from a list of forty. A single winning number paid fifteen times the amount bet, and a combination of three (known as a *terne*) paid 270 times the amount bet. Every two weeks, five numbers were drawn, making for seven possible combinations. Skillfully administered and capitalizing on the popular belief in the redistribution of wealth by chance, the lottery was highly successful. It was abolished in the Year II but reinstituted in the Year VI.

239 An instance of Ménétra's improper use of *malgré* for *grace à*.

everything went according to my desires I always tried to do the right
thing because I foresaw that if I wasn't careful I would be scorned and
subject to slander I set myself above it all and went my own way Still I
made the acquaintance of a charming widow who wanted me to declare
my wife in separation[240] but my wishes were not hers I've never liked
legal proceedings what is more I had children Seeing that I didn't want
to talk about this subject and since she was rich and had retired on
comfortable means promising myself that I would be happier we broke
off She was extremely passionate she died from too much pleasure being
attacked in the lung (??)

Finally in spite of everything it was my old lady who still prevailed
Passing in front of Saint-Eustache and not thinking about her at all I ran
into her We found ourselves face to face I wanted to talk to her She ran
A few days later she sent for me I refused to see her Finally I was
persuaded and little by little she began to behave as usual that is to say
that she always took her share and turned it over to her sister and nephews
So I never had to worry when it was a question of needing a hundred écus
for the business they found friends who would lend to them right away
But those friends were really her secret hiding places One day I caught
her counting out the money I needed the cash was in an alley (and she)
tried to make me believe that somebody had lent her the money I shut my
eyes just to have some peace So I left her to carry the household burdens
and thought only of pleasing my public

One Monday morning my wigmaker invited me to drink some white
wine We drank three half bottles and with them ate eight *petits pains* of
which he had six On leaving he said he had a headache and if I wanted to
we could take a stroll on the boulevard We went I ran into my companion's father who asked me if I was happy with him He was selling tickets
for the French Royal Lottery He had two left It was the day of the
drawing I took the first one he offered me My wigmaker wanted the
second because the one I held was number 1 23 and 84 I kept them We
went up to Nouvelle France we had lunch we walked in the fields we

---

[240] The old civil law made no provision for divorce, which was incompatible with the
religious doctrine of indissoluble marriage, but it did allow *séparation de corps et biens*
(separation of bodies and property), which could be obtained from the civil courts—in Paris,
the Châtelet. The procedure was long and costly, and remarriage was impossible. Ending a
civil marriage was made legal when the Revolution secularized the law (law of 20 September
1792). Ménétra's daughter was therefore able to divorce and remarry in 1802.

went to Little Poland[241] for a drink I heard them shouting out the list
What did I see within one digit of our three numbers I did a jig and I
said We have nine hundred fifty pounds I looked at my ticket there were
only two numbers it was 85 Finally our joy subsided I asked him if he
had any money He answered that he had six livres I took them We had a
good dinner we enjoyed ourselves we went to get the money we split it
we bought a dead sparrow

Then we knocked at my front door A little angry my wife yelled that
both of us had left our shops that his wife had come by more than ten times
that day I told my little boy to (go get her) She came over started
scolding him as all women do because he went out in his slippers wearing
an apron and no hat When I told them about our adventure all of us
regained our good spirits and the lady as she was leaving said to me You
should take my husband on such outings more often

My daughter her mother had with my consent put her out to board My
boy I talked him out of the prejudices that bigots had filled his head with
during his tender years My state (?) my wife went her own way now and
then and made some trips I got used to it

I went often to the Champs-Elysées to watch them play tennis (and)
sometimes I played a few matches When one day Sieur Masson whom I
had known when we were young his father having kept a billiard parlor
opposite my father's shop and I used to go knock some balls around in his
tennis court in the rue Grenelle-Saint-Honoré[242] came to see me upon his
return from England (He) told me that he just set himself up in business
that the duc d'Orléans and the prince de Condé had just made a wager
between themselves the first favors open-air tennis [*battoir*] and the second indoor tennis [*paume*] that he hadn't forgotten me remembering that
I was pretty nimble that they would begin on Sunday after dinner with

---

[241] Petite Pologne, or Little Poland, was a section located just north of the great sewer and
gradually incorporated into the city after the sewer was covered in 1737. Since it lay at that
time outside the customs barriers, it was an attractive location for cabarets and *guinguettes*.
In 1764 it became part of the Madeleine parish.

[242] One of the leading tennis-billiard establishments in Paris, in the rue Grenelle-Saint-
Honoré, run by a family with a long line of such establishments. Indoor tennis was played on
a court 25 meters by 9 meters. The court, or *tripot* (from *trépigner*, to trample) was often
painted black to make the white ball stand out. Widely played in the seventeenth century,
tennis lost some of its popularity in the early eighteenth century. There were 117 tennis
establishments in 1657 but only sixty-some in 1760. The comte d'Artois and various princes
loved the game, which lends plausibility to the episode recounted here. See J. Delay, *D'une
minute à l'autre* (Paris, 1978); see also n. 142.

outdoor tennis and the following Sunday they would play indoors that we
would be six on each side that one team would wear blue scarves and the
other red I agreed with pleasure I told him that I had a jacket but no
white pants and no shoes He told me to come by his place and I would
find everything I needed that we would meet at the Swiss guard's booth
at the pont Tournant[243] where we were supposed to be treated at the
princes' expense

The day came I showed up Everyone gave me a warm welcome I saw
a sumptuously laid table the princes squires who saluted me a number of
crosses of Saint-Louis exhorting each team to do well They tied a scarf
around each of us Me and Masson and the four others we had red
standing for the Prince of Condé We marched in a procession a crowd
followed us hundreds of people were waiting to see the match The person who was playing against me asked me what I wanted to play I
answered Forward glory to all Masson had me put down for twelve
francs in exchange for services rendered I agreed

The match began Masson took the back court I was in second position
the four others were for backup We played marvelously we won the first
match We lost the second All we heard was shouts of Courage in the end
we won everything We were applauded endlessly and the return match of
indoor tennis was set for Sunday We went back to the Swiss guard's
station for refreshment We were welcomed by the lords who were amateurs of tennis and congratulated us I heard several (of them) say to
Masson that they had never seen me before that I was extremely active
and a very ardent player and that I was always after the ball

The following Sunday we were treated like the Sunday before We were
surrounded by lords who encouraged us Masson was foolish having supplied the rackets and tennis balls he went to the court early and amused
himself knocking balls around with the other team he showed them how
to take the ball on the bounce I told him he was making a mistake he just
laughed The match began We lost the first (set) after putting up a good
defense We won the second straightaway So we came down to the wire
We came to deuce often finally we lost Masson was no longer in it he
took the balls even though I asked him he wanted to be in everything and
put them all outside I complained that he had shown them the rebound
shot and angrily threw my racket down and ran over to the Swiss guard's

---

[243] Pont Tournant: a bridge across the moats in the Tuileries between the garden and the
place Louis XV, closed at night and guarded by Swiss guards.

station to dress and go home But I was kept there and a magnificent meal was served though I didn't enjoy it as much as I had the previous one So ended that famous match although Masson asked for a return match

On Saint Mark's day I put on new clothes I went to see Masson In comes the Prince of Condé to play a match and (he) asks if M Dufort[244] has arrived Somebody replied that he wouldn't be long and Masson said to him Monseigneur if you would like to knock some balls around there is a young man here who will keep you amused who was a member of your team in the Champs-Elysées I answered without thinking about what I was saying when Masson handed me a racket that I could not play with Monseigneur Masson grumbled at me but what was said was said I realized my stupidity It was too late and we lost touch

One day at my lace-mender's I ran into one of her cousins who told me that her husband was in business as a master harness maker in the rue des Deux Portes I told her that we were neighbors We had something to eat together I said that I knew her husband that my wigmaker fitted him out I paid her compliments She said she was delighted that her cousin was my girlfriend On Sunday I was at the wigmaker's when her husband came in Since it was more or less my custom to have lunch with the wigmaker I offered him a glass of wine he accepted We got to know one another His wife came I complimented her They said they were going to the château de Meudon[245] and that if I wanted to go with them I would be quite welcome I thanked them They begged me so much that I gave in I went home to leave word that since the next day was a holiday I would be staying overnight in the country

So we left and received a warm welcome That night they had us sleep in two rooms that communicated with each other In the morning the

---

[244] No family by this name was represented in princely entourages at this time. There may be confusion with Durfort, an old noble family with several branches, or with Duport, an aristocratic family from Burgundy which may have had relations with Condé, then governor of Burgundy.

[245] Royal residence unused by Louis XVI. In 1775, the windows and stained glass for the chapel were damaged by a storm. Ménétra could not have gained access except through connections with the castle staff: the porter, gardeners, and guards. It is interesting to note that the supervisor of Meudon and his glazier, Sieur Delaunay, invited to Meudon to assess the damage "the only man in Paris who successfully cultivates the art of painting on glass": see P. Biver, *Histoire du château de Meudon* (Paris, 1923), pp. 45, 292–293. It would be pleasant to imagine that it was Ménétra who made the trip, but the documents do not indicate the name of this expert glass painter, who in any case was not hired. See the letter to the comte d'Angivilliers, directeur de bâtiments, dated 18 September 1775.

concierge went with the husband for a walk in the park I went downstairs I saw a little pig I brought it up to my cousin's door She feigned surprise that her husband was gone and I stood there holding the little animal which was squealing desperately I approached the bed And my husband I kept going I told her to sit up in bed and she would see him in the park I finished what I had begun and left the pig in the room I told (the husband) what I had done as to the pig and refrained from mentioning the rest They came back they saw Monsieur in the room they teased him Everything went quite well The three of us returned home happy and promised to make another such outing

I told the story to her cousin who seemed affected by it and told me to watch out for this woman who could cause us trouble The next Sunday a group of ten or twelve of us went to Saint-Cloud We went in a small boat I played a thousand tricks I sat beside the harness-maker's wife and I saw the husband who was out of sorts talking about the pig I stayed away from her for the rest of the day but at night on the way back she insisted on taking my arm I went along with her wishes We stopped for a drink She drank a bit too much I was with a friend in front of her She called me said some extravagant things praised me in a thousand ways which shocked her husband They blamed me for it I blamed her indiscretion and promised myself to avoid her company

A few days later she went to see my wife and grumbled about her cousin said she was debauching me that if she [i.e., Ménétra's wife] wished she would take her to the house and that she would surely find me there [My wife] believed her and they went off together As luck would have it I was across the street saw them go up to speak to the main tenant I sent someone over to find out what she might have said Plenty of unflattering things about us The next day I ran into her at pointe Saint-Eustache When she saw me (she) said a thousand friendly things asked me to go into a café said that she had many things to tell me I told her You are a Circe and get out of here because I want nothing to do with you after what you did yesterday to me and your cousin taking my wife there Get out Adieu When I saw that my wife had discovered my second home I ordered a move and went all the way out to the rue Jean de Beauvais

One night around eleven thirty passing by a small street called Crucifix Saint-Jacques I saw two men tied to the wall two others crouched in the middle of the street bent over who got up when I passed and two others at the end leaning against a fence I did not lose heart I took out my hammer and set the peen and hurried by A moment later I heard shouts thief murderer I saw two of those crooks come running who had tried to block my way The guard came running after They asked me who I was I told them I saw a man covered with blood whom they had robbed and almost murdered come with another guard I followed them to the police station I described them and since that time I've refrained from coming home so late

One day the executioner asked me to come keep him company as I had done sometimes in the past We drank a couple of bottles of wine together He seemed pensive I asked him what was wrong He answered that he wished the night was over I pressed him He told me that at ten o'clock he had a job to do in the Petit Châtelet I asked him if I could watch He told me to ask I went and had supper with my lace-mender and from there went to the Petit Châtelet[246] I knocked Somebody opened the door I asked for M Henri They told me to wait He came and threw three livres on the table A guard brought six bottles and we all drank together and told jokes when all of a sudden someone knocked at a door I had not noticed before The room was plunged into deep silence Suddenly three men came out one of them dressed in black Someone said There is Monsieur. . . I did not catch the name Henri grabbed him pushed him against the wall (near) a small stool and the poor wretch feeling himself pushed put his feet up on the stool Then a hook and underneath a hood and all at once my man was hanging Henri having given the stool a kick Immediately his brother (?) took him by his private parts and the scene was over Henri ran out and I could not get over what I had just seen I went out I saw that they were putting the victim in a wheelbarrow and I couldn't bear to watch any longer

A short while later I happened to be working in an apartment in the passage du Saumon I saw the person who was to occupy the apartment arrive I recognized one of my old girlfriends from Lyons I greeted her She was surprised We went into another room so that my companion and

---

[246] Opposite the Châtelet, at the end of the Petit-Pont, this was a multistoryed building with vaulted passageway that was used as a prison. A decision was made to demolish it in 1722, but it was not executed until 1782. The prisoners were transferred to the Châtelet. This Goya-like anecdote tells of practices that would hardly have been approved under the criminal code, which required that executions be public in order to serve as a deterrent to crime. For the story to be true one would have to imagine some sort of mysterious affair or more likely a sentence with *retentum*, in which the condemned man could be secretly executed in advance for "humanitarian" reasons and then burned or, more frequently, hanged in public.

her servant would not hear our conversation I asked what happy chance had brought her to live in Paris After we kissed she told me that her husband was in Lyons and that a certain personage whose name and rank she did not wish to tell me had brought her to Paris and that was how she came to have (the pleasure) of seeing me again That she had asked after me but since she didn't know my last name her search might have proved fruitless except that chance had (reunited) us that as for her departure from Lyons she had been forced to leave for many reasons and that she would tell me in confidence that she would somehow find a way to see that we got together I told her about my shop and refrained from telling her about my pranks

I asked about the personage I learned that it was the first vicar of Saint-Eustache one of whose brothers was count of Lyons[247] I wanted to hear her explanation of this matter the first time I went to see her She hid the real story from me finally I wanted to get down to brass tacks seeing that she did not conceal how much she liked me She stopped me with a sigh and reluctantly told me that she was spoiled[248] and that that was partly why she had come to Paris and that this was the secret she wanted to tell me and that it came from the man who kept her who had looked for a job (only) to get himself treated and that he was very careful as she looked enough like him that he could pass her off as one of his sisters I questioned her about her disease I brought her to Henri and he undertook (to treat) both of them

The personage could not avoid making himself known and I along with Henri could not (fail) to be indignant that men who are supposed to demonstrate virtue by their character represent only vice Nevertheless when they finally achieved a state of grace I was the one who tasted the first fruits in any case that was what she wanted me to believe And Madame frequently required visits from the glazier

One Sunday while at the Lion d'Or with two friends a small man and a young woman were at a table behind me The young person had her back to the wall when all of a sudden a stocky fellow carrying a cane jumped on the little man and slapped him saying That's what you deserve for not

---

[247] In the list of canons of Lyons holding a canonry in one of the most prestigious of France's noble chapters, the name cited by Ménétra does not occur. The anecdote is not implausible, given the libertine behavior of some clergymen.

[248] She came to Paris for a course of treatment at Bicêtre or more likely in one of the private clinics that were just then opening their doors. See also n. 184.

letting me dance with that slut and as he said that word moved to slap the man again She threw herself on me I told my man to leave off He answered me When I'm good and ready I asked him if he knew who he was talking to He challenged me raised his cane I wasted no time With his first blow he had already received two or three All the onlookers applauded The tables were overturned the glasses broken The tavern-keeper made him pay Two of his friends told us that whenever he had a glass of wine he was like that that he was friends with the little man who was named Brocq that the fellow I'd been dealing with was a master baker from the faubourg Saint-Martin and that the quarrel was a result of jealousy He apologized to Brocq and didn't want to go off without drinking a bottle with me I agreed He wanted to give me an explanation We shook hands without rancor While this was going on the little man and his girlfriend made their getaway

Almost two hours later I saw Brocq come in with a friend and ask if they could join us that I was a good fellow (they) asked where I lived what I did for a living The next day (he) came to see me We became friends We agreed to meet Each of us brought a girl and we became fast friends I found out that he had a talent for card tricks and that he was in vogue that he never went out with less than three livres and twenty-four sols At home the little fellow received visitors in the morning in a charming office Not an evening went by when he didn't come to see me

One day of Saint Louis I was taking my daughter who was beginning to be very pretty to hear a concert in the Tuileries[249] We ran into each other He took me to see a person in the rue de l'Echelle who had five or six large apartments We were warmly received To our children they gave bonbons and to us all the liquor we could drink She showed us her place of which the last room was full of cats Brocq told me privately that she knew plenty of things She invited us to come see her I promised her and one day I kept my word She told me a lot of truth but I always suspected that it came from Brocq (?)

It was around this time that we put our daughter out to board and my wife made a second trip to her native village as usual taking pains to take the nuggets with her And I stayed home with my little boy Finally my

---

[249] Concerts were given in the Grand Salon des Suisses starting in 1725. From 1773 on they were conducted by Gossec and Legros and very well attended, with normal audiences of 300–1,000 people and an exceptionally large crowd of 1,324 on Easter Sunday in 1787.

wife tired of her village came back home and took up where she left off and I was gentleman enough to take her back

One day seeing that Brocq did not pass by as usual they told me that he had been imprisoned on orders They suspected it was on behalf of the Duchess of Bourbon[250] Going to his nurse where he had been summoned he had indeed told me that he had done card tricks for M de Bourbon and that was his misfortune

Manon the old governess my solid woman found a grocer from the neighborhood of the Hôtel-Dieu who wanted to marry her She confided in me I made no objection I really wanted to know the truth We had known each other for a long time our moods were perfectly matched It would be desirable for men as well as women before tying the knot to live together for a time to see if their moods can really be joined I went to see my competitor He showed me into his office I explained the reason for my visit I told him that he knew what it was all about that if it was for good reasons I would cede to him but not otherwise He assured me quite firmly that he wanted to make his wife legitimate that he knew all about the situation with me and that he would overlook it since he believed me gentleman enough not to make any objection I promised him and gave him my hand that it was all over and I gave him my word of honor because he spoke to me so frankly

Some time earlier my little boy caught smallpox from being too affected by the fact that somebody was doing his portrait (?) It bothered him tremendously that he was obliged not to move and had to keep perfectly still Finally the disease revealed itself Without saying anything to the mother I made the sister drink as often as possible from the same glass I made them eat against their will crusts of bread and both came out of it quite well and without any mark from this deadly disease

Meanwhile Manon informed me that her marriage would take place at Sainte-Marguerite since her mother and father lived in the faubourg Saint-Antoine I did not come despite the invitation The following Sunday she passed by the shop I saw her She glimpsed me I followed her and we met at the Petits-Carreaux She spoke to me about her marriage We went in to drink a bottle She told me that her husband had her body but that I would always have her heart I became inflamed I took her to the cour

---

[250] Daughter of the Prince de Condé, Louis Henri Jean, duc de Bourbon (1756–1830), and his wife Louise Bathilde d'Orléans.

des Miracles[251] and at the home of a willing accomplice I struck a blow at her blessed husband I told her Now I'm happy that's all I wanted be calm take care of your household live well with your husband You have all you need to make things turn out well this fellow must love you because he has long known that you were in my hands and he doesn't hold it against either of us For I was sure that I was going to find another girlfriend She didn't want to leave me even though she was going for dinner in the rue Montmartre at her husband's brother's place

The elimination of this girl (from) my usual routines (left) me in greater perplexity than I ever felt for any woman Several of my friends noticed this and to distract me we made outings together One of my friends who had just recently made the head of that saint sent they said by the pope under the name Saint Victory (?) (and) whose face I had seen my friend mold in wax all the good women and all the hypocrities said that she came from Rome when I had been one of those who had seen her manufactured in the rue Tiquetonne And all those devout folk came to invoke (the saint) and burn candles to this piece of wax in the church of the Filles-Dieu formerly known as *filles du diable* [daughters of the devil] And that proved to me that the priests have always impressed weak minds

Langlois and some friends and I kept going out together I had made the acquaintance of a fellow named M Gaillard who lived near the house (He) was from Geneva traded in watches (and) being a great friend of the famous fireworks artist Ruggier[252] took me to see him often Since he had hot pants he knew the abbesses of several convents with whom he traded gold watches One day I went with him to Henriette de Poissy's in the rue du Pélican He sold two watches in exchange for a good supper There were six of us at table Henriette had her lover and each of us had a girl

---

[251] The Cour des Miracles was a web of narrow streets, courtyards, alleyways, and culs de sac in the Saint-Sauveur parish. Access was via rue Thévenot. In 1667 the lieutenant général de police, La Reynie, rounded up the tramps and beggars who had settled there. It remained a trouble spot until 1787, when the Petits-Carreaux market was built on the site.

[252] No Paris festival was complete without a fireworks display. Fireworks were manufactured by masters commissioned by the king or the city, who, after the fire of 1707, were required to do their work outside the city limits. Volume 1 of *L'Encyclopédie méthodique* (arts et métiers) lists the major kinds of fireworks in use from the seventeenth century on. In the final years of the Ancien Régime the Ruggieri brothers were the kings of fireworks. They imitated Torré, the founder of Vauxhall, and staged lyric pantomimes and celebrations in their gardens in the rue Blanche, which attracted large crowds during the good season. Without access to the family documents it is hard to know which of the brothers—Pietro, Francesco, Antonio, Petronio, or Gaetano—was friendly with Ménétra. See Thiery, *Guide du voyageur à Paris* (1787), 1:144.

Gaillard teased me made jokes at my expense about my mistress who was married Henriette said I was not the sort of fellow to displease the person sitting next to me and who had just bought a watch

So the night wore on the young person in spite of her profession talked quite well (and) said she wanted to help me get over my memories and there I was off again She had a private room outside (the house which) was well furnished and (she) was very friendly to me And (she) gave me a double key and as long as our relationship lasted for I was the one who broke it off she never missed a meeting and when we went out together she dressed up and looked like a good bourgeoise

One evening at the Cadet Buteux with old Gaillard a well-dressed woman with a servant came over to our table to say that she wanted to talk to him He said to her you may after he made them sit down and have a drink say what's on your mind She said that she had just come from his house and that his principal tenant had told her that he was surely at the Cadet Buteux or the Grand Vaingueur She asked him if he had any watches He showed her several They agreed on the price She said she did not have the full amount she paid him and gave him her note on condition that we go eat a dead sparrow I went to order it and a salad I found out that she was the famous madame Madame Saint-Louis who kept a convent in the rue Beaurepaire She invited us to come the next day for dinner We escorted her She bought us ratafia to drink and we promised that we would be at her place for dinner the following day

We kept our word We were two men and eight women The evening was spent at table Each woman went out when somebody called them to their work Me and Gaillard pretended to ignore it He sold another watch to one of the women Gaillard made sweet eyes at mother Saint-Louis We were on our way The girl who had bought the watch had some drinks brought in It was late They invited us to sleep in the house They had a bed made up (in the room) of the Saint-Louis woman and so we made a couple

After two weeks Gaillard said to me Go see Saint-Louis I think she has a little something for you She sent somebody to your shop to order some panes and I gather from what she told me that your companion went to install them I went there one morning She was in bed I wished her well and kissed her and noticed two lumps of fat that somebody was pretending to hide She told me to sit down that she had something to tell me I asked what that might be She told me in confidence that the young lady had been ill since the time we were together

I remembered having the same adventure with Denongrais Arm in hand I showed her that I was in a state of grace In a trice my pants were down it was done in the blink of an eye with a turn of the lock I was riding to the charge She said I was intrepid and that that would not do I went about my business and she accused me of employing the same strat- egem about which I had told old Gaillard and which had once worked so well with the Denongrais woman whom she called a b—— I asked her for an explanation because as far as I was concerned they were equal She answered that she was a widow that she was his mistress and that the other woman had her husband I couldn't believe that in a profession like hers she would have had so much delicacy I pretended to go along with her but I knew what to believe When her whim and mine had passed I went to see her sometimes or when I had nothing better to do And she often reproached me for it but I don't at all like to be tied down

I went occasionally to see Melle de Saint-Léon the Lyonnaise She had taken the name of her dear brother in God One day she asked me to take her out walking that her dear brother the abbot was leaving for the country and that we would have dinner together and so we were off But the proverb is not false Man proposes and the Lord disposes for I cer- tainly proposed to myself to spend a night such as I had spent before with that charming lady We ran into him She held my arm He asked where she was headed She answered with an assured air that she was going for a stroll on the boulevards with her glazier to look around and buy a few prints He answered that he was going to accompany her I bowed to them They returned my bow I left and that was the end of my plans I found ready consolation in the arms of her servant whom I knew I would find at home and with whom I had several times had idle conversations in which I said I loved her more than her mistress who lived with an abbot The charming Thérèse was all aflame I pressed her She told me she was a virgin I told her to keep it and withdrew and a good thing I did because as I was leaving I spotted the quality in the distance on their way back home

A few days later standing on my doorstep I watched sweet Thérèse go to and fro I wished her good evening She shook my hand said that she had many things to tell me I followed her The wife shouted that I could not stay in the house I said I was coming back I arrived I saw a nice meal She said to me after a really warm exchange of kisses that between Monsieur and Madame things were stormy that Monsieur had not set foot in the house since the day or our meeting that a lady friend came to take Madame to the theater that she and her mistress had both tried several times to speak to me I started kissing her some more She poured me several glasses and begged me to take what I had not wanted to even though I was all aflame just as she was I made objections to her She heard none of them and we sacrificed to Cupid She was ablaze We made promises in the heat of passion that we could not keep

The mistress arrived She was delighted to see me (and) had many things to tell me She told Thérèse that she was all red The charming Thérèse said that whenever I came to the house I tormented her She made me go into Thérèse's room so that in case her jealous lover came he would not surprise us together She sent Thérèse on an errand and I was obliged to sacrifice to Cupid again on the same altar but with another priestess

She told me that she had received a letter from her family and one from her husband that she showed me that breathed love and friendship and that she wanted to leave the abbot Since he ran into us together (he) had been treating her coldly and that that would lead to a break between them (since she) had told him one day that she had known me in Lyons I pointed out her indiscretion and without saying anything I left her with her intention to leave the abbot and return to her family which she did I set a date with her at a secondhand dealer's under the roof of Les Halles and the night before her departure it was there that we said the tenderest of farewells She left Paris without saying good-bye to the holy abbot and without receiving his blessing and thus ended my relations with my charming Lyonnaise who had promised to stay in touch but never did unless her letters were intercepted by my wife

The gentle Thérèse found herself without employment I got her a job with a woman who was an actress at the Comédie italienne[253] She stayed there for a long time I saw her occasionally because she had a great deal of respect for me She fell ill I took steps to treat her (She) went to the Hôtel-Dieu to get rid of the burden and died shortly thereafter and I was very upset

[253] After many rebuffs due to the hostility of the rival Comédie française, the Comédie italienne returned to Paris in 1716 and, having renounced the use of Italian, established themselves in the hôtel de Bourgogne. Shortly thereafter the troupe experienced a serious crisis that forced them to try their luck as an itinerant company, and they began staging shows in the Saint-Laurent market. In 1762 they merged with the troupe of the Opéra-comique. The hôtel de Bourgogne's theater was located in the rue Mauconseil in the neighborhood of Les Halles.

Despite my little indiscretions I took care of my business and my wife too Her interest had a lot to do with it Our two children grew the girl became charming My womanizing slowed down and everything was going pretty well Tranquillity began to reign in the house and my wife My wife was constantly on the lookout and made investments on her own account and cheated me and my children out of our share But in order to have peace and quiet I let her do as she pleased (and) never tried to stop her greedy speculation

One day while working on the glass roof of a pearl merchant's shop by his carelessness the ladder slipped and I fell to the street I tried to go home I could not move Friends were obliged to carry me and I found myself confined to my bed having hurt my kidneys severely We had a lot of work The companion left us I sent for another one The next day one came at seven o'clock and between eight and nine arrived the syndic who was a Picard accompanied by Oran who was a jury member with a whole entourage and who began by drawing up an affidavit charging me with a violation because the companion was working without having registered

Even though I was in bed injured and though I told them that it was their clerk who had just sent him within the hour they paid no attention to any of it and both took their vengeance against me the one for having done a job that he could not do the other because his brother had robbed me on the tour of France Finally I was fined fifteen francs I said to them when I went to pay at the office some choice words which they deserved I treated them to my invective The other masters who were present made fun of them I treated them as they deserved The three other jury members were delighted Much as they tried they couldn't intimidate me (and) sensing that I had support they withdrew in shame saying that they were going to bring suit against me I scorned them and challenged them and told everyone present that it was not out of vengeance (that I behaved as I did) All the masters were affected Somebody threw a stone at them They were seen and I had shown them up for what they were Oran went out In the alley of the office I gave him the one-two His wig fell to his shoulders He shouted wanted to call the masters present to witness (but) they all said they had seen nothing so he shouted inappropriately and went off with his shame Some while later all these self-important juries and syndics were abolished[254] My jibes and writings against them pleased the masters who had them copied and distributed

---

[254] As contrôleur général des finances, Turgot, pressed by the liberals, began in 1774 efforts to reform the guilds, which were totally abolished in February of 1776. Freedom of labor

I had long since lost contact with a person I had known when I was with Jérôme master glazier in the rue des Prouvaires Melle Beaufort who had married a fellow named Bouchu employed in the [royal tax] farms One day I came to the corner of the rue des Petits-Carreaux and the rue de Bourbon with several friends to drink a bottle I saw behind the counter a person who was not unknown to me I stared at her She did the same I got up and tried to remember where I had seen this person (who) although of an advanced age still preserved something of the beautiful woman she had once been Finally we went down I paid I said to her Madame I think I know you And me too says she aren't you a glazier At the sound of her voice I took her hand I said to her I knew you under the name of Melle Beaufort and I she answered (knew you) under the name Ménétra One of my friends left I told the other that we were going to drink a half bottle We went into the office near the bar She told me that her brother-in-law was the owner that she was a widow and that she tended the bar that her husband had been serving an envoy in Turkey for five or six years and that it had been a long time since she had heard any news that if I wanted to come see her she would tell me everything that had happened since we lost touch that she lived in the rue Grenier-Saint-Lazare

I promised her and kept my word I found her one morning it was an Ash Wednesday I had spent part of the preceding days with old Gaillard at Ruggieri's where we had danced and had a good time (and) had gone in costume to a ball that he had given several times without spending much I had been a little quick in making the acquaintance of a woman I'd met at

---

became absolute, provided police regulations were respected. Turgot encountered opposition from the guilds and the Parlement of Paris, which refused to register the edict and made itself the champion of corporate society, a complex system in which the guild wardens were merely a cog. But Parlement failed to take account of the serious flaws in the system: the absolute power of the masters, the breakdown of master-journeyman relations, the prevalence of self-interested behavior. Nor was Turgot's reform received enthusiastically by the police, which saw the measure as encouraging restlessness and insubordination among workers. But the *petit peuple* greeted it with an explosion of joy, which Ménétra recounts in his own way. In a number of neighborhoods there were illuminations, fireworks, and signs proclaiming "Long live the King and liberty." There were brawls between masters and journeymen. The lieutenant of police, Le Noir, prohibited the reestablishment of the *jurandes* while suggesting some improvements in the edict. Turgot's fall from grace was followed by a proclamation in August 1776 reestablishing the guilds, which satisfied no one, and whose enforcement was obstructed by all concerned. The crisis of 1776 ws a major turning point in the disintegration of the old monarchy, which was unable to make a clear choice between one kind of society and another. Cf. S. Kaplan, "Réflexions sur la police du travail, 1700–1815," *Revue Historique* (1979), pp. 17–77.

the ball (who had been) one of your so-called decent women who was the last one who would have made me think of it[255] for two weeks Ruggieri made me a present of a kind of water that took care of it so I never felt it again

We struck up a conversation after lunch starting with our old friendship She told me that her father and mother had passed away Unable to live with her husband who was a gambler she had been obliged to divorce[256] she had a house of her own that she rented for twelve hundred livres besides that she received seven hundred fifty livres income on investments with Attorney Darvelay and in addition she had just invested two thousand livres with the city at 10 percent I congratulated her She said to me And you my dear Ménétra I answered her Nothing there is only my wife who takes all the profits we make Oh she said you are still the same you will spend your days this way and you will be the loser for all (your) simplicity and lack of interest in business

For me that was food for thought but what to do about it I did not hasten to reclaim my old rights with her and for good reason and we separated with a promise from me that I would come see her often (which) she received with pleasure assuring me that her door would always be open since I was one of her best friends

Around this time our daughter came back from (the) country boarding school where her mother had put her over my objections Our boy began to learn my trade and to amuse himself as young people of his age will do and (I) had taught him and would teach both of them to put himself above the prejudices that had been instilled in them when they were young

One (day) it happened that I went to see Mme Bouchu's brother-in-law The police were there They threw him out the door I wanted to speak they said either you make bail or pay or else get out of the way I left saying Against force no resistance I went straight to his sister She told me that he was a gambler an unscrupulous man that it was the father-in-law who was forcing the sale that he owed her a lot or otherwise she would have lent him the money to keep his house She said I would see one of her nephews who was an auctioneer and a debauchee a drunk and slave to that most vile of vices that in spite of everything she couldn't get rid of him even though the courts had ordered him to keep away from her

---

[255] Allusion to Ménétra's final bout with venereal disease, apparently cured by a specific provided by one of the Ruggieris.

[256] Ménétra here uses the term divorce, which did not become legal until 1792. See n. 240.

He came in like a hungry dog We were at table (He) made jokes about me I answered He replied acted like a tough guy and I got nasty and (I) stayed away from the house for almost six months I reclaimed my former rights For my birthday she gave me silk stockings and a cord for my cane with gold tassels She gave me a lot of presents I didn't want to accept any of them because I told her that I was in no position to return them All she wanted from me was steadiness and everything went along well I persuaded her to go live near the porte Saint-Denis

Her brother-in-law having eaten up all his funds moved in with her She could not get rid of him He stole from her She closed her door to him We were forced to have dinner and supper in the cabarets either in Nouvelle France or in the rue Cadet He came to ask me to plead in his behalf I got him reinstated and found him jobs here and there through my contacts

One day we were on our way to the square in front of Notre-Dame to a notary to cash a thousand francs both of us Mme Bouchu (?) The grocer (Manon) was on her doorstep saw us invited us to come in and rest our feet These two people were delighted to make each other's acquaintance spoke politely with an eye on me The husband recognized me invited me to come see them and eat their soup I responded to his politeness I was wary of it and well might I be This fellow was seized with jealousy some time later against his apprentice who was wooing his wife I don't know whether she responded for that is truly a woman's secret He was found poisoned and three days later the master died in the same way as his apprentice It was smart of me not to go see them despite his urging I would surely have been the first one that he sacrificed to his jealousy She told me about this and (I) took an interest in her business I advised her to keep her shop but other people who had an interest in the business talked her out of it and she sold out and never got anything from it in spite of the fine promises that had been made to her Seeing that I stayed out of her affairs and six months later she married let me know about it and I behaved just as I had done at the time of her first marriage

The first Paris battalion was just leaving and (I) went to join all the gay blades and revelers of Paris at Saint-Denis[257] Mme Bouchu's nephew was in the grenadiers The aunt stayed away from home I was the only one who knew where she was hiding He finally came to see me and asked me

---

[257] This episode probably occurred as the French troops who would fight at Yorktown were being sent to America via Le Havre, in either 1780 or 1781.

where she was living I pretended not to know but I promised him that I would go to see him off at Saint-Denis She gave me eighteen francs I was to give him twelve francs and spend the other six with him I took with me a fellow named Cordier who had been an auctioneer like him We found him I gave him the twelve francs and we had dinner together He did some foolish things got himself put under arrest And so we wished him a pleasant journey since he was supposed to leave the next day for Le Havre

On the way back we saw a wagon loaded with furniture which was headed toward Paris We walked behind because there was a strong wind and it gave us some shelter We heard a mewing It was a cat in a cage With our canes we amused ourselves by tormenting it The cage came apart the cat fell to the ground he began running as fast as he could The mistress who was seated in the front of the wagon called her cat and wailed We laughed ourselves silly and soon lost sight of her All we could hear were the cries and lamentations of this woman

One Sunday night after seeing madame Bouchu home on my way back to the house I felt somebody grab me two men grabbed me around the neck and one held me from behind by holding my hair another took my cane from my hands when I tried to use it in the square of the porte Saint-Denis They forced me to climb into a coach in which I saw a police inspector and another person When the door was closed I saw as the coach started moving a man who was speaking in a low voice to this individual and who said out loud To the Bonne Nouvelle guardhouse My imagination ran riot We arrived They made me get down The black beast[258] followed me I was surrounded by cops I heard them mumble that they had made a mistake The inspector asked me my name my trade I told them and to prove that what I said was true I said that on the handle of my cane they would find the coat of arms of my occupation I took my watch from my pocket and showed them a similar set of arms They told me that I was free that I could go I wanted an explanation of my arrest They all left and I remained with the watchman After receiving some unsatisfactory reasons I left and I never could find out what it was all about but those gentlemen had made a mistake and that shows that many a crook looks a lot like an honest man

I had fallen ill My former companion believed that I would not recover

---

[258] *Bête noire*: either a police inspector or a *commissaire*. See n. 13.

since I was really sick I regained my strength and felt better Then he too fell ill with chagrin because he had thought he could take my place and he died of it In any case I gave up all my girlfriends and settled down to business

We had another companion who had worked at the house before who was a real blockhead He became infatuated with a person who made him think that she had given him her first favors He spoke to me about it I tried to talk him out of it finally he married as the saying goes both the cow and the calf One Saturday night he said to me Boss I'll be needing you on Monday I pretended not to know anything about his wedding I asked him why When he told me he was getting married I asked him at what time He told me that I was to act as his witness and asked me to advance him twenty-four francs for lunch which would take place in the rue Saint-Sauveur at La Gerbe I gave him the money and (we) went to the celebration

I had left the church because the wedding party kept us waiting too long by the time I got back it was all over I arrived The bride was introduced I gave the usual compliments and finally I gave her my hand I thought it was just to cross the gutter Not at all The groom ran over and said Boss follow me As he said these words he fell down smack in the gutter While he was wiping himself off I said to the bride who had lifted her skirts in front that if I had known I would have taken a carriage A lunch was served Two of the guests said that knowing my companion's resources all three of us should chip in for the lunch I was happy to And that evening we gathered I asked especially for music so that I and my children who were growing up could enjoy ourselves

Some time later a pastry maker set up shop near us he spent a lot of money (and) knew how to sweet-talk my wife who lent him money on condition that he marry my daughter which was like selling her into slavery (?) Her hand was requested with all the usual ceremonies I thought she was still too young to start a home she was barely eighteen besides which I saw something in this (fellow's) face and even in his name Durus I had every reason not to approve his suit but he had the knack of pleasing my wife His hypocritical air his Tartuffe ways and his wicked face about which I was not mistaken prevented me from agreeing

The young person had no will She was sacrificed to the monster by the greed of her mother and it was not long before she repented of her error I told her that to marry our child we needed money She answered me Provided I find six hundred francs cash she will make the sum of twenty-four hundred livres She accused me and confessed to me that since our daughter was born she had been putting aside twelve sols per day And practically in spite of me the marriage was concluded and when I went to the notary to sign the contract my wife used a ruse and I led my daughter to the altar as one leads a lamb to slaughter as the saying goes

Every day I heard reports of them Whenever I tried to say anything my wife told me to shut my mouth Neighbors became involved Not five months had gone by when it all fell apart Every day there were loans that would never be repaid The shop everything was sold and the young lady was reduced to a garret I did all I could and finally we rescued her from the clutches of that ravishing wolf and kept her home with us after that monster had made her endure many cruelties We brought suit I was then obliged to take my daughter accompanied by friends to the civil lieutenant after having brought the police to the house He humbled himself before the civil lieutenant by going down on his knees and kissing his feet crying acting in every way like a Tartuffe and a real hypocrite I told my side of the story and he was sentenced to pay costs and I was allowed to keep my daughter at home

The wife left all this burden to me She didn't show herself as she had for the marriage After he made several scenes I had him arrested[259] one night and (he) spent six weeks in prison People urged me to send him away for a spell and his own mother suggested it to me I didn't want to carry vengeance to such an extreme but to rid [my daughter] of such a creature we went to see the feather dresser of the king of England who needed workers and we were obliged for her tranquillity to banish her from the country of her birth and all because of the grave error of a mother who for fear of losing the money she had advanced was the cause of the misfortune of a friendly and loving young girl of sweet and benevolent character Finally we had to part and the mother watched her leave without emotion that I could see she who had so loved her in her tender youth

Around that time this Marseau who had been one of the ones who

---

[259] With sealed letters issued by the soverign and countersigned by a secretary of state, containing orders concerning a particular individual, generally for exile or arrest. Such letters have been seen as the means by which sovereigns exercised their absolute power, but in reality the letters were issued through intermediaries such as intendants in the provinces or the lieutenant of police in the capital upon demand of families, who used them to get rid of libertines, gamblers, and spendthrifts. All levels of society were involved. Such letters were abolished when the government was reorganized after the Revolution. See also n. 235.

signed my warrant was put under arrest for debt[260] and sent for me When I saw him in misfortune I forgot all the ill he had done to me and avenged myself by trying my utmost to rescue him from such a bad pass Wife relatives friends all had abandoned him I went to see one of my old customers who had been friendly to our family and this good fellow M Legouteux senior who took an interest in the case put up a certain sum and I went to get him out and (he) was released What was in his shop had been sold His wife had taken the rest I went to see her (She) did not want to go back to him He took over another shop and with the aid not of his relatives but of those he had despised he was on the road to recovery when he fell into drunkenness and sank again into the greatest misery

His godmother came to see me gave me some money for his clothes I persuaded him to go to Versailles I gave him the address and a letter of recommendation for M Gerard the king's glazier I got him new clothes and at the sands of Port aux Pierres Saint-Leu[261] on the bank of the river I made him bathe and wash and throw all his old clothes into the water I gave him three livres and kissed him (and) said good-bye after escorting him on his way He came back to Paris and two weeks later I learned that he was dead So ended the last of the Marseaus because three others had passed away with bitterness in their hearts right to the very end And what I had predicted by pure chance came to pass in the case of all four

My dear younger sister passed away and her dear husband did not deign to send for me even though she summoned me at the hour of her death She probably wanted to tell me that she repented for the suffering she had inflicted on my unfortunate father A gnawing worm penetrated her heart and she died calling out to me and in repentance My boy grew up (He) wanted as the saying goes to start breaking out of his shell and went to Beauvais to one of my former apprentices and stayed there for a time And (he) came back home and was warmly received even though upon his departure I who had gone to escort him (he) brought me with recommendation a young man who worked as my companion and they left at the

---

[260] Pierre Claude Marseau, master glazier, rue de la Grande-Truanderie in Saint-Eustache parish, Ménétra's uncle, was declared bankrupt on 5 February 1778 by the court of the *juges consuls* of Paris. His assets at that time were 16,343 livres and his liabilities 15,372 livres (AD Paris, D4, B6, 66, 42.981).

[261] A reference to the Port de la Conférence on the Right Bank, below the old Conference Gate near the Tuileries, demolished in the eighteenth century. The port was used for unloading stones from Saint-Leu (whence the name used by Ménétra) as well as floating logs.

beginning of the job and he came back at the beginning of winter (?) All was forgotten and I was happy to see one of our children because the other was too far away to kiss

Mme Bouchu's nephew came home and the good woman gave him dinner When the man had had something to drink he was not easy to handle and was very insolent The three of us were together after a good supper when a quarrel started Rue Cadet the woman said that a certain shortcut was to be avoided for fear of being murdered by him He answered No but with a volley of blows (?) I turned around His stick was raised over me I parried it with my cane I knocked his stick out of his hands and it fell to the ground whirled around He bent down to pick it up I said You see François I'm a good fellow I don't hit you when you're down (He) didn't say anything I thought it was all over I let down my guard He clubbed me over the head I was hurt I hit him two or three times on the face with my cane He fled yelling for the guard

The next day I met him at the market His face was all bent out of shape I said he was a real brave fellow I repeated this remark in front of his mistress and several other people he knew He said that I would pay I answered Right now The best mourning is over the grave[262] I said to him You're a soldier what is more a grenadier go get a weapon I'll go to the quay to find Robert the recruiter and I'll wait for you on the quay of the Ecole at the Madeleine Bring anybody you like with you He answered that he wanted to fight with clubs His woman tried to stop him Finally I pushed him into agreeing I went into a chandler's and I took two broom sticks We went over by the boulevards and in the rue Saint-Fiacre we took up our positions He fended me off I gave a blow I received one Finally the people watching said that was enough I threw the broom stick away in a rage because they hadn't let me put a mark on him They wanted me to go for a drink with them I said to them With you gladly but with him he's a traitor And he went off with his lady love who was just as fine looking a type as he was So there he was out on the streets again since he knew his aunt would turn her back on him We rested As for the brother-in-law he got himself thrown out from time to time and came looking for me or tried to have me get him a pardon

In the mean time I had a little adventure that might have turned out

---

[262] *Il n'y a pas de plus beau deuil que sur la fosse:* in other words, a dead man's debts are best paid at the graveside.

badly for me A certain harness maker's wife who had not been cruel to me ran into me I told her that if she wanted me to I would go home with her She teased me on the subject I asked if her husband was home She told me that he had had his dinner and gone out I said I would come up She said that she left the key in the door but wouldn't allow me to come in I laughed and apparently on my way in I stepped on the trap door Two strong apprentice harness makers came in and I had only enough time to hide in the alcove to wrap myself up in the curtains and to climb up on the rung of a chair They shouted to see if anyone was there

The mistress arrived was suspicious of what was going on told them that it was her kitten jumping around in the bedroom They maintained that it was a man's step and that when they came in they saw what looked like something moving in the alcove curtains She still maintained that it was her cat The master came in at this point I was not exactly having a good time The subtle woman reminded him that he had given his word and was expected and so I was relieved of the fear of being discovered and what is more by a man who had made mincemeat of ten others like me I praised her for the skill and subtlety with which she had dealt with her husband and for the way she had laid the apprentices' doubts to rest The experience had cooled me off a bit I went home and came back carrying some panes of glass and asked the apprentices in the shop if the boss's wife was upstairs They were still talking about the same subject when the lady of the house opened the trap door and invited me to come up Which showed me that she had plugged up some holes so I could come in and plug up some others From time to time a window pane would be broken I went to take the measurements I took a break and drank a drop and a couple of hours later I came to set my glass and finish the job I had begun She was worth the trouble she had a delightful plumpness well worth my offerings

My boy was maturing We had put him on a monthly salary or rather his mother had He felt he wasn't making enough money he felt the sap of springtime He left us Once again he went off to work for other masters I had the misfortune to break my leg and there I was confined to bed I asked him to come back He made me beg he bargained with us Finally we were forced to give in and (I) remembered and (he) reminded us that six or seven months before he had also left us and (he) had come back all disfigured saying that he had fallen and struck a boundary marker while out jumping with one of his friends I know what I wanted to think about it You don't learn cunning from an old fox I heard news of our dear Madelon from people who came from London who told us wonderful things that she was becoming a charming woman

I met an old mistress locksmith named Widow Liévin who had shared the same landing[263] as Manon She greeted me invited me to come have a drink I agreed on condition that I could treat We started talking about old times and finally we got hot She told me she had always had a hankering for me I asked if she still did She answered only in monosylla bles I figured the deal was signed sealed and delivered I took her home and once again found myself king of the castle She didn't care how regu larly I came but she wanted me to herself We could have lived quietly but it was inhibiting That didn't suit me besides which my character wasn't suited to doing nice little things and even less to living with a woman's caprices and since I didn't find in this one what I had found in the other I didn't rush things and went to see her only when passion got the better of reason

It was just before Lent there was a domino player in the shop A girl he knew sent for a Harlequin costume and a Pierrot costume The one who took the Harlequin outfit (was) my size but with a bit more stomach While they got dressed I hid in another room The boy left I immediately got dressed and with a girl dressed as Pierrot I arrived at the house It was toward the end of the day I teased her I had a good time I tor mented my wife my boy I was not recognized The person who had brought the clothing kept saying that if he hadn't dressed the person himself he would never have thought he was so jovial

I went to see Mme Bouchu who was at the Maison Neuve with her brother-in-law and one of her cousins (because) I had promised I would come for supper I went to their table I joked Nobody recognized me I bent over close to the ear of Mme Bouchu I told her a few of our private secrets She said she didn't know me My friend was below We went to a café He took back his costume and I returned to join the group They told me that a Harlequin and a Pierrot had just left their table who had given them a good laugh and that it was too bad I hadn't arrived sooner that I would have had a good time but she couldn't get over what he had said to her and I had a hearty laugh over it

Around this time an old friend of mine who was a glazier set up shop in

---

263 *Carré*: used in Paris to refer to a stairway landing in a house, which was often a meeting place for residents.

Versailles I ran into him with some neighbors on their way for a drink at the corner of the rue des Deux-Portes when a prostitute named La Maréchale called me from her window to come set some glass for her In his simplicity this worthy fellow thought she was my wife I made him think I had left my shop and I told him the whole story as we drank He said he wanted to go say hello to her and kiss her I told him that he could go up and that he would get a warm welcome He went He climbed the stairs She thought he was a client and set about doing her job I told my friends about the trick I had played He said that my wife was a shameless woman and that if he had a wife like that he would have her locked up I told him that that was the fashion in Paris that we didn't get upset when a friend took our place My friends were choked up with laughter Finally we told him what the story was He had a good laugh over it and said that I always was a prankster

I went to set my glass and told her about the client I had sent her and that I had passed her off as my wife She said I was joking that I wouldn't have dared I proved it to her She was so pleased by what I had said that she asked me again if I would come for supper and said that she would show me that she had had her eye on me I spent a nice evening and a delightful night with this woman in spite of her profession And every now and then she broke a window and that was all the compensation she required for the favors she was often pleased to grant me

While passing by a chapel I heard someone call me A master carpenter came down to invite me up for a drink and to console one of his friends who was a master locksmith with whom he was having no luck he hoped that I might be able to restore his spirits which had sunk when he lost his wife that he lived in the faubourg Saint-Germain and said that he wanted to throw himself into the water that he wanted to do away with himself one way or another I went up I looked at the fellow I tried every way I knew to console him and to talk him out of what he kept repeating he wanted to do The more I told him that there was no remedy for what ailed him that he must resign himself to the will of the Eternal the more he said he wanted to do away with himself When I saw that what I said to him only made him more stubbon than ever I said to him firmly So you want to do away with yourself Here is my hammer there is a nail and take this rope and go into the next room and do your business and let's be done with it And I made like a Norman[264] He didn't say a word and I left

---

[264] An unusual expression, possibly to be interpreted as meaning "I took no interest in the matter, like a shrewd Norman who says neither yes nor no."

A short time later I asked about this inconsolable fellow Imagine my surprise when I learned that six weeks later he remarried

It was around this time that my sister Thérèse remarried in the country at a place called Saint-Prix I went to the wedding with my son He went chasing down the masters (but) he was always careful not to lose sight of the house

One day I went with a friend of mine to a café kept by a fellow named Andreau and saw three white mice in a bottle I told him that those little animals ordinarily ran around like squirrels and that if he wanted me to I would make him a glass cage and he would see the effect no sooner was the cage finished than it was sold I found the white mice and my son and I made all kinds of cages in the style of a Chinese house And we found a seller and sold them at good prices My wife never slept and was careful to conceal the money and as usual for herself and her profit and I did not feel I was making progress Though she concealed what she was up to I got wind of the scheme I complained I found out or Mme Bouchu discovered what she had done giving her sister and her nephews the sum of four hundred livres in income me and my children were left out I wanted to make a stir at home She fell ill She claimed that it was because of the smell of the mice I might have said that the money she had appropriated for herself alone had no bad odor since she had taken care to place it in the hands of her family

While she was convalescing my dear sister who had come to visit her put it into her head that she would be better taken care of if she went to the convent known as La Roquette And despite the one month paid in advance it was necessary in addition to pay her burial fee in case she needed to be interred[265] at Béthanie the convent cemetery As soon as my dear sister said that she would be treated better despite my observations they immediately took a carriage and left She stayed there about two weeks I went to see her with her sister even though I had said I would not go She was annoyed because I said that I was selling cages and she saw that she was not receiving any funds She asked to come back to the house I teased her for an answer because she was complaining that they had made her pay in advance to go to Béthanie we left her for a little while finally one Sunday with my son we went to pick her up in a carriage She

---

[265] Ménétra writes *exhumer* but clearly means *inhumer*. Some hospices and hospitals insisted that burial fees be paid in advance, so that the institution would not be held responsible for them. Béthanie was the name of the place where the cemetery serving the convent of La Roquette was located.

reclaimed what she called her rights as usual and for the sake of peace and quiet I made no objection

So the days passed and our time elapsed eating and drinking at Mme Bouchu's and working at home and come what may I was always looking for ways to keep from getting bored My work allowed me to make the acquaintance of many women and I tried as hard as I could to sacrifice to Cupid Sometimes I was punished for it and always by those goddesses who behave like prudes and act so reserved That gave me food for thought but passion won out

Finally calculation (and) self-interest though never among my vices because I was never of an ambitious character (but) in the end the prospect that if I kept quiet I would have enough to live fairly well in my old age if the Eternal granted me a long life that gave me food for thought and I began then to lead a quieter life and to pay more attention besides which age was beginning to gray my hair I did not give up love entirely but like the heroes of old I rested on my laurels and made sacrifices and oblations to Bacchus though I had never been one of his biggest worshippers and never sacrificed to him except in company

The hope of an easier life in my old age had more influence on me than all the moralizing I had endured and I was enjoying myself and watching my days go by when the French Revolution came suddenly and revived all our spirits And the word liberty so often repeated had an almost supernatural effect and invigorated us all

People rushed to arms and supported those who called themselves the fathers of the people This revolution was supposed to secure the happiness of the French people by confining the king to his throne and returning to all the rights that the parlements the priesthood the nobility had usurped under the leadership of ministers [who were] inept [and] outrageous liars who thought only of their pleasures and their ambition trampling the constitution of the state underfoot or making it serve their whims or to put it better still it [the constitution] was unknown [to them] The debts of the State mounted doubled [There was] nothing to do but (make use) of the wealth of the clergy which could contribute to the State's burden But these immoral men who constituted a second authority by means of all the chimeras invented by lies and sustained by ignorance backed up by fanaticism and superstition these creatures preferred to see the Nation fall into adversity into decrepitude rather than make the slightest sacrifice Thus they were and will always be the cause of misfortune in those nations that they uphold with their ancient Gothic prejudices Men of this kind know nothing but to dominate and wish to rule by their dogmas and fabulous mysteries

The nobles with their old parchments and their ancient gallant knights from whom they claim to trace their ancestry when most of them are descended from servants lackeys [and] coachmen these men could not imagine that a man who was not of this class was made for anything but to serve their whims And (they) did not believe that the Eternal when he created man everything was in the most perfect equality and that they were just as subject as the commonest of men to all the infirmities and even to death All these men left their fatherland Those who remained did all they could to insure its defeat

Everything moved forward They flattered the ambitious and all the ills came gradually to a head Murder drowning everything was allowed Intriguers monopolized all the offices Good men could only mutter for if they spoke they were lost Hatred vengeance everything was permitted and nobody dared open his mouth or even dared to refuse the positions delegated to him in the assemblies in which he was obliged to participate

It was in this state of chaos in which treachery was rampant abroad as well as at home that I began after the tenth of August to appear in the assemblies of my section[266] And when they required the people of Paris to stand guard[267] without distinction I saw that all the votes for the position

---

266 The function of the various administrative organizations need to be clarified. Ménétra first mentions his participation in sectional assemblies. The sections were administrative units set up in Paris in May and June of 1790 to replace the districts, which had themselves replaced the older quarters (*quartiers*). Paris was divided into forty-eight sections, which were first used to organize elections in which the voters were the active citizens—those who paid the electoral tax of three days of work, excluding servants. The sections became the centerpiece of the popular movement in 1791, thanks to their general assemblies, which met freely until 1794, and their various committees. They were beleaguered by the nonactive citizens. Through speeches, petitions, street actions, and participation in demonstrations the sections influenced the policies of the Assembly and the revolutionary government, which counted on them for support until 1794. In March and April of that year the government clamped down and purged undesirable members. This was the turning point, after which discord grew between the sectional movement and the committees, paving the way for the Ninth of Thermidor and the fall of Robespierre. Ménétra's section was Section Number 16, known as the Mauconseil section until August of 1792, when it was renamed the Bonconseil section.

267 Here, the National Guard, which in the summer of 1789 consisted of active citizens able to secure arms. Ménétra, in one of his miscellaneous writings, says that he took part in the Tenth of August, in patrols of the city, and in guard duty that fell to section members. From 1792 on the latter were organized into companies of 126 men, with officers and noncommissioned officers elected by the men. Each section had approximately one company for every 100

of captain were destined to go to me and I opposed this and was named lieutenant and was reappointed three more times despite the cabal mounted by an inept and unscrupulous person

And my daughter had come back from England having had only fifteen days to prepare for her departure found herself in the midst of a feast mounted by the French to celebrate the Revolution[268] Some time after her arrival I obtained her divorce and she linked her life with that of a good man who made her forget the pain and suffering that her monster of a first husband had caused her to endure He was a chief in the war office[269] From there he became chief of armaments at the Oratoire and was sent as inspector general of armaments to Charleville where he stayed for a short time

During this time terror hovered over France and particularly in Paris where everyone lived not only in the greatest penury but also in horror of every kind in (the midst of) murders Everything was in the greatest disorder The French breathed blood They were like cannibals and were real man-eaters Neighbor cold-bloodedly denounced neighbor Blood ties were forgotten I witnessed those days of horror and I witnessed all the attacks on the infamous revolutionary committee[270] When I was named

---

active citizens; thus Bonconseil had nearly twenty companies of guardsmen, since there were 1,700 active citizens. When the National Guard, organized by district battalion, was merged with the sectional guards, military committees and disciplinary boards were set up, as Ménétra describes. The law of 12 Frimaire Year II (2 December 1794) reorganized the Parisian command. The sections were partially disarmed and placed under the control of the army following 16 Vendémiaire Year IV (8 October 1795).

[268] Allusion to the pro-Revolutionary agitation of French citizens living in London, as a result of which they were expelled for fear that they would encourage the spread of Jacobinism in England (prior to 1792).

[269] In the Year XI Ménétra's daughter married Herman Paul Goverts of Marseilles, a wholesaler from a family of Marseilles wholesalers. See C. Carrière, *Négociants marseillais* (2 vols.; Paris, 1969), pp. 724, 923. The current state of cataloguing of the archives has made it impossible to discover the connection, if any, between Paul Goverts and the person with whom Marie-Madeleine Ménétra was living, who became bureau chief in the War Ministry in 1791 and held the various posts mentioned by Ménétra. An arms factory was located in the buildings of the Oratoire de Paris, rue de l'Enfer, beyond the barrier near the Luxembourg.

[270] The section was run by a civil committee and a revolutionary committee. Ménétra acknowledges having been a member of the first but refuses to admit that he belonged to the second. The sixteen-member civil committee was responsible for regular municipal services, supervised the commissaire de police, and enforced all administrative decrees. The chairman of the committee convoked the assembly, which elected committee members and had the right to revoke the committee's powers, a right that the assembly did not shrink from exercising. The civil committees were less political than the revolutionary committees which gradually supplanted them after the Year II. They recovered some of their prestige after Thermidor, for

to take charge of examining their accounts men that I believed to be honest denounced [?—the object of the verb is missing—trans.] in cold blood for an idle word The man was [men were?] immediately incarce- rated and even in many cases guillotined

You my unfortunate friends you will always be present in my memory Respectable Saint Cristau[271] farmer general who had taken a liking to me who often sent his servant to fetch me to eat with him You were destined to perish you were rich The monsters' only grudge was against your fortune My speeches to the assembly everything I did to win people over to your side all came to nought The decent man pitied you but held his tongue

I was there unfortunate Marie[272] for having been naive enough to lend some money you were denounced and you perished All my efforts to save you came to nought and I saw the moment when I would rejoin you when that vindictive man spoke out against me when all I was doing was asking for (your) freedom from men who had betrayed their country Liberty was drowned out by the hue and cry of the honest men who were in the assembly And you poor Barbet[273] you good and loyal man with whom we

---

they were put in charge of such basic issues as food supplies. They were abolished in the Year IV. The revolutionary committees, also known as committees of surveillance, were (from July of 1792 until March of 1793) composed of fourteen members elected by the assembly. Reorganized in March of 1793, they were reduced to twelve members and made responsible for keeping an eye on suspect individuals and foreigners. People had to apply to them for *certificats de civisme* and *cartes de sûreté*. They acted as political police and also played a key organizational role in the democratic sectional movement, and they were in direct contact with the Commune and the committees of the Convention. By late 1793 the Committee of Public Safety was attempting to control the revolutionary committees. It succeeded in doing so by exerting direct or indirect influence on the nomination process, especially after the purge of enragés and hébertistes. Ménétra is referring to someone who belonged to one of the latter two groups when he wrote that in March or April of 1794 "I was named to make them give an accounting." Ménétra was then a Jacobin, close to the Robespierrists. In August of 1794, these committees were placed under the supervision of the Convention's Committee of General Security. They were abolished in Brumaire of Year IV. Note that members of the committees of the Year II were generally hounded in the Years III and IV by moderates and reactionaries, who accused them of having been terrorists.

271 Adam François Parcel de Saint-Christau, a very wealthy *fermier général* and member of a family of financiers, sentenced to death and executed on 19 Floréal Year II (8 May 1794) (AN, W. 362 (785)).

272 Member of the revolutionary committee of the Bonconseil section, François Marié lived at 25, rue Mondétour. He was arrested in Thermidor of the Year II with other Jacobins and Robespierrists of the section who had been denounced by Vallois (AN, F.7 4663, 4774–35).

273 Barbet or Barbey Mathieu, a journeyman hosier, age 37, residing at 16, rue Française. He was arrested and executed on 1 Prairial Year II for counterrevolutionary and pro-royalist

passed an evening now and then Two of the section's well-known stool pigeons dogged your tracks and kept an eye on what you did I warned you you were from Lyons that was a capital sin They got you drinking and made you talk They arrested you took you to the inspector a hard man who only looked for guilty men to show the committee of general security[274] that he was doing a good job as the revolutionary committee in the position to which he had been assigned These men had become barbarous inhuman (They) all made sacrifices ostensibly to defend the fatherland when in fact they were trying to destroy it

I was a guard the day of his arrest I arrived with my company The officer I was relieving told me that there was someone under arrest I went to see Imagine my surprise It was Barbet I had him brought out at once He calmly spent the night with me I questioned him He had no idea why he was imprisoned I was told to keep an eye on this man They took him to the Conciergerie Three days later he died on the scaffold Oh man sometimes I can still see him a single word brings him back to life and a single word that he had a hard time explaining caused him to die And so it was that thousands of wretched men ended their days while the criminal [sic] seized and battened on the fortune of their [sic] fellow citizens The chaplain[275] of our battalion was incarcerated he had mounted the fatal tiers [i.e., had taken a seat in the assembly—trans.] and had written a letter to the assembly I presided Immediately I wrote to that cannibal Fouquier Tinville[276] with the consent of the assembly and the seventeen he was the only one acquitted

---

remarks (AN, F.7 4585, W369). Ménétra is of the opinion that his Lyonnaise origins influenced the sentence. Lyons was at this point suspected of grave crimes, following the federalist and royalist rebellion, which was put down on 9 October 1793. Two informers reported to the Committee of General Security some remarks that he had made, rather vague but given the circumstances sufficiently compromising to cost him his life.

[274] Formed in October 1792 by members of the Surveillance Committee of the Legislative Assembly. An issue in the struggle between the Montagnards and the Girondins, the committee came to be dominated by Montagnards. With Amar, David, Le Bas, and Vadier, it frequently clashed with the Committee of Public Safety after September 1793. After Thermidor it assumed full police powers and with partly new membership led the anti-Jacobin reaction.

[275] Lacking the chaplain's name I have been unable to find any trace of this affair. If the story is true, the letter must have been sent to the committees of the National Convention elected in August 1792, which assumed responsibility for governing revolutionary France under the stewardship of the Committee of Public Safety. The future of the revolutionary movement was played out in the Convention in Thermidor of the Year II. The Convention was supplanted by the directorial assemblies in the Year IV.

[276] Antoine Quentin Fouquier-Tinville (1747–1795). Procureur at the Châtelet in Paris, a

In those days of mourning which true Frenchmen will always look back upon with horror I was sent with the delegates Satin Bayard Adam Lesimple[277] to snatch [Duperon?] from the hands of the *septembriseurs*[278] those cannibals who were massacring everyone in the prisons of Paris It was about time The virtuous Samson Duperon[279] former justice of the peace was dying We arrived and asked (for him) in the name of the section and he was handed over to us I saw those men whose faces and manners proclaimed their humanity (as being) on a par with cannibals

I shall draw a curtain over those days of horror that descended upon France My son was happy He was fighting for his country it was the second time that he returned to the army He risked his life it is true but never got mixed up in all the horrors that were being committed with impunity And those ogres even took pride in their crimes

Finally the murders ended[280] but people were still unhappy This Na-

---

lawyer by profession, he became the principal public prosecutor in the revolutionary tribunal and the key figure in the great trials of Prairial in the Year II. Because of his character, it seems implausible that Ménétra would have taken the direct personal initiative he describes. Fouquier-Tinville was himself executed in Floréal of the Year III.

[277] Jean Mathieu Satin: a rentier, age 44, born in Paris and residing at 11, rue du Renard. An active citizen, he enlisted in the sectional movement in 1791. He was loyal to Robespierre and the commune in May 1793. (AN, carte de sûreté Bonconseil, F.7 4775–13, Arch. Préf. Police, mars-octobre 1791-Bonconseil, BN, 8.⁰.LB. 40 1958).

Pierre Casimir Bayard, feather dresser, age 33, born in Noyon and residing in the rue du Petit-Lion. He held posts in the sectional committees and was an inspector of sewers and lanterns and a *commissaire de police*. A captain in the National Guard, he was arrested in the Year III. He was a Jacobin and even a Robespierrist, but a moderate one, as his deposition for Barbet shows (AN, carte de sûreté, F.7 4585, 4589–2, 4775–32, 4663, W.369, BN? 4⁰ LB 4⁰ 1733).

Jean-François Adam, lace and linen merchant, age 31 in 1792, born in Compiègne and residing in the rue de la Grande-Truanderie. He was revolutionary commissioner of Bonconseil in 1792 and probably a Jacobin. (AN, carte de sûreté, Arch. Préf. Police Bonconseil, 28 December 1792).

Jacques Nicolas Lesimple, rentier, age 36, born in Maultre-sur-Seine and residing in the rue Montorgueil. He was probably a baker and held sectional posts in 1791. (AN, carte de sûreté, Arch. Préf. Police Bonconseil, April and September 1790, October 1791).

[278] Allusion to the massacres that took place in the Paris prisons between the second and the sixth of September, under threat of a Prussian invasion.

[279] A justice of the peace, Jean François Samson Duperon was arrested in September 1792 and saved from the massacres by the *sectionnaires* of Bonconseil (AN, F.7 4589–2).

[280] An allusion to the change that occurred on the Ninth and Tenth of Thermidor in the Year II with the fall of Robespierre, which put an end to the Terror and shifted power to the Assembly, which was divided into several factions, with the remnants of the Jacobins, the reactionaries and royalists led by Fréron and the *jeunesse dorée*, and a large group of moderates. In the sections this was a period of turmoil, with former Jacobins and terrorists under attack.

tional Convention in which everyone had the greatest confidence was and one can say so nothing but a den of slanderers of vindictive men seeking to slaughter one party so as to replace it with another They made the people march according to their passion The tocsin and the general[281] were as people often said the order of the day All these evils had overwhelmed the sections

People watched one another Nobody dared to say what he thought We were constantly under arms sometimes to guard the Convention other times to guard the supplies of food And so it was that a person I had thought to be my best friend attacked me violently for having forced him to join a faction By his stubborness I was forced (?) This creature insinuated to several people to avenge himself that I had signed the twenty thousand and the eight thousand[282] In those days this was a capital crime I was summoned before the assembly and I answered forthrightly that I had never signed anything except a debt The explanation that I gave to the assembly had a singular effect in my favor It was the day new bureau members were chosen I was renominated president by acclamation and by the vast majority of the assembly I tried to get out of it I was so to speak carried to the bureau All the citizens who had been honored with this post made a speech describing the duties they had had to fulfill

I said to the entire assembly Citizens those whom you honored with your votes before me and who served as president have all spoken to you Do not expect a speech from me I ask only that you show me great forbearance and all I ask of you citizens is silence Clapping of hands was heard throughout the hall and my presidency and all the other (posts) with which I was honored passed in the most untroubled tranquillity

To every post that fell empty I was immediately appointed I was named commissioner of general security[283] a post which I held for about two

---

[281] *Le tocsin et la générale*: official signals using drums to assemble armed section members and bells whose repeated long, slow peals gave the alarm.

[282] Two petitions initiated by the Girondins and hence moderate in tenor, protesting the location of a *fédéré* camp south of Paris and the staging of an antimonarchy rally on 20 June 1792. This led to charges of moderatism by the *enragés* in June 1792. The power of the Jacobins put a brake on blind purges. Accused of moderatism in 1792, Ménétra became suspect, and his adversaries passed for extremists. Exonerated, he remained a good Jacobin, as is confirmed by the fact that he signed the petition demanding that Louis XVI be deposed, which circulated in the sections prior to 10 August 1792. Was he elected president of the General Assembly at that time? It is not out of the question; if he was, it would only add further proof that he was a sans-culotte.

[283] Member of the Surveillance Committee, i.e., the revolutionary committee. See n. 270.

months with de Lenoncourt I resigned as member of the revolutionary
committee despite a decree from the committee of general security I
explained myself as follows in my defense (for) in fact I was in the chair
"Citizens the post to which you call me requires a great deal of attention
I cannot accept it given that my son is at the frontier my wife dangerously
ill and my companion has left me to go fight the enemies of the fatherland"

That made an impression and I myself appointed another man Poirier[284]
who became the wickedest of all those monsters who have given mankind
so much cause to moan I was appointed assessor of the peace[285] I presided over the court in the absence of the justice of the peace I was appointed to the commune as vice president for *assignats* in the bankruptcy
of Guillaume who was also commissioner (?) (I was appointed) concilia-
tor of the Petits Pères member of the jury of accusation member of the
jury of judgment with the former baron d'Ognie[286] and citizen Poupart[287]
curate of Saint-Eustache I had them spend the night in the Palace in the
case of the three individuals who were manufacturing counterfeit *assignats*
(and) at my urging the wife did not lose her life but the man and his sister

---

[284] Paul Marie Poirier, tinsmith, age 28, born in Créteil and residing at 6, rue du Petit-Lion.
He headed the sectional secretariat in the General Assembly and was a member of the
revolutionary committee. During the Terror he belonged to the clubs and was a Jacobin
enragé, if we can believe the reasons given for his arrest in Brumaire of the Year III; he may
even have been pro-Babeuf. He is the only militant Jacobin whom Ménétra attacks in these
terms, possibly because of his extremist position in the Year II. (AN, carte de sûreté F.7 4774
48; Arch. Préf. Police, AA. 281, fols. 257–278.)

[285] In other words, deputy to the justice of the peace, elected under the provisions of the
law of 29 September 1790. Deputies were entitled to render final judgment in all cases up to
50 livres; their judgments were subject to appeal in cases up to 100 livres, in cases involving
personal disputes and property and civil cases such as wage and labor claims, insults, brawls,
etc. From 1793 until August 1795 they were appointed initially by the General Council of the
Commune and then reelected to their positions. The almanac confirms that Ménétra held this
post in 1793, 1794, and 1795. (AN, D.III.253–11 pluviôse an III.) De Guillaume was
assesseur in 1792 and 1793 and probably a member of the jury in the *département* tribunal.

[286] Claude Jean Rigoley, baron d'Ogny, arrested in the Piques section at the age of 75 on a
charge of having an émigré son. A petition by the citizens of Millemont in Seine-et-Oise
helped to free him. (AN, F.7 4774 93) There is no trace of his role as a jury member, which
must have been prior to 1792.

[287] The curate of Saint-Eustache, Jean-Jacques Poupart, lived at 49, rue Traisnée. After
the Oratoire he became a parish priest and was at one time confessor to Louis XVI. He was
highly esteemed in the diocese and swore allegiance to the Civil Constitution of the Clergy. A
member of the Provisional Commune in August 1789, he was an elector from 1790 to 1792. He
was never bothered during the Terror and was allowed to reopen his church as a constitutional house of worship in 1795 (AN, W. 257).

were guillotined So they said to me because of your way of looking at things you've made us endure a bad supper and a very bad bed because to each jury member they gave a *petit pain* a cervelat and a half bottle and to sleep a cot with a mattress and a cover And the next day (we) finished our deliberations at ten o'clock

I was also named three different times commissioner of the civil committee and usually I knew how to get out of it I was charity commissioner[288] I also had the job of verifier of defenders of the fatherland commissioner for hoarding which I got out of as soon as I could I was appointed by consent of the citizens who made up the disciplinary council to preside in the absence of the commandant I was part of the central committee for the reception of the citizens of the popular society[289] over which I often presided I was appointed to obtain an accounting from the sectional authorities

I was one of those in charge of examining the accounts of the saltpeter commission of which I was named chairman I was involved for two days in a runoff election for the position of member of the commune For fifteen months I was president of the primary assemblies I was named one of three candidates for police inspector When I saw that all the votes were in my favor I resigned I was also appointed to take charge of examining the accounts of the infamous revolutionary committee And so I was named to preside and to many other posts with which my fellow citizens honored me also in the time of the Terror I was careful not to refuse

I had one enemy Duplessis[290] who with his insidious accusations tried

---

[288] That is, a member of the sectional committee in charge of assisting the unfortunate. In 1790 the curate of Saint-Eustache called a meeting of commissioners to try to bring some order to the distribution of relief. In 1793 the assembly of commissioners drew up plans for dealing with poverty. After July of 1793 the sections chose commissioners to deal with hoarding and food supply, responsible for enforcing the law against hoarding and speculation on foodstuffs (AD, Paris, D. 796. Sd.).

[289] When the Convention reduced the number of sectional general assemblies to two in September 1793, the *sectionnaires* organized popular societies so that they could meet freely. In reality, these were purged sections that worked to prepare for the upcoming general assembly elections. A committee of inquiry eliminated any candidate who might have signed an anti-civic petition. Candidates therefore had to account for their activities since 1789 and had to be presented. Robespierre and the Jacobins kept a close eye on these societies, and in Floréal of the Year II many of them split, including the one in Bonconseil. See E. Mellié, *Les Sections de Paris* (Paris, 1898), pp. 274–285.

[290] Duplessis or Duplessy, a wigmaker residing in the rue Pavée and a neighbor of Ménétra's. A quarrel over a guard is given by Ménétra as the reason for their dispute. (Cf. II fols. 82–83).

to do me in after having been one of my best friends He wormed his way in with the members of the revolutionary committees and every day deliv-ered another denunciation of me So people called his house the little revolutionary committee In the ensuing reactions he cleverly allied him-self with three of my declared enemies One A Nardin[291] because I hadn't spoken in his favor and hadn't opened my mouth for good or for ill at the people's society from which he was excluded B Isidore Langlois[292] the second was the famous pamphleteer because I had reprimanded him in the disciplinary council for not standing guard though he knew well how to denounce people in the section C the third Valois[293] a vociferous impostor and outrageous slanderer who in the wars of the Vendée had been a well-known spy (and) who had lent (?) twelve francs silver to two citizens of our company who had remained in the army in the Vendée (and) who frequently wrote to me to get the money back knowing that I was the person who bore all the burden of the company since the captain was absent (?)

In those stormy times it was necessary to be under arms almost all the

---

[291] Paul Louis Nardin, clerk, age 32, born in Naulet and residing in the rue Saint-Sauveur. After coming to Paris in 1790, he moved in 1793 to 26, rue Pavée, the same address as Ménétra. He was employed by the national estates and served as deputy justice of the peace. He was a *muscadin* who stirred up trouble in the section after Thermidor. (AN, carte de sûreté, D.III.253–254; BN, 8⁰ LB.4⁰ 1728 and 4⁰ LB.4⁰ 1733.)

[292] Isidore Langlois styled himself a teacher, student, and man of letters. In 1793 he was 24 years old and lived at 63, rue Mauconseil. He arrived in Rouen in 1786. In 1794 he lived at 17, rue du Petit-Lion. A fierce supporter of the Revolution, this one-time scholarship student at Louis-le-Grand participated in the events of 1789 with other young students. He was at that time a poor student who intended to study medicine. In 1792 it was he who carried to the other sections the decree of the Bonconseil section demanding that Louis XVI be deposed. Little is known about his doings in 1793, but he was one of those who turned moderate, probably in May, and then joined the counter-Revolution when conscripts were sought for the war in the Vendée. In August 1793 he was arrested and owed his liberation to Thermidor. He then became one of the most talented journalists of the counter-Revolution, publishing espe-cially in *Le Messager du Soir*. He was a *muscadin* and *réacteur*. He died in the Year VIII. (AN, F.7 4774–61 and 4279–21).

[293] Charles Jérôme Valois, or Vallois, fanmaker, lived first at 14 and later at 23, rue Pavée. He was a Parisian by birth, age 36. He followed roughly the same course as Langlois and after Thermidor became one of the leaders of the *muscadin* and anti-Jacobin reaction in the section. Ménétra is mistaken about his military service. He served not in Vendée but in the army of the Pyrenees, where he rose to the rank of lieutenant. Ménétra's confusion may come from the fact that Langlois and Vallois violently protested and even rioted against the conscription of troops for the Vendée. It is known that after returning from the army Vallois served as a spy for the Committee of General Security (AN, Carte de sûreté, F.7 4589–2, 4775–32, 4775–38. BN, 4⁰ Lb.40 1733).

time and because I had several times invited the enmity of that man sustained by his three associates (and) when they took him out drinking[294] I had those four men for implacable enemies Also I was trying in those times of Terror in which all the denunciations the slanders the calumnies (and) in which even the most honest man was incarcerated and most of the time lost his life on the scaffold in which the sensible man did not dare speak up to ask for his friends' freedom I often risked my liberty in those times of Terror to ask for the freedom of several of my friends Everything that I might say in the assemblies on behalf of my unfortunate fellow citizens was turned around by those contemptible creatures in such a way that I had to fear for myself

Those three wretches tried every way they could to find something they could use to attack me because the fourth did nothing but make denunciations when he was home heading up his little revolutionary committee And I was informed of all the plots against me So I stayed on my guard One of those four individuals accused me of having written him a letter in the Vendée which he shortened and distorted and had published in a newspaper edited by one of them They thought I was done for but I kept my wits about me and went to the committee of general security to present a petition on the subject They investigated what I was and who my enemies were They were advised to be more circumspect in the future and not to denounce anybody This document was conveyed to them by the justice of the peace[295] my friend who had urged me to take this course which succeeded as (I had) hoped That held them back a bit but they changed tactics and kept on plotting But in everything they were able to do they found their path blocked and I continued on my way

Finally another upheaval occurred All the parties clashed[296] and their

---

[294] *Gobleter:* to drink, have a party in a cabaret, used by Voltaire in his letter to Thiriot dated 19 November 1760.

[295] Piere Dumeige or Dumeigne, who was a *commissaire de police* in 1792. He was a clerk, age 36, who lived at 41, rue Montorgeuil and later in the cloister of Saint-Jacques-de-l'Hôpital. He was civil commissioner of the section, clerk of the assembly, and from 1793 to 1797 justice of the peace. (*Almanach national,* AN, D.iii.253–254, F.7 4589–2, Arch. Préf. Police Bonconseil, 1792.)

[296] Probably a rather clumsy account of the Days of Germinal in the Year iii, when the most radical sections marched on the Convention to protest the hard times and the reactionary policies of the Thermidorians. The Committee of General Security mobilized the moderate battalions of the sections of the west and center, including Bonconseil. Paris was placed in a state of siege, Montagnard leaders were deported, and terrorists were disarmed and often arrested. Disarmament entailed loss of civil rights and precluded access to public employment; it symbolized loss of liberty.

supporters in the sections rose up My enemies sought to take advantage of
the situation I had been sent as a guard over my objections by order of the
general staff our commandant being a temporary commander and (he) had
designated me for this job My wife had again gone to the country to stay
with a friend finding that she could not live on the ounce and a half of
bread that was allotted to each individual Even though I was commissioner for food supplies I got no more and was careful not to betray my
trust for fear of my enemies who were on the lookout

The adjutant brought me a letter from the general staff announcing that
the commandant and sixty-six men were waiting for me in front of the
armory that it was for a secret mission that would not last more than six
hours I refused to go The commandant came to get me I told him that I
would not march He said he would force me I told him that I had not
had my supper He said that he would take care of it and that I absolutely
must leave immediately

I closed my shop I arrived at the armory with the commandant On the
way (they) gave me a pound-loaf and a large cervelat They told me to take
my men who were three men from each company and give them arms I
was in command He said to me Here are two letters You will open one of
them when you reach the Duplessis prison[297] and the other tomorrow
morning and seize the post and disarm them The general staff leaves that
to your prudence

I told him You've made a mistake (He) gave me the password and just
laughed I left When we were almost at the Petit-Pont a man came up to
me and said Sir a cannon is waiting for you I was not surprised I had
my men split up and pass close to the houses and upon reaching the cannon
I rushed it and surprised the guard I went in I unsealed the letter I
presented it to the post commander I had the cannon put away and took

---

[297] This prison was located in the rue Saint-Jacques in the former collège du Plessis; the
episode can be dated as having taken place in Prairial of the Year III. Following the failure of
the Days of Germinal, the democratic sections were in turmoil, and the Convention feared a
popular movement. According to Tönneson, the prison was the place where actions were
organized, because the many sans-culottes held there were able to communicate freely with
the outside. An escape plot involving the leading patriots was uncovered. Pamphlets written
in the prison were distributed in Paris. As a result, Ménétra and the National Guards from his
then rather "centrist" section were mobilized. He shows the same lack of precision in his
account of the events of the Revolution (cf. II fols. 69–76, fols. 80–100) as in the *Journal*, but
he does tell us that he was with the National Guards that supported the Convention when it
was invaded by *sectionnaires* from the faubourgs and Representative Féraud was murdered on
20 May 1795.

charge of the concierge and the guards At ten o'clock fifteen cavalry and then fifteen gendarmes arrived as reinforcements A man came in to say that supper was waiting across the street I saw a well-laid table I asked two friends to keep me company They allowed me to spend two nights and two days

Meanwhile my enemies were furious at the assembly when the authorities were subjected to the so-called purge vote[298] After the justice of the peace it was my turn One of those monsters called for my arrest He was shouted down The other for my disarmament He was spurned Finally Nardin took the floor and said that my shop had been closed for three days He was interrupted by the commandant [Nardin said] that my wife had left and that I was not ethical enough for the posts I held People shouted Down with him The pamphleteer took the floor and asked that I be suspended from office

That night still unaware [of what had happened] with my friend de Lenoncourt[299] I went to find the justice of the peace who told me the news all three of us went to the adjutant where we found Nardin who tried to make excuses The commandant came looking for us said that he had given a categorical denial to those who had spoken against me and that he wanted to take me to the committee of general security that he had said before the full assembly that if my shop was closed for three days it was because I didn't want to leave the post I had been assigned and that people had applauded and that several citizens had spoken in my favor and that the traitor Nardin could not help praising me and also speaking well of my son whom I had sent to the frontier

We went the next evening to the committee with the commandant who was a friend of Merlin[300] They had us shown in They listened to us

---

[298] Following the events of 1 Prairial, there was a widespread settling of scores in the sections. Subject to scrutiny were all who had been leaders in the Year II, especially those who had been members of the civil and revolutionary committees. 1,200 Jacobins were imprisoned in Paris, and there was a drastic purge of the National Guard. This adds support to the notion that Ménétra, though a Jacobin rather hostile to the terrorist excesses, was nevertheless accused by the *muscadins*. The story also illustrates the solidarity of the National Guards and the intervention of Ménétra's company commander.

[299] Joseph de Lénoncourt, bailiff in the Châtelet, age 42, was born in Champagne and lived at 30, rue Pavée. He is also said to have been former bailiff at the Chambre des Comptes. He held various posts in the section and in the National Guard, where his rank was captain. He was a moderate Jacobin.

[300] Antoine Christian Merlin, known as Thionville (1762–1833), member of the Committee of Public Safety and Committee of General Security after the Ninth of Thermidor, at which time he abandoned Robespierre and became one of the political leaders of the reaction.

They gave me a document signed by the representatives to be (read) at the next assembly I presented it to the president who read it which ordered that I be recognized as a good citizen and that I be retained in the posts that my fellow citizens had entrusted to me Bravos and clapping of hands were heard My enemies were annihilated and I continued in my duties

The revolutionary committees were abolished[301] The citizen breathes (easy) but their [i.e., the committees'] henchmen spread the rumor that they were going to regain power People were constantly saying things to me about them and telling me that I would be one of their first victims The fellow who told me that I had no respect for He was himself called before the disciplinary council The commandant asked me to preside When I arrived I saw that traitor Nardin who asked me if I was going to preside I answered that it was no concern of his He told me that if I wanted vengeance I had all the means to obtain it that Duplessis was summoned and that when they called him I should turn over the chair to a citizen and he would go for sure to the rue du Bouloir[302]

I answered that Tartuffe that I would put the matter on the day's agenda He was called He appeared He insulted his captain He did not appear for guard duty and did not sleep at the guard house which he practiced with me He began complaining that people had it in for him that they wanted to see him dead I told him it wasn't that (and) that he should answer the charges against him He had neither bridle nor bit[303] didn't know what to answer

I said Citizens this being the first time that the citizen appears before you I ask that we move on to the next item of the agenda Many citizens asked for the floor saying that this fellow was a bad citizen who did not perform his service (except) in the cafés and cabarets After much debate one of the citizens said I am of the opinion of the president except that the president should enjoin him to be more diligent in performing his service I put the question to a vote I said these words "being the organ

---

[301] A good example of the chronological incoherence of Ménétra's writing, since these committees were replaced much earlier (7 Fructidor Year II, 24 August 1794) by twelve committees of surveillance for Paris, but the sketch brings out discord that can be traced back to committee membership in the Year II. Here again Ménétra describes himself as a centrist, an adversary of the extremists who were rumored to be making a strong comeback. As we know, however, most had been eliminated in the spring of the Year II. After Germinal and Prairial they were proscribed.

[302] The Committee of General Security had offices there, hence, by extension, the police.

[303] An equestrian phrase meaning that the horse does not respond to the reins.

of the council I order you to appear for guard duty to be more diligent in performing your service than you have been in the past and to stop insult ing your officers"

He went out went to the café at the corner of the rue Française I arrived with some friends He kept on repeating what I had said to him in a facetious and ironic tone I said to him Duplessis I am tired of your nonsense I have been putting up with it for a long time so either shut up or I'll shut you up Do it then says he All right I answered right now I went home I put on a frock coat and put my saber underneath and (I) came back to wait for him He arrived with his weapon in bandolier I went out I thought he was following me Not at all he was slandering me I opened the door I called him Baré junior[304] came out and invited me to forget the whole thing I told him He's been insulting me long enough it's time to put an end of it Tired of waiting and (since) my friends told me he would not come out I went home I treated him as he deserved I missed my chance and still regret that I didn't give him the lead of my saber across the face but some time later Beauchand[305] was not so forbearing he sent him to eat beans (?) that time

I tried to resign all the posts that my fellow citizens had delegated to me when I saw how badly things were going Our company was combined with the company of the Petit Lion I was named to preside I withdrew Nardin put his name in and asked that the person who got the most votes in a single election be made an officer It would go according to the votes One fellow got twenty-one two twenty one nineteen and both de Lenon court and I seventeen We were excluded by cabal mounted by Duplessis People wanted me for sergeant-major I objected People said that the notorious cabalist wanted me appointed corporal I said Citizens citizen Beauchand was commandant and was named corporal and so I don't want to act disdainfully toward him and all the trouble and expense he went to it did not add to his honor when he was named corporal (and) he was teased about it

---

[304] Jean-Baptiste Baré or Baret, junior, caterer and innkeeper at 36, rue Saint-Denis. In Fructidor of the Year II his father was imprisoned for debt and became a *muscadin* upon his liberation (AN, F.7 4586).

[305] Claude Beauchand, upholsterer, age 58 in 1793, born in Annecy and residing at 47, rue Saint-Denis; he had been a resident of Paris for 48 years. Note that he came from a region (Savoy) in which Ménétra probably had relatives (cf. II fol. 12) and that the two men were similar by age and occupation. He was a sublieutenant of the National Guard in 1789 and probably a captain and company commander in 1795–96.

On 13 Vendémiaire[306] this monster accompanied by Baré who like him had been drinking all day came knocking on the door at midnight saying that if I didn't march they would shoot me when they came back from their expedition and all said in big words I came out without a weapon wearing a jacket my hat pulled down At one thirty in the morning (I) found the battalion commanded by Beauchand in the place des Victoires filled with people who never appeared all (being) big merchants I saw the brave Duplessis with his dear friend Langlois who had been named president by the cabal Duplessis was licking his boots I went up to commandant Beauchand I told him that the line troops could besiege them and that they could be surrounded by the five streets leading into the square and I left

The next day the thirteenth the general alarm was sounded I went to the armory (and) to the Assembly where I saw all the new faces shouting like madmen To arms We marched several friends together promising ourselves not to march against the Convention We guarded the national treasury

At five o'clock many people asked if I had left Baré junior who was full of wine repeated the same words he had said the night before My wife urged me to march for fear that something would happen to me I left with a number of citizens who had been given cartridges They loaded their weapons We left We found a part of the battalion I found de Lenoncourt I asked him where we were going he had no more idea than I did Slowly we made our way to the quai de Voltaire De Lenoncourt had not eaten He had been under arms since morning I gave him a piece of bread I climbed up on a hydrant I saw that they were lighting the fuses There were cannons aimed at all the battalions on the quays I told the captain that since the [opposing] troops did not want to fraternize we'd better do

---

[306] Ménétra's account confirms that the National Guards of Bonconseil marched against the Convention in the insurrection fomented by reactionaries and royalists on 13 Vendémiaire. The western sections, seven out of forty-eight, marched on the assembly, which was defended by Barras and General Bonaparte. Ménétra describes an attack launched from the Left Bank, quai Voltaire, which was thrown back by Verdier's cannons. The National Guards were then disarmed. The "new faces" mentioned by Ménétra were those of wealthy merchants, bourgeois, who after several years' absence from the scene returned because of *muscadin* pressure. The insurrection had no unified plan and was led mainly by *réacteurs* and *feuillants* (royalists of 1790–91), without participation by royalists affiliated with the émigré networks, including those of Antraigues. See H. Zivy , *Le Treize Vendémiaire an IV* (Paris, 1898), and D. Woronoff, *La République bourgeoise, 1794–1799* (Paris, 1972), pp. 42–45. See also II fols. 97–100.

an about face I heard voices that were not unknown to me (saying) that anybody who repeated that would get a bayonet in the stomach I said My friend we've got to wait for the event At that moment we heard the shout To arms The cannon were heard across the way the sound of shells What did I see My friend alongside me on the ground the one who was on my left my clothes were full of blood I couldn't see anybody almost The pavement was littered with rifles

Everybody escaped into the houses I took the rue des Vieux Augustins saying My friend is dead I came to another little street I held on to my rifle I did not dare cross the Pont-Neuf I reached the pont Saint-Michel and arrived at the section They clapped Anger got the better of me I sprang for the platform where Langlois was presiding I said How can you applaud (when) they have just slaughtered our comrades on the quai de Voltaire and I said Miserable fellow you are responsible I'm going to plunge my bayonet into your body Saying that I went to do it to sacrifice him to the shades of the [fallen] citizens when an extremely strong master harness maker jumped on me in time saying Ménétra what are you doing

All the bureau officials ran out The next day the bureau was outlawed I was in my quarter it was a wholesale disaster I found de Lenoncourt (who) although he had fallen had no wound I was summoned by my justice of the peace to go to the section to make a proclamation in favor of disarmament Since some of the grenadiers and infantry refused to go along I didn't want to do this and announce such a good piece of news again I found my friend de Lenoncourt and others and we embraced like people who had come back from the other world The brave Duplessis had himself tonsured the next day because he had received a head wound not while advancing but while retreating because the wound was in back I had somebody tell him to hide because my justice of the peace told me that there was going to be an investigation of the wounded As for Baré he was wounded in the arm by a Biscayen[307] and went to La Charité[308] and died at home

I said farewell to all and resigned and didn't want any more posts when they renamed the company Some people insisted that I be made captain (but) I wanted no rank not even a civilian one and didn't want any kind of

---

[307] Denotes a large-caliber rifle manufactured in Biscaye, as well as the projectile fired by that weapon and shrapnel from the artillery fire.
[308] Well-known hospital in the rue de Vaugirard, founded by Mme Necker.

job whatsoever The tenth of August[309] as I was leading a part of the section to the Castle I just missed being run through by the sword of a Swiss guard of the apartments as we had just saved a father his two daughters and his wife whom we took by the arms after they asked that their father's life be spared all three having fallen on their knees I asked where he was and put him outside them in safety I thought to do the same (for the Swiss) by telling him to take off his uniform He tried to run me through wounded me in the hand Avoiding his blows my comrades stuck him with their bayonets and the fellows with pikes soon had him undressed

The ninth of Thermidor I lost a runoff with the wretched and unfortunate Gentelle[310] for the position of member of the commune and so just missed being guillotined The day of the murder of representative Féraud[311] I just missed being run through I parried the blow just in time while I was trying to have the unfortunate fellow's body brought home by a frantic cannoneer who was left almost alone in the rue Saint-Nicaise where they threatened to shell us and everyone fled

The affair of Saint-Eustache in front of the portal owing to Beauchand's imprudence they shelled us heavily All the unpleasantness that I endured from certain parties stirred up by that implacable enemy and that I was clever enough to avoid all those shells gave me food for thought and I quit and didn't want to hear any more about holding any positions of any kind even though they were offered to me my only thought being to

---

[309] The day when the *sectionnaires* seized the Tuileries and thus put an end to the reign of Louis XVI, who, defended by his Swiss guards, several of whom were killed, sought refuge with the Assembly, which was then meeting at the Jeu de Paume.

[310] Antoine Le Jemptel, sometimes written Jemplet (Ménétra spells it Gentelle). He was a clerk-auctioneer at the butter market, age 51, residing at 20, rue de la Grande-Truanderie. He was elected representative of the Bonconseil section to the general council of the commune of Paris, which replaced the municipal government on 10 August, at the time of the final vote that gave control of the assembly to the Robespierrists. He was civil commissioner of the section in 1792 and 1793. He was arrested and executed on 11 Thermidor along with other supporters of Robespierre. See E. Campardon, *Le Tribunal révolutionnaire de Paris* (Paris, 1886), p. 545. Arch. Préf. Police Bonconseil June-July 1790, September 1790, November 1792; BHVP. 100–65 (340); BN, 8⁰, Lc 31 (381).

[311] Jean-François Féraud (1764–1795), deputy from the Hautes-Pyrénées, close to the Girondins, voted for the death of the king, sent on special mission in the Year II; he opposed Robespierre in Thermidor. He was murdered in the Convention chamber on 1 Prairial in the Year III, and his head was paraded around on the end of a pike. Ménétra confirms that he was with his company at the Convention and was threatened by the canons of the insurgent *sectionnaires*.

bewail the fate of my poor boy who was risking his life for his fatherland while it was being betrayed and pillaged by intriguers on the home front

Around this time my wife returned from the country where she had gone to live with friends in the hope of living better than she could in Paris But all France was shaken by the misfortunes associated with the Revolution The selfish man enjoyed himself and the decent man moaned and languished for want of food

Citizen Bouchu fell ill her brother-in-law and her nephew both died at the same time she offered to give me her property on conditions that I rejected and because of my scruples refused She told me that some time ago she had made a will in my favor but that she was afraid that her relatives would not honor it and that all her bequests and donations would be ignored that since I refused to accept her proposition she was going to trade her house for a life annuity in my favor until the end of my days or else she would give it to me in exchange for an annuity until her death

I communicated this offer to my wife who would not agree to it I found a citizen to whom I spoke about it who was Captain Léonard[312] of my company (She) didn't leave me until the deal was complete She had to get divorced That was done She had the misfortune to burn her leg I took care of it She died while talking almost That morning we had had breakfast together She had wanted me to take possession of her jewels my scruples prevented me from taking them and also from accepting a contract for 750 livres assigned income

They came to tell me what had happened She suffocated at the sight of her relatives whom she had never known or met who came from Moulins in Bourgonnais and pillaged everything and then had the place put under seal The fellow who had taken the lion's share came to see me looking for the jewels and money he had not been able to find I refused His good fortune was short-lived because he died a month later from the debauch and pleasure his inheritance had brought him

Our son-in-law arrived shortly thereafter from his administrative du-

---

[312] Louis Léonard, painter and carpenter, age 25 in 1792, born at Feltin and residing first at 15 and later at 12, rue Pavée. He was a captain in the National Guard in 1793. Purged by the popular society for being somewhat weak, many citizens attested to his patriotism. He was deputy justice of the peace. Unless Léonard was reelected captain in 1794, the episode probably occurred in 1793. (AN, D. III 253–254, W. 112.) See A. Soboul, *Les Sans-Culottes parisiens* (Paris, 1958), pp. 702–703.

ties Food was very scarce in Paris He proposed to my wife to persuade me
to leave the shop and come live with him and his wife that what I had
would take care of my entertainment My wife didn't stop talking about it
I played deaf My children made me the same proposition I stated my
objections that I wanted to keep my shop for my son My wife pointed out
that he had always said he did not want a shop of that kind

I felt my strength waning I had constant pain in my left arm companions were rare and demanded high wages Nevertheless I told my wife
that it was always better to have a place of my own Despite all my arguments she still wanted to leave me It was then that I reflected on the
scruples that had caused me to turn down the offers that had been made to
me Finally despite everything I could do or say I had to give in Her mind
was made up I was alone isolated so to speak and I gave in after four
days I sold my shop for just ten thousand francs in *assignats*[313] and left
(the buyer) the greater part of our belongings and received as down payment (only) two thousand francs with the rest payable after six months
when it was no longer worth the trouble to collect

I lived very well We didn't feel the shortage we were well provided
we kept a good table Our son-in-law undertook to pay the armament
workers at Charleville by arranging things with the minister Benezech[314]
with whom he was in contact (and) taking all the iron stored in the house
of the Jacobins in the faubourg Saint-Germain (and) which came from all
the religious establishments And he put me in charge with six men who
weighed and loaded Thus having been a man of glass I became a man of

---

[313] Paper currency issued in 1790, in theory backed by national property confiscated from
the clergy and émigrés. The value of the *assignats* declined steadily, especially after 1794 in
the wake of price increases and speculation. Anticipation of the decline in the assignat was a
factor in the economic crisis of 1795. It may be that Ménétra is describing the situation in the
Year IV, when the louis d'or, fixed at 2,000 livres in Brumaire, reached 5,000 livres by
Frimaire, and when eight billion livres in assignats were placed in circulation in the space of
one month. Hard currency was hoarded and the state was reduced to expedients. In March of
1796 it created a new form of paper money: the *mandat territorial*, which was worth 30
assignats. The value of the assignat had declined to 1/400 of its nominal value. The mandat
collapsed immediately and was demonetized in February of 1797. The monetary situation was
improved by an uncontrolled deflation and measures to alleviate the debt and raise income
from taxes.

[314] Pierre Benezech (1749–1802), son of a councillor in the chambre des comptes of
Montpellier, was a businessman who joined the Revolution in 1789. He was Minister of the
Interior in the Year IV, but, compromised by relations with royalists, he was sacked on 16
Fructidor in the Year V. He then joined Bonaparte and died prefect of Saint-Domingue
(Haiti).

iron but not at heart That lasted around six months at which time my wife fell dangerously ill She recovered

I had not forgotten my old quarter and I saw my acquaintances particu- larly my friend de Lenoncourt My wife took a dislike to her daughter I saw that we were going to have to leave As for me I left on friendly terms and I rented a room and (we) were back on our own thinking of our poor children especially our boy I used friends to try to see him again by making petitions None of it did any good and since that time we have been unable to obtain either a short leave or a discharge The only pleasure we have is to receive news of him (and) to see our children even though it meant going to the country to Montrouge which I did often when we first moved into our room

I was named charity commissioner of the Luxembourg a job I had a hard time getting out of A citizen attached to the Directory by the name of Lepuel being the treasurer of the directors I had several conferences with him He took a liking to me My conversation pleased him (He) promised me a post as government commissioner when all of a sudden the Directory fell[315]

In this new order of things I am most comfortable When the weather is good I go walking The fires of my youth are quenched When I am with old friends I think about all that has happened We recount what we have seen what we have felt the good and the evil that the Revolution has done all the assaults the days the nights the punishments and the fate of our unfortunate friends who perished in the time of Terror when good men feared for their lives We are beginning to see the twilight of the times in which our fathers were happy And I tell myself that when I see my son again my wishes will be fulfilled That is my only desire and my only hope to see both (of my children) established and happy So I call upon the Eternal to grant them peaceful and serene days and that I may see them in my old age free of the suffering that the Revolution has made all of us feel

Unfortunately our fortune is not considerable being just enough for a rather mediocre life because ambition never governed my actions and I was often thwarted in the enterprises that I wished to undertake or that others proposed to me So I gave up any idea of being able to make them happy with our property

---

[315] Allusion to the coup d'état of 18 Brumaire with which Napoleon overthrew the Direc- tory and established the Consulate on 10 November 1799.

I had nothing from my fathers and mothers [sic] nor did my wife Nevertheless we shall try never to abandon our children and to do for them whatever we can to give them salutary advice not to succumb to weakness as I did by imprudence and to place all their thoughts as I do and to call every day upon the Supreme Being to grant us a happy life and a good end

Epistle to My Mind

My mind it is to you that I speak today
account to me for all you have written
You put no date much less day of the month
I believe my mind that you don't know them yourself
no spelling no period no comma
much less any consonant for you all that is not important
All those beautiful sentences and all those big words
tell me are they true accurate or false
You say that you have written without ostentation
and swarms of pages in abundance
What devil suggested that you write your story
all your nonsense pranks and failings
My mind you amused yourself with trifles
you have no fear that your readers will gloss you
What good are your slanders and your calumnies
Though you say you bear no grudge against your enemies
According to you my mind you've written without reflection
and many pages are full of illusions
you take pride in your foolish loves
About such things my poor mind you ought to keep silent
You boast of your glorious exploits
And say my poor mind what you done
You speak to us emphatically of everything
And you make great show of a trifle
You say my mind that you have friends
Do you believe it and in these times do friends exist
To hear you tell you're some kind of Hercules
About everything you say I'm quite credulous
Your mistresses do you say they all loved you
How simple you are my mind to believe it and to think so
You hold our fathers' faith up to ridicule
and paint their ministers as men of no account
They are treated by you as imposters and ambitious men

because truly you don't think as they do
What verve you have my mind you always want to moralize
Leave them alone that's their job because people really do want to listen to them
Does not every man know that the Supreme Being takes care of everything and
   even of yourself
Remember my mind always stay calm
you must see everything say nothing and no speeches
Believe me throw all these papers in the fire
and don't complain or slander our elders
For if you have it in mind as I suppose you do to hold on to them
those who come after you will want to tear them up
They'll say to themselves this mind was a proud doddering fool
He tells his stories in a foul and rotten mood
He will give them to the dairymaid or the grocer
where they will use them you understand for other purposes
They will say this mind was not very well advised
to repeat his household affairs
Do you think your belief impresses us
We know my mind better than you what to think about it
I urge you for your own good to keep silent and stay calm
You're getting old you will be called an imbecile
and they might try to restore your reason
and give you for reward an apartment in the Petites Maisons
And for your own peace and quiet you who pretend to be a fine mind
renounce erase and cross out what you have written

   Year XI, 25 Vendémiaire

Jacques-Louis Ménétra
An Eighteenth-Century
Way of Life

[1]

Childhood, Marriage, Culture

Over the past few decades historians of the family, both urban and rural, have relied on the systematic study of vital statistics.[1] This kind of research has raised many questions, some of which have been cleared up by bringing in other kinds of sources: judicial records (declarations of pregnancy, lawsuits), religious documents (such as requests for dispensation from the rules governing consanguinity, episcopal statutes, confessors' manuals, cases in church courts), and, farther afield, evidence from the medical and moralistic literature, statements by writers, and even studies of folklore.[2] Personal documents have seldom been used, and most of our information about families of low social status has come from observers of other classes bent on instituting some kind of reform. For example, in Paris Sébastien Mercier and Nicolas Rétif de la Bretonne have left us a priceless picture of the life of the common people, but the meaning of that picture is distorted in a number of ways: by the praise of nature in opposition to the corrupting city, by fascination with or aversion to the peculiarities of poverty, or by devotion to some edifying idea of human nature.[3] Texts that describe relatively poor people invariably combine images of denatured, undisciplined man, who must be supervised and disciplined, with images of the city as lethal and pathological, a place of filth that must somehow be restored to natural cleanliness. Accordingly, it is common in such writing for family imagery, and especially comparisons of the mores of the peasant family with big-city ways, to occupy a large place. To establish the principles of family life was an essential first step for those moralists, who hoped to find a basis for ethics and religion in the myth of a harmonious natural hierarchy.[4]

Unlike the tirades of the moralists and the dry statistics of the urban demographers, the *Journal* of Jacques-Louis Ménétra is a lively, spontaneous work that bears its author's uniquely personal stamp. Yet to suppose it

free of bias would be to succumb to a naive and vulgar populism. Ménétra's biases (different from those of the well-bred), his prejudices (different
from those of the scientists), and his assumptions (unlike those of the men
of letters of his time) all helped to shape his vision of the family and to
alter his conception of the affective life. In themselves these biases are
significant, for they form an integral part of a life experience that is intimately bound up with its representation. To put it another way, Ménétra's
distortions show how imagination (*l'imaginaire*) affects behavior. His attitude toward the family wavers between pessimism (which accords well
with the views of those historians who see the family as an instrument for
regularizing behavior, an instrument of socialization)[5] and optimism
(which sits well with the view of other historians, that the modern family
is an outgrowth of developing individualism and of sexual and emotional
liberation).[6]

In any case, the picture that one derives from the *Journal* complements
Philippe Ariès's model of western family history.[7] It suggests another
alternative, a possible working-class family and emotional model and a
sensibility that is neither completely independent of, nor completely de-
pendent upon, ruling-class norms. Ménétra, whose mother died before he
was two, fashions a new myth of a motherless Oedipus, in which the
drama is played out entirely between father and son. Beyond the myth we
can make out the actual web of family relationships through the tales of
childhood adventures and apprenticeship experiences and the ultimately
unremarkable fate of the former companion who settles down, marries,
and becomes procreator and creator in his own right. This singular adventure, which in its own way illustrates the old adage that "there's nothing
new under the sun," no doubt exaggerates the rosier and more righteous
aspects of its hero's character. What is more, it suffers a bit from the lack of
any similar story with which to compare it, with which to establish its
place in the prosopography of Enlightenment Paris.

The image of the father occupies a central place in the *Journal*. The
circumstances dictated as much: Jacques Ménétra, a master glazier by
trade, finds himself a widower with four children. Jacques-Louis was then
out to nurse, as was the custom among Parisian artisans and shopkeepers.[8]
He was two years old when his father was forced to remarry and to tap his
family for assistance. Of his late mother the little boy remembers only
what is appropriate to her role: virtuous and fertile, she probably died in
giving birth to her youngest daughter. The three surviving children were
the fruit of a marriage which, based on averages calculated for Lyons,[9]

lasted some five years: the size of the family was larger than normal and attained the maximum that the artisan class could tolerate, given the economic hardship that supporting a large family entailed. This would explain why the second marriage was childless (or at any rate produced no surviving child) and hints at the use of some form of birth control. Contrary to popular legend and deeply rooted tradition, the stepmother loved the children of the first marriage, and when she died, Jacques-Louis, who must have been around fifteen, mourned her loss. Though the family shell had already been pierced, the father's home remained the center of family life.

Like many young Parisians, Ménétra's child care was intermittent; he was suckled in the suburbs by paid nurses yet escaped the mortality that claimed most infants, thanks to the solicitude of his grandmother and probably also of his uncle and godfather, as well as his father—though in writing his memoirs Jacques-Louis Ménétra rather too carefully avoided the good points in his father's character, which he sought to blacken as much as possible so as to make himself look better by contrast. After escaping the perils of ailing nurses with bad milk, he lived, from the time he returned to Paris after his second birthday until his eleventh year, in the home of his grandmother, a strong woman about whom I shall have more to say in a moment.

We should not make too much of the rift between father and son, which again is rather overdrawn in Ménétra's account: it was not far from the rue des Prêtres Saint-Germain-L'Auxerrois to the rue de la Grande Truanderie where his grandmother lived, and the child attended the little school in his father's parish. There was no break in the continuity of his education or in his emotional life, though his schooling scarcely had the regularity described in the manuals of education *ad usum populi* or in official documents. The boy adjusted to the schism in his life and to living with a surrogate mother. Jacques Ménétra senior, burdened by the care of two daughters whom he seems to have preferred to his son (if the narrator is to be believed), must not have been ungrateful for the help he received in his boy's upbringing from his mother-in-law.

The roles of the elder glazier take shape one after another in the *Journal*, but they were apparently governed by a logic of opposition that was established quite early and consolidated by the conflicts of adolescence. Here we glimpse the clichés of a traditional popular view of the Parisian family. In the first place, the father is responsible for feeding and clothing his family. If he fails in this, if he nibbles away at the money needed for upkeep, he fails in his duty. He fails even more if he stingily refuses the few coins that the child, and even more the adolescent, requires for his own needs. In short, from very early childhood the father-son relationship involved crucial issues of money. This makes sense when we remember what an economic hardship it must have been to provide for three children and two adults in the Paris of the 1750s.[10] In addition, the father is an educator; the representation of the father meting out punishment, his no doubt excessive violence, his predilection for the kick in the behind, the slap, and even the thrashing with cane or rope, all suggest his concern for his child's education and his sense of responsibility. The account of the paternal mission in the *Journal* is one-sided from beginning to end. On the success or failure of that mission the child's fate depends, for the city offers all too many opportunities for young boys and girls to leave the straight and narrow and find their way to the margins of society. It is up to fathers to watch over their progeny. "That made me see that fathers are responsible for their children's misfortune." Spare the rod and spoil the child: the loving parent did not stint on punishment.

But where in all this is paternal love? Does it even exist? To those who have rather hastily concluded that intense emotional investment in one's children is a recent development, a product of reading Rousseau and Dr. Tissot, I shall point to Ménétra's direct testimony which proves that what changed was the form and content of an emotional investment whose existence is beyond dispute.[11] There can be no doubt that in his own way Ménétra esteems his drunkard of a father. If he depicts his father as he should and could have been, his concern is to illustrate the intrinsic goodness of his own nature and the remarkable fact that he turned out well in spite of unfortunate circumstances. Jacques-Louis is careful to set against more bitter memories the episode that occurred in May of 1750 when his father, worried by rumors of kidnappings in Paris, joined with other families in the rue des Prêtres-Saint-Germain to send an escort of stout cooper's apprentices to meet their children at the schoolhouse door. The elder Ménétra's outbursts of temper toward his son were not incompatible with genuine affection, though they do serve to cast the son in a favorable light and to justify his tantrums and escapades.

The paternal authority is not called into question, although it is challenged in any number of revealing confrontations: the father prevents the son from enlisting in the army; the father escapes from a strange episode of arsenic poisoning, a striking "parapraxis"; the father and the son compete sexually for the attentions of the fair Rosalie. Behind the sins of the son and the rages of a father who lives up to his reputation, the honor of the family is at stake. What is more, the power of the father is backed up by the power of the law, enforced as everyone knows by the *lettre de cachet.* The only counterweight to the authority of the father is that of the King: "I no longer belong to you, I belong to the King," exclaims the boy who has just enlisted; yet in order to marry, the independent companion must have his parents' consent, at least until he has reached the age of majority. From these images of conflict, or rites of initiation, we gather that the relationship between father and son was a tense one, combining violence with fierce affection and complicity. Who can forget the ambiquous and somewhat disdainful image of the young man going through the pockets of his reeling father to protect the drunken old man from thieves? Equally memorable are the words of the widower commanding his son to supervise his wife's funeral. In other words, Ménétra's version of the "School for Fathers" accommodates the continuity as well as the incoherence of working-class life (*la vie populaire*). Sooner or later the pupil becomes the teacher. The future will tell.

It remains true that the child has a great need to love and be loved. Here the important role is played by his grandmother (to whom he also refers as his good mother or simply as his mother: the mother of his real mother, snatched too soon from the child's affection). This strong woman fully asumes the roles of the dead mother. Mme Marseau, a glazier's widow and mother of four working glaziers, serves as the vehicle for a eulogy of motherhood; an anthropologist might read this episode as one that throws light on the historical fortunes of matriarchy, as contrasted with the law's emphasis on the paternal line. Behind her we catch glimpses of a sturdy clan. Note, too, that Mme Marseau comes from Dauphiné (she is a Boyer from Valence) and is the Parisian counterpart of that feminine figure that Ménétra occasionally shows silhouetted against the horizon, the shrewd but kindly peasant—or, in another context, the distinguished superior of a convent of nuns. She gives advice and renders judgment; it is her name that one invokes, and among glaziers and glass dealers in the provinces the Widow Marseau of Paris is a name to reckon with. To Jacques-Louis she was both protective and nurturing; she laid balm on his wounds and taught him the rules of proper behavior. In her grandson's memory she is the object of positive primary emotional investment. Note, too, that it is she who secures the young man's future, for after setting up her four sons and marrying her daughter she is still able to pay for her grandson's master's certificate, which assures him some modicum of independence. Her purse is always open for the young companion in the provinces, far away from home.

One anecdote in particular illustrates the importance, in Ménétra's mind, of the bond between this surrogate mother and himself, the chosen, coddled son: the story of a mother in the Cévennes who dies when her prodigal son returns home, which Ménétra hears in the course of his travels, inspires a personal parable, which he casts in a dramatic style rich with echoes of the broadsheet literature, fairy tales, and the Bible— a story of the gratitude of the son who returns to Paris unchanged in all but outward appearance, still good and loyal, in good health and with his pockets full. The full significance of the story, its connection with the vicissitudes of the grandmother's affection and the father's authority, becomes clear when we remember that it ends with the admonition to "go see your father," an order that the young man instantly obeys. The imagined scene of the grandmother's death brings out all the associations implicit in Ménétra's situation as the chosen son. These associations are clearly the basis of his polemic against his father. What is more, they also show that the history of feeling is a complex subject indeed.

Beyond the nuclear family—Jacques-Louis, his parents, and his two sisters—we are also aware of an extended family, composed primarily of relations on his mother's side. Housing conditions had long dictated that each generation live in separate quarters, though this rule was flexible: the elder Ménétra, for example, lived with his daughters—with Thérèse until she moved in with her husband in the faubourg Saint-Antoine and then with the younger daughter after she married a companion from his shop. On the Ménétra side we find two families, probably related through the father's sisters and described as the families of "cousins" (for which read uncles): Charpentra, who is a recruiter, and the notorious Chénier. The latter plays an important role in Jacques-Louis's life: a dealer in dry goods and groceries doing business, according to the *Almanach* of 1769, on the quai de la Ferraille, he was an established and sober gentleman, a source of sound advice. His country house in Vertus was a family gathering place. He had two sons, one who wound up in the Isles and the other, our hero's cousin and pal, in the French guards after a stint in the grocery business: thus Uncle Chénier, like the elder Ménétra, tasted the bitterness of the deceived and disappointed father.[12]

On the side of Anne Marseau and grandmother Boyer Ménétra had quite a crowd of uncles and aunts and male and female cousins, and, later on, nephews and nieces, which made possible some highly improbable adventures and some highly probable liaisons, especially with his young female cousins. In the Marseau clan the four glazier sons and their wives appear in the *Journal* as familiar characters, now as protectors, now as villains.[13] Relationships among the three generations centered on the grandmother, despite the fact that each generation lived separately. The family discussed many complex matters of business and ethics, deciding the future of a spendthrift or mulling over a niece's loss of virginity or the jealous passion of grandmother Boyer. When the latter falls ill the Marseau aunts stand watch at her door, and when she dies these Errinyes of the neighborhood heap invective and threats upon Jacques-Louis, who characteristically resents the whole Marseau family from then on. The tumultuousness of family relationships is here clearly in evidence.

It was in this emotional and troubled environment that Ménétra's childhood unfolded. The *Journal* offers a unique opportunity to observe the various ways in which feelings, knowledge, manners, and practical know-how are acquired. We look on as the components of a culture are assembled and put to use. Ménétra develops loyalties to his neighborhood playmates that will exert great influence over his adolescence and adult life: his nostalgia for these early years suggests that his childhood was active and passionate. The young man's education is not confined to any one locale. In his father's and grandmother's homes he learns the basics of daily living and religion and the emotional routines of a family that is held together by the benevolence of his grandmother, the wrathful tenderness of his father, the timorous jealousy of his sisters, and the anxious affection of his uncles and aunts. In the parish schools he learns the rudiments of scholarship, the rites of the Church and the official religion. In the family workshops as well as on the job in Paris and its suburbs he becomes versed in the practices of his trade by watching others and listening to their advice. In the streets and on the quays he learns the ways of the city— its social customs—and acquires his first experience of life. What is striking about this educational history is that the young child learns so many different, and sometimes contradictory, lessons, and learns them all simultaneously.

Ménétra's *Journal* enables us to understand how children experienced their city. Grandmotherly caresses and paternal beatings complement the lessons of earliest childhood, learned in the miserable quarters of his peasant nurse. The boy's talent, sensibility, precocity, cleverness, and gift for imitation are already in evidence. Mme Marseau, a mildly religious woman given to recounting old legends and something of a Jansenist, passed on to her grandson a gift not unusual among middle- and working-class Parisian women: a taste for storytelling, a fascination with miracles and hence for the extraordinary within the ordinary, together with a desire for the religious simplicity exemplified by "good Monsieur Paris," the symbol of a purified primitive Church and the antithesis of the archbishop and the parish clergy. The boy's early education ended by age seven. Until then the teacher's role was shared: the grandmother, surrogate for the absent mother, imparted tenderness and imagination, the father instilled violence and in some ways realism, for life is not always easy or pleasant. The twin educators symbolize the two sides of working-class life: the anxious hope of innocent pleasures and the harsh realities of earning a living and raising children.

The parish school revealed other realities to Ménétra and opened up new avenues of action. Unusual for its time, the Paris school system offered those who had access to it (almost all males of established families and a good proportion of females) a wide range of choices: the system comprised nearly five hundred schools of all kinds. Culturally, Ménétra was a product of the Catholic counter-Reformation and its educational institutions: the choir schools, parish schools, charity schools, and Church-sponsored boarding schools.[14] He was surely taught by the schoolmasters of Saint-Eustache and Saint-Germain-l'Auxerrois while he was living with his grandmother. When the cooper's apprentices were sent to meet him at the school door in 1750, he was twelve years old. Shortly thereafter he won a place in his parish's choir school. Six places were reserved for pupils with gifted voices; they were to accompany the services with their singing and received both regular lessons and lessons in Latin. Ménétra was a talented scholarship boy. He amused the fathers of Saint-Denis with his precocity. Later, in 1760 at L'Isle-Jourdain, he embellished the Holy Week services with his voice and splendid Parisian hymns. Still later, as a companion, his songs were taken up by other companions in processions and in the inns. An aspect of popular life about which little is known can be glimpsed in these commonplace activities, which combine celebration, religion, and work with a taste for beautiful things and a capacity for emotion. Songs were learned on the benches of the classroom and the choir, and later from sheet music purchased on the streets. Every young boy became familiar with a vast repertoire of hymns, psalms, and refrains and could sing "Onward Christian Soldiers" along with the choir, to say nothing of "Let Your Daughters Screw" (to the tune of "May your sheep safely graze"). As Ménétra puts it in a pun of his own devising: "to be a singer (*chanteur*) is to be an enchanter (*enchanteur*)."

To recap, by the age of fifteen Ménétra, like any other Paris boy, could boast of having mastered four essential skills: reading, writing, arithmetic, and singing.[15] He might have continued beyond this elementary curriculum and entered one of the colleges, as he suggests in an attempt to make his father look overbearing and greedy: the elder Ménétra, we are told, was in a hurry to put his son to work despite the objections of Mme Marseau and "several other people." He might have preceded his contemporary Sébastien Mercier, a pupil of the parish and son of a master furbisher of the quai de la Ferraille, who left the parish playground for Father Toquet's filthy boarding school and ultimately crossed the Seine to take his place on the benches of the *collège des Quatre Nations*.[16]

Ménétra's future was different, because the powerful tradition of passing on the father's trade and the need to join forces and husband resources militated in favor of his becoming a glazier. He did, however, retain vivid memories of his early schooling, memories that combine the dreams of a young choirboy with the harsh realities of apprenticeship. For what was taught with the voice and the ruler in the schools of Paris was not only useful knowledge but also physical discipline: learning to write, a matter of mastering the complicated motions of one's own hand, did part of the job, and silence, supervision, and catechism did the rest. This was an education in which a tincture of learning did duty for knowledge, and in which religion remained paramount. Instruction was based on the catechism and attendance at services. As early as his first communion, Ménétra revealed a curiosity and a talent for discussion that would never leave him. One whole aspect of social life was bound up with religion, summed up in the priest's threefold authority: the youthful Ménétra's confessor reappears as a symbolic witness at the time of his marriage, suggesting the formative power of the parish clergy; schoolmasters of every sort were responsible for inculcating knowledge, manners, adaptability, and patience; and families, mothers and fathers, relied on both confessors and teachers to reinforce their commandments and to discipline the mischievous. The child's freedom lay in the interstices of this threefold hierarchy: it was in the dark regions beyond the reach of these three disciplinary authorities that the people passed on its inventive talents, its ability to manipulate the norms, to "make do"[17] with whatever was at hand.

In the workshop these rules were reinforced. At the same time the young apprentice learned his business and the elementary personal skills needed by anyone who wished to go his own way, manage his own shop, and expand his trade. The workman learned on the job how to handle his tools, how to estimate accurately, and how to work efficiently. One began by watching others, then helping them with their jobs, sweeping up the shop, lighting the way up a dark stairway, preparing snacks, carrying tools, cutting glass—each skill was learned by stages. In Ménétra's case, this apprenticeship took place mainly in the family workshops of the Marseaus and the Ménétras, but the young novice also visited the homes of clients in various parts of the city and its suburbs. Installing glass in a neighbor's apartment, accompanying an uncle to Issy to collect his pay, following another to a job at the abbey of Saint-Denis, all helped the young man to learn his trade, gave him a chance to be of service, gradually enabled him to contribute to his family's upkeep, and at the same time initated him into the world. The apprentice left the protective shell of family and parish and learned to judge for himself which employers and clients were good and which were bad. He could judge where his fortune lay, and eventually he could spread his wings and fly on his own. Then he was ready to seek out new masters. The time of initiation was over; the role of the father as educator had come to an end.

There is no doubt that training of the son by the father was one of the basic forms of craft training in prerevolutionary France. In the present instance, this training pitted son against father in a painful crisis of identity, an essential part of growing up—that communal ritual played out before watchful relatives and neighbors. The tension between father and son was internalized by the exceptional author of the *Journal* to such a degree that it became one of the guiding principles of his autobiography.

Other kinds of knowledge, and other anxieties, were learned from the street urchins who rallied to the cry of "Ménétra-Patatra" in the maze of streets, byways, enclosures, alleys, and passageways that formed the backbone of the old working-class neighborhoods of Paris. The river—its quays, bridges, arches, watering troughs, work sites, ports, and sandy beaches below the Pont-Neuf under the statue of Henri IV and below the Jardin de l'Infante opposite the Louvre—were the scene of childish games and pranks, the place where our young hero first learned to stake out his own territory. There was a sharp contrast between the world of stray children,[18] young and old, who wandered sadly through the streets of the city and along its waterfront, and that of the sons of the common people, of settled artisans, who were tied to their homes by family and work and yet free enough to escape the watchful parental gaze long enough to get into mischief and assert their fragile independence. The evening escapades of young scamps are the preludes to the nocturnal adventures of adolescents, some of them out looking for a good time, others cast out by irate fathers. The cat-and-mouse games with the police and the tirades of the *commissaires* prefigure a later, and more serious, rebelliousness against the constraints of family and society. Boys who shared the first pangs of puberty formed close and lasting friendships.

We need list only a few of the more noteworthy games in which these youths engaged: running, leapfrog, hide and seek, indoor and outdoor tennis (*paume longue* or *courte*), pushing and shoving at the water's edge, racing over wooden barges and onto hay boats, instructive explorations of fishing boats, fishing with the local fishermen, and swimming—all forms of physical training. Playing games brought dexterity and strength and hence confidence, which in Ménétra's case helped to compensate, one suspects, for his small size. Finally, our young man learned how to handle himself in fights and brawls, as city boys tangled with young peasants from the suburbs. This kind of life placed a premium on bravery and taught Ménétra to deal with the many violent situations, ordinary as well as extraordinary, that he would encounter in later life.

There is nothing surprising about the harshness of his experience; such was the nature of the age. A boy falls into the river and drowns, another is stabbed with a pitchfork and dies; a carelessly handled pistol goes off and kills a kitchen maid. Violence and death dogged the steps of young males as they underwent their rites of initiation. Beatings were endured and just as quickly administered. Ménétra conceives an early enthusiasm for fireworks (prohibited, incidentally, by police ordinance) that will stay with him throughout his life, and the sound of firecrackers exploding beneath the skirts of seamstresses and fruitsellers and of Chinese rockets whistling through the air enliven Ménétra's memories of childhood. This rough-and-tumble education in the streets will stand him in good stead later on, when he begins his travels and has to cope with some difficult situations or ride a horse for the first time or suffer the fatigue of travel and the rigors of the companion's lot. This is the price of the ability to partake in some measure of the feast of the body (*la fête corporelle*). Our young man quickly acquires physical self-confidence,[19] as he shows with his bold and confident stride—moralistic observers like Rétif and Mercier would later describe such strutting as seditious. Note, too, his just appreciation of the value of strength, his astonishing feats of jumping and hiking, and his remarkable courage, which is exhibited in a variety of ways.

Ménétra as a young adult is a fine specimen of what this kind of education could produce. His abilities highlight the dividing line between the man's world, with its emphasis on strength and courage, and the woman's world, in which the paramount values are circumspection and timorous modesty: the young males' sound and fury contrasted with the watchful silence of young maidens. Youth was shaped, physically as well as morally, by the street and the family.

His apprenticeship complete, Ménétra took his place among educated Parisians: by 1750, nearly three-quarters of all young men in the city could read and write. This figure exceeded the literacy rate for urban girls, who were always relatively disadvantaged, and also for rural youths of both sexes.[20] What the memoirs show us, however, is the way in which Ménétra turns this cultural capital to advantage. In arithmetic he proves himself skilled; his trade required this, as we shall see later on.[21] Writing is for him a familiar activity, and the memoirs show clearly that the common people of Paris, and in particular the members of the shopkeeping classes, were in the habit of writing letters. The ability to write was not the preserve of the social elite. As it happens, history has preserved the sophisticated products of the epistolary art of the ruling classes. It has been uncommon to save, or even to look for, the badly written, poorly spelled letters that men and women of modest station exchanged among themselves. But such private correspondence did exist. The regular operation of courier services and the creation of the Petite Poste, which distributed mail in Paris, no doubt helped to encourage it. The *Journal* gives us a fairly concrete idea of what these letters must have been like: some discussed family business, some had to do with work, others touched on matters of the heart. For the companion separated from his family, writing was a way of maintaining contact, relaying news, obtaining money, and announcing his impending return. Ménétra maintains his family life while on the road by writing to his sisters, his grandmother, and perhaps even to his father (who, it is worth noting, could also write and sign his name—he affixes his initials to the marriage contract and to the minutes of the guild jury proceedings.[22]

An elementary education is an advantage both in obtaining work and on the job. It is by writing that one makes the best deals, finds the best jobs, obtains the money needed for travel, and comes to terms with prospective employers. Ménétra is capable of keeping the books and maintaining the commercial correspondence of the widows who hire him. He can sign his name. When conflict breaks out this ability singles him out as a person capable of negotiating an agreement. The companion's prestige with his employers, as well as with those of his comrades who do not possess the same advantages, depends on his ability to reap the benefits of this modest cultural capital. He proves his mettle at Nantes, Bordeaux, Niort, and Lyons, both as a negotiator in labor disputes and as first companion. I shall have much more to say on this topic later on, but for now it is worth emphasizing the importance of writing in the Devoir's initiation rites, which included copying out the list of "companions of maître Jacques."

Ménétra knows how to use his advantages in love as well as in business: the poor widow of Nîmes received more than one subtle letter from him, justifying his tardiness and in general putting off the performance of various promises. Ménétra's talent is clear in the letter, no doubt copied from a genuine original, in which he responds to the companions of the Devoir who have criticized him for establishing the "order of the loaf." This episode, incidentally, is a good example of something that worried the moralists, who were quick to attack the common man's "misuse" of education intended to inculcate morality and keep him in line. Ménétra's predilections remind us of the success of epistolary novels and of the vogue for self-improvement manuals, such as the so-called *Secretaries for Lovers and Families,* which there is reason to believe he may have read.

From writing let us move on to reading. What books of the day might Ménétra have read? In five hundred pages of text he cites, without comment, six titles: the Bible; the Parish Missal sent to him by his grandmother and brought to mass on another occasion by a passionate butcher's wife; the *Petit Albert,* a widely circulated book of white magic; and *The Social Contract, Héloïse,* and *Emile.*[23] His silence can only be interpreted as signifying that he read infrequently and as the opportunity arose and that his knowledge of books was superficial. He probably owned some books and may have borrowed others in the castles and abbeys that he visited. Borrowing books was sometimes the pretext for an adventure, as in the case of his wooing of a country curate's maid. He made lucky finds with some frequency, both in Paris and in the countryside. He read the newspaper, or at any rate *Le Journal des Dames,*[24] which was rather common in Paris. In short, Ménétra was a man of some culture.

Must we qualify this further and say that he was imbued with "popular" as opposed to "high" or "erudite" culture, that his culture was of the "dominated" classes rather than of the "ruling" ones? Actually, the *Journal* and the *Ecrits* prove that this is not the right question to ask about Ménétra's creative abilities. Whatever the value of his writings compared with great literature and high philosophy, he embarked on the adventure of writing with the means available to him. His poetics, of course, reflects a

desire to imitate, an amorous or erotic desire, a circumstantial need dictated by events in the world of politics or within his family. The influence
of his probable readings can be detected. He spontaneously uses names and
ideas borrowed from mythology: woman is Circe or Venus; a person who
stands in his way becomes an Argus or a Cerberus; a bed, a sofa, and
Bacchus preside over the libations of old age. Rather than attempt to
identify the original sources of these various borrowings, we would do
better to appreciate the noteworthiness of the effort, which shows that
Ménétra was able to read the books of the learned and make their content
his own. His consumption of literature is creative; we cannot understand
what he was up to by alluding to the intentions of more familiar authors or
by introducing literary-historical standards and periodizations.

Ménétra's attempts to reflect on religion and politics reveal a theological, not to say metaphysical, training, which is not surprising in a pupil of
the Saint-Germain choir school. His vigorous polemics retain the alert,
lively qualities, as well as something of the clumsy naïveté, of the young
adolescent fascinated by religion. His overemphatic repetitiousness and
his profound inability to resolve the subtler contradictions of philosophy
other than by veering sharply and clumsily from one extreme to another
indicate the immaturity of his mind and the limits of his education.

Like the *Journal*, the more theoretical *Ecrits* are governed by a class-
based narrative logic, in which repetition does duty for proof and the
ultimate guarantee of authority is "they say." The imprecision of the language is hardly surprising, given that it is the work of a man accustomed to
the rough-and-ready approximations of the craftsman; and the clumsiness
of the writing, whether deliberate or not, will not shock anyone prepared
to believe that a man like Ménétra could develop a personal style. His
reservoir of information is fed by a variety of sources, from scripture to
fairy tales to almanacs to broadsides to travelers' tales to jokes and moralistic tales. He knows precious little about the Enlightenment, though in one
burlesque play he cites Voltaire, Fontenelle, and Rousseau.[25] The latter,
whom he met, probably had an influence on him, which may be discernible
in the sketch he gives of his political thinking. He is spontaneously attracted to a direct egalitarian form of political organization, especially in
its religious aspects. These brief patches of light suggest that there was
some circulation of thought from high to popular culture, but that it had
little to do with published texts and clearly articulated ideas. Here again
Ménétra is a true representative of the masses of people whose consciousness was just beginning to awaken.

One crucial point has yet to be examined: the formative influence of the theater. It seems clear that Ménétra very early acquired the habit of theater-going. The *Journal* reveals that he knew Taconnet, Carlin, and Gaudon, that is, the elite of the boulevard theaters and the Italian comedy, whose actresses he naturally admired. This experience of the theater developed his fondness for dialogue, and there are many instances in his writing in which he appears as author, actor, and spectator all rolled into one. Think of the unforgettable scene of his abortive enlistment, or of the lubricious sketch of love caught in the act when the Burgundian curate returns home sooner than expected, or of the drama in three acts in which he plays the part of an innocent prisoner before the gendarmes, innkeepers, and peasants of an out-of-the-way village in the Cévennes. His vigorous imagination retains the grace and suppleness of farce and repartee.

On the whole, Ménétra's case proves once more that oral culture and written culture influenced each other profoundly. His whole system of communication relies on constant shifting from one mode to another: he tells a story at dinner, he recounts his pranks to an old Provençal nobleman, then he writes them down. Songs are first written, then sung. Letters are received and read out loud. Farces are written and performed. The *Journal* itself, with its obdurate composition and obscure manner of writing, can be understood only if first read out loud. Ménétra's culture is the culture of everyman: active, syncretic, porous, composed of borrowed and imitated materials. Quilts are not the only example of patchwork art; they are a cultural model.

As his knowledge accumulated, Ménétra reached adolescence and became a companion. Setting out on the tour of France was not really an occupational obligation but a psychological necessity, a way of escaping his mounting emotional problems, of breaking with his family, of putting off the moment at which he would have to establish himself, which required both money and planning. In another respect the tour was a ritual of adolescence, an intermediate stage between puberty and the responsibilities of adult life. After an absence of nearly seven years, Ménétra returns home at the end of the 1760s to face the same issues that he had left behind years earlier: his relationship with his father and other relatives, and his need to establish himself. But the threshhold is crossed and he soon experiences all the usual domestic difficulties while slowly acquiring the virtues of fatherhood.

The permanent conflict with Jacques Ménétra cannot be settled until the son marries. The sequence begins in the summer of 1764 with a first major break between father and son. The father offers the prodigal son the opportunity to move back in and go to work for him and says that he is willing to forget the past, particularly the matter of the grandmother's bequest (remember that Mme Marseau has died in the mean time, probably in 1763). The son replies with a cryptic declaration of filial respect: "I have always respected you despite your temper." But he asserts his independence. Legally he reached the age of majority in 1763, and he is able to make his own way in his profession. Father and son cannot live together, for a reason that is altogether plausible: their personalities clash, and the son is unwilling to work for his father and be paid with empty promises. To be an adult is to work for oneself. Emotional relations cannot be entirely independent of economic relations, and in the elder Ménétra we recognize a man who tries to take advantage of his son and son-in-law, who provide the cheap labor he needs to keep his small shop running. Behind the tense family situation we glimpse the rational calculation of the artisan trying to cope with the difficulties of his economic plight. From this point on, relations between father and son are a mixture of latent conflict and genuine complicity.

Opportunities for this latent conflict to manifest itself are not lacking: the father is inclined to drunkenness and dissipation, he is greedy, he has probably squandered a portion of his son's inheritance on drink, and he has a particularly irritating way of moralizing. The father is put in his place by a kindly police inspector, and the younger Ménétra triumphs by reminding his father of the common moral truth: "I see clearly that you don't love me and that you have never loved me therefore you are a bad father." But complicity between father and son is equally apparent in their everyday activities: Jacques-Louis frequently runs into his father and occasionally shares a bottle with him; he protects him against the insults of the two drunks from Provence; and he helps to work out arrangements intended to make his aging father's life a little easier. Relations improve to the point where the matters of the inheritance and marriage can be settled: the younger Ménétra renounces all his claims to an inheritance, and he agrees that he will receive no share in the dowry.

Ménétra's description of his father's role remains ambiguous; the older man seems at times grotesque, but at other times he is viewed with something like affection. The tone changes gradually as old age, illness, and death enter the picture. The father, having set up his younger daughter by marrying her to his companion and giving them the shop, is thrown out by the ungrateful couple. At this point father and son reverse roles. Now it is Jacques-Louis who takes care of his father, consoles him in his misfortune, and attempts to rescue him from the hospital.[26] The final scene takes place at the dying father's bedside. It exalts the virtues of reconciliation and forgiveness. A tearful tragedy, as the aesthetic standards of the time required, this deathbed scene also has affinities with the painting of Greuze and the plays of Sedaine.[27] In some ways the writing here escapes from its author's conscious control to express deeper feelings, almost justifying the older man's faults: the burlesque and bacchic epitaphs that Ménétra composed around the same time suggest that he fully understood and sympathized with his father's character.[28] In this authentic and unconventional view of a father-son relationship we find, in one bon vivant's tribute to another, awareness of what could never be changed and regret for what never could be. The father's love and the son's are both shrouded in the obscurities of class culture.

The father-son relationship had its impact on other family matters. Let me mention two of these: the defense of the family honor, and the conflicts between the mother's side of the family and the father's. Ménétra little by little assumes responsibility for defending the moral and symbolic interests of the Ménétra family: he tries in one way or another to protect the husband of his elder sister, he lectures his younger sister who thumbs her nose at neighborhood opinion and turns out to be a poor daughter to her father, he acts as a negotiator in honorable marriages and criticizes the choices of future spouses. His efforts are not very effective—he is not much of a diplomat—but they do show his rather high ideal of decent family behavior. Against the Marseaus he defends the Ménétras in a series of conflicts involving the Marseaus' desire to hold on to their share of the inheritance. The Marseaus, with their own sense of honor, do not always appreciate Ménétra's jokes, and relations between the two clans are aggravated by family rivalries in economic and guild matters. Beneath the resentful acrimony of Ménétra's account we glimpse the intensity of intrafamily relationships, in which economics, feelings, and ceremony all play a part. Everyone is aware of the existence of a code of behavior and sensitive to its infractions. We see clearly how difficult it was to reconcile conflicting moral values, feelings, and economic interests.

Also complex were the strategies for setting oneself up in business. There are rational business choices to be made, but emotions all too often get in the way. A twenty-year-old is not interested in amassing capital to start a business. Embarking on the tour of France gives him the opportunity to go from city to city in search of a stable situation; opportunities do arise, but he always decides that they can wait. Ménétra's tour is full of missed chances; but youth must be allowed to take its course. The young companion meets the widows of masters, the daughters of masters, and even the sisters of masters. The good towns are the ones that offer tempt-ing business opportunities: Vendôme, Angers, Nantes, Toulouse, Nîmes above all, Carpentras, and Lyons; in other places there are no good pros-pects. Parisien le Bienvenue lets us see the details of marriage contracts in which the economic aspect of the relationship is almost always sexualized. In the end, family obligations, Ménétra's attachment to his native city, his character, and the companion's way of life conspire to prevent him from settling down outside of Paris.

Marriage becomes a necessity only at the end of a journey filled with love affairs of a sort typical of Ménétra's class, and only when his pressing financial need is taken care of. The choice of a partner is determined by two things: business compatibility and physical/emotional attraction. When he marries an illiterate but thrifty girl from the provinces, who adds more than a thousand livres to the family coffers, Ménétra concludes a bargain that has both its good points and its bad points. He is able to fulfill his destiny, which is to found a family and a business, but at the same time he discovers first the boredom and later the bitterness of a stable domestic relationship. His memoir has something to say about the history of love and sexuality, but it would be necessary to trace the thread back to an earlier time. Here I shall examine only two aspects of the case: how the family was run, and how the love of parents for children manifested itself.

Did Ménétra love his wife? His depiction of Marie-Elisabeth Hénin is not completely unjust to her, because it does reveal the division that existed in his own mind between, on the one hand, his memory of a brief interlude in which true passion and friendship, which underlie the popu-lar conception of marriage, were reconciled, and, on the other hand, his own fickleness and infidelity coupled with the erosion of feeling that is so common a part of marriage. His account of true intimacy with his wife, and of the profound anxiety that he feels when he loses sight of her during a riot on the place Louis XV on the night of 30 May 1770, has the ring of authenticity. His marital conflicts centered on two issues: who was to wear the pants in the Ménétra household, i.e., who would run the family and the business, and how should the children be raised. To the first of these questions Ménétra gave an answer that was certainly in keeping with the most common thinking on the subject. The only legitimate au-

thority in the family was that of the father. God and the law both backed
him up in this, as did popular wisdom: "The good horse and the bad horse
both need the spur."[29] But Marie-Elisabeth felt that this precept was
somewhat out of date, and she was by nature manipulative and inclined to
keep a tight grip on the family purse-strings. Jacques-Louis slowly got used
to this, though he never entirely accepted it, and the storms in their
relationship finally subsided only with the onset of old age. A play, probably written fairly late in life and entitled *A ma femme* (To My Wife),
together with the final pages of the *Journal*, proves that Ménétra and his
wife did achieve a *modus vivendi*.[30] From his experience Ménétra derived
the notion that it might be a good idea for a man and a woman to live
together before marriage: "It would be desirable for the man and the
woman before marrying to live together for some time to see if their moods
can be reconciled." Free of the constraints of law and custom, this was a
novel moral perspective.

Ménétra had four children; two died, two survived. His family abided
by the accepted norms.[31] He tempered his authority with genuine paternal
love. Just as he once loved his wife, he later loved his son and daughter,
more, apparently, than she did. He identified with them, and his *Journal*
shows how he tried to reconcile his violent nature with his true tenderness. There was no reason why parent-child relations should have been
very different in the period 1770-1790 from what they had been in
1740-1760 when Ménétra was growing up. But his love for his children
made him a different man from his father. A devoted parent, Jacques-
Louis supervised the education of his children. He took them to concerts
and out for walks, he cared for them when they were sick, he worried
about securing for each of them a good future and a happy marriage. His
daughter's marriage at his wife's insistence to a hypocritical and brutal
pastry maker made him inordinately angry. He got over his rage only after
he found his own solution to the problem: the separation of the couple and
his daughter's departure for England to work for the royal feather dresser.
The separation from his daughter rends his heart, and news from London
always brightened his days.

As for his son, Ménétra controls his rage when springtime comes and the
young man begins to "chase after the masters" in search of a job. When the
boy goes off to fight for the Republic, Ménétra frets and tries to have him
recalled, yet he cheers his promotion to corporal. To be sure, in all of this
he self-indulgently claims the starring role, at Marie-Elisabeth's expense.
But Ménétra, who knows how to be sincere and is not afraid of looking

ridiculous in situations where his wife wears the pants in the family, states the three principles that guide him in bringing up his children: a father can and should love his children, he can and should love all of them equally, and he can and should help to establish them in life.[32] Here we see how norms were reconciled with everyday realities, with the imperatives of custom and morality. In the final lines of his *Journal* Ménétra describes a tranquil family life and offers a hymn to all fathers: the cardinal rules are to stand by one's children, to help them out economically, and to give them sound advice. Emotion is never far below the surface, as in the account of Saint Martin's Day in 1776 when, on the way to bury his father, he remembers his dead little boy, who was buried on a previous November 11 in the cemetery of the Saints-Innocents. The monotony of Ménétra's final years, the trouble he has in settling down, help us to understand the restlessness and mischief of the life he has left behind. The contrast between the humdrum reality of marriage and fatherhood and the preceding years of pleasure establishes the direction of his life and gives it meaning.

[2]

Pleasures and Games: Jokes, Violence, Sexuality

Ménétra knew every square inch of his native city and traveled all over France. His travels are a precious gift to the historian of culture. They are the source of numerous descriptions and anecdotes, a host of minor details and several major episodes that reveal the nature of Ménétra's imagination and interests. He writes with unparalleled freedom, indeed with a kind of vengeance, but one must first accept the constraints and conventions of his style. The life of the companion was in some respects a bohemian one, governed by a kind of hobo's code, the first rule of which was the absence of rules. The second rule was that fantasy and joking are the most important things in life, and the third that opportunities must be seized as they arise. For all the family supervision and the watchfulness of religious and governmental authorities, the young man was in fact quite free from adolescence on, as we see from the endless series of pranks that turn his life into one long, well-meaning farce, making the passions, as Diderot says, the source of all pleasures.

Ménétra's adventure, the details of the various episodes that he recounts, provide us with an extraordinary tableau of the life of the people; his very manner of recounting his escapades and detailing his good fortune adds zest to this vast portrait. There is no doubt that his memory is at work embellishing and reconstructing his experience, and it is this reconstruction that gives the *Journal* its richness. Ménétra's memoirs are to be read as an attempt to give life and color to days gone by, to substitute the "pleasure of the text" for that of action, at a time when the gulf was widening between the ardor of the senses and a somewhat forced respect for the proprieties. "People tell me every day that at my age I should be tranquil and wise, and that some day I will repent; and yes, some day I will think about it."[1] The passage of time and the experience of climbing the "age ladder"[2] are in the background of the action, the account of which tells us in its own haphazard way a great deal about the texture of everyday life.

We can more easily find our way through this abundant mass of partially reworked memories if we follow three thematic threads: first, the theme of friendship, since it is the author's friends who provide the occasion for laughter and jokes and who participate in or watch various kinds of games; second, the theme of private and social violence, in which physical prowess reveals not only a kind of discipline but also a fascination with death, marginality, and crime; and third, the theme of sexual freedom, which reveals the strategies and conventions of sexual behavior among the working class.

One can argue about the relative importance of these three themes in Ménétra's writing. This is a matter of personal choice and in part a question of resisting the seductiveness of the author's personality. His rather crude recital of innumerable sexual encounters could easily lead to an assessment of the author as a sort of poor man's Casanova and of his work as a history of his conquests, a popular contribution to a genre with whose bourgeois and aristocratic variants we are quite familiar.[3] Such an interpretation might accord well with our current interest in sexuality and its history[4] and with the image of the eighteenth century as a lascivious or libertine age. It is true that Ménétra thinks of little else, but it may be that his obsession with sex is a way of escaping, if only through a kind of sublimation in memory, more pressing concerns: the monotony of work, his dismal family life, and the cooling of "the fires" of youth.

We have no history of the solidarity achieved through laughter, no history of humor itself, despite the central importance of laughter in popular life.[5] Throughout Ménétra's work we see the importance of the ties created by laughter and good times. He reports on the variety of games and amusements to which people turned for relaxation and which differed from generation to generation. And his account teaches us an important lesson, for if we are to laugh with him at jokes that his contemporaries evidently found hilarious, we must recognize the essential distinctions that made these jokes work.[6] For laughter and amusement are above all a matter of shared feeling: one's pals come first.

In the *Journal* we encounter three kinds of friendship: childhood friendships with other boys of the neighborhood;[7] friendships formed in the workplace; and finally mature friendships with a few key individuals, about whom we hear only briefly in the *Journal*. The latter friendships tell us more about the influence of social relations and neighborhood patterns than they do about the basis of working-class sympathies and esteem. Henri Samson, the executioner,[8] Bertrand, the button-seller, the Genevan Gaillard who sells watches in cabarets and brothels, the baker Brocq, a cardsharp who is sent to Fort l'Evêque by the duchess of Bourbon, and Masson, the owner of billiard parlors who organizes the tennis match for the princes, are colorful and talented individuals whose names recur throughout the *Journal*. The author's comrades at school, play, and work probably play a more fundamental role. The companion indicates his awareness of this when he writes, at around age fifty, that "I love and greatly esteem my friends. I think that a friend is as rare as a phoenix. Jean-Jacques often told me so. I believe that they are very rare nowadays."[9]

The crucial relationships were formed at school, in catechism class, and in the rough-and-tumble games of childhood. These childhood friends are the ones who come and go according to the hazards of the road and the accidents of youth. The street urchins from the neighborhood of the Louvre are there to see our hero off when he leaves Paris; they are the sons of shopkeepers and artisans, near and distant cousins, boys who accompanied the author in his first sprees and larks and who worked with him in his first jobs. Their friendships with one another are close, and each time one of them departs a new chapter begins for the others, with new promises and new worries. Each time they escort one of their group from the crossroads of the Trois-Maries to the top of the Pont-Neuf and the barrière d'Enfer at the beginning of the road to Orléans, they are witnessing the end of yet another friendship rooted in the enthusiasm of childhood, in a shared history of childhood pleasures and common experiences, whether tempting the devil or chasing the neighborhood girls. Meeting one of these old friends on the road is always a high point in the life of the companion. This is the case, for example, when Ménétra meets the son of the Swiss of Saint-Germain-l'Auxerrois, Cordier, in Agen where he is selling hardware in the fairs with a woman of dubious reputation, or again, when he meets Du Tillet, who has meanwhile become majordomo to Charles de Brosses, the premier président of the Parlement of Dijon, and who will later introduce Ménétra to the Trudaines, for whom his wife works as a washerwoman.

Other friends do battle with our hero in riots and brawls. Some are identified by name: Robert, Givet, Lapierre. Others remain anonymous: the companion from the shop. We meet the same faces when Ménétra celebrates his return to Paris, now in the exuberance of working-class Paris by night: Turkey Lenoir, who keeps a bar and grill and occasionally works as a pimp; Langlois, the companion who lives in the rue Grenier-Saint-Lazare, who is also something of a pimp and afficionado of the brothel; and Bussie, who works in Elophe's shop in the rue Pagevin near Saint-Eustache. The latter is the victim of a rather bad joke of Ménétra's, which he accepts as being all in good fun: "Go on, my friend, I would go in your place." Ménétra's rhapsodic narrative occasionally evokes some rather enigmatic figures: the surgeon Baron, who dies of nostalgia for Paris, the harlequin Gaudon, the master glazier Gombeaut who appears as a likeable pimp, Véron the starch-maker from the faubourg Saint-Marceau, and above all Ménétra's cousin Chénier, who is ruined by his mistresses and joins the French Guards. To be sure, these friends share good times, but even more than that they live with the intensity of men who have not yet accepted the discipline of the settled life.

Ménétra establishes no hierarchy among his characters; rather, he places them in various revealing situations: settling quarrels, dividing up a treasure, finding a place to hide a friend in trouble and his belongings, asking for a woman's hand in marriage, performing a penance (e.g., the merchant Damour's pilgrimage to Mont Valérien), contracting the pox, joining in a sexual adventure. The youth of the neighborhood formed a solid front against the enemy of fathers, cuckolds, and policeman—in other words, against the establishment. They formed a true, if temporary, counterculture of young bachelors, held together by "the friendship that one cannot share with the jealous or the wealthy."

On the tour of France, the roving life of the companion encouraged the formation of another group of friendships. At each stop along the way work and recreation were combined. A companion's fellows were not necessarily his friends: they might also be the butt of jokes or the object of professional or sexual rivalry. For example, Ménétra, a man of the north, a Parisian, frequently makes fun of the Gascons for their superstition and naïveté. Quercy the Ill-Scrubbed carried the mark of a bad joke on his face; the one-eyed Rochelais who doesn't get the joke pays for the broken glasses. Briefly, then, relations among companions were a combination of friendship and utilitarian accommodation. Several companions might work together. It was more pleasant to travel from town to town in a group. And there was strength in numbers, as when the Dévorants prevailed in the battle with the Gavots.

Those individuals whom Ménétra chooses as friends are distinguished by certain epithets, such as "my friend" or "my comrade," or by certain episodes, as is the case with the Rennais who for more than six months works and travels with our hero from Nîmes to Carpentras. After parting at Montélimar, where the Rennais stayed to work and to recover from the rigors of the road, the two friends meet again in Lyons in 1762 and 1763; the Rennais remains faithful in reverses and stands at our hero's side in success. He even comes out from Paris to meet Ménétra on the road and inform him of his grandmother's death. The brevity of the account suggests the tenderness of the feelings involved.

In the narrative of his wanderings Ménétra the fluent storyteller focuses particularly on other companions from Paris, with whom he clearly felt a solidarity that derived from a common background and shared values. The Parisians had no use for traitors and thieves, like the glazier Oran, who though "a countryman" is unlucky and dishonest. But the hazards of the road and the end of Ménétra's wanderings put an end to these temporary friendships, which do not continue after Ménétra has settled in Paris. It is with a certain nostalgia, however, that he remembers the faces of these old friends and describes their acts and gestures. In a cabaret on the city's outskirts, moreover, old memories are reawakened by a chance encounter with a group of companions, "who invited me to come see them and (said) that they would always take pleasure in my com-pany"—in other words, they would be glad to have him join their Monday revels. Eating and drinking together was a way of savoring a common culture, a fondness for joking, singing, and playing games, for theater and masquerade.

Jokes are repeatedly recounted in the *Journal,* which tells of endless occasions for laughter. "I played some tricks" or "I laughed at all that nonsense" are phrases that Ménétra uses to introduce various situations. Quite often the joke is at the expense of an oafish or naïve comrade, or at the expense of peasants fascinated by the Parisian's glibness. Laughter here is part of a unifying social process; it brings together the local elites—the good curate of Vendôme, the sympathetic and curious rural nobles and bourgeois who take pleasure in hearing the companion recount his pranks and making them "gasp with laughter." In the cultural dialogue it is the backward hicks and artisans who stand opposed to a group of the more liberated. In another sense, laughter is a form of social control: it sanctions deviance from the moral principles of one's age group, it underscores the physical weakness and decrepitude of the drunk, and it makes fun of the incompetent workman who fails to live up to an implicit heirarchy of social, intellectual, and professional standards. An employer who sticks his head through a pane of glass, a companion who falls off a ladder, a comrade who falls off an ass, another friend who goes astray in a touchy situation and is mistaken for a third person, a drunk with an iron collar around his neck, tarts punished by having their buttocks exposed—any-thing is likely to provide the occasion for a joke. One-eyed, hunchbacked, deformed individuals seem to have been especially comical; popular mirth took up where aristocratic farce left off, as in the rather sinister episode involving the hunchbacks of Lyons, who on official orders were brought together in one place for the purpose of having a laugh at their expense, leading to widespread disorders that becaame the subject of popular verse and song. This corrective function of laughter was rather similar to the social inversion that has been associated with carnival, and it is not sur-prising to learn that clowning by companions increased as carnival time approached.

When an earthquake brings houses crashing down, it is an occasion not for grandiloquence but for laughter, which erupts once Ménétra's fear has subsided and the moonlight reveals the incongruous nudity of "two enor-mous buttocks" belonging to the author's employer and employer's wife. A delighted crowd comments upon the amorous feats of a pack of dogs chas-ing a bitch in heat, emptying the shops and bringing everyone out into the street. Bringing a fat pink piglet named Monsieur into the bedroom of a castle is the prelude to a first-rate adventure and a skillful seduction.

Works and days are lightened by jokes having to do with sex and food. There was a good deal of impressive scatological hilarity: a little boy falls into a sewer and his happiness is said to be assured; a farting child reminds onlookers of enemas and douches used for contraceptive as well as diges-tive purposes. When two companions with tattered trousers provide un-usual entertainment to chaste young nuns in Touraine, there is much astonishment. When friends come down with the pox, they console them-selves by joking about "la maladie des corps aux pieds." Bawdy stories are told around the dinner table, to the delight of children and novices. Mén-étra's laughter may not be in good taste, but it is healthy: today as in the past, prigs without a taste for farce can hardly be expected to appreciate it. An old burlesque vision of the world, in which abundance and fertility are exalted along with the destructive, regenerative, cosmic power of time, is here clearly in evidence.[10] Furthermore, the obvious emphasis on physical prowess makes sense of another aspect of the companion's recreation, the love of theater and masquerade.

Dancing, joking, and singing were all regular leisure activities, as was strolling about, either alone or in groups, for relaxation or in search of opportunity. Having a good time and making merry gave life the dimensions of a spectacle. The emphasis on physical prowess explains the enthusiasm for such adult games as espadon and cane-fighting by twos or squads. Foot racing and jumping over hedges and ditches were also popular. The Champs-Elysées were used at this time for such sporting activities. Open-air tennis (*longue paume* or *battoir*) was played in the country before audiences of village notables or in Paris on courts in the rue Grenelle-Saint-Honoré or in the lower part of the Cours-la-Reine. Rowing on the river took groups of friends from Saint-Maur to Meudon and Saint Cloud to La Rapée. Swimming and diving from bridges were good ways to keep cool. Recall that Lenoir, the bar-and-grill owner, won a bet by diving from a bridge. In short, then, the age of sexual ardor was also the age of sport.

The period just before Lent and the hot nights of the Parisian summer were high points of these popular liturgies. Companions strolled through the city's overheated neighborhoods from La Grève to the market (La Halle) and from Saint-Eustache to the Pont-Neuf as well as in the faubourgs. Everywhere Roman candles streaked through the nighttime sky, firecrackers went off, rockets exploded, the canopies of *guinguettes* caught fire, and the cabarets rang with happy voices. Ruggieri, a friend of Ménétra's who gave him a remedy for the pox, became a master of fireworks. The reveling went on endlessly and time seemed to come to a halt in the dark nights so propitious to all the passions. We catch sight of the nights of the poor in brief flashes, which in Paris at any rate reveal elements left over from the sumptuous feasts of the aristocracy and combined with a never-ending spectacle of speech and gesture.

Theaters in the fairs and on the boulevards were extraordinarily popular, as Ménétra attests. From 1750 until the Revolution he went frequently to the theater and even visited backstage. He took his sister and his children to see plays. He was among those avid theatergoers who were responsible for the success of the Italian comedy and the comic opera. He appreciated Carlino Bertinazzi, whose epitaph might have pleased him:

> De Carlin pour peindre le sort
> Très peu de mots devraient suffire
> Toute sa vie il a fait rire
> Il a fait pleurer à sa mort.

[Very few words should suffice to describe the fate of Carlin: all his life he made people laugh, and at his death he made them cry.]

He knew the obscene actor and author Taconnet, whom Mercier preferred to Préville and rated as high as Lekain: the court and the city were
endlessly entertained by stories of his troubles with the law on account of
indecency. Ménétra probably also knew Jean-Baptiste Nicolet, one of the
most talented producers of his day, whose opening of a theater on the
boulevard du Temple in 1759 influenced the orientation of Parisian entertainment for a century to come. He also praises the harlequin Chaumont,
as well as Gaudon, an actor who trained tightrope dancers until 1770. The
broad boulevards that stretched from the north of the city toward the
elegant western sections were a nightly fair in which Ménétra encountered all the ingredients that make up the culture of the masses.[11]

The dance spectacles of Torré and Ruggieri provided a brilliant and
ephemeral backdrop. Wax museums displayed celebrities and monsters.
Tightrope dancers exhibited the suppleness of their torsos and offered a
eulogy to the discipline of the body. The pantomimes of Nicolet, the di-
alogues and farces, the obscene plays and comic operas of the Italians and
of the rivals that their success encouraged satisfied the taste for slapstick
and comedy by depicting the adventures, singing the pleasures, and de-
ploring the miseries of the poor. To Ménétra and other artisans, shopkeepers, laborers, and servants, both the itinerant and the established
theater troupes taught the subtleties of the marketplace and exploited the
whole gamut of emotions. His theatergoing encouraged him to try his own
hand as an amateur actor, and with his friend Bussie he staged two plays in
Versailles for nobles from the castle, bourgeois from the city, and ordinary
people like himself: the *Farce du savetier* and the *Parade des tailleurs*.
During carnival he rented masks and dominoes and went clowning from
cabaret to cabaret. His artless Harlequin and Pierrot disguises suggest a
popular culture of masquerade, a readiness to see life as a drama and the
world as a stage on which all behavior is ritualized and all roles are
dictated by fate. The same zest for laughter and parody and the same cult
of suppleness and triviality inspired Diderot at about this time to write
that great pantomime and masterpiece of critical cynicism, *Le Neveu de
Rameau*. Factitious and fantastic, theater and masquerade allowed every
man to remake his own image and to engage in what Hegel called the
"universal deception of oneself and others"—in other words, to share the
destiny of the poor and homeless.[12]

All these elements of culture were found in the ever-present experience
of violence. Violent scenes occurred every day from childhood on, in the
home, in the family, in the street, in the neighborhood, in the cabaret. In

adolescence, when the young man learns to "fight to the death," the level of violence rises a notch, for now he must prove himself to friends and girlfriends. Ménétra, who is small in stature, is forced to outdo himself. Every brawl becomes a personal rite of passage, as well as a communal obligation incumbent upon all touring companions. The brutality of these comradely brawls helped to strengthen the solidarity of the group, as we shall see below. Here I want to concentrate on the significance of these repeated fights for the constitution of a collective and individual identity. Four-fifths of the brawls described in the *Journal* occur before Ménétra settles down with his family. These fights are therefore primarily bachelor affairs, though married masters did fight on occasion. At age sixty, during the troubled days of the Revolution, Ménétra rekindles the fires of youth sufficiently to provoke the royalists. The motives for these fights (so far as we are able to understand them, because some remain obscure) fall into three main categories: one-third result from rivalries between companions; another third are caused by competition or teasing on the job; and the remainder have to do with women and sex. It is striking how quickly a fight can come about and how fighting in general is governed by a system of rules. Over a period of some fifty years the scenario is always the same: provocation and insults, followed by punches and slaps, followed by possi-ble further combat if either man's honor is not satisfied. At this point the fighting escalates from fists or canes to an organized duel in some remote corner of the city, using a sword borrowed from a friend in the French Guards or from the companion's employer.

This dueling is a far more serious business than the other kinds of fighting. There are only six instances recorded in the *Journal*, compared with some fifty instances of quarrels that are settled before they reach the point of a formal duel. On this point Ménétra confirms the observations of Sébastien Mercier and evidence gleaned from police reports.[13] Brawling and fighting are associated with a particular kind of sociability, which combines an aptitude for violence with a capacity for association.[14] It is a question of staking one's honor in public, a business in which women play a central role. Ardent young men gather around the women of the neigh-borhood, who are also at the hub of routine household activities. Brawls and beatings are part of the everyday scenery, "not so much an anachronis-tic relic of a waning barbarism as a structural factor in the social order."[15] A fondness for posturing, sexual insult, and exaggeration made the work-ing-class brawl a kind of spectacle best understood in relation to other games, rituals, plays, and physical competition. This kind of fighting was not, as moralists and bourgeois sometimes believed, lawless savagery; rather, it expressed a strange and different order, a code of behavior of the masses, of people fascinated by violence, familiar with death, and captivated by the activities of the criminal element with which they were in close contact.

It is well known that the Paris of the Enlightenment was a city of death, a city that endured an infant mortality rate nothing short of a massacre of the innocents and an elevated adult mortality as well. Despite some signs of improvement, various endemic diseases kept the life expectancy low. The young and the not-so-young lived with death at close quarters. The *Journal* reveals an awareness of the nature of modern urban mortality. We witness the death of Ménétra's close relatives, and we have a sense of untold numbers dying anonymously in the wings.

We are even more aware of a widespread interest in unusual or spectacular deaths, a taste for executions and scenes of public torture. Ménétra recounts suicides in his neighborhood, sudden deaths of companions, and stories of memorable murders that he hears in the course of his travels. Each of these deaths becomes an occasion to reflect upon the common destiny of mankind and the fragility of life. No man can escape this law of nature, least of all the criminal. Here Ménétra proves to be an acute observer. He attends the executions of Damiens, of Duhamel and Giroux, and of a thief in Chalon. He collects tales of brigands and of bloody murders in inns. Thus he offers us a wonderful opportunity to understand the attitude of the common people toward crime. In the first place we discover how the imagination transforms reality into symbolism. It is tempting to believe in the authenticity of the story of the brigands of the Cercotte woods, which with the realism of a gothic novel evokes the forests and caves used as hideouts by robbers who emerge from time to time to plunder the plains of the Beauce. "Moonlight jewelers" and "sheriffs' game" really did exist in the country around Paris. Still, when Ménétra claims to have raised a glass with Mandrin on the Dijon road in 1763, when in reality the smuggler and his gang were executed in Valence in 1755, we must assume that he wished to transform a more banal occurrence—he met a band of robbers and drank a bottle with them—into a symbolic image gratifying to those who for ten years had made Louis Mandrin their hero. The reiteration of the anecdote a year later, this time with Mandrin's sister and her henchmen in the starring role, demonstrates Ménétra's solidarity with common people driven to the wall by royal taxation: "Everybody wants to be Mandrin."

The Duhamel-Giroux affair resonates with other aspects of popular attitudes toward criminality.[16] It also shows us the extent to which Ménétra worked over the facts on which his stories were based. The judicial archives tell us of two cases. One involves a miserable gauze maker, age seventeen, the son of a purveyor of fireworks in the rue de Loursine—note the coincidence—who is sentenced to death for a violent robbery planned and executed with the aid of accomplices on the Bicêtre-Gentilly highway. He was hanged in the place de Grève on 5 December 1765. The other is a morals charge, a case of corrupting a minor, involving a female servant, age twenty-three, who was condemned in absentia on 8 August 1763 and probably executed in September 1765 if I have correctly interpreted the following note written on the back of the record of sentence: "Monday 9 September at noon, 20 men of the watch."[17] In short, two unremarkable crimes that turned out badly, whose perpetrators, accused by a host of unshakeable witnesses, had little to offer in the way of defense; note, moreover, that the two trials were separate and the two cases completely unrelated. Ménétra may have mixed them up, he may even, as he claims, have taken the virginity of the Giroux girl before leaving Paris, and he must have heard the proclamation of the sentence of the court and its subsequent embellishment by rumor. But in his fanciful account the two cases take on the proportions of a remarkable criminal conspiracy that poses a threat to the entire population of Paris.

In the bowels of the city (as Ménétra tells the story) gangs of criminals had organized, gangs set apart from ordinary society and living according to their own rituals and laws. Their members were the toughest of criminals and the most alluring of prostitutes. Thus petty thieves became fabulous bandits who wore many disguises, set traps for the unwary, bludgeoned wealthy "johns" who fell into their clutches, threw their bodies into the river, and broke society's most fundamental laws by murdering their mistresses and indulging in cannibalism.

To be sure, organized crime did exist in Paris at this time, as it did in all large cities; but in Ménétra's story it serves only to demonstrate the writer's own fascination with crime, as the pretext for a fanciful tale of fabulous misdeeds that had plunged all the honest citizens of Paris into a state of holy terror. In the neighborhoods of the central city, working people every day came into contact with marginal characters of all kinds—hoboes, thieves, amateur and professional criminals—who on occasion resorted to violence out of poverty or predilection. Battalions of prostitutes stalked the streets—Sébastien Mercier put their number at more than forty thousand. Ex-convicts were not uncommon. People sometimes dealt with known pickpockets on the spot. The prison, like the hospital, was a reality about which everyone knew.[18] Crime was on the rise, stimulated by the chaotic growth of the city itself. The rising crime rate justified repression of the worst crimes; this proved to be quite effective, but it changed the way honest men and women behaved.

People took great pleasure in sensational news. It was not the authenticity of the facts that counted but the aura with which the popular imagination surrounded a story: the right mix of blood, gold, and darkest night could turn the most trivial of occurrences into the most spectacular of crimes. Broadsheets, almanacs, songs, and stories amused and amazed the populace. What is more, these tales of famous crimes and trials actually reassured simple folk, for they proved that the wicked were always punished, that the guilty were wretched and their victims pitiable. No man can escape his destiny. To be a criminal is a fate like any other; hence the crimes of the great criminals are excused, and by contrast Ménétra, whose destiny is different, stands out as virtuous. His interest in punishment would seem to demonstrate its effectiveness; for, as Montesquieu says, the law "brings together various kinds of shame to yield particular types of punishment." On the other hand, "the frequency and ostentation [of public forms of punishment] suggest a certain failure, which may have had to do with the marginal social position of offenders or with the fact that most crime went unpunished."[19] Every fascination has its underside.

Ménétra and others of his class liked to hear stories of robbers, but they did not recognize themselves in the heroes of these tales. To working men—peasants, wage earners, and artisans—the society of criminals was not seen as the bearer of the kinds of social demands which, in other times and places, mobilized what Eric Hobsbawn has called "primitive rebels."[20] Bandits and criminals did not defend the poor, except in legend. Their aims were different from those that governed the working world. And their activities were without much political content, even if they did contribute to social breakdown during the Revolution.[21] The world of thieves, governed by the desire to live high, to carouse, to drink, and to gamble, all without work or discipline, was the land of Cockaigne and the "world turned upside-down" all rolled into one: it was a dream, a temptation, a fantasy. When Ménétra mentions his second encounter with the "Mandrins" in 1764, he says: "They were not looked upon as favorably as Mandrin had been." The observation suggests a suspiciousness on the part of the peasants, perhaps even a rejection of the gang, which the companion from Paris understands quite well.

The amount of space in the *Journal* given over to sexual adventures indicates the importance of sex in Ménétra's real life as well as his fantasy life. It is one of the motivating forces behind his autobiography. Repetitive as these escapades are, they serve to emphasize the contrast between youthful freedom and passion on the one hand and stable married life on the other. The fifth introductory epistle is significant in this regard: "The years of my youth were years of pleasure for me, and each year was a century of happiness . . . you flew and never came back, time when I wrote my story." Having reached the age when the hair turns white and the passions cool, the companion is seeking, not without occasional despair, to restore a vital aspect of his existence. The conventions of autobiography require him to tell the truth, but the effect of writing, the pleasure of telling a tale, magnify these rather ordinary sexual adventures to the point where they read almost like a picaresque novel: this was an age that had a fairly lively appreciation of the libertine or lubricious anecdote.

Ménétra was a man made for love, and ready to succumb frequently to temptation. In the end everyone is obliged to settle down, marry, and raise a family. The relatively uneventful transition from a period of sexual exuberance, of quest for temptation, to a time of idle fantasy and marital adjustment illustrates the essential goodness of Ménétra's character. The lesson of this exotic account of a would-be ordinary man's sexual experience is that no one can avoid growing up—and perhaps, too, that we can bear to grow up only because our dreams and our imaginations are so good at dressing up the past. Ménétra's adventures, for all their chaotic disorder, are hopelessly normal. There are no confessions of childhood masturbation or of such homosexual temptations as he may have felt while playing with other boys or living among his fellow companions.[22] Ménétra begins and ends as a womanizer. His *Journal* suggests three ways of approaching the history of sexuality: we can ask, first, how the regular sexual order is formed; second, how are reality and fantasy combined in love play; and third, what images govern the conceptualization of masculine and feminine roles.

In the *Journal* we see the first signs of a profound moral transformation, which will occur in Paris and in the provincial cities of the tour and in which the principal actors will be the young bachelors of the shopkeeping and artisan classes. Remember that the relevant portion of the text covers the period 1750–65. Ménétra is thirteen years old in 1751. He marries at age twenty-seven, the average age for a young man to marry in the France of Louis XV. The standard accounts of peasant sexuality tell us of a lengthy period of Christian chastity followed by a relatively late marriage, or else they focus on obscure moments of liberation in furtive encounters or illicit but accepted relationships, in individual or group masturbation, in premarital petting, or even, in the case of shepherds, in bestiality. Historians familiar with these accounts may find Ménétra's premarital freedom surprising. The companion has fifty-two sexual relationships prior to his marriage, not counting fleeting encounters with inkeepers' daughters and occasional prostitutes. From 1765 to 1790 he admits to a mere thirteen extramarital affairs.

Also worthy of note is the social setting in which these adventures take place. Ménétra's illegitimate relationships fall into four groups. Five involved women of a higher social class: one lady of quality, the marquise de Gardouche, and three nuns. Three involved peasant women. Six were carried on with servants. And all the rest involved the wives, widows, and sisters of Ménétra's employers or other representatives of the small business and working class—shopkeepers, mercers, butchers (the lovely Pinard ladies!), tavern keepers, café owners, wine merchants, purveyors of carriages, harness makers, locksmiths, laundresses, lace makers. Ordinary social relations here take on a sexual aspect: artisans and servants, workers and shopkeepers, and above all members of the glass trade are involved in two-thirds of the illicit relationships. These relationships are identical in nature to those that might result in marriage.[23] Geographically, most of them take place in cities, and it is convenient to organize these in three groups, each corresponding to a different approach or strategy. First, in the cities of the tour of France, there are the relationships with the daughters and widows of masters. Second, there is the Paris neighborhood, where the sexual market is highly competitive. Here, it is neighbors' daughters, married women, and working single women who are lusted after by young males. Third, there is the rest of Paris, where Ménétra's relationships are mainly with loose women, though the kind of mingling that takes place in the city allows for an occasional sacrilegious or aristocratic affair.

In these relationships, of relatively long duration, the sexuality of the young unmarried male is subject to firm conventions enforced by implicit sanctions. Within the neighborhood, the sexual chase is part of the generational conflict; young men tangle with their fathers and uncles over assaults on the honor of young cousins, nieces, and neighbors. The father's authority over the child's person and property is absolute. Fathers and sons at times vied for the favors of prostitutes and mistresses, at other times defended the honor of their female relatives and hence of the family name.

Ménétra is foolish enough to pit himself repeatedly against various fathers, but perhaps this was the normal state of affairs. Old Pinard, the irascible pork butcher, is incapable of defending his harem, and his wife and two daughters all end up in Ménétra's bed. He embodies all the negative qualities of the typical father worried about his daughters' behavior. Ménétra owes his reputation as a seducer to a couple of episodes in which he naturally figures in a favorable light: he was the only witness.

Before marrying, young males openly kept concubines and thumbed their noses at the sacraments. The power of religion's moral percepts had declined, and we see old practices, such as occasional attendance at mass, confession, and observance of the Easter holiday, coexisting with new freedoms in a population that is not entirely de-Christianized. Concubinage was not a practice enforced by poverty, though poverty did contribute to its spread despite the vigilance of the religious and civil authorities.[24] Rather, it was the impossibility of enduring a prolonged and unrealistic period of chastity that drove young bachelors to take concubines. Marriage could not take place until the heart could be reconciled with business interests. Until then, young men were free to enter into temporary relationships and break them off as they wished. Such practices differed sharply from the much more regular and stable proletarian concubinage; in the latter, just beginning to appear in the lower fringes of society, among those truly oppressed by poverty, the household counted for more than the marriage.[25]

For Ménétra and his friends the idea was to live life in accordance with the rules and to take full advantage of the opportunities for pleasure available during a certain period. The young companion does not shrink from using whores and their madams. Ménétra admits that he has to get used to sharing with other men the time and favors of such well-known prostitutes and "abbesses" as Rosalie, Aurora, Dupré, Beaufort, and Denongrais. As he sees it, the bordello is nothing but a deconsecrated convent.

Friends, moreover, must be willing, even eager, to share sexual partners. Opportunities are seized jointly: two companions consummate a brief affair—which we would consider nothing less than a rape—by the roadside or, on another occasion, in the bushes. A girl who strays into the men's dormitory is shared with other companions after an early-morning encounter. This sharing of women, though not without its jealousies and not incompatible with a certain amount of monogamy, strengthened the ties of solidarity among the companions, as did courting in foursomes and drinking in cabarets: "I'll buy you a bottle and a salad, he took me at my word, and we parted in the hope of becoming brothers as soon as possible." In certain neighborhoods, the exchange of women was governed by strict rules involving the payment of money, rules that were not universally accepted. Ménétra refuses to pay forty écus, but his cousin Chénier agrees. In this case the presence of the French Guards in the story gives added point to what is elsewhere merely symbolic.[26]

Broadly speaking, the existence of a considerable degree of sexual freedom did not mean that sexual relations were not governed by convention or made the subject of fantasy. Among the conventions, note the refusal to "pass for a hats-on type," that is, to marry a woman who had been the mistress of an aristocrat. Men rarely married their mistresses and never married prostitutes, nor did they sleep with the wives of friends. As for fantasies, it is worth singling out one in particular, that of making love with a nun; such ideas, real or imagined, reflect the desires aroused in young, unmarried males by the thought of the "seraglio" inhabited exclusively by the "brides of the baby Jesus." To the man living a polygamous life the sacred logic of the cloister must have remained a rather mysterious thing, and the bachelor's imagination found the whole idea preposterous.

In any event, Ménétra and his companions had no intention of accepting responsibility for their affairs. Duping young girls, beguiling them with false promises, is the normal thing, but once our companion has got what he wants he does not stick around for long, particularly when he sees "the bulge in the petticoat" or when a cousin he has seduced succumbs to "the vapors"—though in one or two cases he does offer the girl his assistance. Stories with unhappy endings are no problem for "women of the world"; they have their ways of dealing with things. This accords well with what historians have discovered about sexuality in the middle of the eighteenth century: the rate of illegitimate births was on the rise, and contraceptive methods used by prostitutes were increasingly diffused among the populace. But the shadow of venereal disease hovers over these illicit couplings. Ménétra admits to ten bouts with "the pox." Injustice, punishment, and death were among the consequences of sexual intercourse. Unfortunate girls died in childbirth in the hospitals.

Paradoxically, there is little sensuality in this tableau of sexual love. Ménétra's style has little of the libertine about it. His audacity was that of his class: he boasts of the number of his conquests, the rapidity of his seductions, the directness of his language, and the straightforwardness of his passion, which dispensed with unnecessary refinement. The clientele of Parisian brothels, with their fetishistic interests, were of a different breed entirely. The range of sexual acts and attitudes is that of

bawdy poetry and song. Erotic verse depicted cuckolded husbands, dissolute priests, eager canonesses, exalted nuns, bold maidens, and naughty
servants in vignettes that glorified the most commonplace effusions.
"Every man screws in his own way . . . every man screws as he can and
not everyone screws as he wants."[27] This doggerel reveals a rather banal
eroticism, whose main interest lies in its hint at the way in which common
people may have viewed the relationship between sensuality and love.

Ménétra does not confuse the two. Sensuality is a matter of abrupt and
youthful passions, of pleasure shared with willing or unwilling partners:
the occasional rape is tolerated. Love, on the other hand, is an enduring
sentiment, a matter of delicacy and of profound and prolonged friendship.
There is a time for pleasure-seeking and chasing tarts, another for love and
for hazarding the seas of matrimony. The relatively small number of extramarital affairs proves that this was the case, even if it also proves that
Ménétra suffered from nostalgia for the freedom of bachelorhood and had
a hard time reconciling the need for fidelity with his temperamental bent
for infidelity.

Ménétra loved his wife before he broke his marriage vows, and it was
only when he could no longer put up with her miserliness and her domi-
neering ways, which impugned his manhood and paternal authority and
provided him with a convenient excuse for philandering, that he began to
run around with other women. Twice, however, with Manon the lace
maker and with Mme Bouchu, he sets up a secondary household more to
his liking than the one ruled by his wife.

Sexual good behavior begins at the age when Bacchus supplants Eros
and a balance must be struck between affection and the whims of the
heart. In any case, for additional proof that conjugal love was possible
among working people in times past, in spite of the obstacles created by
the state of morals, parental authority, parents, and economic need, reread
the story of the widow of Nîmes—seduced, abandoned, but never forgotten. The dream of romantic love predates the nineteenth century, and
eroticism in marriage predates the twentieth. In Languedoc our companion found love and friendship, physical pleasure—the widow had tempting
breasts—and delicacy of feeling combined. The spontaneity of feeling that
he experienced in Nîmes he will experience again in the first few years of
his marriage, but eventually he will be worn down by the monotony of
married life. It is probably best to refrain from generalizing about marital
success or failure.

The key to understanding Ménétra's behavior is to be found in the strict
opposition of masculine and feminine roles instilled in him from earliest

childhood. Ménétra's psychological makeup is triumphantly "macho." Women have little existence in his eyes. They have no real character. He fails to mention the first names of most of his women and the last name of almost all of them, including his wife. Their features are unknown, their bodies invisible. They are friendly and charming, appetizing and beauti- ful—abstract descriptions with little sensuality.

To be sure, Ménétra's style betrays him in the *Journal* as well as in his poetry, where he indulges in all the commonplace conceits of amorous verse. It is literally, as people, that he fails to see his women. Rather than see females as individuals with peculiarities and personalities of their own, he sees them as a group, as figures of secondary interest, as an indiscreet, scheming, garrulous lot, much given to prejudice and superstition. He makes full use of the vocabulary of hunting and commerce: women are prey to be attacked, indeed forced to submit, or else objects to be appraised and exchanged. The cult of virility justifies the man's unwillingness to become attached: every Don Juan becomes a collector. This *machismo* is an enduring trait of Ménétra's character, which is responsible for a number of immodest observations. He likens his exploits to those of Hercules, and at least one sharp-eyed mistress knows how to use flattery to gain her ends: "Since she caught me where I was most sensitive and flattered my pride, I outdid myself." On the other hand, he refuses to allow women to take the initiative and is wary of the most passionate, whom he quickly leaves.

Ménétra's *Journal* provides valuable testimony about an important phase in the history of modern love. He shows us the tension that existed be- tween the gradual liberation of morals and the perpetuation of old customs and laws. To the Christian repression of pleasure he opposes the legitimacy of sex prior to and during marriage. To the condemnation of the flesh he opposes his placid Epicureanism. But at the same time he reveals the weight of custom, of the traditions that must be observed and of the rites that mark the passage from childhood to youth to adult life. Ménétra's adventures reveal a capacity to change, an aptitude for modern life, which must somehow come to an accommodation with the inertia of what al- ready exists, the fixity of social and sexual roles. The autobiography gives us the keys to a personality described mainly in terms of violence and sexuality, but even in these realms freedom had its limits. Unlike the libertines of the aristocracy, the ebulliently healthy Ménétra preferred women of robust flesh. The sexuality of the people was by nature lively and physical, even if its representation in writing was hampered by an- cient and enduring symbols and conventions.

[3]

Work: Fraternal Pleasure
and Economic Value

Some time between 1750 and 1755 the economic fate of Jacques-Louis Ménétra was sealed: he would become a master glazier like his father. And some time between 1780 and 1790 his own son chose the same path, without protest and without major conflict. The transition from boyhood to youth was that simple for young Parisians fortunate enough to be born the sons of master craftsmen or shopowners. The possession of some capital, however minimal, and of some power over workers, coupled with the hope of some degree of upward mobility, distinguished the guild masters from ordinary workers (in the narrow sense of the word), though such differences were not incompatible with collaboration in politics as well as work, and it would have been difficult to draw a sharp dividing line as to cultural attitudes or ways of life.[1] The social and occupational level of Ménétra's memoirs is best defined in relation to the old stratification of Parisian society by groups, corps, and communities. There is much to ponder in this social setting, which forms the backdrop against which we see the working life of three generations of the writer's family.

Ménétra finds in his son the same signs of impatience that his father must have found in him: a way of pawing the ground at work, a condescending attitude toward the skills learned by "watching and listening," and a free and easy way about him that culminates in his "chasing down masters" in search of a new employer. Even before his apprenticeship is complete, the son, like other young men of his age, dreams of independence, a dream whose content is essentially economic in nature. There is no doubt that the master glazier of the rue du Petit-Lion-Saint-Sauveur will in due course be succeeded by his son, just as he himself, without replacing his father in the shop on the rue des Prêtres-Saint-Germain-l'Auxerrois, followed his footsteps in the trade. What made this possible was the stability of the guild organization, which the events and legisla-tion growing out of the French Revolution would in part destroy.

The old fox would not see his grandsons at the workbench; history had decided otherwise. Until the Revolution the future was decided by guilds and *compagnonnages*.[2] The former did not survive the Revolution, but the latter experienced, if not their finest hour, at least their moment of great-est publicity in the struggles born of workers' attempts to oppose the changes wrought by the Industrial Revolution. Ménétra's memoirs bear witness to a period of great importance, when the old corps were under attack by economists and reformers concerned with questions of efficiency and utility, and when working-class values that would survive the politi-cal revolution were still being hammered out.[3] The text throws new light on routine working conditions, on the fraternal life of the companions, on the methods of craft labor, and on the profits that artisans could earn.

To be a glazier in the Paris of Louis XV meant to be a member of the community of glaziers and painters on glass, a community firmly estab-lished by statutes promulgated in 1467 by Louis XI and modified in some respects by Louis XIV in 1666.[4] This was not, as Parisian corps went, a particularly prestigious group: in processions it was placed far behind the Six Corps.[5] The edict of 1691 which reorganized jury elections placed the glaziers at the bottom of the third class. New masters were obliged to pay the king twenty livres. The edict of August 1776—when Turgot re-organized the juries—ranked them nineteenth. This, then, was a minor guild, in terms of both the number of masters—Savary counted 300 in 1730, while the *Almanach du commerce* from 1769 counted only 260 shops[6]—and the prestige of the trade. Based on the value of a master's certificate, the glaziers claimed a middling rank: a master glazier had to pay 1,000 francs, half as much as a draper like Uncle Chénier and one-fifth as much as an apothecary, who sat at the top of the hierarchy of Parisian guilds, but still twice as much as a furbisher like Sébastien Mercier's father, a gunsmith on the quai de la Ferraille, and five times as much as a wool carder, a seamstress, a gardener, or a poor basket maker, at the bottom of the occupational ladder. In the glass trade, the duration of companion-ship was set at six years, unless the worker, after four years of compulsory apprenticeship, preferred to spend his time in the leading cities of the kingdom, from which he was supposed to return with a certificate. Méné-tra was an apprentice from 1753 to 1757 and on the road as a companion from 1757 until 1764.

How his experience related to the statutes is not clear, however. In the

first place, only the sons of sworn masters were free to serve their appren-
ticeships in their fathers' shops. Jacques Ménétra was never among those
elected by the guild wardens to enforce the rules of the profession, not
even after he had been a master glazier for ten years as well as a master of
the confraternity of Saint Mark, which was the religious arm of the
glaziers' guild. Jacques-Louis's apprenticeship was therefore invalid, unless we count the years spent working for other Parisian masters or learning from his Marseau uncles. One of these, Marseau Ile-Saint-Louis,
became a member of the jury during the 1760s. So what we see here is a
family strategy for getting around the strict letter of the guild rules. The
second point to consider is how Ménétra obtained his master's certificate.
He never made a masterpiece: given his character, we may assume that he
would not have remained silent about such an important moment in the
life of any companion. Rather, he became what was called a *maître des
lettres*. In other words, he overcame the major obstacle that prevented
ordinary workers from becoming masters via an indirect route, by buying
"letters" paid for by his grandmother with an advance on his share of her
estate.

The wardens of the glaziers' guild made no provision for the sons of
masters. They granted some privileges to sons-in-law of masters and to
companions who married the widows of masters. But since only two companions were accepted as masters each year, it was clearly an advantage to
be designated, as Ménétra was, a *maître sans qualité*. It was his good
fortune to obtain one of the eight *lettres de maîtrises* that the government
forced every guild to accept in 1722; these certificates had been bought in
by the Parisian guild wardens and were sold by them in order to cope with
financial difficulty. In short, even within his trade Ménétra stood somewhat apart. The son of a master, he did not avail himself of the traditional
benefits of that position, such as the possibility of serving his apprenticeship in his father's shop, and he put in the regulation amount of time. He
did not make a masterpiece,[7] which ordinarily would have precluded his
becoming a master. To be sure, his master's certificate gave him the right to
set himself up in business in any city of the kingdom, even where glaziers'
guilds were in operation, but his opportunities, like those of any companion, were limited by the difficulty of establishing himself: it was necessary
to purchase a shop, tools, and supplies, hence to dispose of a modest
amount of capital. This he found, as we know, in marriage.

In any case, his situation vis-à-vis the guild was always marginal, because *maîtres sans qualités* could not be named to the jury until they had

reached the age of sixty and, even more importantly, did not participate in the deliberations of the organization. This helps us to understand the conflicts that arose between Ménétra and the Paris guild wardens in the 1770s. Some of these conflicts involved direct confrontations: the *Journal* reveals how profoundly the guild hierarchy and discipline were internalized; if need be, the police could also be called upon to help enforce the rules.[8] The wardens thus maintained a delicate balance between equality and inequality. Master and companion were both privileged people, though to an unequal degree. The guild assured them a social position and guaranteed their economic independence by enforcing the masters' monopoly and limiting access to necessary skills; the masterpiece was merely proof of ability to perform the tasks of the trade. The guild governed its own economic province but not the whole of the economy.[9] Independence and discipline were often in conflict in relations between the guild and its members. The outlook of the future master was shaped by his experiences as a companion; some differentiation occurred once the young companion became a master, established his own business, and became a member of the jury. Studying Ménétra's experiences proves to be an ideal way of gaining some understanding of the subtleties of what was a complex and rather confusing situation.

There were considerable differences between working conditions on the tour of France and working conditions in Paris. Companions from Paris arrived in the provinces with a reputation for technical skill to live up to, even if they undertook the tour in the first place to complete their training in the infinite variety of regional methods and procedures.[10] Manpower was in short supply in the provinces, and the network of companions' inns made it relatively easy for employers to call upon workers from nearby towns when necessary. Employer-worker relationships are treated even-handedly by Ménétra, though idealization of his years of freedom is in evidence in this respect as in others. With few exceptions Ménétra's bosses and widows (who retained the full rights of their deceased spouses) were good employers, meaning that they were not overly demanding about their employees' keeping regular hours provided the job was well done; that they shared their tables and their homes with their workers; that they took part in the companions' celebrations; and, not least, that they always stood ready to "drink a bottle" and to open their pockets. The very good masters vied with one another for workers; they protected their companions, helped them escape after brawls, and brought them food in prison when they were caught. On the whole, Ménétra's "wander-years" reveal a community of work and conviviality in which whatever conflicts exist are settled either by negotiation, as in Nantes, or by flight, which nothing could prevent. While not all companions could move upward socially, the institution of *compagnonnage* did sustain the hope of such upward mobility. Companions were in the market not only for jobs but also for possible marriages, the possibility of which served to raise hopes and sustain illusions.

In Paris, on the other hand, there was no shortage of manpower; with one or two companions per shop, some six hundred workers were available. The growth of the city created demand for the services of glaziers. The guild maintained a close watch on the hiring of companions, who were assigned to the various masters by the jury. Thus the independence of workers was curtailed; they were kept under surveillance and not allowed to quit without two weeks' notice. Some were forced to stay for long periods with masters whom they disliked, because authorization to quit was withheld. Workers were identified and assigned to particular jobs.[11] This rule, which was just coming into force, provoked conflicts of which Ménétra has left us his account.

The paternalistic, family-centered ideal that continued to function despite some difficulties in the provincial cities began to fall apart in Paris when the interests of small shopowners and workers came into conflict. Workers resorted to provocation: Ménétra entices two companions away from the shop of Elophe, a master with whom he has had a dispute. He asserts his independence through bravado, insolence, and insult. Nothing good comes of it: the police banish him to Versailles, where he installs glass in the château and stables under the watchful eye of the king's glaziers and constables. He is a schemer[12] and an agitator. But his conflicts with his employers are not so much about wages or hours as about behavior.

For Ménétra, freedom of labor means being essentially independent, subject to no one's discipline and to no restrictions on freedom of movement. On the tour of France he doesn't stay in one place, but leaves one job and one town for another, just as he pleases. In Paris, before he goes into business for himself, he changes employer six times in less than two years, moving from his brother-in-law's shop to old Vilmont's to Elophe's (with Vilmont's consent) to Langlois's (without Elophe's consent) to Bellé's to Jérôme's and finally back to Vilmont's. To be sure, he tries to improve his situation with each change, but above all he wishes to throw off the discipline of his elders, of the established masters, who try in various ways to stabilize the labor supply, whether by force or by an appeal to the feelings when there are daughters, nieces, or widows to put in the way of the restless companion. The chorus of a song written by Ménétra and entitled *l'Ancienne Méthode* illustrates this clash and brings out the companions' ideals: the employer must not be proud or mean and must treat his men politely; he should earn his authority through his skill and not through money or pretentiousness; the good master is a good worker, a man of taste, knowledge, and talent; he eats with his companions, "always something good," served on unchipped plates with metal covers; he supplies butter and salt.[13] If the companion is to be believed, "the new fashion" of lodging and feeding workers makes a mockery of the old ways and creates additional friction between employers and workers.

Ménétra does not forget his years as a companion after he becomes a master. He slowly abandons the companion's way of life but betrays a juvenile outlook in his continued hostility to the wardens of the glaziers' guild, whom he regards as unduly meddlesome. He quarrels with the jury when he fails to pay his inspection fee (which all masters must pay, even those not yet in business for themselves); he disputes the elections and engages in a polemic with the guild bureau over a matter of failing to declare the hiring of a worker within the requisite period. In 1776 he applauded the elimination of masterships. In the course of his career he encounters conflicts, relatively mild in the provinces but more acute in Paris, which divide an "impecunious petty bourgeoisie cut off from the proletarians by the barrier of property; in the period of social crises this petty bourgeoisie always takes the side of property's defenders, though in behavior and taste it remains close to its modest origins."[14] The insubordination of workers, which is denounced by the guild wardens and the police, is closely related to the gradual deterioration of the economy and of social and human relations.[15] Himself an insubordinate companion, Ménétra takes his place among the mutinous masters and attests to the long-smoldering spirit of rebellion that Mercier and Rétif feared and denounced in the years prior to the Revolution.[16] The companion shares with the moralists the notion that in the past, "under the old method," customs and social relations were different and more harmonious. This was probably one of the governing notions picked up on the tour of France.

The *compagnonnages* were in theory clandestine associations but in fact were tolerated by employers and by the police, who kept a close watch on employer-worker relations and monitored assemblies, protests, and travel by workers within and between cities. Ménétra and his comrades are arrested on a vague suspicion in Poitiers. He is stopped for questioning while traveling on the main road through the Cévennes. Since the sixteenth century these associations had been defending the interests, protecting the safety, and seeing to the needs of member companions, who were grouped by occupation in so-called *vacations*. The strength of these associations derived not so much from the myths and secret rituals that have fascinated the historians of esoteric working-class practices but rather from their ability to meet the needs stemming from the chaotic lives of workers on tour as well as to assimilate the practices of earlier youth societies and religious confraternities linked to the trade guilds.[17] Traditional symbolism and myth, drawn from various sources, incorporated a broad, general view of the nature of work that attracted young workers and brought together a number of traditional modes of sociability. This diversity accounts for the quarrels that arose among these various associations, which resorted to force, every man's *ultima ratio*, to assert the primacy of their ideas. Worker fraternity, as Ménétra describes it, had three major aspects: the defense of common interests; the assertion of the excellence of his particular association, the Devoir, and of each of its component *vacations*, or trades, through rites and festival; and defining the nature of social relations among young workers through exchange and competition.

Ménétra was what was known as a *compagnon du Devoir*; he was initiated into this association in the companions' inn at Tours, probably in 1758. This meant that he subscribed to the traditions of the so-called *Enfants de maître Jacques* and the *Compagnons passants* or *dévorants* who were the enemies of the *Enfants de Salomon*, the *Gavots*, and the *Enfants du père Soubise*, known as the *Bons Drilles*.[18] These three traditions of *compagnonnage* must in no sense be regarded as similar to contemporary workers' organizations; rather, they should be seen as movements that unified the practices of the skilled trades. Each *compagnonnage* corresponded in theory to a single trade but incorporated, through associations that varied from time to time and city to city, different *vacations*. Last but not least, the nature of these organizations may well have been shaped by their history of clandestinity, even though they now enjoyed de facto recognition.[19] Precautionary and defensive measures became signs of distinction and a way of asserting a distinctive culture: these included the group discipline and secrecy, the adoption of names designed to confuse the police and establish uniformity within the group, the surveillance of strangers, the sponsorship of petitioners, and retribution against informers and traitors.[20] The *Journal*, which is less detailed in its reporting of the normal internal activities of the *compagnonnage* than are nineteenth-century accounts,[21] focuses primarily on three areas: the monitoring of working conditions, the institutionalization of solidarity, and the details of hierarchy and discipline.

Ménétra benefits from various *compagnonnage* activities intended to protect traveling workers and to secure them jobs. Even before his initiation, at the time of his departure from Versailles, he is taken in charge by a regular network of correspondents, including masters, many of them former companions, and representatives of the *compagnonnage*, who together constituted a system of communication that provided an early form of labor-market unification. Thus his itinerary is determined by job offers transmitted from city to city, from Montreuil-Bellay to Nantes, from Narbonne to Montpellier, from Lyons to Pont-de-Veyle. Wherever he goes his arrival is anticipated, lodgings are waiting, and he is protected. Brief periods of unemployment are rare (though he does experience one such period in Bayonne). The duration of the job is negotiated in advance, and when the time is up the worker is free to leave; there is only one instance of conflict, at Carpentras, in a sample of some thirty jobs.[22]

On two occasions Ménétra participates in schemes to secure better employment and working conditions for itinerant companions. The city of Nantes was boycotted by companion glaziers unhappy with job conditions there. Ménétra and two others workers who remained in the city harass the masters and negotiate an agreement with the guild jury. In Bordeaux the situation is more complex, and Ménétra's account magnifies the whole affair in order to glorify his own role and bring out the fact that workers of all occupations engaged in unified action.[23] This episode is one of a long series of conflicts between the companions and the wardens and masters of Bordeaux over the issue of hiring, but in this case the immediate cause of conflict is the hostility of both workers and their employers to the military obligations imposed in 1758–59 in connection with the war against England. Companions not only flee the city to avoid the drawing of lots for military service, they also engage in a delicate game in which they display signs of real political shrewdness: they are able to take advantage of differences among the local authorities; the intendant, the younger M. de Tourny; the municipality; the parlement; and the governor, M. le de duc de Richelieu.

Boycotts, unlawful assembly, and even riots are common accompaniments of these quarrels. If here as elsewhere in his memoirs Ménétra exaggerates somewhat and overstates the number of workers involved—according to him, some four thousand itinerant companions, when there were no more than six or seven thousand craftsmen of every trade and rank in all of Bordeaux—if he ritualizes the action and the speeches, he nevertheless suggests that the *compagnonnages* did possess an effective capacity to organize for the protection of their members' interests. At times these organizations came into conflict with the organizations of local workers and employers and with urban authorities, thus posing a threat of economic disruption and civil disturbance.

The effects of this solidarity were felt in many ways. Men being pursued by the authorities were helped to flee by fellow companions. The inns and *faubourgs* served in time of need as refuges and hiding places, as when Ménétra became involved in an ill-fated duel in Lyons. More prosaically, a companion from Paris could feel at home anywhere in the country thanks to the warm comradeship of his fellows. Men held in jail for activities associated with the *compagnonnage* received the sum of five sols per day as aid from their comrades. If a man became ill, his fellow companions took him to the hospital and visited him. From their religious and confraternal origins the secularized *compagnonnages* of the eighteenth century preserved a concern with traditional forms of charity, though without the conformism usually associated with such traditions. Of course the hierarchy of the *compagnonnage* was responsible for enforcing the rules and settling conflicts that arose between companions and citizens.[24] This power is depicted in the *Journal* in various lights.

Ménétra, who, after a few months as an aspirant, is initiated as a companion at Tours in 1758, becomes a full-fledged companion shortly thereafter and by 1759 is already first companion in Rochefort. Some time later he is reelected first companion in Bordeaux, and he again serves as first companion in Lyons in 1762 or 1763.[25] As captain, elected for a one-year term (though this term was not rigidly fixed), he dealt with all the affairs of his *vacation,* assisted in his work by the *rôleur,* or secretary-treasurer (an office mentioned only in connection with Lyons), who is responsible for the distribution of dues and benefits among current and former workers. Because of the large number of companions and great volume of business in Lyons, Ménétra is so busy corresponding with the cities of the tour, meting out justice, organizing ceremonies and feasts, presiding over the chambers of the Devoir, and arranging escorts that he is unable to work.

This kind of activity was, of course, a major burden only in the large cities: Nantes, with a hundred or so glaziers, Bordeaux, where the glaziers' guild counted some thirty wardens and more than a hundred companions (counting both locals and itinerants), and Lyons, where Ménétra led sixty-two companions and where there were some fifty-odd shops and twice that many local workers in the glass trade. In smaller cities, such as Angers, with eight masters, Poitiers, with four of five, and Mâcon, with two or three, the companions did not establish such an elaborate organization, and occupational and political disputes were dealt with more informally. In the major cities elaborate ceremonies marked rituals and festivals. Serious incidents sometimes occurred as well.

The *Journal* has a great deal to say about the way in which the everyday life of workers was ritualized. Ceremonies, heavily influenced by myth and indeed by ideology, formed the background to all activities; these ceremonies helped to assure the reproduction of social roles and to strengthen a form of sociability that was a culture unto itself. Ménétra remembers two things about his initiation as companion. First, the companions have him recopy the "roll" or statutes of the Devoir and the list of arriving companions, probably in a book in the chamber of the Devoir: writing becomes initiation when it is used to copy the regulations of the organization. Second, he is "baptized," and his new name is both utilitarian and symbolic. As is well known, these baptisms involved a ceremony, educational in purpose but religious in essence, which borrowed the symbolism of Christian baptism, including the passion of Christ and such ritual objects as water, bread, and wine. By retelling the initiatory myths and reliving the torments of Maître Jacques and the legends associated with the beginnings of the Devoir, the companions learned the significance of their solidarity and in a sense rehabilitated manual labor, adducing their own system of moral, indeed spiritual, values in opposition to the prevailing values of a society that held manual labor in contempt.[26] The companion's baptism was a rite of passage, marking the definitive entry into a trade and an age cohort as well as symbolic initiation into an ideology of fraternity that may have had a somewhat more democratic cast among the Enfants de Maître Jacques and a rather more elitist cast among the Gavots. The same duality is evident in other rites of the companion's life.

For example, Ménétra shows us how the practice of escorting departing companions out of town served a practical purpose. Sixty stout companions formed a worthy bodyguard. But these escorts had an obvious symbolic purpose as well, and in some cases the departures were mere shams, pretexts for mounting an escort whose real purpose was to celebrate with

music—violins and oboes—and concrete acts the inevitable reality of separation. The scope of these escort ceremonies varied with the size of the
town and the rank of the departing companion, but all were intended to
give some permanence to memories which, inevitably in a society dominated by instability, were all too fleeting.

We find the same duality in the chambers of the Devoir: it was here that
aspiring new members were received; affiliates were initiated and eventually made full-fledged members (as in Ménétra's case at Tours); ceremonies, burials, and festivals were planned; and conflicts were settled.
The most important thing to note is the sacred atmosphere that prevailed
in the chambers, and the hierarchical way in which they were organized:
companions were seated bare-headed according to their seniority, while
the first companion presided with his hat on and with a book and paper in
front of him. Before the new aspirant is allowed to share in the riches of
the Devoir, he must demonstrate awareness of the boon he is about to be
offered. Ménétra's allusions and markedly discreet attitude show that he
was a true companion and defender of the honor of the Devoir, i.e. of the
petty secrets that contributed to the unity and strength of the organization, such as ordeals of initiation, recognition signals, and salutes.[27] He
submits to the ritual for the last time in 1764 at Châteauvieux near Orléans. When he resigns—and is dismissed—a chapter in his life comes to
an end with the completion of his tour of France, and the tone of the
Journal changes. It is then that we begin to see how the lives of young men
of Ménétra's age were shaped by the companions' culture and to understand the true significance of the tour of France.

The companions' culture was based on certain forms of sociability identified with specific locales or places. While on the tour Ménétra generally
finds lodging in inns, usually located in the *faubourgs* where they were less
subject to police scrutiny than in the cities. It was in these inns that the
chambers and *cayennes* assembled the members of the different trades.
These establishments were managed by so-called "mothers" and their husbands, or "fathers," who kept their lodgers apprised of the news and of
available jobs, advanced sums of money, and made credit available with
the pledge of a man's comrades as collateral. In robbing one of these
"mothers" the glazier Oran committed an unforgiveable crime. All the
companions met after work in the cabaret to eat, drink, sing, and relax.
There was sharing even in sleep, as men slept in rooms with several beds or
in dormitories. Every man knew what his fellows were up to, and life
normally revolved around oral traditions such as storytelling and singing[28]

and other activities such as letter-writing and copying the rules and "rolls" of the Devoir.

Brawling and festivals served a dual purpose: they reinforced the solidarity of the group in a spectacular fashion and they affirmed the importance of youth and strength. In storytelling what mattered was not so much the probability of the details as the significance of the whole. Exaggeration is evident in Ménétra's stories of Bordeaux and Angers, but major brawls involving companions did exist; one could cite any number of examples.[29] These incessant skirmishes—Ménétra mentions at least ten—provided a collective and ritualized way of settling disputes among hot-headed youths and, further, between organizations of companions that differed over such concrete matters as control of employment as well as over underlying issues of ideology. The fratricidal battles of the tour were also a provocative way for a counterculture to assert its existence in the face of an established official order. Bourgeois and militia allowed companions to batter one another; mounted posses pursued both victors and vanquished who fled town after a battle; priests buried the dead when they found them; and companions tried to rescue the seriously wounded and sometimes even to hide the bodies of the slain. Ménétra's account of his great deeds exhibits a concern with organization which was probably more imaginary than real but which discloses an ideal: that of controlling, of commanding in a military sense while at the same time regulating the occurence of these great clashes with the adversary, these gigantic battles in which blows with canes, hurled rocks, and hand-to-hand combat were supposed to demonstrate the physical superiority and uphold the honor of the Devoir.

The companions' festivals develop similar themes though in a more pacific key. Any occasion could serve as pretext for a festival: a Sunday off, a religious or civil celebration, a *Te deum,* the "passing of the bean" for Twelfth Night in Nantes and Mâcon—all these were occasions for banquets, balls, processions, music, and song. Even funerals ended up as celebrations owing to their ceremonial trappings and the custom of honoring the deceased with a large meal. The feast days celebrated by the various trades—e.g., Saint Ann's day, 20 July 1761, in Avignon, and Saint Luke's day—gathered carpenters and glaziers in a celebration of the triumph of the Devoir.

For Ménétra Saint Luke's day in Lyons is a personal triumph as well. As first companion in charge of planning the celebration, he assigns all the roles—to the first companion, the senior companions, the "mothers" and "fathers," the full-fledged companions, the affiliates, the aspirants, the former companions, the itinerants passing through, the employers and their families; he also concludes the arrangements with the authorities. The plan of the festival is to unify time and take possession of space. It lasts nearly a week, night and day: the city is occupied shop by shop in ceremonies involving the hanging of floral decorations and the drinking of toasts; there is a solemn procession as well as a demonstration of the Devoir's power and dignity; there is a high mass and an offering, and a ball followed by four or five banquets worthy of Pantagruel. If one were to give a broad interpretation of this ceremonial, one might say that it en-acted the reconciliation of order and disorder. Youthful violence was tamed, and the proprieties were respected in spite of extravagant drinking. At the same time, all the trades of the city were brought together, all the *vacations* of the Devoir united, in a ceremony that included workers of all ages.

The symbolic meanings of the festival rendered it a celebration of the values of abundance; the very nature of the economy of waste characteris-tic of the period of *compagnonnage* is clearly in evidence. Ménétra's words demand careful reading. One value dominates all others, even strength: namely, generosity, the capacity to give. All the activities of the compan-ions are based on the sharing of wealth, and it is easy to understand why the companion so detests misers and thieves, who regard individual ownership as more important than communal circulation and redistribu-tion. Everything must be lavish and ostentatious. Forget about saving: a penny earned is a penny spent, a gift received from an employer is a pretext for treating him immediately to a drink. Escorts, after-work meet-ings in the cabarets, and above all holidays were opportunities to display the symbolism of belonging and giving, to extol the values of liberating consumption, and to condemn penny-pinching. In Tours five hundred days' worth of wages are lavished on one *Te deum* and the ensuing liba-tions. In Lyons the first companion donates one hundred days to the festival, and the other companions throw the equivalent of more than two hundred days' wages "into the coffers," to say nothing of the debts con-tracted—more than three hundred livres all told, not counting the cost of banquets and gifts from employers. Ménétra receives twelve livres from his employer and turns right around and offers supper to all the members of his *vacation*; he has guests for a snack, pays for the violins and other entertainment, and his loan is gone in an instant.

Ménétra's age cohort is not interested in saving. It learns to live on borrowed money according to an ethic of gift-exchange that does much to promote group solidarity.[30] This perpetual potlatch is an extension of practices we encountered earlier, such as sexual exchange and an intimate communal way of life filled with festive celebrations and carnivals. A gift economy structures both social conflict and generational conflict—the employer is both a bourgeois and a former companion—as well as customary collective practices. It is easy to understand why this economy of seduction and dissipation might have worried not only religious and civil authorities but also moralists and even economists.[31] The rituals of *compagnonnage* delayed the moment of establishment in business by making it impossible for the young companion to accumulate any savings, suggesting a rejection of the rules of commercial society and the labor contract at the very time when those rules were beginning to take hold.

The transition from youth to adult responsibilities was also an economic conversion. These two stages of life were linked together, however, by a community of work and an ideology of qualification. For most workers the purpose of *compagnonnage* was not to create a "labor aristocracy" but rather to transmit traditional skills from one generation to another: "It was the matrix in which many craft skills were formed."[32] The tour of France was the only kind of technical school there was. To us, the glazier's craft is a fairly common one, requiring no great amount of specialized preparation; but to say this is to forget that the introduction of glass windows completely changed the way in which homes were heated and lighted. Nor should we forget the artistic and educational importance of stained glass, which in modern times came within the purview of the guild of glaziers and painters on glass. Ménétra illustrates both aspects of his trade: the archaic outlook of a craft sure of itself and its tradition as well as the modernity that slips in despite the regulations. This was of course the dilemma faced by all the crafts and one of the major problems posed by eighteenth-century economic growth.[33]

Ménétra tells us a great deal about the most important skills and techniques of the glazier's trade. The skills to be used on urban and rural construction sites were first learned in the shop. The glazier worked in a jerkin, leather pants, and an apron, a costume that he rarely changed, even though this convenient work outfit, with its large pockets for holding loose change, nails, and a small hammer, made it easy for the police to identify the companion out for a good time. On the road the apron could be rolled up in a bandolier and the hammer used as a light weapon. Hammer and nails were the indispensable tools for routine work, namely, installing panes of glass in wooden sashes prepared by a carpenter, with nails that hold a strip of paper or reinforce the cement used for installing windows, a mastic made of thick oil and chalk. Also indispensable was the diamond cutter mounted in the end of a wooden handle or in a plane-like holder for cutting large pieces. A common worry was that of having one's diamond stolen by thieves on the road. In the shop we find such additional equipment as furnaces and stoves, tripods for holding pieces of glass to be heated and for melting lead and resin pitch, a large table whitened with chalk and known as the *patron*, shelves for holding rulers, compasses, ingot molds, lead-drawers, tongs, mastic knives, squares, knives, brushes, and all the other tools of the trade. Hung on the walls or kept in a storage shed were the sashes to be installed, which sometimes had to be cooled after the lead was run in by taking them out into the street to be doused with buckets of water.

The glazier's trade involved a number of distinct tasks and hence an implicit, though not rigid, division of labor, in which every man was supposed to know how to do every job. There was nothing out of the ordinary about the work, which involved taking measurements, setting panes, gluing paper, decorating glass in a partition or shop window. Ménétra performed such tasks under the watchful eye of Rousseau in his furnished rooms in the rue Plâtrière. Numbers of less illustrious clients—merchants, neighbors, prostitutes, tavernkeepers—also called on his services. The glazier was a sort of jack-of-all-trades. Greater skills were required of those who collaborated in the construction of new buildings with carpenters and even architects, and still greater skills for the repair, maintenance, or completion of leaded and stained-glass windows in abbeys, convents, castles, aristocratic greenhouses, the king's stables, and the galleries of Versailles. The glazier was also a specialist who knew how to color glass, set glass in lead, draw border designs, cut intricate shapes, and work with large glass panels. It was these skills that made him a kind of artist, though he was not a glass-blower and claimed to be a practitioner of the "old method" as opposed to "fashionable ways of working."[34] The art of glazing demanded quickness and skill, agility for working in churches and monastery refectories, and a good eye.

On the tour Ménétra demonstrates his sure hand. He leaves behind him any number of minor masterpieces: a glass *écritoire,* a small case, the bishop's arms in stained glass at the Carpentras hospital. In Montereau he puts his employer to shame by installing eighty large glass panels in fifteen days. He is enthusiastic about the stained glass windows in the Auch cathedral, with their colorful instruction in the verses of the Bible. He is a shrewd connoisseur who keeps a sketchbook and visits shops in search of ingenious ways of doing things. He lends his book to friends to show them what he has learned and ultimately loses it, much to his regret.[35] This shows how the love of fine work and knowledge of the skills necessary to accomplish it were transmitted. It also shows how a rather modest profession could acquire and spread modern methods and techniques.

Ménétra was the heir of the Parisian craftsmen who built Versailles and who, during the eighteenth century, were employed in various projects by the king, some routine, some designed to enhance the prestige of the monarchy. To the southern provinces of France he carried both the skills of his trade and his habitual manners. Country curates and nobles, splendid abbeys, and modest convents all contributed to the diffusion of modern ways of working with glass.[36] Ménétra took to provincial cities and towns the latest in thinking about windows, namely, the use of large panels of flat glass, of roughly the size still in use today, the principles for working with which were first laid down by Savot and later by Félibien and Blondel, repeated in 1750 by the *Encylopédie*.[37]

The only good glass was made in France, indeed in Paris, and the only right way to use glass was that developed in Paris. For a great change was under way, which had altered the capital during the seventeenth century and had spread, by the beginning of the eighteenth century, to such large cities as Lyons, as fabric and oil-paper windows gradually disappeared and the use of windows with small panes became less and less common. This trend spread to smaller cities and even villages via such important centers as Toulouse and, too, through the influence of Parisian companions. To be sure, this change of methods and techniques was gradual. Eighteenth-century building maintenance records from Lyons prove that every kind of procedure was employed there and every shape and quality of window could be found. But it is true in general that ways of living change slowly. People gradually got used to better visibility, improved lighting, and better protection against cold. Ménétra was a participant in this silent revolution.

He was clearly on the side of modernity, as we see from his many experiments with new ideas aimed at increasing his profits (glass cages, a glass treadmill for white mice, glass frames for prints) as well as from his efforts to champion free enterprise against regulation. His tour of France had taken him to the centers of colonial and commercial capitalism, where profits soared during the eighteenth century. In Nantes, La Rochelle,

Rochefort, Bordeaux, Nîmes, and Lyons he learned how the most enter-prising artisans profited from the feverish commerce of their time, install-ing glass in the king's vessels, shipping panels of glass to the islands, main-taining and repairing arsenals, hospitals, and nobles' greenhouses. He may have picked up some business sense from the coppersmith Rigandier, who installed lanterns in the city of Montpellier: Ménétra defended his bold maneuver against the unemployed companions and timorous masters who had not bid on the city contract.[38] Around 1765 he joined in a similar project with old Vilmont in Paris. In both cases he was participating in work that would change the nature of urban life by improving street lighting.

In business for himself Ménétra was always on the lookout for a good deal. He was an excellent tradesman, "quick and easy-going," and his wife was a good manager. He tried to introduce Alsatian glass (Baccarat) to the Parisian market, but this innovation violated guild regulations, with which he had clashed earlier by using his authority to cover the activities of an unauthorized master in the faubourg Saint-Antoine:

In order to succeed Ménétra has to buck the statutes that governed the glass market, which granted a monopoly to Norman glass makers and limited the quantities that could be bought wholesale. His dispute with the "fat cats of the jury," about which he composed a song in 1773–74, challenged the pettiness of the regulations and the way in which an oligarchy could dominate the market and retain power through elections limited to a closed circle of cronies and through manipulation of the guild finances.[39] In 1776 he exultantly addressed himself to the ex-jurors and syndics of the guild as follows: "You former bachelors of glass/Themis recognizes your faults/your monopolies unjustly exercised/they and you will rightly be struck down/and smashed in a single blow."[40]

With these words the enterprising artisan applauded Turgot's liberal initiative. He was for competition, free enterprise, and profit. Despite the rules he opened a second shop in the rue Pavée, since he needed to expand in order to make and sell "the little manufactured glass objects" that made him successful. He, his wife, and his companions had "a great deal of employment."

In Jacques-Louis Ménétra's career as a craftsman we see the stakes of economic change on a modest scale, along with the perennial conflict between the innovation that brings profit and the desire to cling, tech-nically as well as economically, to the status quo, a desire fostered and legally protected by the guild system. The wardens of the glaziers' guild do not perceive their conservatism as a brake on progress; rather, they see it as the only way to keep the trade functioning and as a way of inculcating the moral principles on which the guild's strength is based: namely, that success comes from self-denial, from dogged savings out of moneus earned, and not from expansion of one's business. Ménétra's personal drama offers a curious parallel to this social conflict: Marie-Elisabeth Hénin is a believer in saving, in putting a little something by week after week. Her economics are modeled on the economics of the guild wardens and the parsimonious *rentier*; Jacques-Louis is a champion of free enterprise, a believer in spending money to make money, in taking new initiatives, in leaving people free to do as they please.[41]

Both as a companion on the tour and as a worker in the shops of Paris, Ménétra works in order to live and have a good time; he does not live in order to work. Set up in business with the help of Marie-Elisabeth's dowry, he took his place among those who were helping to free up a stagnant economy. He gives a splendid eye-witness account of the economic attitudes of the working class and small shopkeepers. The companion dreams of profits that he can spend ostentatiously in a lavish display of generosity and conviviality. He does not know how to count. The master works to increase his profits by shrewd dealing and gradual expansion of his business, but he retains from his younger days certain habits, a certain carefree attitude, and a predilection for spending whatever he earns. He is a hesitant capitalist: he does not want to count. His wife, who invests everything she has, her time as well as her small capital, in the glazier's enterprise, is a good manager who plays an essential economic role: she runs the shop. Yet her imagination, the range of her vision, is that of the guild warden and the *rentier*: she counts too much. In this conflict of generations and roles we see, in the biography of one man, an image of the larger problem of the urban economy in the Age of Enlightenment.

[4]

Spaces and Places,
Time and Action

Knowing something about work skills helps us to reconstruct popular culture by enabling us to understand what a worker's everyday experience must have been like, and how he saw the world. Yet it makes no sense to view such skills in isolation from the culturally determined thought processes and life patterns that shape our experience of space and time.[1] Ménétra's *Journal* tells us about the rhythms of social life, about forms of social behavior. There are passages in which we glimpse indirectly the traditions and practices of the collective memory. In the first place, Ménétra enables us to understand how people of his class situated themselves vis-à-vis the constructed geography of the city and the countryside, in a concrete relationship with the surrounding landscape, or, to put it more abstractly, in a mode of seeing and not-seeing.[2] Second, he gives evidence about the way in which the people of Paris apprehended time. And third, he provides material for an analysis of the ordinary gestures that reveal how men and women related to their bodies, an analysis that may help to shed new light on the role of appearances in popular culture.[3]

To know the city: on this point the *Journal* forces us to confront certain problems of methodology. For what exactly does it contain? Names of places (La Rapée), of neighborhoods (La Halle), popular designations (la Barrière Blanche), a cryptic address (recall that the numbering of houses in Paris came rather late and did not really take hold until the beginning of the nineteenth century).[4] In some rough sense we can use the clues in the *Journal* to reconstruct the topography of the city. The resulting map sums up, rather flatly to be sure, the author's direct perceptions and even motivations. We can reconstitute his system of spatial representation, for example, although the nature of the source introduces certain distortions, for undue importance is attached to places which the author visits repeatedly and the general orientation is determined by his memory and hence by the motives that underlie his decision to write an autobiography. A quick comparison of the places most often mentioned before 1765 with those that occur most frequently after the date makes it clear that there is a structural opposition in the *Journal* between the territory of sin, in which Ménétra's premarital life is centered, and the familiar neighborhoods in which he lives out the humdrum routine of his later years.

It remains true, however, that this is the only known document from a person of this class to detail the sights and sounds of the city and the places that meant most to a common man. It makes sense to distinguish three periods in Ménétra's life: the years prior to his departure on the tour of France, the period 1763–65, and finally the long stretch from his marriage to the Revolution, at which time topographic notations for the most part disappear, except where they are incorporated into accounts of events that the author did not always participate in or witness directly.

For the child and adolescent Paris is a city with two centers: his father's house and his grandmother's house, the river and the Pont-Neuf. About other places there are only scattered indications. Jacques-Louis Ménétra was born in a house on the rue des Prêtres-Saint-Germain-l'Auxerrois where his father lived and kept shop until he was quite old. Between the time of Jacques-Louis's return from his suburban nurse's until his departure on the tour of France, his memory focuses mainly on the locations to which he has the strongest emotional ties; he also remembers the scenes of his earliest work experiences and of his childhood play. What we glimpse here is the Paris of stability, the Paris of settled families concentrated in the narrow and overpopulated streets of the central city.[5] The population density in the old central parishes—Saint-Jacques-le-Majeur, Saint-Germain-l'Auxerrois, and Saint-Gervais—was 800–1,000 inhabitants per hectare. The citizens of *la Ville,* as these old right-bank neighborhoods were still called [as opposed to *La Cité,* the cathedral city on the Seine islands, and *l'Université* on the Left Bank—trans.]—shopkeepers, artisans, merchants, bourgeois, and even some people of higher rank, for there was still no strict social segregation—all lived in close proximity to misery, poverty, and violence: more than 20 percent of the inhabitants of the old parishes received assistance in the late 1780s. The zone with the highest incidence of violence in the third quarter of the eighteenth century extended from the Louvre to Saint-Gervais along both sides of the river.[6]

Thus Ménétra grew up in the thick of Paris life, in the center of trade and commerce, of markets and manufactories, of popular disturbances that were quick to flare up and just as quick to die down, in an area where large numbers of people worked and relaxed. His neighborhood, his street, were the centers of his world, and it was here that the experience of his senses taught him how to live, how to occupy the space around him.

Let us begin with the sense of sight: he noted subtle social differences in the way people lived, and he became accustomed to the contrast between the black mud of the city streets and the white plaster of the buildings under construction. He also gained familiarity with the variety of dress and sights, with the changing light on the Seine and the different appear-ance of the river at different times of day. His ears revealed other con-trasts: the gentleness of his mother's voice, the hum of gossip on the landing or in the alley, the explosive laughter of his father's companions, his father's impetuous anger, the sounds of riot, the clatter of carts and carriages over the pavement, the drone of the priests and cantors and the seraphic responses of churched urchins under the vaults of the collegial of Saint-Germain, the explosion of rockets and firecrackers, and the music of the night mocking the solemn music of the choirs.

Ménétra has little to say about the sense of smell, yet we can imagine the stench of a time remote from our own, when the practice of hygiene involved mainly superficial washing rather than careful grooming of hid-den body parts, when latrines and cesspool drainers were a part of the everyday landscape, when perfumes, heavily laced with musk, masked the sweat of aristocrats and the unique odor of prostitution. The sense of taste was also important. Ménétra educated his palate at the family table, where workers shared with their employers' families the spicy dishes pre-ferred by working people. The first glass of white wine was drunk at dawn, and the first bottle of cheap, vinegary wine tasted in secret in a cabaret. Ménétra also reports on the cardboard taste of the sacred host and on the *brioche* and canary bread offered him by the chambermaid of one of his female conquests so that he can while away the time.

Ménétra is not directly concerned with the sense of touch, which does not engage the memory in the same way as the other senses. But as he learns how to handle himself physically he does experience his first amo-rous embraces, which alternate with his parents' hugs and cuffs on the ear. Note that Ménétra loses his virginity with a lady of quality, that is, in a relatively clean and hence rather voluptuous setting.

We see how the young man comes to discover his city by walking, to learn its streets and byways. As a child and adolescent he crosses the city via intricate and subtle routes that take him from the rue de la Grande-Truanderie to the rue des Prêtres-Saint-Germain, from the quays of the Right Bank to the Ile de la Cité, from the Ile Notre-Dame to the place de Grève, from the ramparts of the collège des Quatre Nations to the Pont-Neuf. He crosses the Seine only twice to wander through the alleyways of the Saint-André-des-Arts parish and to explore the faubourgs of the Left Bank. Ménétra's Paris was less than ten kilometers in circumference and occupied a little more than five square kilometers, a small portion indeed of what was an immense city, covering nearly a thousand hectares. His routes were determined by his work and leisure activities, by the recreations of his friends and the web of family relations.

When it came time for him to seek out master glaziers, he went first to his uncles. And it was his uncles, again, who urged him to leave the city and discover the surrounding countryside, the circle of gardens, swamps, and fields that girded the city, the meadows and thickets that Paris was slowly eroding. By his uncle's side the young Parisian is capable of covering the twelve kilometers between the faubourg Saint-Germain and Issy in two hours. In Saint-Denis and Vertus he finds a way of life different from what he has known in Paris, full of peasant carts, livestock, truck gardeners' wagons, and the smell of rye and wheat in late June.[7]

The young man's city has many different aspects. His memories cover the entire map. An occasion of one kind or another, a wide circle of acquaintances with people of every sort, take the glazier to almost every quarter of the city. Only Saint-Paul in the Marais and the Luxembourg on the Left Bank are not mentioned. The time to take full possession of the city is the period before marriage; the young man makes his way through a never-ending spectacle of wealth and culture, through a scene of lively animation and vivid social contrasts, through scuffles with friends and tangles with the police.

After six years on the road, six years of moving from town to town and city to city along the tour, the chance to get to know the city once more is like a second education for Ménétra, indeed almost a second birth. His personal geography no longer revolves around one or two central poles; the lay of the land is determined, rather, by the necessities of work, amusement, and fleeting sexual affairs. It is in this period that Ménétra is constantly changing his residence, moving first from his father's house to his grandmother's, then for a short while to Rosalie's in the remote parish of Saint-Sulpice behind the abbey of Penthémont, then living with various people, then moving in with his brother-in-law in the faubourg Saint-

Antoine, then renting a small room in the rue du faubourg Saint-Jacques behind the Sorbonne, then returning to the Right Bank after a temporary exile and moving into a small attic apartment in the seventh story of a building in the cloister of Saint-Germain-l'Auxerrois, and finally fleeing the police and hiding out in old Vilmont's shop in the rue de Saint-Louis, between the rue de l'Echelle and the rue Saint-Honoré—in three years he lives at no fewer than seven addresses. The companion has no home; he lives a life of instability, which reflects the instability of his employ-ment. His travels take him from working for Vilmont, whose main work-shop is located in the rue du Vertbois in the quartier Saint-Martin,[8] to Elophe's shop in the rue Pagevin, quartier Saint-Eustache, and from there to Jérôme's in the rue des Prouvaires (same quartier), back to Elophe's, from there to Langlois's in the rue Grenier-Saint-Lazare (quartier Saint-Martin), again back to Elophe's, then again to Langlois's, and then again to Jérôme's. Then he goes to work with his brother-in-law in the faubourg Saint-Antoine, and later enters into a partnership with a master in the rue de Charenton, before returning to old Vilmont and finally going back to his father. In two years, six or seven employers, only one of them on the Left Bank (Bellé in the rue de la Harpe), and twice that number of engage-ments broken and then renewed.

Once back in Paris the companion seems unable to end his travels, and he reproduces the mobility of the tour in the city and even beyond when the opportunity or the need arises: to Versailles in quarantine, to Fontenay-aux-Roses, and to Sceaux with the widow Morel; to Châtillon and Montigny-sur-Yonne to glaze Trudaine's castles, and to Mont-Saint-Hilaire near Etampes to work on the collegiate church there. In the course of these wanderings he gains further experience of work and of people and learns new ways of seeing and doing, new ways to present himself, and new forms of speech; he sees, remembers, and imitates different kinds of behavior. All in all, these experiences turn out to be crucial for effecting a personal and communal transformation—communal in the sense that Ménétra told others about his experiences and taught them what he had learned.

Recreational ramblings followed a different pattern. One option was to stroll into the center of town, to the neighborhood of his birth and sur-rounding areas, between Les Halles, the quays, the rue Saint-Martin, the rue Montmartre, and the rue Saint-Honoré. Another was to go beyond the barriers into the faubourgs and outlying villages. A third possibility was to travel along the river from Charenton to Saint-Cloud. This was where the cabarets and taverns were located, as well as the bordellos, some in the raunchier old neighborhoods, some more distinguished establishments (popularly known as "convents") in aristocratic streets: the house run by Denongrais is in the rue Feydeau. This was also the section where one went to see shows and to watch people on the boulevards: a vast area stretching from the rue Royale to the barrière du Temple that offered all the temptations of a traveling fair, a fair that by 1750 had settled in permanently, where people liked to stroll along streets lined with trees, houses, small theaters, and smart cafés. This was mainly a night district, where men went in search of loose women, drank in disreputable company, and played hide-and-seek with the police, police spies, and the night watch. Knowing the terrain, the side streets and short cuts, made the latter into an amusing game.

Porcherons, Nouvelle France, La Courtille, and Charonne—these comprised the Paris of the *guinguettes* where people went in the evening after work and on Sundays to dance, flirt, "make acquaintances," and in short to have a good time. Gradually these activities spread to the neighboring villages—Vaugirard is mentioned five times—where an exemption from the *octroi* made wine cheaper. And then there was the Seine—the River—which flowed through the city, bringing Parisians what they needed. Pleasure-seekers were drawn to the water, and the river's inlets were crowded with *guinguettes* and inns. Legal and illegal activities flourished.[9] Ménétra, Chénier, and their girlfriends went boating both up- and downstream in search of sheltered spots for amorous adventures. The boat was moored under the Pont-Neuf in the heart of the city, left in the safekeeping of the Samaritaine boy whose sister succumbs to vice. It enables Ménétra to broaden his horizons, to flee the urban spectacle and escape into the nearby suburbs with their princely residences, to Saint-Cloud where fireworks are set off at the estate of the Orléans, to Sèvres, and even Meudon. The city and the river sustain the last flames of youth.

After his marriage Ménétra moves to the rue Petit-Lion in the parish of Saint-Sauveur. Ten or fifteen years later he opens a second shop in the rue Pavée, less than two hundred meters away, and that is where he is living when the revolutionary censuses are taken. From now on this neighborhood becomes his village. It is here that his professional and amorous activities are concentrated. True, he does make brief excursions to other parishes, and old habits lead him back to the wild territory of the boulevards and *guinguettes*. A sign of the times: the rural area outside the city is shrinking, though Ménétra does mention a couple of quick journeys

through it, such as the pilgrimage to Mont-Valérien, the walk with Rous-
seau to the Pré Saint-Gervais, and the excursions to Saint-Denis and
Meudon. The master glazier does not go out as often as he did in the past.
He takes on the airs of a rentier-bourgeois, going to the café de la Régence,
watching young men play tennis on the Champs-Elysées in the company of
Rousseau, taking his children for a walk in the Tuileries, where they attend
a concert. For recreation he visits the elegant sections—the rue Saint-
Honoré, the gardens of the Palais-Royal—while the old business streets—
the rue Saint-Denis and the rue Saint-Martin—are still the focus of his
professional activity. The river has all but disappeared. Ménétra's life
narrowed, being confined mainly to the quiet neighborhood which in 1790
became the section Beauconseil, where the people of the neighborhood
met in political rallies.

The political changes did little to alter the old forms of work and recreation, but old age and the Revolution did ultimately help to disrupt Ménétra's settled way of life: during a period of political disputes among the
sections, he goes and joins the section du Luxembourg in the rue des
Cannettes. He saw this act as an expatriation appropriate to his new
circumstances as an elderly rentier, a considerably calmer figure than the
youth we have come to know, a man disillusioned in many ways and
concerned mainly for his own and his family's well-being. He does not,
however, consider going even farther and moving to the country: people
die in the country, or at least that is what happened, if Ménétra is to be
believed, to his friend the surgeon Baron. The greater part of Ménétra's
life had been lived in the city; his experience of the tour of France did little
to alter the deepseated habits of this city boy pround of his urbanity,
indeed reveling in the glory of being a citizen of Paris.[10]

Traveling on foot for seven years from one end of France to the other
provided another kind of initiation. Ménétra's springtime departure symbolized a break in the continuity of his life, while his summertime return
marked a kind of renewal. His travels, moreover, reinforced his sense of his
own worth. Like so many novels of his day, Ménétra's memoirs disclose the
contrast between the city and the provinces. Unlike the novelists and
economists, however, he has no intention of using this contrast to mount
an indictment of the city. What does he show us? A France reduced to
human scale, traversed on foot in short stretches along miserably muddy
or dusty roads. It is mainly the south of France that we see: 2,000 of the
2,500 kilometers of his journey are south of the Loire. The itinerary is
fixed by tradition: Ménétra avoids regions where guild traditions other

than his own predominate and stops in the cities designated by the Devoir where work is available.[11] The distance covered daily and the length of time spent at each stop along the way are determined by how tired he feels and above all by what opportunities are available: a pretty girl or a good job can deter him from moving on.

Some of his side trips are interesting, for they demonstrate his curious and adventurous spirit. He twice visits Brittany, for example, but finds it not much to his liking: Ménétra detests the ocean, the navy, the gendarmes, and the wayside crosses. Gascony and the Basque regions are merely glimpsed in the course of a brief pilgrimage partway to Saint-Gavot (i.e., to Santiago of Compostella). Holy wandering is not to Ménétra's taste. He spends some time in the Sologne with a friend who lives in Romorantin. But for the most part he follows in the footsteps of other companions who have gone before him, storing up impressions and good stories as he goes. His narrative of the tour is organized around two themes: the virtues of Paris and the discovery of differences between his native city and a rural landscape that calls for close observation.

Since Ménétra prefers the city to the countryside, three-quarters of his stops of any length are in towns of more than 2,000 inhabitants—cities in the parlance of the time. Cities distinguished for their active trade and rapid growth are his favorite stopping places, and he is drawn to market towns.[12] In this urbanized setting the companion is so much at home that he notices few interesting or unusual details and does not comment on local monuments.[13] Except for work, his life is organized in much the same way as in Paris, revolving around the workshop, the construction site, the inn or cabaret, and the evening stroll. There is little individual characterization of workmates and local residents, except for the author's personal friends and the occasional butt of a joke or participant in some important affair. Outside the city, he takes little notice of peasants and none at all of their work. He almost always shows them at rest, in inns, on the road, or in the evening in some hospitable farm house; occasionally a peasant will unleash dogs and servants on the vagabond companion. His limited rural vocabulary—farmers, shepherds, shepherdesses, villagers, good folks—underscores his remoteness from this alien world, which he judges almost entirely on the basis of the hospitality afforded him. Yet on two occasions we find him somewhat more observant: at Aucamville, near Toulouse, where he spends a winter among peasants, craftsmen, domestic servants, and game wardens, as well as curates, monks, and minor nobles; and at Montigny, where he discovers rural forms of relaxation and the stratification of rural society. What strikes him, moreover, is that people listen to him "with eyes wide open" and admire the way he speaks French; in other words, the more or less cultivated provincials are drawn to qualities associated with the prestige of Paris.

In a few passages we find Ménétra paying some attention to the environment and exhibiting some rudimentary perception of the variety of nature and of the farms and cities he visits. The forests, those refuges of thieves, appeal to his imagination, as do the hedged fields of the *bocage*, which make such good hiding places. The sea, the wind, and the coastline provide the occasion for some picturesque descriptions. Roads are "terrible" in two places: Brittany and the Cévennes. The plains of Saintonge are "marshy" and "pestilential." Olive trees, oddly enough, protect travelers from rain and lightning. There are a few tourist excursions: to Sainte-Baume; to the companion's "magic mountain," Mont Ventoux,[14] which he must have climbed in a state of some inebriation since he claims to have discovered a lake at its summit; to the Fountain of Vaucluse; to Salon and the tomb of Nostradamus; to Aix at Corpus Christi; to the boat bridge at Arles and the Pont du Gard. He is fond of farmhouses: warm, dry places good for making love. He likes fountains. He feels warmly about horses, asses, and cats, which he teases, but he is wary of dogs and wolves: in short, his bestiary is as limited as his powers of observation. Even this tells us a great deal: we see only what our cultural background enables us to see. An urban type, Ménétra sees nature only where she is tamed, pruned, reduced to a mere adjunct of man. He shows no trace of a utilitarian or pre-Romantic attitude toward nature. Thus the Cévennes embody all the evils of the wilderness: arduous travel, winds, freezing temperatures, forests, wolves, thieves, isolated, dangerous villages, dialect-speaking religious fanatics—in short, Hell on earth! This is not to suggest, however, that he has no feeling for the picturesque, as when he notices, back in Paris, "the green trees" of the Pré Saint-Gervais which he visits in the company of Jean-Jacques; but this, one suspects, merely signifies the acceptance of yet another convention. "I love the country, it delights and pleases me, I taste every kind of pleasure," he writes in a poem—but still, he would not want to live there!

Common folk could be as unaware of the social reality of space as anyone else, for that reality is the product of collective representations. Ménétra enables us just to glimpse the deeper reality of the Ancien Régime, because his *Journal* is the work of a Parisian who is not yet nostalgic and not at all denatured.[15] He interprets space first of all in terms of his daily activities, his work and recreation. Here his description is charged with symbolic references to such monuments as the Pont-Neuf (symbolizing recreation), the Châtelet (symbolizing imprisonment), and the Hospitals (symbolizing disease and death). But there is also another reading of space, shaped by odd occasions and encounters as well as by certain conventions, from which he acquires a new enthusiasm for things natural as long as those things remain subordinated to the needs of the city.

A similar conventionality shapes Ménétra's representation of time as well as his need to escape from its dominion. Determined to be original, Ménétra refuses to follow other journal writers and autobiographers who use dates and significant events to set their lives in the context of their times.[16] What the *Journal* shows us indirectly, therefore, is the way in which the progress of time was perceived; what it gives is not an intellectual abstraction but a sense of how time was actually experienced, a feeling for duration.[17]

A creature of the city, Ménétra was little affected by the seasons. Seasonal conditions are mentioned fewer than ten times, and then only in connection with travels, to indicate when walking became difficult or when the weather was so good that the day's journey could be especially long. It snows once, in Dijon, and in Paris it freezes once and the Seine becomes dangerous. The month of October is the only month mentioned—one time. After leaving the isle of Yeu Ménétra is within a few days back in Niort, "naked and full of vermin." But his memory must have played tricks on him, because it seems highly unlikely that his adventure at sea could have lasted "three months" at this time of the year. Hence this remark is of little value for understanding how he perceived the changing of the seasons.[18]

If Ménétra is indifferent to the seasonal rhythms characteristic of old rural societies, is he preoccupied with watches and clocks? Is he eager to rationalize his daily schedule? In three hundred pages we find the precise time mentioned fewer than twenty times, and even here the references to time are highly stereotyped: five and six o'clock in the morning are mentioned five times, eight o'clock is mentioned once, ten o'clock in the evening five times, and eleven o'clock twice. These indications of the time are really no more precise than saying morning or evening, dawn or dusk. Ménétra is familiar with watches: in 1763 he returns to Paris with a good suit of clothes and some money in his pocket, and he buys himself an imitation gold watch, a cheap item but one that shows that the use of watches had become commonplace.

Owning a watch was perhaps a matter not so much of practicality as of prestige.[19] Eighteenth-century inventories of working-class property reveal the diffusion of a new custom: in the early 1700s fewer than 20 percent of them indicate the possession of a watch, and these pertain primarily to domestic servants; by 1790 the figure has risen to nearly 50 percent.[20] Henceforth the people of Paris, the modest craftsmen, have access to the world of mechanized timekeeping, which enables them to keep better track of the passage of time, to organize their days, to create time, to fabricate it. The watch is also an assertion of individuality, a symbol of success and of access to another world.[21] Mlle Beaufort, a kept woman, has two gold watches and makes a gift of one of them to Ménétra. Prostitutes in several bordellos buy watches from the Genevan Gaillard, who plies his trade in the cabarets and "convents [i.e., houses of prostitution] protected by the police." This fashion sustained not only Swiss watchmakers but also some 400 horologists in Paris and its environs, to say nothing of the thieves who stole watches from well-to-do citizens.[22] When Ménétra is arrested and taken to the guardhouse, this time by mistake, he proves his rank by showing the glaziers' coat of arms engraved on the handle of his cane and on his watch case.

In fact, however, Ménétra's temporal memory exhibits an equal indifference to measurement, chronology, and the rhythm of the seasons—a common attitude at this stage in history, when natural rhythms had ceased to dominate but rationalized time had not yet fully taken hold.[23] In this period of interregnum the conflicting influences of merchants, the Church, and independent individuals like Ménétra vied with one another. His life is one of spontaneity, and approximate time references are all he needs. With the passage of years he gradually discovers that life has become more difficult: lovers are less easy to find, anxiety for the future overshadows the whims of the moment, the body flags. The younger generation repeats the same cycle: his son "experiences springtime in his turn," his daughter marries. The rough and ready recital of the past becomes bogged down in the litany of the quotidian. Temporal indications serve as rough milestones as the story unfolds; they give shape to the story and bestow upon it an aura of authenticity essential to autobiographical writing.

Ménétra was certainly familiar with the church's manner of keeping time, since he had served at mass, attended services, and sung vespers. But what did he take from this experience? Three holidays had particular significance for his trade: the carpenters' feast of Saint Ann, and Saint

Mark's and Saint Luke's days, honored by the glaziers. Two others were days of commemoration for him: the feast of Saint Bartholomew of Angers, which may have been the day of the great brawl, though this has not been verified, and Saint Martin's day, when his father and son were buried. Ménétra's temporal concepts were in the process of de-Christianization, as we shall see presently; his world view was increasingly secularized. The continuity of church time was a matter of indifference to him; in the Church calender he noticed only the days of rest and celebration. Mardi gras were more important to him than Ash Wednesday. Easter is mentioned in connection with a pleasant sojourn in a wretched little town in Languedoc, where the companion was able to dazzle an audience of rather backward, or as he would say, "fanatical" peasants. His confusion over the significance of Easter is a sign of his own disaffection with religion. For him, Corpus Christi is only a spectacle, and baptisms and marriages are opportunities for living it up.

The only days mentioned by name in the *Journal* are Sunday (thirty times), Saturday (five times), and Monday (four times); Sunday is never described in a religious context but always as a day of freedom. Sundays and holidays become symbols of leisure. The regular rhythm of prayers and festivals that enabled peasant communities to relive the events celebrated in the Bible, the time of the "books of hours" and religious services of the Christian past, is no longer the time in which our Parisian artisan moves, even though these temporal habits were instilled in him in childhood and he occasionally refers to them in passing: monks chanting matins, believers going to church, himself as first companion obliged to make sure that other companions attend Sunday services.[24]

It is difficult to say whether this was an individual change or a collective one: the *Journal's* spotlight shines on only one actor. But two things are certain. First, it is not easy to abandon a culture: passing remarks prove that Ménétra was thoroughly familiar with church time. Second, we can see from his account how the way of life of companions and craftsmen shaped their world view and gradually freed them from obeisance to the rules of religion.

The life of an urban craftsman was divided into two parts: the time spent on the job and the time spent in recreation. Parisian craftsmen, whose craft traditions had reached their apogee, were deeply devoted to the values of their trades and displayed that devotion at work and play. More than three-quarters of the references to time in the *Journal* are either to work time or to leisure time. Time is referred to in no more than one way. In the first place there are references to the succession of days, to the repetitiveness of the work routine, using words and phrases such as to-morrow, the day after tomorrow, at that time, in those days, a short while later, one day, that day, a few days. These express a ritual monotomy to which Ménétra has become accustomed; they indicate not so much an obligation to work in exchange for days of rest as the natural framework of temporal existence. Such words and phrases occur eighty-five times. Words such as Saturday, Sunday, and Monday evoke the alternation of work and recreation.

Next, we note terms that indicate the beginning or the end of a con-struction job or period of employment or relationship with a friend or girlfriend—a limited period of time with approximate beginning and end. Memory creates a kind of stratification that accentuates periods of me-dium length: expressions indicating a period of two to eight days occur approximately ten times; periods of two weeks to a month occur about twenty times; one to six months, nine times; a year, twice. The companion lives from moment to moment, and in his memory the past appears fore-shortened, abbreviated in such a way as to enable him to survey the passage of time. Finally, we encounter a series of words that indicate the distribution of tasks and recreations throughout the day: morning, dinner, after dinner, evening, bedtime, supper, and night, to say nothing of the siesta of a certain monk in Carpentras; there are eighty-five occurrences of this type.

In this analysis of a life's passing one thing stands out clearly. There is an obvious connection between the instability of the companion's life and his piecemeal perception of time: three-quarters of the terms noted occur prior to 1765. After Ménétra settles down and starts a family, things change in this respect as in so many others, even if many masters, like Ménétra himself, live at times as though they were still companions. This overlapping of work time and "real life" expresses a simple relationship to time first learned in the years of apprenticeship and bachelor freedom. On the whole, the time required to do a job means nothing to the good workman; what counts is the ability to get the job done. If necessary, he will work all night (the practical joke that Ménétra stages in Vendôme enables him to demonstrate his adherence to the craftsman's code of honor) and make an ostentatious show of his capabilities: "I told him to go see the porter and let me work, a good opportunity to show the boss that I could do in a trice what it would have taken him two days of hard work to finish, with his awkward way of going about it." In this there are elements of boasting and an implicit admiration of physical strength, but it may be that it shows "more understanding of human nature than the measurement of work in units of time." There is as yet no strict boundary between working hours and leisure hours. The work day expands or contracts as needed.[25] Sunday extends into Holy Monday. To economists, moralists, and priests, this was profligate.

After Ménétra becomes established in a business of his own his behavior continues to be influenced by old habits, as several anedotes illustrate. He takes off at carnival time. He closes his shop to accompany a friend on a penitential journey. He hangs out with companions on "Mondays." One Monday morning he goes off drinking with his wigmaker, with whom he empties three half-bottles; he then consumes eight *petits pains,* cures his headache with a stroll along the boulevards, buys a lottery ticket, goes up to Nouvelle France for lunch and a drink, takes a walk in the country, returns to the city for dinner and to toast the drawing of his lucky number in the lottery, returns home late to a cool welcome from his wife, who is angry with him and his friend "because we abandoned our shops." To be free to work or to take time off: that is the companion's ideal, and many a modest craftsman established in trade missed that freedom of youth and tried to recapture it. During the Revolution Ménétra mentions that he was criticized for "having closed his shop for three days," which is taken as a sign of immorality. The free-wheeling spirit of *compagnonnage* survived in some master craftsmen, who rebelled against the discipline of work. Ménétra, the champion of freedom, defends the "waste" of time as well as the more official leisure of holidays. In opposition to Rétif and other writers he favors the disorder of idleness and the right to be lazy.[26]

Thus the worker's world, before he settled down, was one characterized by instability and mobility in space and fragmentation in time. Former companions who lack the money to set themselves up in business, as well as master craftsmen who formerly belonged to the *compagnonnages* and who refused to accept the discipline of the guild wardens and the strict morality of their class, remained more or less faithful to their youthful way of life. They meet and are reconciled, for example, in the St. Luke's day banquets in Lyons. Life for all of these men is a conflict between the social forces of integration (the family and the shop) and those of disintegration, freedom, profligacy, and physical pleasure.

What the *Journal* has to say about food, the body, work, and entertainment helps us to understand the subtleties of this situation. Drinking and eating were two aspects of the young workman's pleasure against which

moralists were quick to rail.[27] For Ménétra no business deal is complete
until it has been sealed with a meal of chicken or salted fish, a calf's head
or a fish stew or a salad and a leg of lamb, topped off, of course, with a
bottle of wine. From the morning glass of white wine to the last glass
raised at night, the paths of work and drink frequently cross, and the
hours of leisure are still more sodden. Sundays, holidays, and Holy Mondays provide the occasions for innumerable toasts. The companions' ban-
quet meals are washed down with Muscadet, Bordeaux, Clairette, and
various cheap wines from Languedoc, Beaujolais, and even Mâcon. The
tour of France is also a wine tour. In Paris cabarets and *guinguettes,* in the
city and its suburbs, the wine flows freely. Fireworks-illuminated celebrations, amorous outings, and family weddings are all irrigated with rivers of
cheap wine. Wine plays a fundamental role in the popular culture. Wine,
shared along with bread and food, retains a symbolic force derived from
the gospel.

The Church was not wrong to charge, as it did as early as the seventeenth century, that the rites of *compagnonnage* counterfeited the ceremonies of religion.[28] These rituals established a tradition of conviviality.[29]
But, notwithstanding Michelet's opinion to the contrary, it was not "illus-
ion in drink" that the companions were seeking; what they wanted, rather,
was a way to affirm their solidarity. During feasts and ceremonies it was
the first companion's responsibility to ensure that drink did not dull the
men's minds.[30] Were the toasts that were exchanged challenges to rivals or
fraternal salutes? Drunkenness was not a problem with youths but rather
with their fathers, with old men with their noses firmly to the grindstone.
Young people were more amazed than worried by their drinking capacities.
They did not share the belief of the religious and civil authorities that
wine was a cause of crime, family breakdown, and tax evasion.

Another way of expressing the same youthful spirit was the combination of the pleasures of the table with the joys of sex. Sexual escapades
were generally preceded or followed by meals. For young men and the
young women they seduced, this openness was the antithesis of the sexual
prudishness of village life. Groups of young men no doubt prided themselves on their freedom and discussed sex at length, in a manner at which
we can only guess from the small samples to be gleaned from Ménétra's
Don Juanish ramblings. The approved manner among young companions
is quite macho: ravish and tell, share a girl and then tell ribald stories
about her. This is yet another way of drawing the group together, of
protecting it against life's necessities and the coming of maturity.

The waning and collapse of physical strength are major concerns of the *Journal*. We hear of accidents, venereal disease, and the diseases of old age. The five or six accidents that Ménétra describes are related to his work: he falls down a stairway, breaks his leg three times when ladders fall and scaffolds collapse, and injures his back in a fall from a stained glass window. There is pride in this account of wounds and bruises, which prove courage in the face of the dangers of the workplace as well as the battlefield. These glorious injuries are like paintings of war.

A round dozen acknowledged bouts with venereal disease mark Ménétra's sexual itinerary, from the first prostitute to the last kitchen girl, whom he shares, along with her affliction, with two neighbors. Ménétra has his own way of displaying the game he has bagged. Recounting his stories of sex and its dangers, he draws a simplistic moral from his experiences: every coin has two sides, there is no pleasure without its counterpart. He learns prudence from the "little presents" given him by make-believe prudes, and as he grows older life begins to teach him lessons of discipline. Yet at the same time it becomes more difficult to live. Ménétra falls ill and is treated for a nervous disease. He is impotent and loses confidence in the doctors of Paris. He calls upon the good offices of Henri Samson, the public executioner, who has him on his feet again in two weeks, proof that the executioner, that connoisseur of the human body, is well-versed in the tenets of an unoffical medicine, a medicine in which working people believe and which runs circles around that practiced by authorized physicians. For Ménétra this bout of illness is a harbinger of further ills, which slow down all his activities and, as Philippe Ariès has so well observed, point up the common habit of establishing a connection between human biology and the facts of nature.[31]

The different cultures of class and age group continually clash and interact, from the years of apprenticeship through the adventures of youth to the autumn years of the aging master craftsmen. Private life and public life constantly interfere with each other in a whole series of locales about which a word or two needs to be said to conclude this meditation upon time and space.[32]

The popular locales in which Ménétra's life unfolds witnessed three distinct forms of sociability. One revolved around the home and family, first in the father's household and later around Ménétra's own hearth. In old Paris the family household stood for stability, symbolized by the family meal and the welcoming warmth of the fireplace in the evenings. Though Ménétra gives no descriptions, he does illustrate the way in which daily life was lived in cramped quarters and conditions of poverty (which were somewhat better for artisans than for ordinary workers). Life was lived publicly, witnessed by everyone in the neighborhood. Relationships were begun in the stairways, the squares, the alleyways where one went to answer the call of nature during the day (in an outhouse or open latrine) and which were locked at night.[33] Prominent tenants, lesser neighbors, and neighborhood shopkeepers knew everything about everybody, protected the honor of the house as well as of their daughters, and gossiped endlessly.

This neighborhood solidarity extended to the street, to the workshops and stores that opened onto the passageways and surveyed nearby houses and cabarets. From the alley one went into the shop. From the street corner a pretty girl watched. Relationships began. Rumors spread—one mobilized the entire neighborhood in 1750 to deal with the police spies who were allegedly kidnapping children—and there was much gossip about neighborhood love affairs, business deals, successes and failures. Parents received reports of their children's mischief. Neighbors commented upon an impending marriage or gathered to remember the dead. The neighborhood was like a village, in which everyone knew everyone else and people who worked together also gathered together for entertainment.

The typical Paris shop occupied a ground-floor location. Many also had entrances from the building courtyard and side corridor. Some contained a separate office, where meals where served and owners sometimes slept. Employees sometimes ate with the master, who lived in a few cramped rooms. People came to the shop to eat a delicacy or sample a bottle of wine. Neighborhood clients came to talk business or the weather or to discuss a beautiful print. The wigmaker comes to Ménétra's shop looking for the glazier, and the pork butcher comes to avenge himself against the man who made him a cuckold. Shops were centers of news and observation. With their doors and windows wide open, the people inside could identify strangers, always suspect in any neighborhood, or follow the movements of a lover or a pickpocket. The street was the common avenue of communication: Ménétra left his shop to travel to a work site or to consume a bottle in a nearby or distant cabaret.

In the companion's life, indeed in everyone's life, the tavern stood for instability. It was the place of loose morals, the refuge of conviviality, and the temple of consumption. The inns encountered along the tour, the cabarets of old Paris, and the *guinguettes* of the faubourgs all performed the same function: they were the places where one met old acquaintances and sinned with new ones. In the culture of the companion, and in the popular culture of leisure, the cabaret was the anti-church. All the reformers lined up in opposition—the Church, the police, the economists—because taverns, they believed, sapped the energy of workers and wasted capital.

Ménétra, a child of Paris, was also a child of the taverns, where a thousand things were bought and sold, legally and illegally. Taverns were places to mingle with the crowd, to seduce women, to dance; they provided a lively setting in which people of different classes could mingle: the master in his mask, the companion, the thief, the decent women and the "woman of the world"—in contrast to the café, where the atmosphere was relatively tepid, calm, and orderly. Ménétra mentions a hundred cabarets but only one café: the Régence where he plays checkers with Rousseau. Even then, he goes only after he has reached a certain age and in the company of a regular. For him and his companions the cabaret is the place where disputes are settled and friendships and love affairs are toasted. This is the night world made tame, a place wrested in battle from disapproving authorities. In the web of small taverns from Magny to Porcherons—the Veau qui Tète and the Trois Maures at Les Halles, La Gerbe and Le Grand Vainqueur, Le Lion d'Or and La Pantoufle—a thousand acquaintances are made and unmade, a thousand stories unfold.

And it is in this turbulent setting that we encounter the subterranean world of dissidence and crime. Ménétra crosses the frontiers of a world that seems alien and dangerous to the moralists but is familiar and easily accessible to working people. When new forms of discipline were imposed by the Revolution, sans-culottes, sectionnaires, and national guardsmen would celebrate the military victories of the people and their armies in the cabarets, or relax there among members of different factions. After Thermidor Ménétra goes to the taverns to provoke his enemies; the social function of the cabarets survived political upheaval, but that upheaval inaugurated long-term changes in the way people lived. Ultimately, society and politics did have an impact on daily routine, as everyday habits were transformed.

The Social World

In prerevolutionary society the place of Jacques-Louis Ménétra was defined not in any simple way but in terms of a complex set of indicators that
had as much to do with the social imagination as with legal and economic
realities. He proclaimed himself a commoner without ancestors; in other
words, he deliberately placed himself at the bottom of the social scale, far
from the clergy and the nobility who occupied the leading positions.[1] A
citizen of Paris and son of a Parisian, he claims, with full awareness of
what he is about, membership in the class of artisans and the estate (état),
or trade, of glazier. With his determination to write an original kind of
autobiography he rejects the whole panoply of symbols—the coats of arms,
blazons, and honorable ancestors—on which supporters of the Ancien
Régime prided themselves. It was not only the nobility to which these
symbols appealed. Every one, from the seigneur of ancient lineage to the
newly arrived bourgeois, saw such symbols as signs of ancientness, which
given the dominant ideology of the age were felt to be deeply gratifying.
But Ménétra is resolutely determined to be the product of his works. He is
an individualist, a man of the future, who has no need of roots to be any
man's equal.

Although his vision of the old order may have been distorted by the new
circumstances of the revolutionary era in which he rewrote his journal, it
does illustrate how the transition from a society of orders to a society of
classes was perceived by a representative of the lower social strata: the
petty bourgeois, artisans, shopkeepers, and working people of the city. His
account enables us to see how social distinctions were actually experienced, to appreciate the way in which hierarchies that seem so clear in the
legal treatises were actually perceived, and indeed perturbed, in daily
practice. It shows us in a variety of ways how ordinary people related to
the authorities, at a time when utopian philosophers and government

officials were hard at work developing new ways to shape, punish, police, and control the masses.[2] Finally, the few pages of the *Journal* that illuminate, like a brief flash of lightning, the years of the Revolution powerfully evoke, with their syncopated style, the way in which people's lives were disrupted by events. We discover how one patriot watched, from a safe distance, as history veered out of control.

Ménétra was an artisan. In the hierarchy of ranks within the Parisian Third Estate his position was near the bottom, far below the men of learning, even farther below the wealthy merchants and bankers of the capitalist class, indeed below even other artisans practicing trades honored by tradition and economic success and consequently ranked highest by contemporaries and given a place of honor in formal processions.[3] As a guild master, he ranked above the masses commonly referred to as *le peuple,* "all trades and professions of toil and manual labor," because he owned a small share in the means of production and had the capacity to run a business and act as an entrepreneur, with the prospect of succeeding if he abided by the rules of the artisans' moral economy. Yet this "microcapitalist" lived, from the time he started working in 1750-55 to the time he started his own business in 1765, as a companion, sharing the concerns, the work, and the pleasures of other workers in his trade.[4] He straddled a class divide whose import must be understood in both economic and cultural terms.[5]

Ménétra was at first a wage earner whose income depended on the jobs assigned him by the master craftsmen for whom he worked. He left his family's shop, where as an apprentice he garnered a very small wage, to seek a modicum of independence. It is not clear how much he earned in this period. His income consisted partly of regular wages paid by the day or by the piece, partly of what he pilfered, traded, or received as gifts from his relatives. A bag held all his belongings, and packing his bag was a symbolic act signifying his mobility and independence. In inventories of the property of deceased companions, this bag is sometimes the only item left. The theft of one's bag was a tragedy.

We find many informative allusions to money earned on the tour of France and afterward, allusions that tell us a great deal about the diversity of prerevolutionary "wages"—the word does not do justice to the complexity of the situation. Companions were sometimes paid by the day, particularly when they intended to stay in a place for a short period of time or when they were waylaid by an acident, an illness, or a brush with the law. In such cases the *compagnonnage* paid compensation of five sols

per day.[6] This was a minimum available to all and sundry, sometimes supplemented by gifts from friends in the Devoir or small loans from an
employer. Some employers were more generous: the prior of Montdoubleau
paid twenty-four livres for one month, though admittedly he was pres-
sured by the sheriff. The Princess of Condé gave twelve francs for fifteen
days during which Ménétra was unable to work. In addition to these
indemnities we should probably count the food and lodging provided by
the employer, who was obliged to continue to provide for the disabled
companion. Employers sometimes sent generous sums to workers to enable
them to travel to the place of employment: Ménétra receives twelve livres
to go from Montreuil-Belley to Nantes, from Béziers to Montpellier, from
Avignon to Bédoin. If this amount is correct, it would have been more
than enough to cover the companion's costs, even though he was obliged to
pay for food and lodging out of pocket. In a sense this was an employment
bonus. When the king mobilized a number of craftsmen to work on naval
vessels, he granted them fifteen livres for the trip from Rochefort to Brest,
which was a less generous bonus. If the distance was covered in a week,
the companion would have had a scant livre per day for himself.

Companions were also hired by the week, the fortnight, or the month,
and occasionally (as in Lyons) for longer periods. The oral contract, as
Ménétra remembers it, covered a number of points. First, there was a base
pay, figured by the day or by the month, and augmented with allowances
for food and perhaps lodging. In Carpentras Ménétra earns sixteen livres
per month. In Paris his father offers him eighteen francs per month, and
Elophe, Langlois, and Jérôme offer thirty-five sols per day, without provision of room and board. The nuns of Saint-Thomas offer twelve sols at
first, later raised to twenty in order to keep the glazier on the job; he is fed
but not housed. Great nobles, concerned to retain skilled craftsmen in
their employ, offered still more: twenty-five livres per month with room
and board from M. de Laborde, and thirty-five livres from M. Trudaine.

All in all, the companion earns more than the construction worker (the
standard of reference in reports on wages), but it is difficult to estimate
what his annual income was because we do not know how many days he
worked. Supply and demand caused wages to vary, and piecework bonuses
and gratuities may have increased his earnings. With twenty-four livres
per month and good board the companion felt satisfied, and this is the
amount he pays his brother-in-law to work for him. As long as he does not
have to pay rent he can live comfortably, but since he is often forced to pay
for his own lodging his wages are really borderline, significantly less than

he could earn as a domestic servant—but this is something he absolutely refuses to contemplate. Alternating between periods of work and periods of unemployment, Ménétra samples the bourgeois life, the ideal of the Parisian working man: to spend one's time doing nothing, like a *rentier*.

Third and last, companions could also be paid by the job, as Ménétra was in Montpellier and while working for Vilmont. Using his contacts and skills the worker helps to build up the business. He is paid fifteen livres per month, six livres per hundred lanterns that he makes, and a bonus of twenty-four livres, plus good food and lodging. The Table below summarizes the amount he would actually have earned in three and four month periods, based on the reasonably certain data for Montpellier.

	three months	*four months*
fixed bonus	24 livres	24 livres
monthly wage	45 livres	60 livres
600 lanterns	36 livres	36 livres
room & board based on 1 livre/day estimate	90 livres	120 livres
	195 livres	240 livres
actual no. work days	60 days	80 days
actual daily wage	3 livres	3 livres 10
annual wage	750 livres	850 livres

This sum is equivalent to the profits that Ménétra hoped to obtain from three months' business (800 livres), and it is more than the capital that a typical Parisian proletarian of 1789 could claim to possess after a lifetime of hard work.[7] In short, the companion's income depended on his skills and enterprising spirit. It was subject to negotiation when economic and trade conditions permitted. And it suffered when times were hard. It was a composite of various elements, which varied with the circumstances. Finally, it was directly related to the companion's behavior. In times of need he worked hard. Desire to better himself encouraged ingenuity and doing extra work on the side. In a climate that discouraged expense and ostentation (Ménétra took good care of his clothes and appearance), it was possible to put some money aside.

To set oneself up in business one needed a shop. Ménétra and his fiancée bought theirs for 300 livres from a glazier named Bruno. This was not a top price. Some shops sold for as much as 800-1,200 francs. When the couple appeared before the notary, they declared their capital to be 3,300 livres: Marie-Elisabeth's dowry and real property worth 2,300 livres and an additional 1,000 francs for Jacques-Louis's master's certificate.[8] With this amount of capital it became possible to cross the frontier into new economic territory: it took an inheritance on the male side and savings on the female side to reach this point. Marie-Elisabeth was the daughter of a wool comber, a poor worker or craftsman from La Neufville in Picardy. Her marriage to Jacques-Louis was a relatively rare example of geographic and social exogamy, found in only one-third of all marriages in Paris in the middle of the eighteenth century.[9] Ménétra was a winner financially, but he married a social inferior, an illiterate provincial who, like many girls beyond the age of majority, had probably been a servant.

Economically, the young couple was on a par with most other Parisian couples of the master craftsman and merchant class: 65 percent of this group married with more than 1,000 livres, with 23 percent having between 2,000 and 5,000 livres. They stood well above the impoverished masses (20 percent of the population married without a contract and 25 percent with less than 500 livres) and well below the opulent minority of the *haute bourgeoisie* and nobility. The Ménétras were firmly petit bourgeois and moderately well off.

The couple benefited from the growth of the city. Construction in Paris boomed, and business generally fared well. Glaziers enjoyed good times between 1765 and 1790. With the help of some minor speculations Ménétra prospered. On one admittedly unusual occasion he accepted a bill for 1,350 livres. In 1785 he married his daughter with a dowry of 2,400 livres. The bridegroom was a pastry maker. This time the marriage was completely endogamous. Based on what Ménétra says, we can calculate the amount that his capital increased over a period of eighteen years. His wife said that she had saved twelve sols per day. Twelve sols per day × 365 days per year × 18 years = 3,946 livres, or if we count only working days, 12 × 250 × 18 = 3,700 livres.

Such was the meager result of much thriftiness, but it was enough to provide Marie-Madeleine with a dowry appropriate to her social status. The family fortunes would have amounted to 5,000-6,000 livres at the very least, counting the shop, merchandise, and family furniture, perhaps as much as 8,000-9,000 livres if we allow for the 3,000 livres of capital that Mme Ménétra had placed in *rentes* sometime before 1789. In 1778

Uncle Marseau went bankrupt with 15,000 livres in liabilities and 11,000 livres in assets.[10] Leaving aside his business failure, the level of wealth is approximately the same. Finally, prior to the major devaluation of the assignats, the couple sold the business for 10,000 francs. This sum placed Ménétra among the common run of established craftsmen-shopowners, the near bourgeoisie. With such a fortune one lived rather poorly by modern standards but reasonably well for the time.[11]

It has been worth going into these matters in such detail because comparable documentary evidence is scarce and the case of Ménétra shows clearly how difficult it is to place any man's life within a set of neat categories. Before we can understand how an individual becomes socialized we must investigate how he comes to terms with the social realities of his time. In other words, we must follow the lead of Mercier and Rétif and look beyond the social categories to the underlying behavior and economic realities. We must see how different social groups relate, using demographic and cultural information detailed elsewhere.[12]

Ménétra's society cannot be described in terms of a rigorous system of classification. It is fluid, changing with the character himself, whose social perceptions shift as he grows older and takes on new roles. The values of this society accentutae, to varying degrees, both change and stability. From his time on the road Ménétra recalls innumerable examples of upward social mobility. A young man disappears from his village, and when he returns he is an officer of the king's army, riding a beautiful horse. Fireside storytellers perpetuate legends of rapid social ascension. In Paris Mlle Beaufort marries a clerk in the royal administration who vanishes in Turkey, but her case is an instance of a very special kind of social mobility, that of actresses and prostitutes. On the other hand, the disintegration of the Pinard family proves that it was also possible to descend in social status: the pork butcher becomes a police spy and his wife runs off with a farmer. Yet one of his daughters goes to Lyons with a watchmaker and the other, a kept woman, travels abroad in the entourage of a wealthy financier. Similarly, Ménétra's friend Chénier, born rich and married even richer, receives from his intended, the profligate daughter of a wealthy scrap and paper dealer of the faubourg Saint-Marceau, a dowry of 6,000 livres—three times larger than Ménétra's—but he goes bankrupt and is forced to enlist.

Social relations in the city were infinitely complicated by the influence of appearances and by the tricks of fate that made some fortunes and unmade others. In fact, the city produced striking examples of inequality, while the opportunities for equality were much more subtle and difficult to discern. In this confused situation Ménétra is in his element. He has his own ranking, different from that implicit in the "society of orders," where each man's rank corresponds to his legal status, and different, too, from the ranking by wealth associated with class society. Ménétra judges each man according to his personal worth. He does not indiscriminately despise wealthy nobles and clerics, nor does he see companions and masters as embodying all the virtues of the spirit of libery. Ménétra is a Parisian, influenced by the egalitarianism of the city, with its constant mixing of men of different rank and fortune. What matters to him is the way a man behaves. At this point it may, I think, be useful to give a few examples illustrating this empirical sociology, which Ménétra evolved out of his own experience.

First consider women. For the most part the weaker sex is described in pejorative terms. Yet most of Ménétra's sexual relationships are with women from his own socioeconomic group—workers and artisans: this fact does not alter the previous observation. There are a few exceptions that confirm the rule: the good widows, who embody the hope of success, and the women who he dreams would make ideal wives such as Manon the lace maker and above all Mme Bouchu, who belatedly acquires the virtues of the good woman living on her income. But two exmples show that Ménétra was not mistaken about the real social hierarchy: the abbess of Beaumont-les-Tours, Henriette Louise Marie de Bourbon, aunt of the Prince of Condé, who is impressive and yet maternal in her ceremonial garb, and the Marquise of Ballainvilliers, who, when the glazier Elophe permits himself to become overly familiar with her, teaches him, with the aid of her servants, that the *galant* liberty of the Parisian male has its limits.

At work and at play, in the shop as well as the cabaret, the prevailing atmosphere is egalitarian, embracing even the *bourgeois* or boss, who is judged on the basis of his friendliness and generosity. If the employer violates the rules that establish an equilibrium between masters and companions, he pays for it: his men plot against him, take off from work, and play tasteless tricks on him, as is the case, once again, with Elophe. Most of Ménétra's friends also come from his own or comparable socioeconomic groups. Anyone who is affable gets high marks from Ménétra. The examples of Baron the surgeon, Lenoir the roaster, and Rousseau, who is willing to be intimate with a modest artisan, all show that people could live together in harmony in spite of differences of knowledge and wealth.

Ménétra's attitude toward the peasantry is similar. Culturally backward and fanatical in religion, the peasants cannot of course pretend to be a match for a sharp-witted Parisian. But they are good people, victimized by priests and brigands, capable of extremely good behavior as well as extremely bad: one day they will give you a warm welcome, the next day they'll turn the dogs loose; one day they are kind and friendly, inviting you to celebrate a holiday with them, the next day they are nasty and quarrelsome and slam the door in your face. In Montigny Ménétra discovers the true hierarchy of rural society as it is displayed in a peasant celebration. At the summit is the lord, an outsider, a Parisian like Ménétra himself, then the bailiff, the priest, the notables, the younger notables, and the game warden who tricks him. He sorts out these various personalities with the aid of a rudimentary characterology, which probably draws its force from popular broadsides and satire like the *Misères* and *Sottises,* which enable the companion to take his bearings. At the bottom of his hierarchy he places the domestic servants, above whom he ranks certain friends of his, like Du Tillet.

Toward the privileged orders Ménétra's attitude wavers from respect to hesitancy to outright rejection. The regular and secular clergy alike are generally condemned: the bishops of Carpentras and Agen, the monks of Saint-Denis and Grandselves, the recollects of Lyons, the prior of Montdoubleau, the vicar of Saint-Germain-l'Auxerrois, and various confessors and preachers all come in for a share of Ménétra's criticism. His anticlericalism (about which I shall have more to say in a moment) is deep seated and stays with him from childhood to old age. Note that he may have been influenced by an early experience that drove home the contrast between those who work and their betters: he is with his father when the latter explains to the curate of Saint-Germain-l'Auxerrois that if he, Jacques Ménétra, were to do no work, he would receive no pay. A few ecclesiastics are spared his enmity, however: the lay brothers of Grandselves, a holy hermit in Languedoc, the chaplain of the lord of Vénasque, the curate of Montigny, and his hypocritically religious cousin. These are people who by and large accept the rules of popular sociability: they like to drink, laugh, and argue. Of course his favorites are the nuns, for reasons that have little to do with religion.

This leaves the nobility, which Ménétra sees in a rather confused manner. He mixes up titles and transforms a marquis into a duke. He sees things from the outside and is mainly struck by the symbols of authority, the ostentation of power: the crosses of Saint-Louis, blue ribbons, swords in saltire, trains of eager courtiers and servants. To be sure, the glazier does rub elbows with the Parisian aristocracy, but he waits in the anteroom and does not climb the formal staircase. He is, however, a good observer, who doesn't believe everything he's told and doesn't allow himself to be taken for a ride. No friendship is possible with high-ranking nobles who frequent low company in the bawdy houses or recruit strong young men to bolster their tennis teams. Of such men one must be wary. Our companion prefers the lesser rural nobles, who are more open and are amused by his Parisian manners. M. de Gardouche of Toulouse, an officer of the guards always ready to do a favor, the Count of Bouillac, whom Ménétra cures of his fever, a minor Provençal noble—these were men who, it seems likely, invited Ménétra to dine at their table rather than with the servants. The Parisian workman, though not unaware of signs of hierarchy in provincial manners ("in the fashion of the region inferiors rode on horseback ahead of superiors"), appreciates gestures that make possible a less unequal relationship with the nobility.

In sum, Ménétra's sense of the social structure was based more on his moral asessment of behavior than on legal or economic status. The latter forms of status are not absent or unrecognized, but behavior and imagination make a difference, so that each man is ranked according to his abilities. On the good side the companion places those who overlook social differences, who are generous hosts and benefactors, and who know how to laugh drink, eat, and listen. On the bad side he places those who refuse to accept him, who find fault, who accumulate wealth and guard it jealously, along with their hypocritical and unjust servants and daughters. Ménétra aspires to an equality of esteem and sympathy, an equality that is still thwarted by the privilege and inequality inherent in the hierarchy of rank and wealth. He is a Rousseauist. What is at stake is the companion's very being: he is caught between the assertion of individual freedom and authoritarian constraints that reflect the weight of reality. Here we glimpse the origins of a true grass-roots politics, learned through the interactions of everyday life from earliest childhood.

Ménétra shows how people of small means lived. He sees the other side of events that historians generally find out about through police archives. He tells us a great deal about the operations of the police, who, on orders of the royal government, kept the population of Paris under close surveillance. We see the daily confrontations between working people and the forces of order, whose province expanded daily to include work, business, recreation, morals, and family life. What is at stake, ultimately, is the preservation of a social order. For the companion and his comrades there is no option but to try to outwit the vigilance of the police, always quick to note the activities of young men such as these. This trouble with the law is a fairly familiar affair, sometimes just a game, sometimes escalating to actual violence. Young men led the cops a merry chase through the nighttime streets and ridiculed them with their jokes; the Paris watch and guard, no more than a thousand or so men who patrolled the streets on horseback and on foot from dusk to dawn, checked the cabarets for signs of trouble and intervened if called upon by the citizenry. There were many popular terms for the police: *tristes-à-patte, pousse-culs, lapins-ferrés, parents de la pelle à feu* (the latter, meaning literally "relatives of the fireplace shovel," is presumably a pun on the "tongs" who—as we would say in English— "pinched" our wayward youth). Not all of them were bad fellows, either: some were known to bend the elbow a shade more than was reasonable and to stagger as they made their rounds. Ménétra does not have it in for them so much as for their immediate superiors, like Fleury, a corporal of the watch and bachelor about the neighborhood, a rival in love of Ménétra's who receives punishment "in the Parisian manner" at Père Lachaise, or like Denongrais's pimp and lover, a drunkard whom our companion is obliged to tolerate. Such cases were not unusual.

At the summit of the police hierarchy, the lieutenant of police was a remote, inaccessible figure to whom fathers could apply to have their dissolute children imprisoned. Ménétra and Chénier were clever enough as young men to elude this threat, but when the companion became the head of a family in his own right he wielded the same weapon to rid himself of his son-in-law. The meeting of Louis Thiroux de Crosne, who was lieutenant of police until 1789, with Ménétra and his son-in-law Durus the pastry maker is no doubt made up—the case would have been dealt with by a *commissaire* and been disposed of through regular legal proceedings—but the fact that Ménétra brings in this august and much-feared personage shows what prestige he enjoyed.[13] The journal-writer describes four or five different *commissaires,* including Rochebrune, who works out of the police station in the rue Geoffroy-Lasnier. By 1770 there were some twenty or so police inspectors in Paris, but working under them were more than 300 official informers and spies. They were even more hated and feared than the police officials themselves. Their power and their presence increased steadily, not only in the pages of the *Journal* but in reality as well. Some were honest and impartial, others not; some vigilant and active, others less so; but for the companions and working people generally they were the enemy, from whom nothing good could be expected. They represented the arbitrariness of a complex social order. A word from one of them and a companion could wind up incarcerated in the Châtelet, his mistresses in the Salpêtrière, and his dissolute friend in Fort l'Evêque. The prestige and power of the police were formidable.

The *Journal* also shows us the subtler aspects of the relationship that developed "on the street" between the police and their clientele. The *commissaires* of the Louvre district knew a Ménétra who in his youth ran with a dubious crowd, yet they treated him leniently. Ménétra, for his part, did not live in terror of arrest. He knew how far he could go, given the slipshod methods of the police, the ambiguity of social roles, and the uneasy coexistence of the stable and the unstable. Both in Paris and on the road Ménétra faced the forces of law and order as a man who fought every day to defend his freedom, which for him was an active rather than a passive virtue.

At first his reaction is one of insubordination and juvenile insolence, but with maturity it became a refusal to submit to any form of regimentation. Among the various forms of repression that the companion meets in the course of his travels and comes to detest are the navy, the provincial militia where he learns to handle firearms on behalf of his employer, the urban militiamen who look down from the ramparts upon brawling companions, forced labor for the king, and the brigades of the *maréchaussée*, which patrol the kingdom's highways. Fights, bad jokes, and work disputes could all end up before a local judge in the provinces or a *commissaire* in Paris.

Ménétra, if we are to believe what he says, always comes out all right. He casts himself in the role of ringleader because he is able to read and write, talks well, and looks as though he knows what he is about. Note, however, that in the wake of major episodes, as at Angers, Poitiers, and Tours, he slips out of town as fast as he can, no doubt rather skeptical as to the true generosity of the authorities. His refusal to knuckle under or to accept discipline is not incompatible with a measure of fascination with the power of the government. Ménétra would like to see himself as a good tactician and organizer, but he also has the wariness that comes from having been soundly drubbed. The deep antagonism between civilians and the military is also at work.

The people did not like the army and detested the militia. They feared war as much as plague or famine, and it took a revolution to change this. The civilian-military conflict emerges in the *Journal*, collectively in the refusal to enlist and individually in the decison to desert as well as in

Ménétra's frequent quarrels and duels with those who strut about with swords at their sides. Here the *épée* symbolizes both a social function and a place in the hierarchy of privileges which in theory, at least, belongs to the nobility. Ménétra seizes upon this symbol when he comes up with the neologism *épétier*,[14] which underscores his contempt for men who, as a group, are united by their offensive attitude toward the people: the master of Nantes, the libertine *chevalier* of Paris, the former companion from Franche-Comté who enlists in a regiment of Lyonnais, and a whole brigade of French Guards. To Ménétra the *épétiers* are detestable characters, and he avenges himself "in the Parisian manner." Yet at the same time he is somewhat envious. Ménétra uses his membership in the fire brigade, reorganized in 1785 by M. de Morat, as a pretext for wearing an *épée* of his own. This is a sign of the confusion of ranks.

Finally, Ménétra execrates the French Guards, upon whom the Parisian authorities relied increasingly in the second half of the eighteenth century to back up the police. Between the detachments of guards and the populace there developed an ambiguous relationship made necessary by the uneasy balance of power and the need to reach some kind of accommodation. Billeted at first with local citizens, many guards were moved by the royal government after 1770 to barracks in the faubourgs and suburbs. Some worked in other occupations and so vied with civilians for jobs. Ménétra mentions one guard, a glazier by trade, who cleverly took advantage of his dual status. On the Pont-Neuf and in the faubourg Saint-Marcel he took it upon himself to stop and check the neighborhood girls. At the same time the guard was someone with whom the people were intimately familiar, someone they observed in many settings from the guardhouse to the cabaret. Ruined, Chénier and Givet trade their freedom for a uniform, but such cases were increasingly rare. These soldier-policemen, some of whom were also petty criminals, were beginning to be recruited more and more outside Paris, as Chaigneau has shown in his history of the Guards.[15] To the people of Paris they became increasingly identified with arbitrary and alien authority.

The army could be heavy-handed in its repression, and, what is more, from 1782 on it routinely assisted the officials of the royal tax farms, who were universally detested. Ménétra proves that the French Guards did not enjoy the popular prestige that historical legend has conferred upon them since 1789. The Guards joined the Revolution because of conflict between the rank-and-file troops and their brutal superiors, exacerbated by popular pressure and by a few mutinous solders and noncomissioned officers. In

Ménétra's eyes they remained a bunch of fine talkers, braggarts, and wom-anizers. Force was still on their side. One had to be suspicious of them as of all authority.

Therein lies the key to the political morality of the companion as he lives through the final years of the Ancien Régime: suspicion and independence, conformism and fatalism are its most prominent features. Ménétra rejects the discipline of the military just as he rejected that of the guild wardens. He protests against the advantages bestowed by privilege, birth, and wealth: "I am not of the stature of the great, nor am I of the slightest, I am a kind man, I am not at all to be feared."[16] He is also a rude Rousseauist, who admires Jean-Jacques as an affable fellow, a victim of prejudice and false friends, and a man of probity and knowledge. Yet he is capable of remain-ing skeptical about Rousseau's affectation of toilsome poverty ("He amused himself copying music") or about the rather too ostentatious disgust with which the *philosophe* refuses a gift and an invitation to dinner ("I could not keep from smiling").

In other words, Ménétra, unable to change the world or to get rid of the army or of "Madame la police," attempts to come to terms with it in such a way as to protect his own liberty, his freely chosen relationships; no man's fool, he enjoys the autonomy of mediocrity. As he puts it on several occa-sions, "I never liked to be hindered in any way, much less to lose my freedom." He continues: "Seeing that they wished to compliment me I made my escape . . . being little disposed by nature to accept congratula-tions and even less to respond to them." For the same reason he refuses to wear livery, despite the material advantages that the servant's position offered and even though he was perfectly capable of defending that posi-tion against its detractors. For, as he says, misfortune had placed him in the same class as valets and servant girls, and anyone might commit the kinds of crimes so often laid at their door: "They are human, don't forget."[17]

Similarly, the settled master, like the companion of earlier years, exhibits proper conformist attitudes: he takes part in a *Te Deum*, accepts the deci-sions of the magistrate, invokes the supreme authority of the king, views the inauguration of the statue of Louis XV, attends the fireworks display held to celebrate the marriage of the future Louis XVI, and celebrates in doggerel (which he nevertheless has framed under glass) the young king, the queen, and the dauphin.[18] He submits to the authorities by dint of his own skepticism and the power of the law, but he never takes their side.

The theme of the three Harlequins, developed in the *Journal* and in subse-quent writings,[19] expresses in metaphoric terms his innate politics, his

belief that equality, man's natural condition, has been effaced by histor-
ically imposed hierarchies. Harlequin—symbol of freedom in popular culture, embodiment of the crude physicality that polite society found so
offensive, poet of muscle and personification of an imagination that is at
once trivial and brilliant—Harlequin becomes a manipulator of men. The
first Harlequin, the executioner, carries out, in the place de Grève or the
cellars of the Châtelet, the decrees of justice—and criminality is a fate that
can easily befall life's losers as well as its genuine criminals. The second
Harlequin, the archbishop in his cathedral, symbolizes the harsh power of
religion and its cleverness in duping the populace by word and deed. It is
of small importance in this connection that Christophe de Beaumont, the
pious adversary of the *philosophes* and an upright man of faith, was not
guilty of the turpitude of which Ménétra accuses him on the basis of various
tales. Finally, the third Harlequin, Carlin, shows on the stage at the fair
how the people could be amused.

Ménétra's three Harlequins may well hark back to the origins of the dia-
bolic myth of Harlequin, king of thieves and seducers, black and supple,
dupe and deceiver, who slinks his way through the social pantomime. The
three Harlequins surely embody the mistrust mingled with genuine admiration with which the ordinary man, with all his weakness, views authority
and religion. They also justify the mixture of conformism and independence that is Ménétra's personal hallmark: to deceive the *commissaire* but
above all to be just in one's own dealings, to abide by the rules governing
the behavior of the dispossessed, to reconcile reason and reputation, to mete
out quick justice with one's fists, to amplify rumor and aid deserving fugi-
tives. But such opportunities are rare, and for the rest a man must live
according to the times; he must wait for the storm to pass and keep repeating to himself that "against force there is no resistance."

Armed with such principles and worried about his fortune, Ménétra
"enjoyed himself and watched the time pass" in the calm of familiar surroundings and despite occasional famliy problems. The Revolution bursts
into his *Journal* as it must have burst into his life, like a thunderclap in a
clear sky. From that moment everything changes. His writing, which was
in any case not always coherent, loses still more of its logic: the first—
person account proceeds from the point of view of one family to that of the
militant revolutionary and from there to general musings upon the years of
revolution, only to fall back into an apparently illogical diatribe against
rather mysterious adversaries. Ménétra did not conceive the Revolution;
he experienced it in his own way, and all we can do is attempt to clear up
some of the major points in his account.

Of one thing there can be no doubt: Ménétra is a patriot. He joined the Revolution if not at once then at least fairly soon after it began ("People ran to arms"), though he gives no direct account of his participation.[21] The *Journal* immediately takes a Manichaean and simplistic attitude. The vocabulary he uses—full of words like Nation, Fatherland, the French people, Equality, Liberty—is that of revolutionary petitions and the revolutionary press. His discourse divides people into two groups: on one side are those who are working to secure the happiness of the French people, the "fathers of their country," meaning, presumably, deputies and citizens supporting the Revolution, and on the other side their adversaries—Parlement, the Clergy, the Nobility ("the emigrants [sic] sold out France!"), and dishonest ministers.

In the list of the *Most Prominent and Stormiest Days of the Revolution*, he gives a good account of his political evolution, without ever mentioning his role. Of 14 July 1789 he says: "This day was supposed to lead us to liberty and give us laws worthy of a great nation." On 6 October 1789, the day the royal family returns to Paris, he sees "the love of the French for their sovereign." On 10 August 1792: "Since the French people wished to regain its rights, if the court had won out, the people would have been decimated and would have succumbed forever to the harshest slavery." On 8 Vendémiaire in the year I: "The Republic was proclaimed, all good citizens looked forward to peace and plenty."[22]

There is nothing surprising about Ménétra's political itinerary. Like much of the Parisian petite bourgeoisie and *le peuple* as a whole, he made the switch from loyal royalist to republican without difficulty. If we take him at his word, it was by enlisting in the National Guard, which was organized in July of 1789, that he worked actively for political change. On 10 August 1792 we find him at the Tuileries with his battalion and comrades from his section, leading them into battle.[23] He claims to have been elected lieutenant for a time and later, when the National Guard was reorganized after Thermidor, to have been made a noncommissioned officer, possibly a corporal. Finally, he says that he was a member of the committee of discipline,[24] which, though not impossible, cannot be verified, since the Paris National Guard archives have disappeared.[25] His story rings true: Ménétra could easily have paid the *capitation* of six livres to become an active citizen and the four louis (eighty livres) necessary for equipment. What is more, this was a perfect opportunity for him to reconcile his secret attraction to weaponry and his love of violence with his more sublime love of liberty: although the national guard initially excluded the poor from its ranks, it functioned as a democratic institution.[26]

If these surmises are correct, then from 1789 to 1795 Ménétra did his duty, leading patrols and supervising the guard at various sites entrusted to his battalion, such as the corn market and the Duplessis house of detention.[27] He also took part, he tells us, in all the major confrontations: on 2 September 1792 he goes to the Abbey to save Judge Duperron from massacre.[28] On 31 May 1793 he supports the Montagnard Convention.[29] On 9 Thermidor, as second in command of his company, he is responsible for protecting the committee of general security and helps persuade his section to join the Assembly against the Commune and Robespierre.[30] On 1 Prairial (20 May 1795) he is part of the armed force that protects the Convention against the rebellious faubourgs.[31] In Germinal he guards the Duplessis house of detention, where the committees feared that unrest was being fomented by imprisoned sans-culottes.[32] Finally, on 13 Vendémiaire in the Year IV (5 October 1795), he is mobilized, with no enthusiasm on his part, to march against the Convention ("they forced me," as he puts it) and on the quai de Voltaire is peppered with grapeshot by artillerymen from Verdière when, after the bombardment of Saint-Roch, Danican, Lacretelle, and insurgent sections manipulated by royalists mount a fresh assault.[33]

First and foremost, Ménétra was a citizen-soldier, a defender of the legality of the Assembly and supporter of the principle of government by elected representatives. In his eyes the Republic was beautiful when "she assumed an imposing air that made the despots tremble." In such moments "the people showed itself to be great."[34]

Another point about which there can be no doubt is that Ménétra was a sans-culotte and sectional militant. He assures us that after the Tenth of August he attended the assemblies in which the active and passive citizens of the section Mauconseil (renamed Bonconseil in 1793) met and deliberated. He was also named several times to important posts.[35] Of the 13,000 residents of the section, 1,700 were active citizens and 4,000 passive. Socially, the section comprised large numbers of workers and artisans; authority was often delegated to shopkeepers and simple craftsmen. The section's meeting hall, the church known as Saint-Jacques-de-l'Hôpital, held a crowd of 900 on 10 Ventôse in the Year II, when the action of the sections was at a peak, and 300 for the election of *commissaires de police*.[36] During the Years II and III, the Bonconseil was typical of other central Paris sections whose history and climate have been reconstructed by Soboul, Gendron, and Tönneson. By studying what happened to the section as a whole we can understand what happened to Ménétra as an individual. His course was erratic, jolted this way and that by the assembly's sudden changes of position, by the clash of different factions, and by the force of individual leaders who emerged from obscurity.

Unfortunately the assembly minutes have disappeared, and such scattered sources as are available—copies of affidavits, printed petitions to the Assembly, police files, committee papers—are insufficient to provide detailed confirmation of Ménétra's account.[37] Yet the sources do illuminate what he has to say and help us to understand its significance. It will be useful to divide the period into three parts. From 1792 until the spring of 1793, Ménétra's section was among the most active in the sans-culotte movement. It helped to organize the Tenth of August and demanded that the king be deposed. Ménétra claims to have signed the address to the Assembly, which petitioned against the Girondins, eliminated the moderates, and gave power to the Montagnards. By June 1793 the purge of adversaries and the disarmament of those suspected of disloyalty were complete.[38]

From the summer of 1793 until Thermidor, the section supported Robespierre and was moderately "terrorist." There were violent clashes, however, between the most extreme sans-culottes, the so-called *hommes à 40 sols* who received an indemnity for attending meetings, and the *citoyens honnêtes*. Petitions by the latter faction in the Year III brought back violent conflict, encouraged by the terrorist faction, which divided the citizenry into two hostile classes.[39] Yet the section did not support the Enragés,[40] even though in the election of 23 Ventôse in the Year II it relieved of his command in the National Guard one Captain Léonard, Ménétra's friend and neighbor, who was deemed too moderate.[41]

The members of the Bonconseil section were concerned both to defend their democratic institutions (with protests against the dissolution of the popular societies[42]) and to remain loyal to the Mountain (as they showed with their letter of congratulations on the founding of the cult of the Supreme Being).[43] It was at the beginning of Messidor that moderate sentiment hostile to the revolutionary government begn to reemerge, sentiment strong enough, it seems, to have caused the section to take a wait-and-see attitude on the Ninth of Thermidor.[44] Bonconseil, with its revolutionary committee and general assembly disconcerted by the division between the Convention and the committees, caught off guard by the resurgence of opposition, and tired of purges and the Terror, allowed Robespierre and the insurgent Commune to fall.

After the fall of the Mountain, Bonconseil was one of the sections of

Paris in which reactionaries and royalists, moderate champions of the Convention, and Jacobins clashed with one another.[45] During the Year III anti-terrorist measures, a purge of sectional institutions, and disarmament of notorious Robespierrists were all carried out. There were memorable battles between patriots and returnees of every stripe: federalists, clandestine royalists, Brissotins (or *foutriquets aux culottes serrées,* as one untranslatable slur had it). Young *muscadins* [literally, dandies, a word first applied to the royalists in 1793—trans.] squared off with popular militants. The section did not veer toward reaction but remained as loyal to the assembly in Germinal as it had been in Prairial. Gradually, however, the former Jacobins, including Ménétra's friend Bayard, were forced out and in some cases even arrested. In Vendémiaire the fighters of Bonconseil gave half-hearted support to the *jeunesse dorée* and the Royalists, who were backed by the bourgeois sections in the east and northeast. Eventually they were disarmed, and Ménétra along with them. Thus ended the adventure of the sections.

Our task now is to locate Ménétra more precisely against this general background and to examine his conduct for signs of his political beliefs. In this there are three main difficulties. First of all, his account was written while the sans-culotte movement was on the wane. It was probably begun during the reactionary period 1794-95 and later completed and reworked along with the author's "Writings on the Revolution," no doubt to exonerate himself of all guilt. The *Journal* and its companion papers are a plea against accusations that loom in the background but never emerge. Ménétra is rather discreetly attacking a fleeing target. Second, his thinking is distorted by still deeper feelings, namely, his terror of the Terror. Ménétra spent the Year II in a blue funk. He was one of those petits bourgeois of whom Karl Marx did not shrink from writing that they "shit in their pants." After Robespierre's downfall Ménétra, fearing the vengeance of the reactionaries, was forced to justify his recent behavior, possibly in the general assembly where he was attacked, possibly to himself alone.

And there is yet a third problem, which derives directly from the first two: his style is that of the *muscadins* and enemies of the Revolution and thus completely masks his target. Ménétra speaks of the Montagnards in exactly the same terms as the royalist clique that was then seeking, with the aid of bludgeons, to impose its authority on a section whose militant fervor was waning more and more with each passing day. He sees nothing but cannibals, bloodsuckers, man-eaters, and ogres on the one side, and virtuous, banished, betrayed, and murdered representatives of the people on the other. These are the same images that were being used by the enemies of the government of Public Safety to justify the reaction, at a time when militants found themselves threatened by "new and unknown faces."[46]

It is difficult to penetrate behind this style and to separate what is profound disillusionment from what appears to be the product of a persecution complex.[47] Some of his statements seem to have been made out of desperation to conceal his Jacobin past. To mention only the most important: although he signed the petition to depose the king, was found innocent of moderatism in 1793, and served as civil administrator for several months, he vehemently protests that he was never a member of the Revolutionary Committee, which suggests that someone had at least proposed that he become a member. He was a candidate for the Commune of Paris in the 1793 elections. We find him in "the core group (*noyau*) of citizens for acceptance into the Popular Society." This can only refer to a group of militants assigned to purge the membership of the sectional societies after 9 September 1793. He states that he was among those who forced "the authorities of the section to account" for their actions, so that he was still a partisan of the purges in the spring of 1794, when the Committees reasserted their control over the sections, now cleansed of "blood-suckers," Hébertistes, and Enragés. Later he is accused of having supported the pro-Jacobin petition of Dijon. If he defended the Mountain, he fervently hopes that no one will remember: "In those times of Terror I was careful not to accept any posts." Thus his patriotism, he would have his readers believe, was merely conformism and his past attitude merely an error, the product of a plot. But who was accusing him?

Consider the men he denounces. Isidore Langlois, a man of letters who in 1795 was not yet twenty-five, a hungry student who had been a partisan of moderation in May of 1793, who had been arrested shortly thereafter, and who was saved by Thermidor: he would become one of the most talented journalists of the counter-revolution, one of the instigators of Vendémiaire.[48] Charles-Jérôme Valois, a fan maker in the rue Pavée, a neighbor, former volunteer, and lieutenant in the third Battalion of the Eastern Pyrenees: he was a spy for the Committee of General Security prior to Thermidor, hence an adversary of the Jacobins, who backed the Committee of Public Safety. He became one of the leaders of the reaction in Bonconseil.[49] Nardin, an employee of the national estates: another neighbor, an assistant to the justice of the peace and a protagonist in the agitation of the moderates that disrupted the Bonconseil assemblies in the

Year III.[50] As for the last name in Ménétra's list, the traitor Duplessy, a wigmaker, nothing is known except that he lived in the same street as Ménétra and was also one of those pushing for Vendémiaire.[51] In other words, Ménétra's enemies are the enemies of the former terrorists and even of the moderate Jacobins.

On the other hand, his friends, with the exception of the sans-culotte Poirier whom he attacks for reasons that remain obscure, all numbered among the victims of the Revolutionary Tribunal, such as Barbet,[52] Saint Cristau,[53] and Rigolet d'Ogny,[54] or among the moderates in September 1792, such as Bayard,[55] who would become a *commissaire de police,* or, again, among the moderate sectional authorities, such as Léonard,[56] Beauchamps, the justice of the peace,[57] Dumeige, Delénoncourt, a former bailiff and captain of the National Guard,[58] and Marié, who lived in the rue du Petit-Lion and was a member of the committee of surveillance, arrested on 7 Thermidor by order of the committee of general security. Let me also mention, to conclude this list, the unfortunate Gentelle,[59] who was elected to the Commune instead of Ménétra and was executed after Robespierre and his supporters. Notice two things about this list: all of Ménétra's friends were committed Jacobins, some more moderate than others, and all lived, as did the men on his list of enemies, within a hundred meters of our author. Ménétra's politics had to do with the settling of local scores stemming from opposition on the vital issues of the day.

Ménétra, then, was doubtless a Jacobin[60] by dint of his social origins and longstanding libertarian beliefs. He refused to countenance two things: the disloyalty of the turncoat—he will not forgive Valois and Langlois for their undeniable treason—and the political violence that destroys the harmony and transparency of personal relations. If his account of the Terror emphasizes fear and denunciation above all, it reflects the internal breakdown of the sans-culotte movement and shows how heavily the shadow of the guillotine weighed on everyone. His writing is full of nostalgia for the exalting time when the Revolution captured the imagination of Europe and triumphed over the "enemies of Liberty." He is an authentic republican, disillusioned by the excesses of the great Terror of Prairial, as devoted as he can be to the Assemblies which for him embody representative government, and eager to expunge the bad memory of that day when the reactionaries tried to "expatriate the good men," that is, the true patriots. His political consciousness separates him from the extremists who for a time expressed the demands of the masses as well as from the bourgeois who had no difficulty living with factonal squabbling and who changed camps as easily as they changed clothes. He was naîve: "I have seen the Revolution close up, but for a sensitive man it was a terrible lesson."[61] In his old age he applauds Bonaparte,[62] the republican general, just as he earlier championed military patriotism. His son is fighting on France's frontiers where the real problems lie and where it is possible to distinguish between the good citizen and the party politician.[63] When the Ninth of Thermidor put an end to the Terror, Ménétra was pleased, but when he saw that squabbling and corruption continued, he expressed, in his account of an alleged plot against himself, the disillusionment of a class that was neither entirely bourgeois nor entirely proletarian.

To the ongoing debates and controversies over the true meaning of the democratic phase of the Revolution Ménétra offers the voice of the disillusioned militant, of a man incapable of understanding the political purposes of the Terror and uncertain of his ability to make the final sacrifice. Yet even as he reveals the psychological trauma inflicted by the Terror, Ménétra exemplifies the loyalty, not of the profiteer, but of the man faithful to the principles of liberty, equality, and patriotism. Perhaps it also takes dreamers of this kinds to make a revolution.

[6]

Religion and Personality

During the Revolution Ménétra settled an old score with the priests, "those immoral men who made a second authority by means of all those chimeras invented by lies and sustained by ignorance with the aid of fanaticism and superstition." The ambition, hypocrisy, and greed of the clergy became for him the keys to understanding the revolution and the difficulties of the Republic. It would accordingly be easy to blame his harsh judgment of religion on the wave of de-Christianization that swept Paris and all of France in the Year II.[1] On this view, Ménétra was presumably a militant in the struggle against religion, and the *Journal* a retrospective interpretation of his own, and France's, history, rewritten in the light of subsequent upheavals. But then it must seem very surprising indeed that in the pages devoted to the Revolution (except for the few lines of introduction which shed invaluable light on its causes) there is absolutely no discussion of the anti-religious positions taken by the Bonconseil section or of the sacrilegious acts of the sans-culottes, nor is there any mention of the deconsecration of churches or of the staging of provocative festivals by the revolutionary authorities.[2]

On the contrary, the *Ecrits*, which complement the *Journal*, are for Ménétra an occasion to reflect on "natural Religion,"[3] on *théofilanthropie* [sic],[4] on the return of the priests, and on Bonaparte's religious policy: "O Bonaparte, you see that the French are mere children. You have plumbed the depths of their beliefs and feelings. They are crazy about chimeras and *quirielles* [probably for Kyrie] and come what may love to go to chapel."[5]

Far from typifying sans-culotte anti-religiosity, Ménétra should be seen, I think, as a man who gradually turned away from the official Catholicism of his day and who saw his lifelong preoccupations finally taken up by the Montagnard Convention and the Directory; then, when the Roman Catholic priests returned around 1800, he discovered yet another reason for disillusionment. The *Journal* shows us how it was possible for a man of the people to abandon the dominant religion and reflect in his own way upon man's fate. It is no paradox to study the religiosity of this *bon vivant* fond of wine, women, and song and devoted after his own fashion to the cult of the body. For by so doing we can understand how, as the working population drifted slowly away from the Church, carried as it were by social and economic currents, it was possible for at least one man to develop, for all his contradictions, into a free thinker whose rationalism is in many respects different from our own. In other words, we witness another religious culture coming into being.

The difficulty of the writing has to do with the fact that Ménétra worked out his ideas with the help of sources that he never cites. Statements that he makes spontaneously in the *Journal* and with greater deliberation in some of the *Ecrits* (*Sur l'Etre suprême*,[6] *Sur Rousseau*,[7] and especially in the twenty or so pages that he devotes to his *Recherches sur la vérité*,[8] 1766–1776) reveal the substance of a more erudite and very ancient critique of religion. Hence we cannot do as Carlo Ginzburg has done in the case of Menocchio, the sixteenth-century Friulian miller, and study how information flowed from high culture to low, how influences and texts were distorted as they were taken up by oral tradition and recast in the writings of self-taught men of letters in pre-industrial towns.[9] No cultural act of any social class is ever completely isolated and autonomous. The *Journal* does at least permit us to see how a working philosophy was constructed from observations of ordinary religious behavior: Ménétra ponders the treatment of heterodoxy, derives from his observations an indictment of intolerance and fanaticism, and finally attempts to establish a basis for his own religious and moral principles.

On one level, Ménétra's *Journal* shows us how the similarity between popular superstitions and prejudices and the rites and mysteries of the Church could lead to anticlericalism. Ménétra's choice is deliberate and reasoned, a product of doubt born of a situation in which "the ordinary religious person is a believer without always knowing what he believes; he lives in a world which is that of the Church and which he is incapable of leaving to go live somewhere else."[10] But Ménétra's attitude is deeper than that; he does not merely refuse to bow before the hierarchy or thumb his nose, as many of the lower classes did, at the catechism and the priests.[11] He challenges the doctrine and the institution but continues to feel the need to believe.

Numerous features of Ménétra's writing illustrate the power that re ligion held over him in everyday life and the difficulty that he encountered in attempting to shed its trappings. In part this difficulty was surely not of his own choosing, since one of his reasons for choosing to write autobiography was his fervent wish to establish himself as a man born free of prejudice, rational, and anticlerical—as if the sacralization of individuality required a desacralization of religion, a sharp break with traditional teaching that one finds nowhere else in his thinking. He grew up in the shadow of the Saint-Germain cloister. As an altar boy he became familiar with church ceremonies, regularly heard mass, and studied his catechism assiduously if rather impatiently. This early steeping in religion explains many things: for example, his facility with biblical allusions, as when he explains the windows of the Auch cathedral or hurls an ironic gibe, "be fruitful and multiply," at a copulating couple or, again, after the earthquake in Bordeaux, when images of the Last Judgment come naturally to his mind. Perhaps even more it explains his manner of argument and discussion, borrowed from the Paris "priesties" (*prêtraille*) among whom he spent his early years. At age twenty-seven, when he needs to confess on the eve of his marriage, Ménétra seeks out a man who had been his priest in childhood and resumes what must have been a long-standing argument.

The omnipresence of religion in his childhood was a part of the prevailing climate. The Catholic counter-Reformation was then at its peak. Paris had some fifty parishes, collegiate churches, and convents, and innumerable chapels: in 1789 there were more than a hundred places of worship in the city, structuring the sacred space of the capital and affording Parisians the comfort of religious ceremony and charity.[12] This concentration of religiosity surely lent itself to conformism as well as deviance, for collective piety thrived on institutionalized and supervised ritual as much as it did on specific attitudes transmitted by way of the family and class milieu—the forces of "group conformity and oral tradition" were both at work.[13] As a child Ménétra was imbued with legends current among devout women, to which he was introduced by his grandmother and his aunts. He knew all the sign language of Saint-Médard and was already aware of the irrationality of "miraculous miracles": he recounts in detail the affair of the Virgin of the faubourg Saint-Antoine.

The suspiciousness of the Paris clergy and of enlightened reformers toward popular religiosity, whose organic forms of expression were the object of repression, probably contributed to the mass disaffection with religion[14] that lies at the root of Ménétra's anticlericalism. Saint-Germain-l'Auxerrois was an anti-Jansenist parish, and its curates, Labrue

(1687–1747) and Rausnay, were men guided by the strict and efficient orthodoxy of such pastorals as the *Règlements des Compagnies de Charité* (1737) and the *Offices propres à l'Eglise de Saint-Germain-l'Auxerrois* of 1745 and 1747.[15] In a sense, Ménétra's religious education was acquired on a battlefield, and the heat of the battle may have disturbed him and raised many questions in his mind. Around him swirled the fragrant odor of the candles offered to the Virgin in the rue aux Ours, the sounds of mumbled psalms, now melodious, now shrill, the tumult of theological argument, and preachers' threats of hellfire and damnation. None of this was lost on him, and none of it forgotten. The companion and, later, the bourgeois would bear the imprint of this early education throughout his life.

Many signs indicate how deeply religion was instilled in the young man. His actions, however, are indecisive rather than assured. The mature man thinks back upon his first communion, which in those days was taken at age fifteen or sixteen. The companion occasionally goes to mass, hears a *Te Deum,* or distributes a blessed loaf of bread. In prison at the Châtelet he falls on his knees during mass in the chapel. Two or three of his acts make clear that he had learned the lesson of faith: he quickly has baptized a child born on the road; he is shocked by the contemptible treatment of a dead man who is thrown in a corner and abandoned without vigil or prayer; he has his relatives buried in sanctified ground.

Such behavior was no different from anyone else's, even though one does suspect that an insidious transformation of religious practice was under way in the Paris of the Enlightenment. Indeed, sexual behavior was becoming more liberal in spite of religious taboos. Wills left by residents of the city indicate a waning of the faith: requests for masses decline, there is less and less interest shown in the fate of the body, and the very language is increasingly impoverished.[16] If pious customs continued to be respected, it was due partly to routine, partly to the work of the clergy. Ménétra's entire family goes to Notre-Dame to hear the first mass said by a cousin: "All my relatives watched him officiate with veneration." Ménétra's anticlericalism stemmed not from his family or work environment but from his own character. What is more, the religious climate that prevailed in Enlightenment Paris made available a whole range of possibilities for religious choice, and this very freedom encouraged a clear statement of acceptance or rejection of the Church.

There can be no doubt that Ménétra's intellectual capacities enabled him to ponder this choice on his own, aided by his inherited tradition and personal observations. Jansenism and its attendant controversies probably helped shape his character: individualism and a sense of the equality of individuals, not to say of democracy in religious practice, were not merely doctrinal issues but ways of seeing the world that may have made themselves felt in pastoral attitudes and forms of worship.[17] To write that such concepts as grace and reason made no sense to the poor is to show ignorance of the intellectual capacities of simple people.[18] Ménétra's breaks with tradition show, to the contrary, ample critical capacities, which are brought to bear in three important areas.

First, there is the cultural barrier represented by Latin, which, since he cannot cross it, he attacks: "believing according to the priesties that a man isn't worth much unless he knows that dead language." He is critical, too, of the theology of the day, always quicker to seek refuge in authority than to attempt to persuade: "I sometimes asked questions of the priests who always answered in monosyllables either to close my mouth or shut me up by saying these are mysteries." In Ménétra there is something of a disappointed vocation. Second, he makes much of hypocrisy, of the Church's deception, a theme that he develops in disquisitions on the clergy's greed, its liking for money, and its skill at duping people and then taking advantage of their ignorance.

All of these themes are evident in the anecdote about his stepmother's burial. This might be read as a good example of a priori anticlericalism seizing upon a fact of everyday religious life: economizing with partially used candles, saving money on lighting at the expense of the faithful. But the real problem lies deeper: the young man and his father are participants in a larger battle between the curate, Le Bris, and his church council concerning burial costs and other expenses that had to be borne by church members.[19] The archbishop of Paris, Msgr de Vintimille, and the *Parlement* actually intervened in the dispute, as we know from a memoir submitted to the *procureur général* of the Paris *Parlement* entitled "Sur les exactions qu'on fait à Saint-Germain-l'Auxerrois et sur les abus qui s'y commettent" (Concerning the exactions made at Saint-Germain-l'Auxerrois and the abuses committed there).[20]

Anyone could have found a great deal to criticize in this inequality in the face of burial: the price of ornament and decoration ranged from 150 livres to 5 livres and that of burial, including coffin, from 250 livres to 30 livres, not counting the labor of the gravediggers, bell-ringers, and lighting expenses, which ranged from 20 livres down to 35 sols. Families found the abuses committed by the parish clergy intolerable. Some priests went so far as to collect fees forbidden by episcopal regulations and charged for a full service and a sermon which was in fact a part of the service for the dead and therefore should have been free. They allowed the verger and beadle to charge small sums. They prescribed services sung by six cantors with musicians. They refused to allow partial ringing of the bells and encouraged generous use of candles, while using old wax and misrepresenting the number of candles actually burned. And last but not least, they refused to pray at charity funerals. In these charges leveled by the faithful there is ample evidence to confirm Ménétra's account and to suggest what the climate in the parish must have been like, with splendid and profitable services supporting a traditionalist and perfunctory clergy whose behavior outraged parishioners, somewhat tainted perhaps by Jansenism and eager to see greater simplicity and equality in the practices of the Church.

Finally, Ménétra's break with his upbringing involved yet a third domain: ill-conceived intervention by the parish clergy in affairs of the family and the heart. Ménétra in later life refused to allow priests to penetrate the secrets of his family and no longer permitted anyone to dictate his behavior. He would not tolerate such license by the confessor of the widow in Nîmes with whom he was living. The abbot's approach, his insinuating character, his constant presence (owing no doubt to his concern to maintain a newly converted Protestant in the path of righteousness), his reprimands, and what must have been his constant assaults on the lady's conscience finally persuade Ménétra that he has no alternative but to break off his engagement and leave the widow's house. From this episode we learn two things: Ménétra practiced his religion very little ("I did not go to church"), but he claimed to believe in a personal creed of his own ("I am as good a Christian as you") free of the prejudices that he found in others of his class. In his own way he joins those who, in this same period, saw a link between personal destiny and freedom of religion, who considered the self and the conscience to be primordial categories.[21]

Here he parted company with family and friends and moved toward more educated and literate company, close, in fact, to the *philosophes*. He sails under the banner of reason and, like any good Voltairian or enlightened priest such as J.-B. Thiers, he sniffs out popular prejudice and superstition. He finds the opportunity to assert his own freedom of thought and behavior, as distinct from the cultural backwardness of the people among whom he lives. Oddly enough, in this respect he is on the side of the official Church, and indeed he wins the approval of a good priest in Vendôme who comes close to agreeing with the Parisian companion that his parishioners are a bit backward. We are treated to some good stories of popular credulity: a princess who bathes in the blood of children to cure herself of an illness, divination, magical invocations, appearances of the devil, use of black magic on the job and talk of a pact with the devil, some tricks of white magic, black cats, ghosts in the forest or the dark of night, the threat of sudden death if one inserts a knife into a slit in the tomb of Nostradamus, infernal deities of construction and of the mountains, and "grimaces, contortions, speeches." To all of this Ménétra responds with common sense; the masculine soul, he believes, is superior to the credulous spirit of the weaker sex and of children. In short, he exhibits the argumentative rationalism typical of the Paris-educated mind. Thus popular superstitions are for him merely a sign of barbarism, a product of our ancestors' simplicity and ignorance.

Ménétra is a dyed-in-the-wool progressive who believes that mankind improves with age. Then, too, as an enlightened pupil of Parisian catechism he knows that one must distinguish between the miraculous and the supernatural and that there was, in our ancestors' religion, a primitive simplicity that has, alas, disappeared. He can easily identify those priests and "ambitious" schemers, those "men steeped in lies," those impostors whose behavior is based on the exploitation of credulity. Priests fool the people; they take advantage of a "host of absurd inventions" in order to foster belief in "the divinity of their words."[22] Ménétra assembles in his work all the themes of antireligious philosophical thought, which were given wide currency by popularizers and which had been available in manuscript in the libraries of erudite libertines since the seventeenth century. In some of his anticlerical diatribes we may be hearing echoes of the *Catéchisme du curé Meslier* or the *Nouveau système de religion chrétienne* of Pierre Cupé, curate of Bois, not to mention innnumerable collections of *Free Thoughts on Religion, New Thoughts on Free-Thinking, Discourses on Miracles,* and *Critical Examinations of Religion.*[23]

All this suggests that antireligious ideas were widely circulated in manuscript, printed, and oral form in the cultivated fringes of the *peuple* and petite bourgeoisie. If this is correct, Ménétra may have a great deal to tell us about a whole atheistic, materialistic, and antireligious tradition, as remarkable a phenomenon in its own way as the de-Christianizing violence that erupted in Paris and the provinces during the Terror. The personal, sometimes chaotic way in which Ménétra uses these themes makes it all but impossible to accurately assess the importance of any particular influence. Only in one case, in his discussion of the *Traité des trois im-*

posteurs (Treatise on the Three Impostors), which appears in his reflections "On Sects" in *Recherches sur la vérité,* do we find something more:
"Moses who was the first of the impostors who made up Judaism like
Jesus who came after him made Christianity and thirdly Mohammed who
made the religion of those who rule by fire and blood in the East."[24] Now,
we know from abundant evidence that the *Treatise on the Three Impostors*
was one of those antireligious tracts that circulated clandestinely. Editions
of the *Treatise* dated 1719 and 1721 exist, and several subsequent reprint-
ings prove that it was widely read in spite of being banned.[25]

The foregoing discussion leaves two questions unanswered: How could
Ménétra and others of his class gain access to this type of literature? And
must we conclude that his ideas were merely a poor reflection of a culture
whose true sources lay elsewhere? These same two questions were raised
earlier, in Ginzburg's study of Menocchio, the sixteenth-century miller. To
the first the only response is in the form of a hypothesis. To judge from
postmortem inventories, official booksellers' catalogues, and the contents
of the hawker's basket, the reading matter of people of Ménétra's class was
almost entirely devoid of such scandalous and heterodox works. The anticlericalism conveyed by colportage and almanacs did not go beyond limits
tolerable to the government, and it was combined with old traditions of
ribaldry and humor involving priests and their servants, chaplains and
nuns, monks and their donkey—hardly worse than any number of common
proverbs.

On the other hand, philosophical books and manuscripts traveled via
contraband routes. They passed from bold booksellers, who acquired them
in Switzerland or Holland, to liberated amateurs and knowledgeable and
professional readers: ecclesiastics, men of letters, and even erudite police
officials.[26] They were costly and assumed a familiarity with literature rare
among the poor and middle classes. It seems reasonable to assume that, for
an unlettered man of modest means, access to this clandestine literature,
which became increasingly widely available in printed form after 1780,
could have been gained in only two ways. Either he borrowed books and
manuscripts from a well-stocked library or he heard about them thanks to
a heterodox oral tradition based on samples, copies, and excerpts from
works intended for the educated minority.

As a companion, Ménétra wandered from castle to abbey, from out-of-
the-way presbytery to convent. The curate of Montigny-sur-Yonne lent
him books, as we have seen. He visited aristocratic manors, bourgeois
houses, and the *hôtels* of the Paris aristocracy, where books were known to

circulate from library to servants' hall. Domestic servants being excellent intermediaries,[27] he could have had many opportunities to read prohibited editions. He may have borrowed forbidden works from such friends as Du Tillet, major-domo of the Trudaine *hôtel*, Baron, the mysterious surgeon and fireworks master of the faubourg Saint-Antoine, and M. Henri, the executioner. He might, in this way, have made sketchy partial copies of some of these works, discussed them with others, exchanged them for similar works with people who shared his peculiar taste. There is no reason why there could not have been a popular channel for the diffusion of philosophical texts, including excerpts and summaries which probably circulated more freely than the works themselves. The assumption that this was the case seems preferable to the alternative hypothesis, that such ideas, whether right or wrong, simply descended from on high.

Nor do we have a better answer to the second question raised above, viz., whether Ménétra's ideas reflect, in some attenuated form, an alien culture. In any case, it is important to notice the originality of his approach rather than of his thought.[28] His unusual experience is significant because it derives from two voluntary acts. He attempts, first of all, to free himself from a traditional way of understanding the world. Second, he tries to organize the materials of his experience (and probably also of his reading) to create a personal world view. In this regard it is impossible to view the *Journal* in isolation from the *Ecrits*, for, taken together, they disclose the fragmentary character of Ménétra's thinking and throw new light on his actions, which constitute a "search for the truth" in the deeper sense of the term. His interest in the truth is developed primarily through his critique of churches and his fascination with heterodoxy.

Ménétra's critique of religion was guided by several images that shaped his view of the clergy and led him to question the mysteries of the faith. In the clergymen of his day Ménétra saw only the weaknesses. In his eyes all clerics were proud and cruel: the bishop of Agen traveled the highways, whisked along by his galloping team and not even pausing as he offered perfunctory blessings to the "fanatical peasants" he passed along the way. The vice-legate in Avignon committed "the greatest of atrocities." Our northerner discovered baroque piety and saw it as fanaticism. From an unfortunate incident in the courts he formed an unshakeable conviction: "The ministers of a gentle and benevolent God know nothing but ambition and vengeance."[29] In championing Christ without the Church, Ménétra shows that he has read the Gospels carefully. Priests are pleasure-seekers who think of nothing but gain. Ménétra denounces the avarice of monks—

the prior of Montdoubleau, the recollects of Lyons, the Bernardines of La Fontaine-de-Vaucluse[30]—as well as of the secular clergy: "to anyone who gives them plenty of that metal, even the greatest of criminals, the gates of Paradise are open, though they be closed forever to the poor and indigent."

Libertinage was rampant in the Roman Catholic Church: a priest of Saint-Germain-l'Auxerrois has himself whipped by a female penitent, another is caught in a brothel, a canon openly takes a prostitute for his concubine, and even Christophe de Beaumont is given a mistress by our author, even though that pious archbishop, unlike many other prelates, was perfectly capable of getting on without the aid of women.

The important point is that Ménétra, who shared the taste of his times for anecdotes about the sexual life of the clergy—tales that delighted the readers of police gazettes as well as government ministers and even the king, to say nothing of the *philosophes*—based his stories on undeniable facts.[31] In Paris between 1755 and 1764 a thousand ecclesiastics were arrested for debauchery. This state of affairs convinced Ménétra of two things: that all clerics are secret libertines and that their behavior was in conflict with the moral requirements of their estate. He does not insist upon the clergyman's "right to love," as others would do during the Revolution whenever clerical debauchery came to light; he simply wants the men of the Church to cease their hypocrisy. His sexual fantasies, which frequently center on convents that his imagination filled with voluptuous beauties, suggest that this happy bachelor may have regretted not being a father; matters of procreation were certainly on the minds of demographers of the time, who denounced male and female celibacy in the Church.

The companion's fantasies were also influenced by a legendary, perhaps popular, vision of the cloistered woman, according to which she had three main functions: to alleviate suffering (as do the sisters of St. Eligius at the hospital), to pass the time in otherworldly pursuits (as do the nuns of Tours and Agen), and finally, to impair the virility of the companions who serve them (consider the strange episode of the beverage served by the daughters of St. Thomas).

On the whole, however, hypocrisy remains the clergy's fundamental vice. All clerics live behind masks and exploit the fear and terror of ordinary men. The *grosses calottes* (wealthy priests) and even Ménétra's own newly ordained cousin live untroubled and unworried (and isn't this the dream of the poor?), but at the expense of alienated mankind, which they pretend to educate and guide toward salvation. In the eyes of one who has never been a fanatic, to live well is the priest's only ambition. Ménétra takes his place in the long line of those who, having rejected institutionalized religion as oppressive and unduly privileged, ended up rejecting the whole edifice of theology and the sacraments.

In this regard, Ménétra's argument with the curate of Montigny is unforgettable, for it draws on arguments that have been associated with anticlericalism ever since there has been a Church, arguments that Ménétra claims for his own and bolsters with rational criticism. The Church, he says, is intolerant when it should be tolerant. It insists that there is no salvation outside the Church and hence that idolators and heretics are doomed to perdition. The Church is venal: it trades in sacraments and indulgences. The Church victimizes the ignorant with its absurd rites and mysteries. Ménétra goes straight to the heart of the matter: there is, he says, no real presence or incarnation,[32] no Hell ("the great oven doesn't scare me"), no Purgatory, and hence no remission from sins to be granted by judges wearing cassocks rather than robes. A man earns his salvation by himself and not thanks to preposterous inventions and lies that fool only the simple-minded. Reason prevented Ménétra—as it did Voltaire—from believing that a person can chew and digest his God, and it also prevented him from believing that one religion is worth more or less than another. His critique of dogma and discipline[33] leads naturally to praise of tolerance, which is the fruit of experience. As for the embarrassed response of the Burgundian priest, "You are enlightened; the people, for the sake of governments, must always live in ignorance"—what response could it have elicited, other than scorn? "I answered him: So be it."

It is interesting to hear this speech spoken by a man of modest means, and still more interesting to see his enthusiasm for a controversy in which he pulls all the strings and his opponent is without ammunition. One senses that he feels greater admiration for the Dominican in the Comtat who refuses to grant absolution to his friend from Rennes, or for Father Basuel, who refuses to hear his confession and sends him back to the principal official without illusions or indulgence. Ménétra is not a man of tepid disposition. He proves this by his solicitude for Protestants and Jews—the intolerance of the Church strikes him nowhere so forcibly as while he is on the road, visiting areas where these alien religions are a visible presence.

He discovers the Protestants quite early, around 1759, one night in an inn near Moissac, where the good folk swallow his stories along with his remedies for fever. His next encounter with Protestantism occurs in Nîmes with Mme Fricaut, an experience which he finds most stimulating because of the many priests who hover around that recent convert to their faith. Then, in 1763, during his second stay in Nîmes, he encounters the Protestants again and becomes even more interested in their religion. Finally, as he makes his way through the Cévennes, he meets a different kind of Protestantism. From these close contacts the Parisian raised in the Catholic religion retains mixed memories, which tell us a great deal about his reactions and about the way in which experience shaped his polemics.

Note, however, that in his anti-dogmatic musings he attaches no special importance to the reformist current, though this does not mean that he has not read or thought about religious reform. What he notices first is that the Protestants of southern France, among whom he lives at a crucial point in time, are the victims of unequal treatment; in both rural villages and cities they are closely scrutinized by the Catholic clergy and the authorities. The *procureur fiscal* of Saint-Hippolyte-du-Fort would like nothing better than for the companion Ménétra to denounce the stiff-necked Calvinist heretics who have caused a disturbance in the inn; he refuses.

Keep the issues in mind: for the French Protestants, this was a time of retreat, of covert persecution, and of some tension between urban notables, who were content to dissemble their religious practice, and peasants attached to the "traditions of the desert," who gave refuge to pastors from Geneva sought by the *maréchausée*.[34] A decisive turning point had been reached in the final crisis of French Protestantism. Ménétra passed through Languedoc and the Cévennes while Pastor Rochette, executed in 1762, was preaching in the Montalbanais. After leaving Toulouse he stopped at Montpellier and was there when the Calas affair erupted in 1761. He crossed the Cévennes mountains at a time when Protestants of modest means and their outlawed pastors, worried about what the Genevans were up to and about the politics of Rabaud, were ready for a negotiated compromise. In short, the companion heard and saw a great deal, and he knew what he was talking about when he told the curate of Montigny that "they have made men suffer who worshipped the same God as we do, except for a few matters of opinion." He knew what Protestants had to endure after the Revocation of the Edict of Nantes.

In Nîmes he went beyond the role of mere curious observer. We find him frequenting the Protestant bourgeoisie. He discovers that the leading Protestants are kind people and that some of their daughters are less prudish than those of the Catholic bourgeoisie. With Protestants he has "pleasant conversations" that he prefers to the vicar's sermons, "which made my head ache." What is more, he attends clandestine services and is reproached by the widow's confessor for frequenting the Camisards. In short, allowing for a certain idealization in his portrait, which is skillfully contrived to bring out the contrast between the edifying religious sim-plicity of reformed worship and the exuberant fanaticism of Nîmois Ca-tholicism, it remains true that Ménétra felt comfortable among the Huguenots. He does business with them and ponders their fate. Their religion is proscribed and they are not allowed to hold office. Ménétra's initial sympathy develops into informed comprehension. His interest in Protestantism continues when he moves to Saint-Hippolyte: his employer is a good Protestant, and evenings, sitting around the fire, he is told of the persecutions that the Protestants have endured over the past fifty years and that are still fresh in everyone's mind. Both at work and at play his relations with members of the reformed religion are good.

But his feelings toward the Protestants turn sour when, in the course of living side by side with members of this oppressed religious minority, he discovers the fanaticism of the persecuted. One night Ménétra is greeted at an inn with shouts of "There goes a papist." Jeered at and heaped with insults intended not so much for himself as for Saints Augustine and Jerome, who to Ménétra's dismay are dismissed as "louts," he becomes involved in a brawl: "Those madmen wanted to kill me." When saved by gendarmes, he refuses to denounce the cabaret theologians who assaulted him. Two points are worth noticing: first, even a nonbeliever could fight to uphold the reputation of the Church Fathers, and second, there are decent people in both religions. Ménétra's real point is to demonstrate his willingness to treat people equitably regardless of their beliefs, something that the Catholic and secular authorities were scarcely willing to do. Ménétra later avenges himself for this insult: he lectures the companion from Saint-Hippolyte about tolerance and reminds him that the rule of the Devoir is never to offend any man's religion. He never converted, never joined either the confession of Augsburg or that of Geneva. His experience with Protestantism concludes with two remarks. He mentions that in 1764 he visited Geneva in order to see "my ancestors' native land," which is his only mention of these forebears.[35] And in 1781 he notes his belief that Rousseau is a "good Protestant" and worthy of sympathy as a victim of persecution.

His attraction to Judaism derives from a much briefer encounter. In the spring of 1761 he spends several months in the Comtat Venaissin. He arrives there an anti-Semite and leaves convinced that the Jews of the

Provençal ghettos are the victims of injustice. In Carpentras he plays tricks on the residents of the arena, and in the country he robs a Jew who is not wearing his yellow cap. Much to Ménétra's surprise, the victim of his crime is treated by the consuls as the guilty party: the Jew is punished for not wearing his cap and Ménétra goes free. Yet his curiosity about the Jewish communities here and in Avignon leads him to break the ban in order to visit beautiful Jewish girls on whom their families keep a sharp eye. In search of masterpieces he visits shops in the narrow ghetto streets. His eyewitness account gives us some idea of the atmosphere in the ghettos, of the confinement and crowding, and of the quarrelsome and thoroughly inequitable relations between Christians and Jews.[36]

Behind all of this lies the unequal legal status of the Jews, fairly stringently enforced by the papal authorities. Jews were daily humiliated, not only by being forced to wear external marks of their status but also by restrictions placed on their activities. Some, obliged to enter into frequent contact with Christians, were kept under close surveillance. None of this meant that compromise was impossible: we hear of Christian nurses for Jewish babies and of the economic development of the Jewish community.[37] The companion's harsh words for the lot of the wretched Jew, his outrage at the way Jews are persecuted, are not misplaced. We have evidence that such persecution as he describes did occur, particular during Holy Week and processions.[38] If there were no pogroms, there were "Jew hunts," and childish games sometimes ended in tragedy. In all this Ménétra finds yet another occasion to denounce the fanaticism and intolerance of the Catholics and hence to formulate his own notion of tolerance.

In the *Journal* Ménétra explains how he arrived at the idea that in practice all religions are equally valid, and in the *Ecrits* he attempts to reflect more deeply on this point and to justify his assertions. He imagines himself lecturing the fanatic Catholics of the Comtat and their priestly rulers about their behavior. According to Ménétra, the cruelty and contempt of Catholics toward Jews is unjustified for three reasons. First, Catholics contradict their own teachings by "smiting the Jews" with the symbol of a religion of redemption and love. Second, they forget that the Jews are "our brothers in the eyes of the Eternal." And third, in a confirmation of his religious training, Ménétra points to the biblical tradition and proclaims the unity of monotheism in support of his case: with its dogma and ceremony, Judaism is the father of Christianity. In his *Recherches de la vérité* he reaffirms his belief that Catholicism and Judaism share a common root, but only in order to brand both as "impostors."

Now he says that the Genesis story is a fable, a romance, an invention that priests of every religion foist upon the faithful. Moses, the "first lawgiver," is also the "first impostor," responsible for making God wicked, vindictive, and unjust. He is the first priest, for which Judaism deserves no special privilege.[39]

Ménétra's position with respect to Protestantism is different. In his later reflections he does not dwell on his experience of the Protestant faith, which he now sees primarily as offering further confirmation of his practical judgment: fanaticism can exist anywhere. Accused of being a "papist," Ménétra answers that "if I were I would be proud of it." There is no reason to denigrate any particular religion, for one is worth just as much, or as little, as another. Saint Jerome and Saint Augustine are the fathers of Calvin and Luther. The ritualism involved in the companions' tribunal over which Ménétra presides as first companion points up the importance of religious questions in the companion's world. Saint-Hippo-lyte, a Protestant, cannot be admitted to the Devoir. In this case Ménétra is willing to live with the glaring inequality, but through his good offices Saint-Hippolyte is accepted as a legitimate adjunct of the Devoir and is authorized to work in Lyons and to participate in the companions' festivals and open meetings. Given the Catholic ambiance, this amounted to nothing less than de facto toleration.

Ménétra's tolerance was a matter of practical necessity and coexisted with his condemnation of all revealed religions: all were based on fraud, all imposed their ridiculous practices and beliefs, and all were discredited by their fanaticism—"all religions are guilty of massacre."[40] Nevertheless, Ménétra feels the need to believe and to articulate a morality of his own. We can identify three stages in the maturation of his beliefs. In the *Journal* he is satisfied to make do with a rough and ready practical credo, based on a few simple principles. In the *Recherches sur la vérité* and the letter "To a friend who asked me what the Supreme Being was," he expresses his doubts and the state of his thinking on the matter. Finally, in "On sects" and "On *théophilanthropie*," written subsequent to the Revolution, he articulates his ultimate creed.

The religiosity of the *Journal* is striking amidst all the tomfoolery and mischief. The bachelor companion and even the settled shopkeeper of fifty lives by a morality of the moment, a sensual Epicureanism that thumbs its nose at the ordinary morality inculcated by religion and society. To have a good time, to get what every young man wants, to enjoy oneself as much as possible—these are the maxims by which Ménétra lives. As he puts it,

"Where there is inhibition there is no pleasure." Yet Ménétra sees himself as living according to certain rules, so that it is an error to see his behavior as libertine. These rules derive, first of all, from the solidarity of *compagnonnage,* with its balance of mutual help, social control, and individual liberty. They come also from proverbs, from the morality found in the literature of colportage and the simplistic verities of the almanacs: every bully meets his match, uneasy lies the sinner, do unto others as you would have them do unto you. The most important thing is to love one's parents and children, for, as the saying goes, like father, like son. A promise is a promise in business as well as friendship. Ménétra has his cousin the priest say, "For all our madness we never exceeded the bounds of honor," and he himself says, "I was incapable of any baseness." These statements set forth a wholly secular morality: "You do no harm to your neighbor, you are a friend to all men, that is the real point."

Ménétra's morality is sufficiently vague as to embrace any and all situations. It is justified by a fatalism connoted by belief in the signs of fate and in the intervention of benevolent Providence. This, as the reader will recall, is one of the keys to Ménétra's autobiography: like his childhood friends, our hero was exposed to wicked companions and to the temptations of crime. But no one can escape his destiny: the wicked are punished, the good protected. "If I have been what I am, it is the Eternal who has protected me." What happens is what is already written: Ménétra's beliefs are compounded of the popular notion that each individual has a fixed and determined fate coupled with vague reminiscences of Augustinian predestination. Ménétra's youth was spent partially in a Jansenist, partially in an orthodox milieu; he attended religious services. Moralism and fatalism combined to produce a simple credo, which he defends on three occasions: in the argument with the village curate, when his cousin the priest takes confession, and when Father Basuel refuses to hear his own confession. Religion is an individual affair: "Belief is your own business." One must worship God, for Providence is the source of all good: Ménétra is twice spared by lightning. And finally, one must respect one's neighbor. Such is the simple credo with which Ménétra chooses to end his *Journal.*

Yet this approach to religion deserves to be looked at more closely. We need to consider further the meaning of this popular deism, which is only marginally related to the philosophical critique of religion, here reworked and reconsidered to produce a personal view that is not so much a passive reflection of more learned men's ideas as an active assertion of Ménétra's own thinking. In *Sur l'Etre Suprême* and *Recherches sur la vérité* we see a

Ménétra who questions himself and solidifies his thinking, as well as a man who is not alone: his religious reflections are in fact a response "to a friend who questioned me."[41] The *Recherches* allude to discussions with other people. What is more, the encounter with Rousseau reminds our author of passionate discussions about "the existence of God" and "the beliefs of our ancestors."[42] Ménétra doubts the ability of theologians to explain the existence of God (explicitly mentioning the theologians of Leyden in yet another indication of Calvinist influence on his thinking). Their long words are not for him. After all these discussions he remains certain of one thing: if all religions are equally valid, then none should enjoy a position of privilege over any other. Only one thing is important: monotheism, *Credo in unum Deum.* He can take or leave the rest. What is more, no one can define divinity, which proves itself by creation: "I say that it is through this being that we exist and that everything on this immense globe exists; but to understand the supreme being, worship it and let them say what they will; no one can say more about such an obscure point; we must recognize and believe in an eternity; if you believe in it and you do good, your soul will exist forever; that is the real point."[43]

Ménétra's hesitation, repetition, and backtracking are an integral part of his quest for certitude: "I am seeking the truth and cannot find it; when I think of my fate and my creation I cast myself into a labyrinque [sic] of thoughts, which sometimes makes me think that existence is a dream and that at the end of my days [I shall find] happier ones; [at] other times I think that I was born as nothing and that I must end [as nothing] and that everything that the great men have written about creation and nature is pure invention and nothing more; when my imagination brings me to believe in another world I look about and ask myself if anyone has ever come back from it."[44] The effort to reach some final conclusion about his own fate and that of mankind does not conceal from Ménétra the serious-ness of his anguish. His thinking does not plumb the depths of some hidden layer of popular mythical belief; it works with the lessons of his reading. Here he rehearses the great hypotheses: solipsism, the nothingness of abso-lute materialism, the religions of salvation, the anthropology of the re-warded double. He chooses what suits him and constructs his own truth, his own vision of the world.

The companion, Epicurean yet righteous, and the petit bourgeois, skep-tical yet just, are justified by faith and works—a legacy that is difficult to throw off, even if one finds it easy to reject mysteries, dogma, and inter-mediaries. In the end, when all is said and done, we are left with the radical scouring that has turned the able pupil of the Council of Trent's catechism into an adept of individual religion and a deist. Ménétra's God is a combination of the Great Watchmaker, creator of the Universe, and the benevolent Supreme Being, who is present everywhere and not just in the temples. His religion is more than just morality, for it requires prayer and thanksgiving: "worship the eternal, invoke the Supreme Being."[45] These are necessary because man must "remember the sins to which he is inclined." Therein lies the true religion and the true faith, which alone can distinguish "good from evil without mystery." Accordingly, it is "when life comes to an end that our soul will enjoy the happiness that awaits it and our body will return to the bosom of the earth from which we have sprung, without engaging in a thousand disputes that at bottom amount to nothing, without afflicting us and tormenting us as our end approaches."[46]

By now it should be clear how Jacques-Louis Ménétra could have rejoiced in the downfall of the clergy at the time of the Revolution while standing aloof from the intolerant, de-Christianizing movement led by extremist sans-culottes agitators who had turned away from Christianity even before taking up arms against it.[47] For two principles continued to govern his behavior: to think and listen to reason and to respect the beliefs of others. A few remarks suggest that he was close to the constitutional clergy. One of his friends was Poupart, the former Oratorian, confessor of Louis XVI and curate of Saint-Eustache in 1789, who took the oath and brought his clergymen along with him, a man who enjoyed such prestige among the people of Paris that he was repeatedly elected to sit in the assemblies and was left untouched during the Terror.[48] Ménétra's choice of words suggests that he was more an observant witness than an active participant in the Mountain's efforts to establish republican sects and Churches of the Supreme Being. Even more, he seems to have identified with the *théophilanthropes*.[49] His deism coexisted easily with the theism of a Benoît Lamothe or a Valentin Haüy. Believing as he did in the need for reasoned religion, he was gratified by the moderate policy established in the temples of Paris during the Year V (1797). His moral sense was satisfied with the general precepts contained in the sages' code of ethics.[50] He may have identified with the "fathers of families"[51] who presided over the modern liturgies that were gradually instituted at Saint-Germain-l'Auxerrois, where the old vicar, Chassant, was able to reach a compromise with the constitutional clergy, and at Saint-Eustache, where the two religions coexisted.[52] In the Year VII Saint-Eustache was consecrated to Agriculture owing to the proximity of the grain market; Saint-Germain was consecrated to Gratitude owing to the proximity of the Louvre, the "national palace dedicated to the sciences and arts that have rescued the people from barbarism and therefore deserve its eternal gratitude."[53] Ménétra may have been pleased by the very ambiguity of *théophilanthropie,* which was both a religion of social harmony and an instrument of anti-Catholic sentiment. His reflection ends on a pessimistic note: "The priests are coming back, ready to prevent the continuation of natural religion."[54]

At the end of his autobiography the companion's image is still vivid. He remains loyal to the spirit of liberty that has all along been his guide and sees in Bonaparte the republican general who will save the fatherland and the religion of tolerance. This, we may believe, was as far as his religious and political experience carried him. Capable of hope but also of doubt, incapable of taking a broad political view yet equally incapable of renouncing the freedoms he regarded as essential, caught midway between the spontaneity of the populace and the learning of the lettered, he waited.

Epilogue

After spending several years with Jacques-Louis Ménétra, I still find it difficult to locate the central thread of his personality, as difficult as it is to locate eighteenth-century Paris, the city with which the companion lived in familiar intimacy, beneath the Paris of today. To follow Ménétra on his daily walks between Saint-Eustache and the Seine is today to encounter one scene of destruction after another. All that is left of the old Paris are a few names, a few alleyways that huddle in the shadows of Saint-Germain-l'Auxerrois.

Inside the church, which has remained unchanged for two centuries, safe from the extravagances of the surrounding civilization, it is perhaps easier to find our man than anywhere else: Ménétra preceded us here, as a small, argumentative choir boy in the 1740s and later, lurking behind the pillars, as a bold and shameless adolescent. In later years, as an established artisan and head of a family, he may have brought his wife and children here on one of those haphazard walks he liked so well.

Conjuring with ghosts is not orthodox historical methodology, yet it can help us to trace the outlines of a vibrant reality, a reality as vital as any of the reconstitutions that historical method superimposes upon the density of an actual life, by turns dazzling and obscure.

A more reliable way of coming to know Ménétra, perhaps, is to read the *Ecrits* and the *Journal* that first brought him to our attention. Yet no matter how well a life's major events are preserved in memory, a memoir can only contain so much, and actual remembrance inevitably becomes mixed up with dreams and fancies. Reading through these texts is both an enriching and a disturbing experience, for if we ask too many questions about the roles our author claims for himself, about the characters he chooses to interpret for our benefit, there is a danger that the man himself will elude our grasp. Facetious and mocking, he always claims the starring role and yet intends no deception in his attempts at self-revelation. His gift for seeing people and things, coupled with his zest for life, offers us a rich supply of intense and genuine sensations, a quiet Epicurean delight—the fruit of a keen sensibility. With his calm, self-assured refusal to bow to the imperious mediocrity of everyday life and, strongest of all, his fierce love of liberty, he lived out his days free of greed and innocent of the will to dominate.

His style, too, was strong stuff. How close to us this man of the eighteenth-century seems when he proclaims that every man has a right to happiness! How seductive he is as a storyteller, an adventuresome, gregarious, simple man eager to show us the strength of his desires and the pain of lingering regrets! His simple certitude is a guarantee of authenticity.

And that is not all. A truly fraternal soul, Ménétra hoped to write for both his time and his class: such a desire was by no means commonplace. He plunged into the adventure and challenge of writing with total personal commitment and complete fascination with his subject: himself. In this respect the career of this man of the people resembles that of Rousseau, whom he knew and who captivated him as man, author, and friend. To write, then, was simply to express what one life could be; it was, by dint of extraordinary effort, a way of making words the faithful if fleeting mirror of existence—a moment by moment account of life as it was lived.

Ménétra's abiding quality was surely his confidently reiterated desire to understand not only himself but other people and the world at large. For all its contradictions the aim of his undertaking was to seek the truth and the absolute. The central question that his work raises for us is one of justice in a world where people do not fall neatly into categories of good or evil and nothing is clear-cut.

Jacques-Louis Ménétra's deep conviction—as well as the imperious quality of his lonely attempt to capture his life in words—stands out clearly against the noisy political background, even as the chaos of history disrupts his life and the lives of his peers, and the severity of the revolutionary reckoning takes the dreamy idealist by surprise. Ménétra's easy gregariousness invites us to keep an open mind in interpreting people, events, and history. He convinces us, for he has the talent of the heart.

D. R.

Paris, 1977–1982

Notes to Introduction
and Commentary

Foreword

1. Alain Lottin, *Vie et mentalité d'un Lillois sous Louis XIV* (Lille, 1968); Nicolas Contat, *Anecdotes typographiques,* Giles Barber, ed. (Oxford, 1980); and Valentin Jamerey-Duval, *Mémoires,* Joan Marie Goulemot, ed. (Paris, 1981).

2. See Albert Soboul, *Les Sans-Culottes parisions dn l'an II* (Paris, 1962) 197–198.

Introduction

1. F. Ferrarotti, "Les biographies comme instrument analytique et interprétatif," *Cahiers internationaux de sociologie* (1980), pp. 227–48.

2. A. Lottin, *Vie et mentalité d'un Lillois sous Louis XIV* (Lille, 1968).

3. V. Jamerey-Duval, *Mémoires, enfance et éducation d'un paysan au XVIIIe siècle,* with an introduction by J. M. Goulemot (Paris, 1981).

4. R. Lecotte, *Essai bibliographique sur les compagnonnages* (Marseilles, 1960).

5. A. Perdiguier, *Mémoires d'un compagnon,* complete edition, with an introduction by A. Faure, (Paris, 1980), pp. 19–20.

6. D. Bertaux, *Histoire de vie ou récit de pratique? Méthodes de l'approche biographique en sociologie* (Paris-Lausanne, 1981).

7. P. Lejeune, *Je est un autre, l'autobiographie de la littérature aux médias* (Paris, 1980), especially "L'autobiographie de ceux qui n'écrivent pas," pp. 229–316.

8. G. May, *L'Autobiographie* (Paris, 1979), pp. 197–198

9. P. Lejeune, *Le Pacte autobiographique* (Paris, 1975), pp. 241–242.

10. For further light on this parallel, see Goulemot's introduction to Jamerey-Duval, *Mémoires,* pp. 82–85 and 96–105, and P. Lejeune, *L'Autobiographie en France* (Paris, 1971), pp. 63–66.

11. In the *Miscellaneous Writings,* probably recopied at a later date, the names are no longer in the margins.

12. The adventure with the mistress of the French guard is foreshadowed twenty pages before it is actually taken up.

13. Archives of Paris, copy of birth certificate, 13 July 1738; in II fol. 12 we read: "I left for Geneva eager to see where my ancestors had lived," suggesting that the family was native to Savoy.

14. Archives départementales (henceforth abbreviated AD) Maine et Loire, G. E., Les Ponts-de-Ce, Paroisse Saint-Aubin.

15. Archives municipales (henceforth abbreviated AM) Bordeaux, AD, Gironde, G. 1570

16. AM Montpellier, B. B. 1757–1759 and B. B. 1759–1761.

17. The hypothesis that there might have been a jubilee in 1761 is incorrect.

18. Archives nationales (henceforth abbreviated AN), Minutier central, XIX, 18

June 1765.

19. AD, Paris, copy of birth certificate, 9 May 1767.

20. E. Forster, *Le Dernier Séjour de Jean-Jacques Rousseau à Paris* (Paris, 1921), pp. 7–11, and AN, Minutier central, XIX, 1771.

21. AD, Paris, Fonds des faillites, D4 B6, carton 66, dossier 4298.

22. AD, Paris, copy of birth certificate, 25 vend. an XI. Also found was Ménétra's *carte de sureté,* in AN, F⁷ 4787, record of the *section* Mauconseil, 4th book, fol. 25. His name appears under the heading of justices of the peace in the *Almanach national* for the year III and under the heading of assessors for the years IV and V.

23. II fol. 39, *Mon humeur et ma façon de penser.*

24. Ferrarotti, "Les biographies," pp. 228–299.

25. Carlo Ginzburg, *Le Fromage et les vers* (Paris, 1980), pp. 14–21 [translated into English as *The Cheese and the Worms*—trans.]; R Chartier, "L'histoire au singulier," *Critiques* (1981), pp. 72–84.

26. P. Thompson, "Des récits de vie à l'analyse du changement social," *Cahiers Internationaux de Sociologie* (1980), pp 249–68.

27. Ginzburg, *Le Fromage,* pp. 35–38, and A Farge, *Le vol d'aliment a Paris au XVIIIe sièle* (Paris, 1974), pp. 118–9.

28. S. Kracauer, *Das Ornament der Masse* (1960).

29. R. Bastide, *Sociologie des maladies mentales* (Paris, 1965); E. de Dampierre,"Le sociologie et l'analyse des documents personnels," *Annales. Economies. Sociétés. Civilisations* (1959), pp. 442–54.

30. D. Roche, *Le peuple de paris, essai sur la culture populaire au XVIIIe siècle* (Paris, 1981).

1. Childhood, Marriage, Culture

1. For a good survey of an abundant literature, see A. Armengaud, *La Famille et l'enfant en France et en Angleterre du XVIe au XVIIIe siécle, aspect démographique* (Paris, 1975), and F. Lebrun, *La Vie conjugale sous l'Ancien Régime* (Paris, 1975).

2. J.-L. Flandrin, *Familles, parenté, maison, sexualité dans l'ancienne société* (Paris, 1976).

3. D. Roche, *Le Peuple,* pp. 30–35, and J. Kaplow, *Les Noms des Rois, les pauvres de Paris à la veille de la Révolution* (Paris, 1974).

4. G. Benrekassa, "Le Typique et le fabuleux, histoire et roman dans *La Vie de mon père,"* *Revue des Sciences Humaines* (1978), pp. 32–56.

5. J. Donzelot, *La Police des familles* (Paris, 1977), and P. Meyer, *L'Enfant et la raison d'Etat* (Paris, 1977).

6. E. Shorter, *Naissance de la famille moderne* (Paris, 1977).

7. P. Ariès, *L'Enfant et la vie familiale sous l'ancien régime* (Paris, 1960), and D. Hunt, "Parents and Children," *History* (New York, 1970).

8. Kaplow, *Les Noms,* pp. 140–161, and Roche, *Le Peuple,* pp. 85–89, 242–255.

9. M. Garden, *Lyon et les Lyonnais au XVIIIe siècle* (Paris, 1970), pp. 96–106.

10. Roche, *Le Peuple,* ch. 3: "Fortunes et infortunes populaires."

11. In a different context, P. Thomson, *The Edwardian: The Remaking of British Society* (London, 1975).

12. II fol. 34. The epitaph composed by Ménétra at the death of his Uncle Chénier reads: "Here lies a merchant/ selling trading and exchanging/ Had he found you on his hands he would have bartered you/ recognize in him Toussaint Chénier."

13. Since I am unable to reconstruct the family's genealogical tree, let me at least mention the addresses of the various uncles as indicated in the 1769 *Almanach du commerce.* "Uncle Marseau," that is, most likely, Louis François Marseau, Ménétra's godfather and witness to his marriage, lived in the rue Saint-Louis in the Ile of the same name. Uncle Pierre Claude Marseau lived in the rue de la Grande-Truanderie, possibly with Ménétra's grandmother; he is best known for his bankruptcy. And there were two other uncles, one living in the rue

Saint-Avoye and the other in the rue des Petits-Champs.

14. R. Chartier, D. Julia, and M.-M. Compère, *L'Education en France du XVIe au XVIIIe siècle* (Paris, 1976), pp. 45–85.

15. For an overview see Roche, *Le Peuple,* chp. 7: "Les Façons de lire."

16. B. Arsenal, Ms. 10579.2, vol. 4, fols. 109–110, *Le Parnasse Saint-Jacques,* in which Sébastien Mercier vividly describes the atmosphere associated with the various classes in Paris. Note that Mercier was born in the parish of Saint-Germain-l'Auxerrois in 1740.

17. Roche, *Le Peuple,* ch. 8: "Les Manières de vivre." M. de Certeau, *L'Invention du quotidien* (Paris, 1980), vol. 1: *Arts de faire.*

18. A. Farge, *Vivre dans la rue à Paris au XVIIIe siècle* (Paris, 1979), pp. 62–65.

19. Here I am following, with insufficient detail to be sure, the program of Marcel Mauss, *Sociologie et Anthropologie* (Paris, 1950), pp. 365–383.

20. In 1715 61 percent of men and 34 percent of women in the lower classes could sign their names. In 1789 the figures were 66 percent and 62 percent respectively. As for peasants recently rounded up by the police in 1785, the indices drop to 40 percent and 7 percent.

21. Note that Ménétra's wife cannot sign the marriage contract, yet she is perfectly at home with the account books.

22. AN, minutier central, xix. 28 June 1765; BN, F22960, 3 November 1753.

23. Note the following image, suggestive of some broader knowledge of novels: "An old castle . . . like the castles described in novels."

24. ii fol. 117, Letter or response to a brochure entitled "Eulalie," *Journal des Dames,* 1779 (which I have been unable to locate).

25. ii fol. 20, *Critique des Jurés,* and ii fol. 145, which allude to a literary and philosophical dispute in which Ménétra defends Rousseau.

26. P. Chaunu, *La Mort à Paris, XVI, XVII, et XVIIIe siècles* (Paris, 1978), pp.

166–196. I would stress death in the hospitals more than Pierre Chaunu does: nearly two-thirds of the deaths in Paris occurred outside the home. Most of these were newcomers to the city, but Ménétra's account proves that Parisians of long standing also died far from the families, though family members felt guilty about it and tried to make amends.

27. Ménétra knows something about art: framing and selecting prints are activities with which he is familiar.

28. ii fol. 33: Four epitaphs, the last of which gives a crude summary of the family's economic history: "My father drank up everything or gave it away / my first brother-in-law ate it all / my second brother-in-law kept it all / and me, I didn't inherit a thing and I don't give a damn." The first three all mention the father's enormous capacity for drink: "Here lies Jacques Ménétra / died while drinking / from here to heaven there are 1700 cabarets, and he won't skip a single one without regret."

29. Flandrin, *Familles.*

30. ii fol. 130: "I also reached the door and went away saying my *mea culpa.*" Cf. also ii fols. 38–40, *Ma façon de vivre et de penser:* "I love my children with affection" (translated literally).

31. Roche, *Le Peuple,* ch. 3: "Fortunes et infortunes populaires." Garden, *Lyon et les Lyonnais,* pp. 150–155. Here again conception seems inevitable: four children in forty years of marriage!

32. Flandrin, *Familles,* pp. 128–169.

2. Pleasures and Games

1. ii fol. 19.

2. M. Philibert, *L'Echelle des âges* (Paris, 1968).

3. Exciting and indispensable: J. Solé, *L'Amour en occident à l'époque moderne* (Paris, 1976), pp. 12–13.

4. M. Foucault, *Histoire de la sexualité,* vol. 1: *La Volonté du savoir* (Paris, 1976), pp. 18–22.

5. There is an outline of such a history in P. Burke, *Popular Culture in Early Modern*

Europe (London–New York, 1978), pp. 116–148.

6. Comparison may be made with the novelistic art as practiced by Diderot in Le Neveu de Rameau or Jacques le Fataliste; cf. E. Walter, Jacques le Fataliste (Paris, 1975), pp. 41–49.

7. Medieval examples may be found in J. Rossiaud, Histoire de la France urbaine, vol. 2 (Paris, 1980).

8. ii fols. 42–43, dedicatory letter dated 15 July 1775.

9. ii fol. 39: "My temperament and manner of thinking."

10. M. Bakhtin, L'Œuvre de François Rabelais et la culture populaire au Moyen-Age et sous la Renaissance (Paris, 1970); Ginzburg, Le Fromage et les vers, pp. 11–12.

11. M. Albert, Les Théâtres de foire, 1660–1789 (Paris, 1900).

12. D. Diderot, Le Neveu de Rameau (Paris, 1950), J. Fabre, introd., pp. lxii–xcv.

13. Roche, Le Peuple, ch. 7: "Ways of Life."

14. A. Farge and A. Zysberg, "Les Théâtres de la violence à Paris au XVIIIe siècle," Annales E.S.C. (1979), pp. 904–1,015.

15. M. Maffesoli and A. Pessin, La Violence fondatrice (Paris, 1978), pp. 19–20.

16. For the Giroux case, see AN, Y. inv. 450; AD, iii, 11 (sentence); Y. 10267 (trial). for the Gilbert and Duhamel case, see Y. 10269 (trial) and X2 A830 (appeal).

17. AN, AD, iii, 11.

18. A. Abbiateci et al., Crimes et criminalités en France au XVIIIe siècle (Paris, 1971).

19. See the fundamental work of N. Castan, Justice et répression en Languedoc à l'époque des Lumières (Paris, 1980), pp. 252–253.

20. E. J. Hobsbawm, Les Bandits (Paris, 1972).

21. N. Castan, Les Criminels de Languedoc (Toulouse, 1980), pp. 278–324.

22. There may be an allusion to sodomy as practiced in the cities in Ménétra's mention of the propositions of an aristocrat.

23. A. Daumard and F. Furet, Structures et relations sociales à Paris au XVIIIe siècle (Paris, 1961).

24. Kaplow, Les Noms, pp. 110–113.

25. M. Frey, "Les comportements concubins à Paris au sein des classes populaires," Aimer la France (Clermont-Ferrand, 1980), 2:565–578; Farge, Vivre dans la rue, pp. 108–109.

26. J. Chagniot, "La Criminalité militaire à Paris au XVIIIe siècle," Annales de Bretagne (1981), pp. 326–345: "Lettre de Sartine à Chaban aide-major", 24 October 1770.

27. ii fol. 160.

3. Work: Fraternal Pleasure and Economic Value

1. Kaplow, Les Noms, pp. 61–62; Roche, Le Peuple, ch. 2: "To Know the People."

2. E. Coornaert, Les Corporations en France avant 1789 (Paris, 1968), and Les Compagnonnages en France du Moyen Age à nos jours (Paris, 1966).

3. W. E. Sewell, Work and Revolution in France: The Language of Labor from the Old Regime to 1848 (Cambridge, Mass., 1981).

4. R. de Lespinasse, Les Métiers et corporations de la ville de Paris (Paris, 1879–1897), 4:745–754, "Statutes and regulations."

5. A. Franklin, Dictionnaire historique des arts, métiers et professions exercés dans Paris depuis le XVIIIe siècle (Paris, 1906), pp. 291–296.

6. J. Savary des Bruslons, Dictionnaire universel de commerce (Geneva, 1744), vol. 4. The difference is explained by the fact that the Almanac of Commerce lists only shops and not licensed masters. It would be surprising if the number of glaziers in Paris declined between 1730 and 1770, given the feverish construction during the period.

7. For this one had to file one's apprenticeship license (cost: 30 livres), be assigned a masterpiece (cost in fees paid to masters: 20-odd livres), defend the masterpiece (cost of the examination: 64

livres), and finally, purchase the master's certificate for 1,000 livres and pay the required tax of 40 livres. Thus a total of nearly 1,200 livres had to be spent.

8. S. Kaplan, "Réflexions sur la police du monde de travail 1700–1815," *Revue historique* (1979), pp. 17–77

9. J.-C. Perrot, *Genèse d'une ville moderne, Caen au XVIIIe siècle* (Paris, The Hague, 1975), 1:321–345.

10. Perdiguier, *Mémoires*, pp. 10–11.

11. Kaplan, "Réflexions," pp. 24–26.

12. *Ibid.*, pp. 33–35.

13. II fols. 140–143.

14. Faure, introd. to A. Perdiguier, *Mémoirs d'un compagnon*, p. 12.

15. Kaplan, "Réflexions," pp. 70–71.

16. Roche, *Le Peuple*, ch. 2; S. Mercier, *Tableaux de Paris* (Amsterdam, 1788), 12:323–324.

17. J. Lecuir, "Associations ouvrières de l'époque moderne, clandestinité et culture populaire", *Histoire et clandestinité, Privas colloquium, 1977, Revue de Vivarais* (1979), pp. 273–290.

18. Coornaert, *Les Compagnonnages*, pp. 175–205.

19. Lecuir, "Associations," pp. 284–285.

20. G. Martin, *Les Associations ouvrières au XVIIIe siècle (1700–1791)* (Paris, 1900), pp. 91–124.

21. Barret-Gurgand, *Ils voyageaient la France, vie et traditions des compagnons du tour de France au XIXe siècle* (Paris, 1980).

22. In the consular archives of Carpentras, which have come down to us almost complete, the only missing notebook is that for the semester of January-July 1761 during which Ménétra experienced his difficulties. Cf. BM, Carpentras, FF60.

23. J. Cavignac, *Le Compagnonnage dans les luttes au XVIIIe siècle*, Bibliothèque de l'école des chartes, 1968, pp. 377–411.

24. Kaplan, "Réflexions," pp. 42–58; Martin, *Les Associations ouvrières*, pp. 124–180. In E. Martin Saint Léon, *Le Compagnonnage* (Paris, 1901), pp. 65–66, note an instance of employers being placed on an index by a letter written in May 1753 by the companion glaziers of Tours to those of Or

léans. This indirectly confirms the strength of *compagnonnage* traditions in the area of France in which Ménétra began his tour.

25. Cf. Nicolas Contat, known as Lebrun, *Les Anecdotes typographiques*, G. Barber, ed. (Oxford, 1980). This text illustrates the workings of the *compagnonnage* system in Paris printing shops.

26. C. M. Truant: "Solidarity and Symbolism among Journeymen Artisans, the Case of Compagnonnage, Comparative Studies," *Social History*, 1970, pp. 214–226.

27. Faure, introd. to Perdiguier, pp. 15–16.

28. Ménétra recorded five songs from the tour of France. The first features the rivalry between Dévorants and Gavots for control of Tours, the second is to the glory of Tian (gratins of herbs) from Carpentras, the third sings the praises of the glaziers of Orléans and condemns the weakness of sailors, the fourth contrasts Parisian customs with those of the tour, and the fifth celebrates the great exploits of the companions of Auxerre.

29. Martin, *Les Associations*, pp. 40–44, 96–97; Barret-Gurgand, *Ils voyageaient*, pp. 149–184, 267–288.

30. Mauss, *Sociologie et Anthropologie*, pp. 145–225.

31. Martin, *Les Associations*, pp. 62–63, cites the *Encylopédie méthodique. Police*, 2:607.

32. Faure, introd. to Perdiquier, p. 9.

33. J.-C. Perrot, *Genèse d'une ville moderne*, 1:321–322.

34. II fol. 141: "To set straight in lead / do it well but take your time / Solder clean all around / that was the old method / curdled joints, full of prisoners / badly cut and badly greased glass / crumpled, poorly soldered lead / that's the fashionable way of working / Filled with science by design / for architechture of the most refined / to paint one's glasses with an art divine / that was the old method / Now things have changed / men are accepted as masters for money / Without taste, science, or talent / those are your fashionable new regulations."

35. II fols. 140–142.

36. R. Cottin, "La fenêtre et le verre à Lyon aux XVIIe et XVIIIe siècles," *Mélanges de travaux offerts à Maître J. Tricou* (Lyons, 1972), pp. 111–137 (a fundamental work).

37. L. Savot, *L'Architecture française* (Paris, 1624); F. Blondel, *L'Architecture française* (Paris, 1673); A. Felibien, *Des principes de l'architecture* (Paris, 1681).

38. BM Montpellier, BB. 1759–1760, fols. 108, 599 and DD. 310 *bis.*, 19.

39. The innovation was both technological (involving the introduction of a new raw material) and commercial (glass would be bought directly from the manufacturer in Alsace and Lorraine, without dealing through the guild). He passed the deal on to a third thief, Lobjois, a master glazier in the rue de Sèvres; perhaps he made a profit on it. Note, too, the role of the merchant Vatencle, probably a wholesaler.

40. II fols. 20–31 and fol. 48: "Vite au contrôleur français la liberté est en France, vite au contrôleur français et de tous les états, l'on peut faire à souhait."

41. Coornaert, *Les Corporations*, pp. 165–177, 236–245; Perrot, *Genèse d'une ville moderne*, 1:322. The protest against the glass monopoly is illustrated by a decree of the lieutenant général de police, Berryer, dated 8 March 1753 (Report on the Regulations concerning the glass trade in Paris): "There were communities that in fact deserved favoritism, because they contributed to the perfection of the arts and to the increase of commerce, but this was certainly not the case with the glaziers. These were simple manual laborers whose entire skill consisted in cutting glass to the size of the frame made by the carpenters, a skill that could be learned in a week or two. Surprisingly, one tolerated their power over the public to such a degree that no one was allowed to order glass to be delivered or to take glass from a warehouse for private use. . . . Nothing would seem more contradictory to public liberties." AN F. 12, 100, Cf. F. 12, 58, 85, 89, 55, and BN, MS., FF., 22959 and 22960:

4. Spaces and Places, Time, and Action

1. L. Febvre, *La Terre et l'évolution humaine* (Paris, 1922), and G. Gurvitch, *La Multiplicité des temps sociaux* (Paris, 1958).

2. H. Lefebvre, *Le Droit à la ville* (Paris, 1968), pp. 185–189.

3. F. Loux and P. Richard, *Sagesses du corps* (Paris, 1978). Roche, *Le Peuple*, ch. 6: "Le Vêtement populaire."

4. Roche, *Le Peuple*, ch. 7, and especially J. Pronteau, *Les Numérotages des rues de Paris* (Paris, 1966).

5. Roche, *Le Peuple*, ch. 1: "Espaces et populations," and Kaplow, *Les Noms*, pp. 21–24.

6. Farge and Zysberg, "Les Théâtres," pp. 888–901, cf. map 1.

7. Rétif de la Bretonne, *Les Nuits de Paris* (London [Paris], 1788), 7 vols., pp. 2493–2494.

8. Addresses in *Almanach du commerce* (Paris, 1769), article "vitriers" (unpaginated).

9. Farge, "Vivre dans la rue," pp. 49–53.

10. II fols. 38–40: "I am a resident of Paris, I was not born in the country."

11. Barret-Gurgand, *Ils voyageaient*, pp. 43–60.

12. See maps. Perdiguier, *Mémoires*, pp. 109–393, sees mainly in terms of paragraphs headed "Beauties of . . . ," regular lessons in what there is to see.

13. *Ibid.*, pp. 130–131, 335.

14. Barret-Gurgand, *Ils voyageaient*, pp. 53–55, and especially J. Vidalenc, *Un Aspect de la vie ouvrière au XIXe siècle, le pèlerinage des compagnons du Devoir du tour de France à la Sainte-Baume*, Congrès National des Sociétés Savantes, Lille, 1955 (Paris, 1956), pp. 280–295.

15. Goulemot,   pp. 14–16.

16. The execution of Damiens, the battle of Saint-Cast, the Bordeaux earthquake, the inauguration of the statue of Louis XV, the riot of May 1770, the abolition of the guild wardens, and the events of the Revolution are the only ones he mentions.

17. L. Febvre, *Rabelais et le problème de l'incroyance au 17e siècle* (Paris, 1947), pp. 430–432.

18. H. Lefebvre, *Critique de la vie quotidienne* (Paris, 1958), pp. 52–56, contrasts cyclical time and linear time, or country time and city time, which is an oversimplification.

19. Concerning the spread of watches and clocks, see L. Mumford, *Technics and Civilization* (New York, 1963), and C. Cipolla, *Clocks and Culture, 1300–1700* (London, 1967).

20 Roche, *Le Peuple*, Ch. 6: "Ways of Reading," and Farge, "Vivre dans la rue," pp. 82–150.

21. E. P. Thompson, "Temps, travail, capitalisme industriel," *Libre (1979) S, pp. 3–64.*

22. C. Aubry, *La jurisprudence criminelle du Châtelet de Paris sous Louis XVI* (Paris, 1971).

23. Thompson, "Temps," pp. 18–38; K. Thomas, "Work and Leisure in Pre-Industrial Society," *Past and Present* (1964), 2(9):50–66.

24. J. Le Goff, "Au Moyen Age: Temps de l'Eglise et temps du marchand," *Annales E.S.C.* (1960), pp. 417–433, and "Le Temps du travail dans la crise du XIVe siècle, du temps médiéval au temps moderne," *Le Moyen Age* (Paris, 1963), pp. 597–613.

25. Thompson, "Temps," pp. 21–22.

26. Kaplan, "Réflexions," p. 54; Roche, *Le Peuple*, conclusion.

27. Martin Saint Léon, *Les Compagnonnages*, pp. 30–50; Lecuir, "Associations," pp. 279–284.

28. Lecuir, "Associations," pp. 281–282; G. Durand, *Vin, vigne, vignerons en Beaujolais à l'époque moderne* (Lyons, 1979), pp. 10–30.

29. P. N. Stearns, "The Effort at Continuity in Working-Class Culture," *Journal of Modern History* (1980), pp. 626–655 (a very important article for the bibliography of the subject and for reflection, though it draws too close a connection between the practices in question and the constitution of the industrial working class; in Paris the former came much earlier than the latter).

30. Martin Saint Léon, *Les Compagnonnages*, p. 51.

31. P. Ariès, *L'Enfant et la vie familiale sous l'ancien régime* (Paris, 1960), pp. 10–20.

32. Roche, *Le Peuple*, ch. 8: "Manière de vivre"; Farge, "Vivre dans la rue," pp. 26–41, 72–77, to compare Ménétra with other sources.

33. Garden, *Lyon et les Lyonnais*, pp. 4–22.

5. The Social World

1. For the interpretation of Ancien Régime society, see R. Mousnier, *Les Institutions de la France d'ancien régime*, 2 vols. (Paris, 1974–1979); and J.-C. Perrot, "Rapports sociaux et villes au XVIIIe siècle," in D. Roche, ed., *Ordres et classes* (Paris, 1973), pp. 141–166.

2. Roche, *Le Peuple*; Farge, *Vivre dans la rue*, pp. 193–245; Kaplan, "Réflexions," pp. 17–18, 74–76; and the forthcoming thesis of Marie E. Bénabou.

3. Kaplow, *Les Noms*, pp. 59–75.

4. J. Peuchet, *Mémoires tirés des archives de la police* (Paris, 1883), 1:204–210.

5. F. Furet, "Pour une définition des classes inférieures à l'époque moderne," *Annales E.S.C.* (1963), pp. 459–474.

6. A livre was equal to one franc or twenty sols.

7. Roche, *Le Peuple*, ch. 3: "Fortune et infortune populaire."

8. AN, Min. Cent., XIX, 28 June 1765.

9. Daumard and Furet, *L'Education*, pp. 57–93.

10. AD Paris, Marceau bankruptcy , doc. cit.

11. See Roche, *Le Peuple*, ch. 3, for a comparison with the standard of living of an industrial worker, and Kaplow, *Les Noms*, pp. 120–140.

12. Perrot, "Rapports sociaux," pp. 143–150; Roche, *Le Peuple*, ch. 3: "Connaître le peuple."

13. No trace has yet been found in records of civil proceedings.

14. II fols. 7, 13.

15. Chaigneau,   p. 344–345/

16. II fol. 39.

17. II fol. 177 (Response to the *Journal des dames*).

18. II fol. 47: "With a Dauphin our wishes have been granted, Friends he comes in the good season of the grape harvest, Long live this illustrious Bourbon blood, Think about drinking, singing, and speaking lines, Honor and joy for all France, He brings us and comes with peace, Our desires and our wishes shall be fulfilled." (Verses placed under glass in celebration of the birth of the Dauphin, 1781.)

19. II fol. 123.

20. For the French Revolution, see M. Vovelle, M. Bouloiseau, D. Voronof, *Nouvelles histoires de la France contemporaine*, 3 vols. (Paris, 1972).

21. II fols. 69, 72–73, 102–103.

22. II fol. 102.

23. There is no history of the National Guard during the Revolution: cf. L. Girard, *La Garde nationale au XIXe siècle* (Paris, 1964), pp. 3–4, 7–9. Worth consulting though quite inadequate is C. Comte, *Histoire de la garde nationale* (Paris, 1830); for eyewitness accounts, see Cadet-Gassicourt, *Les Quatre Âges de la Garde nationale* (1818); and see also G. Aclocque, *André Arnould Aclocque, commandant-général de la Garde nationale, 1748–1802* (Paris, 1947).

24. II fols. 86–87.

25. Aclocque, *André Arnould Aclocque,* pp. 63–65, 153–163. Ménétra's section was stationed with that of the center in the place du Caroussel on the Tenth of August; he does not describe the retreat of the sectionnaires in the first phase of the battle but only the pillage of the castle during the third phase, after the arrival of reinforcements and the defeat of the Swiss guards.

26. E. Mellié, *Les Sections de Paris pendant la Révolution française* (Paris, 1898), pp. 245–275 (a work of fundamental importance).

27. II fol. 82.

28. II fol. 102; AN, F.7 4589 (2). Judge Samson Duperron's declaration does not mention Ménétra, but he may have been "one of the citizens" who came with Bayard to claim custody of Duperron and thus to save him from the massacre.

29. II fol. 102.

30. II fols. 76–78 and 94–96; and A. Soboul, *Les Sans-Culottes parisiens en l'an II* (Paris, 1958), pp. 998–1,012.

31. II fol. 82.

32. II fol. 91; cf. K. D. Tönneson, *La Défaite des sans-culottes, mouvement populaire et réaction bourgeoise en l'an III* (Paris, Oslo, 1959), pp. 365–370; F. Gendron, *La Jeunesse dorée* (Paris, 1981), pp. 63, 129–199.

33. II fols. 91, 98–101, 102; Gendron, *La Jeunesse dorée,* pp. 299–320; H. Zivy, *Le Treize Vendémiaire an IV* (Paris, 1898), pp. 90–95.

34. II fol. 73.

35. President of the sectional assembly, probably in 1793 (Ménétra was exonerated of having signed both the petition of the 8,000, opposing the establishment of a *fédéré* camp below the walls of Paris, and the petition of the 20,000, opposing the *journée* of 20 June 1792 which was prejudicial to the interests of the Girondins). Commissaire de sûreté générale (which he is probably confusing with the post of commissaire civil, since two lines earlier he states that he had refused the post of commissaire de surveillance on the section's revolutionary committee). Deputy justice of the peace (confirmed by the *Almanach National* for 1794–1795–1796). Commissaire de bienfaisance (member of the committee responsible for distributing aid to the poor). And perhaps delegate of his section to the Commune of Paris charged with matters pertaining to assignats and food supplies. See A. Soboul, *Les Sans-Culottes,* pp. 581–650; Mellié, *Les Sections de Paris,* pp. 158–166, 178–222, 234–245, 273–275. There is nothing in the papers of the Comités de bienfaisance AD Paris S–D 687.

36. Soboul,   *Les   Sans-Culottes,*   pp.

588–590.

37. Mellié, *Les Sections*, pp. 308–315; A. Soboul, *Les Papiers des sections de Paris* (Paris, 1950); Tönneson, *La Défaite*, pp. 390–400; Gendron, *La Jeunesse dorée*, pp. 333–340.

38. Mellié, *Les Sections*, pp. 114–116; Soboul, *Les Papiers*, pp. 43, 100, 200, 206, 245–247.

39. Soboul, *Les Papiers*, pp. 22, 24–25, 41, 43, 48 (Election of 20 June 1793: cf. Bibliothèque V. Cousin, MS. II91), 68, 78, 192, 196 (de-Christianization), 308, 376, 410, 430; BN, LB 40 1733 (20 Germinal Year III).

40. Soboul, *Les Papiers*, pp. 555, 565 (AN, F.⁷4603), pp. 572–574, 593, 675, 706–707 (Lullier affair—AN, F.⁷ 4774–27), pp. 773, 783, 871.

41. Soboul, pp. 702–703.

42. *Ibid.*, p. 911.

43. *Ibid.*, p. 926.

44. *Ibid.*, pp. 965, 998–1,022.

45. Tönneson, *La Défaite*, pp. 39, 69, 72, 92, 98–99, 179–182, 191–192, 208, 227, 250, 267, 318,339; Gendron, *La Jeunesse dorée*, pp. 14–15, 42, 52, 65, 81, 127, 135, 181–185, 201, 245, 255, 299.

46. II fols. 88–90.

47. II fol. 79: "My answer to the invective of the most inept and intolerant of men . . ."; Fol. 83: "My answer to a denunciation, the honest man has no venom and does good, my enemies were those of the Republic."

48. AN, F.⁷ 4787 (4) F 25; 4774–61, 4279 d–21.

49. AN, F.⁷ 4787 (4), 4589-2, 4775–32, 4775–38.

50. AN, F.⁷ 4787 (4), D III 253 254, BN, 8⁰ Lb–40 1728 and 1743. II Fol. 89.

51. AN, F.⁷ 4787 (4); Duplessis or Duplessy was a wigmaker. This may be the same fellow who accompanied Ménétra in the spree described before II Fols. 89–91.

52. AN. F.⁷ 4785, W369.

53. AN, F.⁷ W 362 (785).

54. AN, F.⁷ 4774–93.

55. AN F.⁷ 4787 (4), F⁷ 4585, 4589-2, 4775–32, 4663.

56. AN, F.⁷ 4787 (4) D III 253–254.

57. AN, F.⁷ 4787 (4), W 369, D III 253–254.

58. AN, F.⁷ 4787 (4), BN LC–31 381.

59. AN, F.⁷, 4787 (4), A.P.P. Nov. 1792, Sept. 1790, July 1790. BN,8⁰ LC–31 381.

60. II fol. 77: "I do not wish to blame the honest citizen who belonged to this society, for at the high point of the Revolution they were the saviors of France."

61. II fol. 69.

62. II fols. 78, 103, 125, 127–129.

63. II fol. 93.

6. Religion and Personality

1. M. Vovelle, *Religion et Révolution. La déchristianisation de l'an II* (Paris, 1976); C. Langlois, "A l'épreuve de la Révolution," in F. Lebrun, ed., *Histoire des Catholiques de France du XVe siècle à nos jours* (Toulouse, 1980).

2. Soboul, *Les Sans-Culottes*, pp. 296–315.

3. II fols. 55–58, 104–116.

4. II fols. 65–68.

5. II fols. 125, 134–135.

6. II fols. 40–43.

7. II fols. 53–54.

8. II fols. 55–65.

9. Ginzburg, *Le Fromage*, pp. 18–20, 176–178.

10. B. Groethuysen, *Les Origines de l'esprit bourgeois en France* (Paris, 1927), pp. 15–20.

11. A. Dupront, "De la religion populaire," epilogue to *La Religion populaire* (Paris, 1980), pp. 411–419.

12. Kaplow, *Les Noms*, pp. 192–217.

13. Dupront, *La Religion populaire*, p. 413.

14. Chaunu, *La Mort à Paris*, pp. 216–217.

15. M. Baurit and J. Hillairet, *Saint-Germain-l'Auxerrois* (Paris, 1955), pp. 145–146.

16. Chaunu, *La Mort à Paris*, pp. 432–454.

17. M. Cottret, "Le Thème de l'Eglise primitive," (thesis: University of Paris X, 1978).

18. Kaplow, *Les Noms,* p. 209.

19. BN 4⁰ Z Le Senne 1023 (3), decree of Mgr de Vintimille, regulation and deliberations of the church council, 16 May 1745.

20. BN, 4⁰ Z Le Senne 1023 (6).

21. Mauss, *Sociologie et Anthropologie,* pp. 359–361.

22. II fols. 104–105 "concerning the sects that have insinuated themselves through the agency of a thousand impostors."

23. I. O. Wade, *The Clandestine Organization and Diffusion of Philosphic Ideas in France from 1700 to 1750* (New York, 1967), pp. 11–19.

24. II fols. 40–42.

25. Wade, *The Clandestine Organization,* pp. 124–140; G. Brunet, *Le Traité des trois imposteurs* (Paris, 1867).

26. R. Darnton, "Le Livre français à la fin de l'Ancien Régime," *Annales E.S.C.* (1973), pp. 735–744.

27. Roche, *Le Peuple,* ch. 6.

28. Ginzburg, *Le Fromage,* pp. 70, 110–111; Chartier, *L'éducation,* pp. 80–81.

29. II fols 56–57.

30. II fols. 60.

31. M.-E. Bénabou, "Amours vendues à Paris à la fin de l'Ancien Régime, clercs libertins, police et prostituées," in *Aimer en France,* pp. 493–502.

32. II fols. 60–61, 107–109.

33. It is further developed in II fol. 104 S–11, *Sur les sectes* (the Incarnation, the Immaculate Conception, the Trinity, and sacramental practices).

34. E.-G. Léonard, *Histoire générale du Protestantisme* (Paris, 1963–1964), 3:20–29.

35. II fol. 12.

36. Cf. the fundamental work of R. Moulinas, "Du ghetto pontifical à la nation française, les juifs d'Avignon et du Comtat Venaissin au dernier siècle de l'Ancien Régime" (typescript in 6 vols., Aix-en-Provence, 1979).

37. *Ibid.*

38. *Ibid.*

39. II fols. 40–44, fols. 55–65.

40. II fol. 61.

41. II fol. 40.

42. II fols. 53–54.

43. II fol. 42.

44. II fol. 55.

45. II fols. 62–64.

46. II fol. 64.

47. Bouloiseau et al., *Nouvelles histoires,* pp. 195–196.

48. Biographical information made available to me by E. Ducourdray.

49. A. Mathiez, "La Théophilanthropie et le culte décadaire 1796–1802," *Essai sur l'histoire religieuse de la Révolution* (Paris, 1903).

50. *Ibid.,* pp. 40–66, 84–94.

51. *Ibid.,* pp. 95–103, 171–182.

52. *Ibid.,* pp. 117, 124, 169.

53. *Ibid.,* p. 169.

54. II fols. 65–69.